THE LOSS OF HINDUSTAN

THE LOSS OF

HINDUSTAN

THE INVENTION OF

INDIA

MANAN AHMED ASIF

HARVARD UNIVERSITY PRESS

Cambridge, Massachusetts

London, England

First Harvard University Press paperback edition, 2023
First printing

LIBRARY OF CONGRESS CATALOGING-IN-PUBLICATION DATA

Title: The loss of Hindustan : the invention of India / Manan Ahmed Asif.
Description: Cambridge, Massachusetts : Harvard University Press, 2020. |
Includes bibliographical references and index.
Identifiers: LCCN 2020008165 | ISBN 9780674987906 (cloth) |
ISBN 9780674292338 (pbk.)
Subjects: LCSH: Nationalism—India—History. | Europeans—Attitudes—
History. | India—Historiography. | India—Public opinion—History.
Classification: LCC DS435 .L67 2020 | DDC 954—dc23
LC record available at https://lccn.loc.gov/2020008165

To my teachers who gave me the gift of Hindustan: C. M. Naim,
Muzaffar Alam, and Shahid Amin

CONTENTS

NOTE ON TRANSLITERATION AND TRANSLATION

I have retained the diacritical indication for the presence only of the letters *hamza* (') and *'ayn* ('). I have omitted the Arabic definite article as well as used -i for the Persian *iẓāfa*. When citing from sources, I have left the text unaltered. All translations, unless noted, are mine. All dates are rendered in Common Era (CE).

THE LOSS OF HINDUSTAN

1

INTRODUCTION

The End of Hindustan

WHAT HAPPENED TO HINDUSTAN? The Portuguese, Dutch, British, and French who visited, settled in, and conquered the subcontinent since the sixteenth century used Estado da Índia, Nederlands Voor-Indië, British India, or Établissements français dans l'Inde to denote their colonial holdings.[1] Often their maps depicting these settlements labeled parts of the subcontinent as "Mogor" or "Mogul India" to refer to the major native polity of the Mughals.[2] In these renderings, it was explained that the Mughals, who claimed to be the kings of all the kings in southern peninsular Asia from the sixteenth century down to the nineteenth century, were called Shahanshah-i Hindustan (emperors of Hindustan). Hence, until the late eighteenth century, Hindoostan or Indostan was regularly embossed in cartouches on colonial maps. The European travelogues, histories, philological works, operas, and plays that wanted to signal their authenticity or knowledge of "Oriental languages" would also use this same word, with its varied spellings, as the "local" name of the subcontinent.[3]

Yet, in the early nineteenth century, the word Hindustan begins to fade from the colonial archive. The major histories of the subcontinent, written in the early parts of the nineteenth century, were now histories of "British India." With the British East India Company (BEIC) ascendant,

the Maratha or the Sikh polities did not invoke Hindustan in their political claims.[4] There was a brief last resurgence of Hindustan in 1857.
The rebels and revolutionaries who opposed BEIC rule rallied to the flag
of the Mughal king, Bahadur Shah Zafar. He was, once again, hailed as
the Shahanshah-i Hindustan—clearly there remained an idea of Hindustan. After violently crushing the revolution, Queen Victoria took
British India under her direct rule and assumed the title of Empress of
India, sending Bahadur Shah Zafar to die in exile in Burma. His contemporary the poet Mirza Ghalib recognized the momentous change in
the fate of the subcontinent with this verse: "Hindustan sayah-i gul pa-e
takht tha / jah-o-jalal-i ʻahd-e visal-e butan nah puchh" (Hindustan was
the shadow of a rose at the foot of the throne / the grandeur, the splendor
of that age of union with the gods, don't ask!).[5] And so, per Ghalib,
Hindustan became the past.

Yet, Hindustan lingered even after the formal end of the Mughal
polity and the entrenchment of colonial British India. The people of the
subcontinent continued to be called, and called themselves, Hindustani.
The early twentieth-century world encountered Hindustanis who were
taken as indentured labor to the Caribbean and the Americas or who
traveled on their own to Europe. North Americans experienced "Hindustanee" students, activists, and lawyers who came to California and
Vancouver and rallied against imperial Britain.[6] This glimmer of Hindustan as an idea of anti-colonial politics was also present in the subcontinent. It was the idea behind the Hindustan Socialist Republican Association, created by anti-colonial revolutionaries like Chandrashekhar
Azad and Bhagat Singh in 1928. It emerged in a slogan asserting independence as *Jai Hindustan ki* (Victory to Hindustan)—the rallying cry
for Subhas Chandra Bose's Free Hind Army in 1942. Later, when the Republic of India issued its first postage stamp on August 15, 1947, the day
of independence, it depicted the tricolor flag, with Emperor Ashoka's
dharma chakra, and Bose's anti-colonial slogan, shortened to *Jai Hind.*

Many of these ideas of Hindustan are now lost in the mists of time.
Over these many decades since the Partition, the conventional understanding has calcified that Hindustan is either a simple Hindi word for
"India," an articulation of Hindu chauvinism, or, more rarely, something
associated with the bygone era of the Mughal polity—itself understood

by the Hindu Indian as a demonstration of the imperial violence of foreigners.

The erasure of the precolonial idea of Hindustan has meant that it is taken as a truism that there was no coherent concept of peninsular India before British domination.[7] What is nominally understood by this is that the British were the first to control or claim the entire territory of the southern peninsula. In this line of telling, the subcontinent before British colonization was an age of "regional kingdoms" with no coherent notion of territoriality nor the political control over the entire peninsula. The only noted exceptions are of Ashoka, from the third century BCE, whose realm included Kabul, or the Mughal king Aurangzeb, who extended Mughal rule in and beyond the Deccan in the late seventeenth century.

Such conventional wisdom, these historiographic truths, are mistaken. Certainly, the Mughals did not create the concept of Hindustan. There already existed an idea that Hindustan was a place of territorial integrity that encompassed the entire subcontinent, and that diverse communities of believers lived in this place.

Take as a small illustration this Persian inscription from 1325 found in a step well in Batiyagarh, Madhya Pradesh, in Central India.

In the reign of king Ghiyathuddin wa-Dunya
the foundation of this auspicious edifice was laid
May such a king live as long as this world lasts
Because in his reign, the rights of none are lost
In Hindustan all are grateful for his justice
In Turkistan all are fearful of his supremacy.[8]

Here Hindustan is depicted as a political collective (all who recognize the king's justice) and as unique (distinct from the land of the Turks), long before the Mughal imperium.[9] Clearly, there is more to the story of Hindustan.[10]

This book is animated by a set of simple questions: What was the idea of Hindustan? When did it come about and what made it powerful enough to persist for nearly a thousand years? What role did it play in organizing ideas of place, of history, of community? These questions are straightforward, but they are frustratingly difficult to answer. To study the erasure of concepts or ideas is a difficult task, especially when it happens gradually and when the erased concepts are replaced by some hegemonic or majoritarian truth. What was the name of "America" before the settler colonials arrived? Can we even imagine how to answer that question? Even when we can understand that "America" or "Australia" is an erasure of precolonial naming and being and we can understand that the indigenous peoples of the "Americas" were not "Indians," we let these labels persist.[11] We are thus content with the convention that while Pakistan came into being in 1947, "India" was something that stretches back to an "ancient" period. That is to say, "Early Pakistan" or "Early Bangladesh" seem incongruous, but "Early India" a seemingly unproblematic periodization. This is puzzling, since there is critical engagement with "South Asia" as a twentieth-century geopolitical toponym.[12] What remains remarkably absent from such debates is the idea of Hindustan.

How does one, then, write the history of something that is not even realizable as missing or cannot even be fully articulated?[13] Colonization refuses the colonized access to their own past. By imposing a colonial language, it retards the capacity of indigenous languages to represent reality. It claims that the languages of the colonized lack "technical" or "scientific" vocabulary. It removes the archives, renders history as lack, blurs faces and names.[14] Thus, the colonized face a diminished capacity to represent their past in categories other than those given to them in a European language, or provided to them in an imperial archive. This rupture, brought about by the colonial episteme, erases the fuller memory or awareness of the precolonial. Now, a "translated" term for an indigenous concept is deemed sufficient to stand in for it by an academy more inclined to maintain citational coherence than the truth of history. The discipline of history, itself a colonizing tool, is resistant to the demands of the colonized.

When there is no disciplinary recognition that something has been erased, the history of a concept must first deal with the act of political forgetting. Political forgetting superimposes the present over the past such that all the conveniences and prejudices of the present overshadow the complexities and lived-in realities of the past. Political forgetting is an ongoing process that happens in the shadow of the inventions of origins.[15] Take, for instance, the efforts by the Republic of India to reclaim street or city names at first given by the British: Bombay to Mumbai in 1995, Calcutta to Kolkata in 2001. More recently, the reclamation has turned to the Mughal: the city founded as Allahabad (or Illahabad to its residents) by the emperor Jalaluddin Akbar in 1583, which is at the confluence of the Ganga and Yumna Rivers, was changed to Prayagraj by the elected government of the province in 2018. Now, Allahabad is a colonial word, and the Mughals a colonizing force.

Such political forgetting is not unique to India in the subcontinent. We can look to Pakistan, where few contemporary Pakistanis recall that there was once something called "East Pakistan." The state of Pakistan has erased from its textbooks and its official narratives any indication of the existence of an eastern wing to its territory. Few Pakistanis connect the country of Bangladesh with a nation born out of Pakistani violence against the people of East Bengal in 1971. In order to imagine a Hindu-only Republic of India or non-Bengali Islamic Republic of Pakistan, the project of political forgetting targets minorities to deprive them of history, of the right to narrate, of the capacity for recognition in the collective. One is reminded of Walter Benjamin's warning that *"even the dead* will not be safe from the enemy if he wins."[16]

Political forgetting is an act of writing history. The political forgetting that this book explores concerns the idea of Hindustan. I am interested in Hindustan as an object of historical study, that is, Hindustan as the active or passive subject of history writing. There is the political forgetting that is understood via the study of how Europe worked to erase Hindustan in its own practices of history writing.[17] Under the guise of a purported universalism—the field of world history—it stripped "Hindustan" from geography and supplanted it with another concept, "India." The colonial episteme collected, archived, organized, and excerpted textual and material forms to create histories of India. By "colonial episteme" I mean a domain of knowledge constituted beginning in the sixteenth century by the Portuguese, French, Dutch, German, and British about the subcontinent. Europe's making of "India" itself as a geography, and the ways in which historical change takes place in that geography, is the first and necessary act of political forgetting of Hindustan. In order to describe the idea of "Hindustan,"

I simultaneously show the construction of the idea of "India." Keeping the colonial episteme in view foregrounds the work of history writing and shared assumptions and ideas across genealogies of knowledge production.

Parallel to the colonial story is the history of the histories of Hindustan. The idea of Hindustan, as a political and spatial concept, was in the works of history written between the tenth and the nineteenth centuries. These are the Arabic, Persian, Sanskrit or Prakrit, and later Urdu sources in which the peninsular subcontinent is imagined, described, and peopled as Hindustan. This is the story of Hindustan that disappears under colonial works of history.

But I am getting ahead of myself. Let me pause and walk through these concerns and claims one at a time. Let me begin with a telling of the fractious ideas about Hindustan from the beginning of the twentieth century and how they shaped the political forgetting that is our contemporary moment. I then turn to the work of history in this loss of Hindustan as an idea. To do so I delve into the first and most consequential European "History of Hindustan," by Alexander Dow in 1768, which defined early modern and colonial history writing on the subcontinent. In this discussion of the constitution of European history and the field of the philosophy of history, we see the instruments of the erasure of Hindustan. Next, I introduce the monumental history by Muhammad Qasim Firishta written in the early seventeenth century, upon which the European histories on India relied. It remains the singular most important history of Hindustan inside and outside the subcontinent. This Persian history, and its own intellectual genealogy, constitutes the bedrock—a sedimentation—for this book.

THE END OF HINDUSTAN

In 1904 in Lahore, a young revolutionary and anti-colonial activist, Har Dayal, organized a gathering at Forman Christian College for like-minded students.[18] He invited his friend the young poet Muhammad Iqbal, who was teaching at Government College, to the gathering. Iqbal inaugurated the meeting by singing a newly composed poem, "Hamara

Desh" (Our homeland) with the rousing first line, "Sare Jahan se Achcha Hindustan hamara" (Better than the whole world, our Hindustan). The reception was rapturous. One listener scribbled the poem and immediately mailed it to the leading Urdu weekly, *Itihad*. It was published in the first issue of August 1904:

> Better than the whole world, our Hindustan
> We are its nightingales, it is our Garden
> When we are in exile, our heart remains in this homeland
> Think that we exist, where our heart exists
> That tallest of all Mountains, neighbor to the sky
> It is our guard, it is our caretaker
> A thousand rivers play in its lap
> They make our gardens the envy of Paradise
> O flowing Ganga, do you remember those days?
> When our caravans landed on your banks?
> Religion does not teach that we hold grudges against
>   each other
> We are Hindi, Hindustan is our homeland
> Greece or Egypt or Rome have all been erased from the world
> To this day remains, our name, our presence
> There is some reason, our existence has not been erased
> Even if Time has been our enemy for centuries
> Iqbal! there is no confidant of ours in this world
> Who can know our hidden pain![19]

The anthem was eventually published in Iqbal's first poetry collection, *Bang-i Dara*, in 1924.[20] Iqbal had celebrated Hindustan as a collective for *all* people living in it. The poem gave Hindustan a geography that was defined by its mountains and its rivers—recognizing the Himalayas and Ganges, the two central sacral entities in Hindu cosmology, as one of the primary definitions of Hindustan. It was an affirmation that the people were Hindustani first and Muslim or Hindu after. It asserted that Hindustan was a civilization akin to Greek, Roman, or Egyptian civilizations. It was a song of power: a declaration of the formidable nature of what it meant to belong to the subcontinent.

Iqbal's Hindustan was a continuation of the idea of Hindustan that existed for hundreds of years, most spectacularly as the claim of the Mughal emperors. His anthem was wildly popular. It became a song of the masses—a song beloved by children as much as by political leaders. It was sung at the opening sessions of the Indian National Congress. It was the favorite song of the activist and anti-colonial leader M. K. Gandhi since his days in South Africa in 1909. He was moved when he heard it in August 1947.[21]

The first decades of the twentieth century saw important shifts to the idea of Hindustan. Iqbal's own 1924 *Bang-i Dara* includes another poem, "Tarana-i Milli" (Patriotic anthem), which posited the Muslim nation as one constituted both locally and globally—that is, not merely in Hindustan: "Chin o Arab hamara, Hindustan hamara / Muslim hain hum, vatan hai sara jahan hamara" (China and Arabia is ours, Hindustan is ours / We are Muslims, our homeland is the whole world).

In 1930 Iqbal would further refine his notion of Muslim belonging when he delivered the presidential address to the All India Muslim League. He argued for a "Muslim India within India," defining India as "the greatest Muslim country in the world. The life of Islam as a cultural force in the country very largely depends on its centralisation in a specified territory. This centralisation of the most living portion of the Muslims of India, whose military and police service has, notwithstanding unfair treatment from the British, made the British rule possible in this country, will eventually solve the problem of India as well as of Asia."[22] This "Muslim India" had certain similarities to the Hindustan of the Mughals, for Iqbal hearkens back to Akbar's polity: "I have no doubt that if a Federal Government is established, Muslim federal States will willingly agree, for purposes of India's defence, to the creation of neutral Indian military and naval forces. Such a neutral military force for the defence of India was a reality in the days of Mughal rule. Indeed in the time of Akbar the Indian frontier was, on the whole, defended by armies officered by Hindu generals."[23] While Iqbal had argued that the Muslims were global as a community, in this speech, especially in his portrait of a frontier guarded by Muslims—Turkistan is kept at bay. He makes the point that "Muslim India" would provide Islam "an opportunity to rid itself of the stamp that Arabian Imperialism was forced to give it."[24]

The Partition of the subcontinent in 1947 created the Islamic Republic of Pakistan and the Republic of India. The two nations immediately went to war. Under the military dictatorship of Zia ul Haq, Iqbal was designated the national philosopher of Pakistan. Iqbal had died in 1938, but the idea of a federated subcontinent had died before him. His "Tarana-i Hindi" had little purchase in the Pakistan in which I grew up. In my Pakistan, the word "Hindustan" was only associated with the word "Hindu."

Where Iqbal demonstrates a slow evolution in the idea of Hindustan, from an exemplary and inclusive space to a multi-political federation, Vinayak Damodar Savarkar provided a sharper reconceptualization of the subcontinent as a place solely for Hindus. Savarkar, widely understood to be the philosopher for Hindu supremacy, was arrested for sedition in London and sentenced to life imprisonment in the Andaman Islands in 1911. After his release in 1924 until 1937, he was under house arrest in Ratnagiri in Maharashtra. On January 30, 1948, Nathuram Godse, one of Savarkar's followers, assassinated Gandhi.

Savarkar was deeply invested in the idea of Hindustan. In 1908, he composed his own poem, "Amucha Priyakar Hindusthan" (Our beloved Hindusthan), in Marathi and delivered it in London. It has some resonance with Iqbal's vision as it too started with a declaration of Hindustan's supremacy over other nations. It also acclaimed the Himalayas and the Ganges. Yet it was markedly different in that it held both the British and the Muslims as equally outside colonizers:

> O Beautiful Hindusthan! Our very soul you are!
> O, beloved Hindusthan
> The most delightful one of all you are!
> So many Lands seen and heard of
> Beside her, all so very small do seem!
> Puny are Egypt, China, and Japan, Britain very much a hell,
>   I deem!
> Here the Goddess of Freedom readily bestowed
> Heroic Vikram to rout the *mlecchas* with zeal.[25]

In declaring that the Hindus of "Hindusthan" will resist all conquerors, Savarkar gave the example of the impure, unclean *mleccha* Greeks who were defeated by Vikramaditya in the first century CE. However, the historical memory evoked by word *mleccha*—the Sanskritic term for impure outsiders—would just as often be understood as a reference to Muslim invaders.

Savarkar expanded this conception of Muslim invaders in his essay "Essentials of Hindutva," first published in 1923. The essay was his attempt to define what "Hindu" meant, to coin a new word "Hindutva," and, in the process, to redefine and reimagine Hindustan.[26] In "Essentials of Hindutva," Savarkar argued that "Hindusthan" was the internal name of the subcontinent, and not something given to this territory by outsiders—he chose to spell it with an "h" to highlight the transliterated Sanskrit suffix *-sthāna* (place) rather than the Persian *-stān* (place). In doing so, Savarkar was forcibly rejecting the idea, raised first in the late eighteenth century by European philologists, that the words "Hind" and "Hindustan" were foreign words (non-Sanskritic in origin) that had entered the subcontinent from Pahlavi or Old Persian and, later, from the Arabic "al-Hind." Savarkar disagreed that "Hindustan" was a term coined by outsiders: "Long before Mohammad was born, nay, long before the Arabians were heard of as a people, this ancient nation was known to ourselves as well as to the foreign world by the proud epithet Sindhu or Hindu and Arabians could not have invented this term, any more than they could have invented the Indus itself."[27] Similarly, "Hindu would be the name that this land and the people that inhabited it bore from time so immemorial that even the Vedic name Sindhi is but a later form of it."[28]

In order to define "Hindutva," Savarkar first defined "Hindusthan." He began in geographic terms, arguing for its territorial integrity, and then along religious (Vedic and non-Vedic) and civilizational (Sanskriti) lines:

> The geographical sense being the primary one, has, now contracting, now expanding, but always persistently been associated with the words Hindu and Hindusthan till after the lapse of nearly 5000 years if not more, Hindusthan has come to mean

the whole continental country from the Sindhu to Sindhu from the Indus to the Seas. . . .

Hindusthan meaning the land of Hindus, the first essential of Hindutva must necessarily be this geographical one. A Hindu is primarily a citizen either in himself or through his forefathers of "Hindusthan" and claims the land as his motherland.[29]

Savarkar argued that, in the long history of "five thousand years," "Hindusthan" was a place of peace and beauty until "Mohammad of Gazni crossed the Indus, the frontier line of Sindhusthan and invaded her." This invasion set up the "year to year, decade to decade, century to century" conflict between Muslim invaders and Hindu resistors.[30] This invasion, and the resistance to it, gave birth to the civilization that Savarkar called "Hindutva": "in this prolonged furious conflict, our people," became "Hindutva, i.e., Hindudharma that was being fought out on the hundred fields of nettle as well as on the floor of the chambers of diplomacy."[31] Once Savarkar had defined "Hindusthan" as having a five-thousand-year-old history, and declared the 1000–1800 CE period of Muslim rulers as one of conflict that defined the nation of Hindus, he ended his argument with the final point that contemporary Muslims remain outsiders to "Hindusthan." He declared that the Muslims born in "Hindusthan" were the result of forceful conversion and, secondly, that the Muslims had internalized the oppressor's faith and no longer had fealty to "Hindusthan":

In the case of some of our Mohammaden or Christian countrymen who had originally been forcibly converted to a non-Hindu religion who consequently have inherited along with Hindus a common Fatherland and a greater part of the wealth of common culture are not and cannot be recognized as Hindus. For though Hindusthan to them is Fatherland as to any other Hindu yet it is not to them a Holyland too. Their Holyland is far off in Arabia or Palestine. Their mythology and Godmen, ideas and heroes are not the children of this soil. Consequently their names and their outlook smack of a foreign origin. *Their love is divided.*[32]

The Muslims of the subcontinent were either themselves foreign or converts to Islam, and in either case, their fealty lay to a foreign god in Mecca. Savarkar extended his argument about Muslim outsiders in his other historical works, such as *Hindu-Pad-Padashahi, or A Review of the Hindu Empire of Maharashtra* (1925) and *Bharatiya Itihasatil Saha Soneri Pane* (Six glorious epochs of Indian history; 1971).

Such conceptions of Muslim othering were not limited to ideologues. Jadunath Sarkar (1870–1958), a historian of the eighteenth century and of the Mughal period, gave his lectures in Madras in 1928, published under the title *India through the Ages,* and stated clearly that "Muslims cannot merge in Hindu society and creed."[33] Sarkar asserted the foreign and unassimilated nature of Muslim rule in India:

> The Muslim conquest of India differed fundamentally from all preceding invasions in one respect. The Muslims came to India as a new element which the older inhabitants could not absorb. . . . Therefore, Hindus and Muhammadans, as, later on, Hindus and Christians—had to live in the same land without being able to mix together. Nothing has enabled them to bridge this gulf. The Indian Muslims have, throughout the succeeding centuries, retained the extra-Indian direction of their hearts. The faces are still turned, in daily prayer, to a spot in Mecca.[34]

Sarkar's framing of the Muslims as foreigners with their "faces" turned to Mecca was an indictment *tout court* for being Muslims in the subcontinent. His assessment of the Muslim past was similar: "Another equally important characteristic of the *Muslim element* in India was that from 1200 to 1580 their State and society retained its original military and nomadic character—the ruling race living merely like an armed camp in the land."[35] For Sarkar, the Mughal period was a study in contrast against the "universal peace" produced within the subcontinent during British rule.[36]

The Hindustan of the late 1920s was drastically different from the one imagined in Iqbal's 1904 poem. The notion of Muslim otherness was firmly established. Even Iqbal's own 1930 speech admitted that Hindustan could only be imagined as a counterfactual: "It might have been a fact in India if the teaching of Kabir and the Divine Faith of Akbar had

seized the imagination of the masses of this country. Experience, however, shows that the various caste units and religious units in India have
shown no inclination to sink their respective individualities in a larger
whole. Each group is intensely jealous of its collective existence."[37]
Throughout the 1930s and into the 1940s, the arguments for separatism
grew stronger—albeit with great resistance from Muslim intellectuals.[38]
After the Partition, the postcolonial states of Pakistan and India continued their progress toward majoritarian hegemonic ideas. A strain of
historians in India remained wedded to the idea of a Muslim colonialism
over India. As T. V. Mahalingam put it in a presidential address to the
Indian History Congress in 1951:

> It is not that the Muslim did not make vigorous attempts to
> bring India under their sway. But their conquest of India was
> slow, partial, and difficult because of the determined resistance
> of the Hindu rulers in North-west India. Nagabhata I, the founder
> of the Pratihara dynasty at Bhinmel, is said to have defeated the
> Valacha Mlechchas (the Balucas). The attempt of the Arabs to
> conquer the Navasarika country (Southern Gujerat) was checked
> by Avanijanasraya Pulakesi, for which he received the title of
> *Dakshinapatha-svadgaarnna* (solid pillar of the *Dakshinapatha*)
> and *Anivartaka nivartayitr* (repeller of the unrepellable).[39]

Similarly, Pakistani historiography after Partition embraced the colonial narrative, though reversing its valence—the Golden Age was the age
of decay. The first textbook produced by the government under the di-
rection of the Pakistan History Board in 1955 set up the Arab Conquest
of Sind as the beginning of history for the subcontinent.[40] Pakistan,
under various military dictatorships, and the Republic of India, under
the Bharatiya Janata Party's (BJP) rule in 1998–2004 and since 2014, have
continued to strengthen these narratives.

THE DISCOVERY OF INDIA

The title of Shahanshah-i Hindustan, as mentioned earlier, came to an
end when the British Crown deposed and exiled the last Mughal king,

Bahadur Shah Zafar, in 1858. When Queen Victoria declared herself "Empress of India," the Crown articulated a different understanding of the territorial and political sense of the subcontinent. How did the British colonial regime first encounter Hindustan? How did India come to stand in for Hindustan? The formative acts of political forgetting of Hindustan were done long before Iqbal and Savarkar began to reassemble Hindustan in the twentieth century. The story of Hindustan's forgetting begins in the eighteenth century.

The British East India Company had factories, villages, and commissions in Calcutta, Madras, Bombay, and Surat, as well as in many smaller coastal towns of Karnatak, in the beginning of the eighteenth century. It was already more successful than the Dutch Company. By 1784, it owned Bengal, Awadh, Karnatak, and was moving up from Gujarat toward Delhi. By 1803, Delhi had fallen to the BEIC.[41] Over the course of the eighteenth century, the BEIC, its private contractors and merchants, and the British Crown were all engaged in a multifronted effort to contain, control, and dismiss Mughal, Maratha, Sikh, and French power.

Alongside the acquisition of territories was the capture of texts and knowledges throughout the eighteenth century. It featured colonial or para-colonial figures, often rendered as "Orientalists"—such as William Jones, Anquetil Duperron, John Z. Howell, Nathaniel Halhed, Charles Wilkins, and so on—who set about the task to acquire, digest, and reproduce knowledge about Hindustan.[42] It was in this production and assimilation of knowledge about Hindustan that India came into being.

The creation of British India over Hindustan was predicated on the very same principles that Savarkar would espouse some two hundred years later: that the true history of India was five thousand years long, and that the Muslims in India were foreigners, whose only relation to the native inhabitants was one of despotism. The "five-thousand-years-old" narrative was critical to the colonial project of seeing British India as a geography and a people suspended in time. The effort of the British jurists to create law from "ancient" Sanskrit texts was to acknowledge that the *Gentio* or *Gentoo* of Hindustan—meaning the non-Muslim majority—existed in a continuity of "customary practices" that represented the timelessness of Hindu society. The practice that had the earliest, and most robust, hold on the colonial imagination was that of the immolation of women on the deaths of their husbands. The practice of immolation, and the role of women in general, would constitute a central obsession of the eighteenth-century philologists.[43] In this colonial episteme, immolation was the persistence of an idea of womanhood that demonstrated the timeless nature of the five thousand years of India's past. Muslim despotism, forced conversion, and temple destruction were the markers of Muslim foreignness to Hindustan. The outsiders, best represented by the Mughal rulers, were fanatic, lecherous, and violent, while the Hindu populace had long suffered under their rule.

The British search for, and discovery of, a comprehensive history of Hindustan was the single most important step in the making of British India as a conceptual category.[44] To be sure, the Hindustan that was being sought in the books of history was not a new entity. The Portuguese, English, German, French, and Dutch merchants, travelers, missionaries, and mercenaries had given, since the sixteenth and seventeenth centuries, histories and ethnographies of Hindustan. The establishment of British dominion in the mid-eighteenth century in Bengal and the simultaneous loss of the American colonies, however, resulted in an urgency to understand the new colonies in Hindustan. This was the moment at which Alexander Dow stepped forth, bearing the first "History of Hindustan."

Lieutenant Colonel Alexander Dow (1735–1779) crystallized the displacement of Hindustan in the discovery of India as a historical and political subject. Dow was an officer in the BEIC's Bengal Infantry. In the process of learning Persian, he acquired and transported to London a series of Sanskrit and Persian manuscripts from Bengal and Bombay. One of the texts he brought to England was a Persian history, popular throughout the eighteenth century as *Tarikh-i Firishta* (The history by Firishta). It was written by Muhammad Qasim Firishta (b. ca. 1570) in the first decades of the seventeenth century at the court of Ibrahim 'Adil Shah II in the Deccan. In 1768, Dow published his first rendering of Firishta's history in two volumes as *The History of Hindostan; from the Earliest Account of Time, to the Death of Akbar; translated from the Persian of Mahummud Casim Ferishta of Delhi: Together with a Dissertation*

Concerning the Religion and Philosophy of the Brahmin with an Appendix Containing the History of the Mogul Empire, from Its Decline in the ca. 1570 Mahummud Shaw to the Present Times.[45] This was the first comprehensive history of Hindustan in English, and it profoundly changed the practice of history writing in Europe.

Dow dedicated his text to King George III. His dedication, written a mere eight years before the loss of the American colonies, is worth parsing out a bit. Dow wrote:

> Sir, the History of India is laid, with great humility, at the foot of the throne. As no inconsiderable part of Hindustan, is now in a manner comprehended within the circle of the British empire, there is a propriety in addressing the history of that country to the Sovereign.
>
> In the history of Hindustan, now offered to your Majesty, the people of Great-Britain may see a striking contrast to their own condition; and, whilst they feel for human nature suffering under despotism, exult at the same time, in that happy liberty which they enjoy under the government of a Prince who delights in augmenting the security and felicity of his subjects.[46]

In his dedication, there are the two clearly articulated aspects of his history: that it filled a need created by the king's newly acquired possession of the subcontinent to understand the political history of Hindustan. Secondly, the people of the subcontinent, imagined by Dow as solely Hindus, required a separate dissertation, distinct from Firishta's political history of Hindustan.

Dow elaborated on the themes of possession of land, the possession of history, and the role of British knowledge-making in the new colony in his preface. It was while he was learning Persian, he writes, that his teachers suggested to him that he translate a work of history, and they gave him "the history of Muhammad Qasim Firishta of Delhi." Dow's wrong attribution of Firishta to Delhi did serve the idea that Hindustan was synonymous with Mughal polity—he was placed at Jahangir's Mughal court. Dow then claimed that his decision to translate this work, and to supplement this history with "such books, and authentic histories as were necessary to compleat the History of Hindostan" was a project that the Mughal king had himself approved.[47] Yet, Dow also inserted the originary difference that separated the Muslim from the Hindu—the question of language. Dow asserted that though Firishta's text was specifically given to him as a unique history of all of Hindustan, Dow believed it was "very far from satisfactory" as a history, because Firishta was "not acquainted with the Shanscrita [Sanskrit] or learned language of the Brahmins, in which the internal history of India is comprehended."[48] In other words, according to Dow, Firishta's history was a complete history that was constitutionally incomplete, by virtue of its sectarian difference.

Dow delineated the history of Hindustan from the history of India. The former belonged to the Muhammadans, or the Mughals, and the latter to the Hindus. The first was external, and the second internal: "The prejudices of the Mahommedans against the followers of the Brahmin religion, seldom permits them to speak with common candour of the Hindoos. It swayed very much with Ferishta when he affirmed, that there is no history among the Hindoos of better authority than the Mahabarit. That work is a poem and not a history."[49] Dow believed that proper history could only exist in prose and that Firishta had been wrong to consider Sanskrit texts such as the epic *Mahabharata* to be history, for it was not prose. It is for this presumed lack in Firishta that Dow inserted before his rendition of Firishta his own dissertation on the "customs, manners, language, religion and philosophy of the Hindoos."

Dow's *History of Hindostan* was an immediate sensation. From the English, it was rendered into French and German in 1769 and circulated widely. Buoyed by this success, Dow returned to this *History* and, in 1772, published further excerpts from Firishta, and extended the period down to the eighteenth century. He added another essay titled, "A dissertation on the origin and nature of despotism in Hindostan," and a plan for the company to wrest political power in Bengal through property reallocation.[50]

Other colonial officers stepped up to affirm the importance of Firishta and to take part in rendering other sections of the massive work into English. In 1786, James Anderson published a rendition into English from Firishta in *Asiatick Miscellany*.[51] Anderson's extract focused on the history of Malabar. Anderson highlighted that portion as a history of Muslim arrivals in Hindustan. In 1794, Jonathan Scott, Persian secretary to Governor General of India Warren Hastings, rendered into English Firishta's section on the Deccan. Scott dedicated to the "Chairman and Court of Directors of the East India Company this attempt to add to the Publick Stock of Hindoostan History."[52] Finally, in 1829, John Briggs did another rendering "from the Original Persian of Mahomed Kasim Ferishta" and published his four-volume *History of the Rise of the Mahomedan Power in India, till the Year A.D. 1612.* Briggs surrounded his text with exhaustive notes on the landscape and peoples of Hindustan. For this purpose he employed "Meer Kheirat Ally Khan," who had "his whole life devoted to the study of Indian history" and who "travelled for several years successively throughout Deccan, and made copies of every Persian inscription."[53]

These soldier-scribes of the BEIC—Lieutenant Colonel Dow, Lieutenant Anderson, Captain Scott, and Lieutenant Colonel Briggs—identified Firishta's text as the most comprehensive history of what they considered to be Hindustan: the history of Muslim arrivals and their dominance over the Hindus.[54] Their renderings of Firishta were appropriately in the vein of military campaigns, conquests, and domination. They appended to their renditions extensive essays and exegeses on the origins of Muslim fanaticism and temple destruction, the character of the Hindu people and those who had been forcibly converted, as well as the ways in which the current Mughal polity was oppressing the population of British India. The wide readership of Dow, and later Briggs, consisted of historians and philosophers who looked not only to the Persian text rendered into English but the gloss provided by these officers, which came with its own claim of authenticity and expertise.

From Dow, and others, the claims to the first history of Hindustan, or histories of first arrivals of Muslims to the subcontinent, caught the attention of historians and philosophers of history. Edward Gibbon's sixth volume of *The History of the Decline and Fall of the Roman Empire* (1776) and Joseph Priestley's *Disquisitions Relating to Matter and Spirit* (1777) both cited and used Dow's *History of Hindostan* for presenting a political as well as a theological history of Hindustan. The synthetic histories also picked up this valuable primary source—such as Thomas

Maurice, *The History of Hindostan* (1795), and James Mill's *The History of British India* (1817)—and relied exhaustively on Firishta. The "raw material" of Firishta, delivered via Dow and others, was generative in provoking ideas of periodization, political geography, racial difference, and world history in European thought.

Dow's *History of Hindostan* not only shaped the writing of history, it also played a pivotal role in the emerging discourse on the philosophy of history. Dow, who was from Scotland, was a close correspondent of David Hume. Hume introduced Dow's text to Voltaire and to Immanuel Kant. In 1756, Voltaire had published his *Essai sur les mœurs et l'esprit des nations*—translated into English in 1759 as *An Essay on Universal History, the Manners and Spirits of Nations,* and labeled as "a philosophical history of the world." As he continued to revise the *Essai,* Voltaire sought more historical and ethnographic information about British India. Voltaire's revisions of the essay in 1769, 1775, and 1778 all depended on Dow's *History of Hindostan* as Voltaire's chief source of information.[55] Voltaire saw Dow—and John Z. Holwell's *Interesting Historical Events, Relative to the Provinces of Bengal, and the Empire of Indostan,* published in 1765—as providing the real information about the five-thousand-year past of India.[56]

Immanuel Kant had begun lecturing on the philosophy of history in 1756. In 1784, Kant published his *Idee zu einer allgemeinen Geschichte in weltbürgerlicher Absicht* (Idea for a universal history with a cosmopolitan aim). Kant, like Voltaire, was invested in thinking about the place of various peoples in history. In Kant's vision, history was not a capacity given to all peoples of the world. Rather, history required "a learned Public that has endured uninterruptedly from its beginning up to our time . . . back beyond it everything is *terra incognita;* and the history of nations that lived outside it can be begun only from the Time when they entered into it."[57] Kant cited Hume's contention that Thucydides was "the sole beginning of all true history," for, Kant agreed, Greek thought had endured across time. The inhabitants of India, Kant believed, did possess a five-thousand-year-old past. They were, however, repeatedly "interrupted" by foreign invaders, and hence were one of the many nations whose past belongs to what Kant termed an unknown land.

Kant's student Johann G. Herder elaborated this further in his *Ideen zur Geschichte der Menschheit* (Ideas for the philosophy of the history of humanity) in 1784. In staking out his own racio-spatial notion of universal history, Herder also relied on Dow to portray the Brahmins as a "political tribe" that kept the people ignorant: "For thousands of years this influence [Hinduism] on the minds of men has been singularly profound; for in spite of the Mongol yoke, which they have for long borne, its importance and doctrines still remain unshaken."[58] Herder cited Dow's 1772 dissertation to his 1768 *Hindostan.* The people of Hindustan would have remained in their ignorant bliss, deemed Herder, with barbarous customary practices such as "burning of wives on the funeral pyres of husbands" but for the interruption of "warlike Mongols" and the "covetous adventurers of Europe."[59]

The bifurcation of Hindustan's past as a history of Muslim despotism and that of the backwardness and timelessness of Hindus reached fruition in works on the philosophy of history by Georg Wilhelm Friedrich Hegel and Friedrich von Schlegel. Both relied on the work of Dow, in his rendition of Firishta and his appendices, to write these imagined colonial facts as natural laws of the philosophy of history. From Hegel's 1822–1823 *Vorlesungen über die Philosophie der Weltgeschichte* (Lectures on the philosophy of world history) in Berlin: "The Hindus have no historical perspective and are incapable of any historiography.... Because the Hindus have no history in the subjective sense, they also have none in the objective sense. Precisely because the Hindus have no *historia,* they have no authentic history."[60] Hegel cited Dow, Mill, and other histories to argue that Hindus had no history, and the history of India could not be found in any Muslim text. This Germanic notion of Indians, as people incapable of thinking historically, had firm scholarly purchase. A final illustration can suffice from the romanticist and Indologist Friedrich Schlegel. In his 1823 *Vorlesungen über Universalgeschichte* (Lectures on universal history) in Vienna, he summarily dismisses everything that happened after the arrival of Muslims to the subcontinent: "Of the political history of India, little can be said, for the Indians scarcely possess any regular history.... The more modern history of Hindostan, from the first Mahometan conquest at the commencement of the eleventh century of our era ... is unconnected with, and incapable of illustrating the true state and progress of the intellectual refinement of the Hindoos."[61]

The European project of writing a world history thus utilized Dow and the multiple and reiterative citations of his *History of Hindostan*. This field, which called itself "the philosophy of history," argued that the place of India in world history must be understood in two related ways: the violent interruptions of Muslim invasions that started historical time in India, and the subsequent retardation of progress among Hindus, seen as the sole inhabitants of the subcontinent. Later historians were governed by the dictates of this philosophy of history that had already predetermined histories of Hindustan through these categories and with this conceptual language.[62] Dow and his *History of Hindostan* profoundly shaped the European understanding of Hindustan and the people who lived in it. Nineteenth-century English soldier-scribes would continue the task of parsing Firishta for constitutive aspects of the Muslim medieval.

Firishta's *Tarikh* entered Europe as a distorted fragment in 1768 and, over the next fifty years, shaped the discourse around history writing. Now, I turn to Firishta himself. Who was Firishta, and what was his history before Dow's rendition? What was this work that was both the most successful history of Hindustan and the instrument for the colonial dismantling of the very concept of Hindustan?

FIRISHTA AND *THE LOSS OF HINDUSTAN*

The historiography of Muslim histories has traditionally split along the lines of the languages in which the histories were written, that is, between Arabic, Persian, and, later, Ottoman Turkish, or by major political formations—the 'Abbasid, the Safavid, the Mughal, the Ottoman.[63] In 1968, the world historian Marshall Hodgson considered two Muslim exemplars as historians—one writing in Arabic and one in Persian: Tabari (d. 923) for the 'Abbasid and Abu'l Fazl (d. 1602) for the Mughal.[64] Hodgson illustrates the tendency among modern historians to make a certain distinction between "Arabic historiography" and "Persian historiography," and later "Ottoman historiography."[65]

Firishta, who wrote in the Deccan, far from the Mughal polity in the early seventeenth century, is largely absent in contemporary scholarship on historians of the precolonial period. Other than a brief note in Peter Hardy's *Historians of Medieval India* (1966), Firishta does not appear in any of the aforementioned seminal works. Firishta's erasure is such that the "Indo Persian Historiography" chapter in the recent "Persian Historiography" volume of Charles Melville's *A History of Persian Literature* (2012) does not even mention him in the two-page subsection called "Provincial Histories." There are certainly no monographs on Firishta nor a robust attempt to situate him in any broader study on the historiography of Muslim societies.[66]

These are strange omissions, considering that Firishta's *Tarikh* was the most important historical work in eighteenth- and nineteenth-century Hindustan and was foundational to European historical thought. The *Tarikh* was popular almost immediately after its completion, judging from the extant copies in manuscript libraries across the Deccan, the northern subcontinent, and Europe. The surviving manuscripts of Firishta, in the European collections, are copious—the most complete extant manuscripts are from 1633, 1639, 1648, 1703, 1728–1729, 1750, 1762, 1795, and many from the nineteenth century.[67] Beyond manuscript copies, there are nearly fifty unique histories, written in the eighteenth and nineteenth centuries, which are summaries and derivations of Firishta's *Tarikh*.[68] Further still, Firishta is the central historical source for any number of major Persian, Urdu, Hindi, Sindhi, Bengali, and Marathi histories on the early modern period from the nineteenth century. Thus, Firishta's history is a text that has shaped both the European and the subcontinental practice of history writing. It is ever-present in footnotes, in paratextual apparatuses, but it is itself unaddressed and untreated as a project of history writing.

Who was Firishta? He did not leave any sustained autobiographical account, and what we know of him is parsed only through his two major works—the *Tarikh* and his work on medicine, *Dastur al-atibba*. Based on Briggs, writing in the early nineteenth century, the conventional take is that Firishta was an immigrant from Astarbad (now Gorgan in Iran by the Caspian Sea).[69] This is, however, doubtful. Firishta was likely born in or around Ahmadnagar where his father had moved during the Nizam

Shahi polity.[70] His name was Muhammad Qasim. He once refers to himself, in his *Tarikh*, as "Astarabadi" (meaning his ancestors hailed from Astarabad) and once as "Hindu Shah." However, in all references to himself he says he was commonly known as "Firishta." He began his career at the Nizam Shahi court as the captain of the palace guard.[71] In 1589, Firishta moved to Bijapur, to the court of Ibrahim 'Adil Shah II. Firishta's patron, 'Adil Shah, built a new city called Nauraspur and also wrote a treatise on musical theory and songs called *Kitab-i Nauras*.[72] We do not know when or where Firishta died.

However, we do know a lot more about Firishta's immediate political, social, and cultural world, the early seventeenth-century Deccan of Ibrahim 'Adil Shah II (r. 1580–1627).[73] On the western shores of Hindustan, the region we understand as the Deccan plateau comprised a series of nested and overlapping polities, from the cities and forts of Ahmadnagar (1496–1636), to Golkonda and Hyderabad (1496–1687), Gulbarga and Bidar (1347–1538), and Bijapur (1490–1686). Abutting them was a polity centered at Vijayanagar (1346–1565). All of these polities emerged in the fourteenth century and lasted until the end of the seventeenth century. The Mughal state (1526–1858) emerged from Kabul, and eventually its capitals spread between Agra, Fatehpur Sikri, Delhi, and Lahore. The Deccan polities were nominally incorporated under Mughal rule by the late seventeenth century.[74]

The Deccan was a world that faced the Indian Ocean and was simultaneously a crossroads for all of Hindustan. Its location facilitated a cultural world built by the movement of diverse peoples and ideas both from outside Hindustan and within Hindustan.[75] These interactions gave rise to new languages (Dakhani), art forms, and political structures— Firishta's "new" history was itself a result of this milieu. However, this "middle plateau" was also the buffer for polities of north or south and saw constant campaigns from armies within and without Hindustan. Firishta's *Tarikh* emerged in this mobile, multilingual world.

Tarikh-i Firishta is the first comprehensive history of Hindustan in terms of time and geography. There are at least two recensions existing—one dated 1608 and another 1614, though there are dated events in the manuscripts that are as late as 1623–1624. Firishta labels his history *Gulshan-i Ibrahimi* (Garden of Ibrahim) and *Naurasnama* (The book of the newest flavor)—both gestures to his patron. In his conclusion he refers to his book simply as *Tarikh-i Firishta o Shahnama* (Firishta's history and book of kings). The work runs to over a thousand folio pages—a recent critical edition is in four volumes. *Tarikh-i Firishta* has a long preface, followed by twelve chapters. Eleven chapters are organized as histories of rulers across Hindustan in different places—Lahore, Delhi, the Deccan, Gujarat, Malwa, Khandesh, Bengal, Multan, Sindh, Kashmir, and Malabar. The last chapter is about the Sufis and religious scholars of Hindustan. A short conclusion reflects on the qualities of Hindustan as *janat-nishan* (a marker of Heaven on Earth).

Firishta's history realigns the major axis of the historical writing tradition that he inherited. He eschews the genealogical table approach, wherein history was written first as a series of births—beginning from the first creation of Adam. He eschews, as well, the royal household version, where the seat of power rests with a family, and a historian's task is to chart the rise and fall of families. His history is uniquely a history of place first and foremost. After the spatial reframing for a discussion of the past, Firishta constitutes his archive from sources written and spoken, Sanskrit and Persian, from oral histories and travelers' tales. He is keen to incorporate dissenting voices, and eager to resolve conflicts in his own tabulations. Firishta's text is oftentimes overwhelming to the reader, for the pace of events rarely slows down. Firishta, as a historian, sometimes sits in judgment and sometimes lets the contradiction remain on the page. He is taken by the story, and distrustful of the monarchs.

Firishta's *Tarikh* is the most comprehensive and substantive rendering of the concept of Hindustan, even as it was written in the Deccan, far from the control of Mughal sovereigns.[76] Here, I argue both for Firishta's originality and his comprehensiveness in thinking about Hindustan. *The Loss of Hindustan* is explicitly a history of how the concept of Hindustan, most meaningfully captured in Firishta, moved from the subcontinent to Europe and was taken up in the project of the formation of Europe's philosophy of history. Subsequently, it was the influence of Firishta's text that shaped the colonial knowledge project, and the contours of how British India emerged over the nineteenth century. Firishta, I demonstrate, was the lynchpin for this monumental transition from Hindustan to British India. My history holds tightly to this thread of

Firishta, as I investigate the pre-seventeenth-century Hindustani histories that Firishta read and the post-eighteenth-century colonial histories that read and deployed Firishta.

The Loss of Hindustan is a history of the *Tarikh-i Firishta* and its intellectual world. It is a book that is situated within the extensive historiography of the Mughal imperium and the Deccan polity. It is, however, not *about* the Mughal or Deccan polities. This book is about the scope, the parameters, and the themes that occupied Firishta's *Tarikh*— the archives and genealogies of history writing, the imagination of place, and the people who inhabited Hindustan. It is also not a work of political history, and I do not reconcile the events and dates provided by various historians, including Firishta, to create an account of "what happened." As an intellectual historian, I pursue primarily how and why it was understood to have happened and what that understanding did to the craft of history writing itself.

The Loss of Hindustan sees Hindustan through the eyes of Firishta's *Tarikh* in order to crystallize a vision of a concept that is now opaque at best. It is only through an intellectual history of history writing that one can see the work of a concept like Hindustan in full effect. Firishta's history is one of the most important works of history writing about this concept called Hindustan. For that reason, as much as for reasons of scope, this book is not a treatment of all the histories, epics, romances, poetry, and architecture in the Deccan, let alone in the region known as Hindustan.

Instead I argue for the analytical importance of rethinking the historiography of the colonial period even as we reassess the historical traditions of Hindustan. The contemporary historian of the precolonial periods of the subcontinent has long had a tense relationship with the colonial historiography. Many continue to rely on the renderings made available by colonial military officers; many travel to the libraries and holdings in Britain, Germany, or France to access Hindustani manuscripts without remarking on this disjuncture in their scholarship. This is perhaps most acutely felt in the U.S. and European academies, where, after the Saidian critique of Orientalism, there is a re-entrenchment of the idea of a philologist sitting above the political contexts of colonialism.[77] My aim is not to rehash these debates. Rather, I want to argue for a methodological shift for the historian of the medieval and early modern periods in the subcontinent. I would like to insist that the material and intellectual frames of colonial knowledge-making be thoroughly investigated in any effort at a history of the precolonized world. In other words, I would like to show how we *know* the precolonized is shaped irrevocably by the colonial knowledge-making machinery. There is simply no doubt that there is a material impact of colonial collection, cataloging, archiving, listing, sorting, genre-making, and framing on the very texts, epigraphs, and artifacts upon which we rely for telling the histories of the precolonial periods in the subcontinent.

It is important to recognize that the de-glossing of this history cannot proceed without formally reshaping how we write the history of the subcontinent—how we understand periodization, source languages, and their relationship to communities and identities, and, most importantly, the imprimatur of colonial knowledge practices on the archive. If the legacy of James Mill or Leopold van Ranke to the process of writing history is to demarcate epochs and eras, to insist on the primacy of archival presence, and to separate "what happened" from "what was imagined," then this project joins other decolonial thinkers in writing against the normative strictures of the discipline. This book is, thus, a purposeful staging of the unrest that exists between the colonial episteme and histories of Hindustan, between countervailing discourses, between a politics of domination and one of recognition.[78]

The chapters that follow juxtapose the colonial imagination of the histories and peoples of India against the world-making in histories of Hindustan. The chapters are structurally organized in three sections.[79] Each of the chapters foregrounds the European entanglement with the telling of history in British India. Each moves back in time to the comity of intellectual traditions that preceded Firishta, properly reading them as histories of Hindustan by Hindustanis. Firishta's history acts as the last word for each of these chapters. While the archive, the space and place, and peoples of Hindustan are some of the major themes explored in specific chapters, the book pointedly engages the question of violence and historicism throughout.

The Loss of Hindustan is critical of the past as we have received it. It questions our analytical and methodological assumptions. Yet, writing about Firishta also allowed me to engage with the many historians of medieval Hindustan who wrote during the colonial and early postcolonial period. I found that many of them had a fearless composure, even as they predicted and faced the violent distending of the subcontinent in 1947. Somehow, I found comfort in their ethics and their resolve. For those of us who tremble at coming apocalypses of water wars and climate-led forced migrations, there is much to learn from their engagement with this deep past.

2

THE QUESTION OF HINDUSTAN

HOW DOES ONE THINK ABOUT HINDUSTAN AFTER COLONIALISM? The previously colonized subject faces a stark challenge when it comes to writing history. The disciplinary histories in classrooms and research institutes are often written by the erstwhile colonizers, yet are paradoxically the only legible forms of recognition afforded to the colonized. The previously colonized subject also learns history through originary myths. These myths are prevalent in *lieux de mémoire,* on grandmothers' knees, inside political, social, cultural, ethnic, and linguistic identities. These originary myths, whether or not they are an invention, do not *feel* as such. They feel lived in, even natural. In the subcontinent, the radical difference between Hindus as insiders and Muslims as outsiders is one such naturally felt history that has also significantly shaped disciplinary history.

So how do we think about the history of the subcontinent when colonial historiography continues to hold such discursive power? When we think of history as cause and effect, as change over time, as rise and decline, we become imbricated in the arrangement of a "before" and an "after." The central issue for the history of the subcontinent is that our prevalent and predominant "befores" and "afters" are an inherited teleology created by the European sciences of history under colonialism. The challenge historians face is that they have to provide a history of continuity that is not ipso facto a history of stagnation or of martial determinism.

The colonial episteme arranged the history of India around the notion of "five thousand years." Within this enduring idea, there were two
organizing concepts—that of a "Golden Age," which featured a majestic
Hindu polity and monumental Sanskrit epics and initiated the five thousand years of unchanging Hindu society, and that of medieval Muslim
"invader" kings, who pushed India into darkness and maintained their
power through despotism. History as a field of knowledge lies at the
center of these constructions of the past.

The structuring of this assessment lies in an interlocking quadratic
formulation that can be most succinctly expressed as follows: India's past
is five thousand years old, during which there was a Golden Age, best
epitomized by Emperor Ashoka, who ruled over the entirety of the subcontinent. That Golden Age was disrupted and destroyed by Muslim
invader Mahmud Ghazni, who launched seventeen invasions on the subcontinent and destroyed many temples, including the temple at Somnath. Ghazni inaugurated a dark age of Muslim despotic rule, with
the only respite in that eight hundred years of tyranny being the enlightened rule of Jalaluddin Akbar. It was British colonial rule that
provided a means to an end of Muslim hegemony and the advent of
liberal secularism after Partition. The five thousand years, the Golden
Age of Ashoka, the seventeen raids of Mahmud Ghazni, and Muslim
despotism—this is the central logic in the philosophy of history that
has organized the colonized historiography of Hindustan. It is this
episteme that needs to be properly historicized in order to undertake
the project of reassessment.[1]

For, in the colonial episteme, it is the Muslim medieval that is demonized, elided, ignored, and put up as the literal Dark Age between the
Golden Age of ancient India and the modern liberal age of British rule.
The general sense regarding the histories written in Persian in the subcontinent during the second millennium was that they were written by
outsiders; were too complicit with despotic power; were written by individuals to uphold or glorify the ruling elite; were mired in conventional and superfluous language; were biased against those who were
not Muslim. These histories were thus perceived to be tinged with
bias, sectarianism, and blindness to scientific knowledge. Mountstuart

Elphinstone's 1841 *The History of India* is a perfect embodiment of this structure of thought. It is subtitled "The Hindū and Mahometan Periods," with the book itself divided into two distinct sections labeled "Hindus" and "Mahometans."[2] The critique of this colonial episteme was a project even in the early twentieth century by historians such as Mohammad Habib, Shafaʾat Ahmad Khan, Tara Chand, and R. P. Tripathi. Several generations since have dismantled the colonial paradigm for India's modern history brick by brick—most famously under the Subaltern Studies collective. However, the construction of a medieval and ancient past for India under the colonial episteme has come under renewed attention recently.[3]

When conceptualizing how to think of Hindustan it is important to take seriously the intellectual genealogies of history writing, in Persian, from the eleventh to the nineteenth centuries and to put Europe in its "proper" historical place by demonstrating how universal claims of history do specific violence to our understanding of the past in colonized geographies.[4] At the heart of this book is a call to reassess and relearn Hindustani historical writings from the eleventh century to the twentieth. The need to reassess or relearn arises precisely because these texts have been rendered as biased, limited, lacking the necessary valid insights into the pasts or presents that they purportedly address—they are outsider texts, removed from the lived realities of the subcontinent.

Before I turn to the rich archive of Arabic and Persian histories, I want to start by offering a reading of a set of historiographic frameworks that have overdetermined how we interpret the history of the subcontinent: the paradigm of five thousand years of changeless Hindus and of the Muslim invaders and despots. The two frames are codependent, linked from their very inception in the colonial episteme and throughout the production of its history. This book contests both of these frames. In the second half, I make an argument for a world of Hindustan that can be found in Arabic and Persian histories. This world has a living connective tissue that stretches from the northwest subcontinent to the south, which touches the Indian Ocean, and provides a genealogy of historical thought for Firishta.

THE MAKING OF INDIA

The Constitution of the newly independent Republic of India, adopted in 1950, named the country in its first article: "India, that is Bharat, shall be a Union of States."[5] This new state embraced the colonial notion of an ancient Golden Age. Jawaharlal Nehru, the first prime minister, argued that this new nation's first and ideal ambassador was actually the Emperor Ashoka, who had ruled in the third century BCE. Ashoka's *chakra* (the dharmic wheel) was placed in the center of the tricolor flag of the Republic of India, while the Sarnath capital, with its four lions facing the four cardinal points, became the republic's emblem. Nehru had moved for the *chakra* to replace M. K. Gandhi's *charkha* (spinning wheel), which had been featured on previous flags. Nehru argued for Ashoka's significance to the new republic on July 22, 1947, when introducing the design of the flag: "It is well that at this moment of strife, conflict and intolerance, our minds should go back towards what India stood for in the ancient days and what it has stood for, I hope and believe, essentially throughout the ages in spite of mistakes and errors and degradations from time to time."[6] Where Nehru had long held Ashoka in admiration as a unifying figure, others at the constitutional debate interpreted Ashoka in starkly majoritarian ways. Mohan Sinha Mehta from Udaipur read Ashoka as a nativist: "Am I far wrong in saying that the chakra of Asoka represents the Indian States, because since the time of Asoka, the Great, the whole country has *not* been under Indian rule, ruled *by Indians for Indians*? At any rate, some of us would like to look upon it with that sentiment."[7] The insistence on "Indian" here was to underline that the Muslim rulers who had ruled in the subcontinent, just as much as the British colonial rulers, were not Indians.

To Nehru, Ashoka meant solidarity in a time of immense crisis and violence. In the purported "Golden Age" of Ashoka, Nehru saw a foundation for this new republic. Nehru had a deep and abiding interest in history and had already written influential works on the subject: *Glimpses of World History* (1934) and *The Discovery of India* (1946). While Nehru was jailed between 1930 and 1933 by the colonial state, he held India and Hindustan to be near synonymous. As he explained in a letter to his daughter, Indira Nehru, later published in *Glimpses of World History:* "Have I told you, or do you know, how our country came to be called India and Hindustan? Both names come from the river Indus or Sindhu, which thus becomes *the* river of India. From Sindhu the Greeks called our country Indos, and from this came India. Also from Sindhu, the Persians got Hindu, and from that came Hindustan."[8]

Yet, Hindustan was not mentioned as one of the names of India in the Constitution. It is thus important that, at the outset, we take a look at India as a semantic label. Much is made of the fact that both the words "Hind" and "India" are inventions of outsiders describing the subcontinent. In contrast are labels such as "Jambudvipa" or "Bharatavarsa," which represent emic or internal spatial labeling. The anxieties of insider / outsider, between languages that "belong" to the subcontinent and those that do not, permeate much of such debates. The Sanskritic labels preserved in Vedic texts speak often of a cosmological conception of place—an all-world encompassing space. There is no delineation of insider / outsider in such a cosmology. There is also no sense of the political belonging and exclusion that modern invocations of these terms rely upon.

Incidentally, South Asia is another geopolitical appellation that caught on in the post-1960s, which internalizes the nation-states and denotes a geography composed of India, Pakistan, later Bangladesh, Sri Lanka, sometimes Nepal and Bhutan, and, much more rarely, Afghanistan.[9] Thus, South Asia as a metonymic space grows or shrinks based on the boundaries of the constitutive states or the politics of the speaker. It is legible only when placed against East, West, or Central Asia. There is no internal logic. No one in the subcontinent has ever claimed to be proudly "South Asian." How South Asia entered the lexicon of the post-Sputnik era is a story covered elsewhere, and outside of our remit.[10] If "South Asia" and "India" are particular "outsider" constructs that came to be adopted, how was "Hindustan" erased? This is the elision that stands out in particular. When, as scholars, we make an implicit or explicit spatial argument for "India" or "South Asia" (for the precolonial subcontinent) without focusing on the role of language and sectarian temporalities, we participate in this erasure of "Hindustan" as a decidedly attendant precolonial geography of the subcontinent. In effect, the making of "India" and the unmaking of "Hindustan" are twinned processes. "India," as a word, came to be linked specifically by the Indologists with Sanskrit texts (and thus with Vedic cosmologies). This linking of India with the Vedic past coincided with the linking of Hindustan with the "Muslim" despotic political regimes.

As the British East India Company (BEIC) first advanced into the subcontinent, it already imagined the Mughal king as despotic and careless. When William Hawkins, an early English merchant, arrived at the port city of Surat in 1608, he noted, "At my coming on the shore, after their barbarous manner I was kindly received, and multitudes of people following me, all desirous to see a new come people, much nominated, but never came in their parts. As I was near the Governour's house, word was brought me that he [the Governor of Surat] was not well, being I think, rather drunk with affion or opium, being an aged man."[11] Hawkins's narrative depicts a Hindustan that is filled with people of "barbarous manner" and with an aged governor that is high on opium. When Hawkins makes it to the Mughal emperor Jahangir's court, these same two countervailing descriptions heighten his narrative. Jahangir received him with the "kindest manner," yet Hawkins describes him as indolent with his vices, unable to restrict his passions, and cruel to his nobles. Hawkins narrates a long anecdote concerning Jahangir having a man beaten to death for accidentally breaking a dinner plate. Jahangir is, like the governor of Surat, negligent of his populace—he spends his time watching elephants kill each other, and countless human beings are killed in the process. In Hawkins's telling, Jahangir ruled in a despotic manner with coercive power; a network of spies stretched across his realm. The Mughal king—the chief interlocuter for the English Crown and company—entered English discourse as a villain, a caricature, a king with ungoverned land. Over the long seventeenth century, the Muslim rulers of Hindustan would become the proverbial "despots" of European Enlightenment.[12]

Hawkins's vision carries over to William Jones (1746–1794), who arrived in Calcutta in 1783, to work as a judge for the British Supreme Court of Judicature in Fort Williams in Bengal.[13] In an early work, *Grammar of the Persian Language* (1771), Jones translated *hindu* as "black" as well as an Indian.[14] The European conceptions of race as a hierarchy and of Atlantic slavery shaped Jones's attitude toward Hindu: he sees them as "black," an enslaved population, within the subcontinent. When Jones updated this grammar in 1783, he also included a sample Persian "extract from the memoirs of the Emperor Jahāngīr, written by Himself," intended for the student to practice translating into English. The passage contains a description of the city of Agra. It reads, in the Persian, "Agra is the oldest city in all of Hindustan by the banks of the River Yamuna."[15] Jones left the passage from Jahangir untranslated in his book. Hence, the proverbial colonial student would read "Hindustan" in Persian and write "India" in English. This minor detail, of "Hindu" becoming "Indian," and "Hindustan" remaining untranslated, from a widely used pedagogical text of the Indologist Jones, captures precisely the process of this eliding of "Hindustan" as a concept.

It was not that Jones did not know of the word "Hindustan" or did not understand the usage. In 1783, he was appointed a jurist by the BEIC, and, during his journey aboard the ship, he sketched out his agenda for his stay in Calcutta. He headlined the list, "Objects of Enquiry during my residence in Asia." In the ordered list, item number five was "Modern Politics and Geography of Hindustan."[16] Therefore he was actively involved in the making of British India. For him, "Hindustan" and "India" may have shared the same or overlapping geography but were certainly separate cosmologies. In 1786, by the time he was giving his "Third Annual Discourse" for the Asiatick Society, Jones had completely disambiguated India from Hindustan: the former was Hindu, the latter Muslim. In this presentation, he connected the dots between Sanskrit, Pahlavi, and Greek to stress that "Hindustan" was a "foreign nomenclature" given by the Persians to the subcontinent. The philological argument started with Sindhu, an already specifically denoted location within the cosmology of Jambudvipa: a geography that surrounds the river Indus, a substratum of Bharatavarsa.[17] The "Sindhu," from Sanskrit, Jones argued, becomes "Hindav" in Old Persian or Avestan, "India" in Greek, "Hodduv" in Hebrew, and later "al-Hind" in Arabic. Much of this philological claim of Jones was conjectural—"Sindhu" in Sanskrit and "Hindu" in Avestan did not mean "Indus River," nor was there any reason for the word to *move* from one language to the other. Rather, both terms meant "frontier" and were not loan words at all.[18] The logic for Jones's claim, of course, was not simply philological but racial.

The argument for the term "India," thus, as an "indigenous" name for the subcontinent is itself a project within the colonial episteme. Jones stressed that while there were many Indias; or, rather, different parts of the subcontinent were labeled India in the Avestan, Greek, and Roman sources, one could now be sure: "By *India*, in short, I mean that whole extent of country, in which the primitive religion and languages of the *Hindus* prevail at this day with more or less of their ancient purity, and in which *Nágari* letters are still used with more or less deviation from their original form."[19] It is clear that Jones's linking of a particular language, its script, and a unitary faith and geography was critically a colonial project and began long before standard histories of language or historiographic schisms indicate. In fact, the nineteenth-century and early twentieth-century debates about Perso-Arabic script being foreign to India reflect the continuing hold of the Jonesian framework.[20] Jones had specifically linked India to a notional primitivity and a script that represented said indigeneity. Or, as Karl Marx would later put it, here was India reduced to "undignified, stagnatory, and vegetative life," by the "barbarian egotism" of the Oriental despots.[21]

It is also to Jones that we ought to credit a chronology for this Hindu place called India. The idea that India as a civilization is "five thousand years old" is now a truism. Here is an oft-repeated joke among Indologists: "I was in a rickshaw in India and I saw an ancient monument that I did not recognize, so I asked the rickshaw driver: 'What building is that?' and he answered 'It is a famous temple from the Ramayana and it is five thousand and twenty years old.' I said, 'Wow, that is very specific dating, how can you be so sure?' and he said, 'Ji, it was twenty years ago that I was told it was five thousand years old.'"[22] The point in the telling is to mark the way in which the totemic past (five thousand years) and the material past (the monument) intersect with the retelling of that past in India. The punch line is clearly the "twenty years ago"—the accretion of the small passage of the present to a monolithic past.

Where did we get this number of "five thousand years"? Jones's production of a primitive past for India was the product of a deep infatuation with figuring out the age of things—as we will soon see. The specific notion of "five thousand years" is, thus, traceable to Jones's long poem "The Enchanted Fruit; or, The Hindu Wife," from 1784, published in *Asiatick Miscellany* in 1799. The 287-couplet-long poem was part of a series of hymns he wrote as imitation of Sanskrit texts, while he was learning the language.[23] In this poem, Jones is overlaying the story of Draupadi and her five husbands from the *Mahabharata* with biblical time—the tasting of the forbidden fruit by Eve in the Garden of Eden and the Flood of Noah from the Bible. The equivalence between Draupadi and Eve allows Jones to merge the Christian story of the Fall of Man to the *Mahabharata*—linking the originary woman's appetite and the sexual deprivation of the Hindu wife. These linkages between deviant womanhood gave not only a chronology for India's history but also an illustration of the role of sexuality in Hindu society.[24] What is important to mark is that this poem is subtitled "The Hindu Wife," and that it pivots on the confession of Draupadi to sexual desire outside of her marriage with the Pandavas. In using the figure of the prototypical "Hindu Woman," Jones marks sexual enslavement as the division between India and Hindustan.

In "The Enchanted Fruit," Jones re-creates a story line from the *Mahabharata* concerning Draupadi, who was married to the five Pandava brothers. Jones recasts this story as the story of Adam and Eve. While on a walk with Draupadi and his brothers, Arjun shoots down a plump fruit, which is sixty cubits up in the air, dangling from a majestic tree branch. The fruit falls to the ground. However, the tree and the fruit did not belong to Arjun but to Krishna. Thus, in shooting down the fruit, they had committed a crime against Krishna, who vows to punish them, unless they each confess a crime, with the condition that Draupadi is the last to confess and that she hide nothing in her confession. With each confession, Krishna offered that the fruit will rise ten cubits into air, and with Draupadi's last confession, it will rejoin the stalk. While each of them admits to some version of a biblical sin (rage, deceit, and so on), Draupadi at first confesses to vanity and desire. The fruit rises, but stops two cubits short of reuniting with the stalk. She was clearly not telling the whole truth. After being subject to opprobrium, she finally confesses to lust, to having been tempted with desire for another man, a Brahmin, who had kissed her cheek. This confession of a transgression reunites the fruit to the stem.[25] Thus, with such juvenile versification, the prurient Jones provides a founding history for India.

The hymn is peppered with botanical taxonomy, Sanskrit terms in italics, and Jones's excessive annotation. The poem opens "'O lovely age, by Brahmens fam'd / Pure Setye Yug in Sanscrit nam'd," with an invocation of a golden age:

> when females of the softest kind
> were unaffected, unconfin'd
> And this grand rule from none was hidden;
> WHAT PLEASETH, HATH NO LAW FORBIDDEN.[26]

This was the time, Jones labeled, as belonging to India. In this pure age, the women were free to move and had freedom to pursue their pleasures— even marry up to five men—and were not subject to restrictive laws. Thus, for Jones, the first primary distinction between the two worlds—the Hindu India and the Muslim Hindustan—was the confinement of women. To illustrate his claim, Jones brings the "swarthy nymphs of Hindustan" to testify on the present state of Hindustan; for they can see far beyond their contemporary "short-sighted" man. They sing that they belong to the Kaliyuga (Dark Age), which was filled with women-haters and oppressive laws—that is, the Muslim man, who drags his harem full of enslaved women, stuffed in cages, and perpetual victims to his lust and rage. Here is the speech of the enslaved Hindu women in Jones's tongue:

> Not bound by vile unnatural laws,
> Which curse this age from *Cáley* nam'd
> By some base woman-hater fram'd
> Prepost'rous! that one biped vain
> Should drag ten house-wives in his train,
> And stuff them in a gaudy cage,
> Slaves to weak lust or potent rage!
> Not such the *Dwáper Yug*! oh Then
> ONE BUXOM DAME MIGHT WED FIVE MEN.

> True History, in solemn terms
> This Philosophick lore confirms.
> For *India* once, as now cold *Tibet,*
> A groupe unusual might exhibit,
> Of sev'ral husbands, free from strife,
> Link'd fairly to a single wife![27]

The Hindustani women, for Jones, are women who are simultaneously nymph-like, enslaved, enraged, and lustful. These are women whose confinement by the "one biped vain," in a harem alongside ten others, represents this Dark Age, the current Age of Kali. India's past was a lovely age when a woman was free to marry five men—the contrast could not be starker for Jones. This Golden Age of freedom in contrast to the current enslavement of the Muslim present, asserted Jones, was the "true history" of "*India once.*"

The question then arises for Jones on how to demarcate the time of the golden India from the vile Hindustan. To do so, Jones needs to provide a complete chronology, which he does:

> But, lest my word should naught avail,
> Ye Fair, to no unholy Tale
> Attend. *Five Thousand* years ago,
> As annals in *Benares* show,
> When *Pándu* chiefs with Curus fought[28]

Jones attached a footnote to "years" to explain how he came to the figure, as well as to give it a particular resonance as an "Indian" polity: "A round number is chosen; but the *Caly Yug* a little before which *Crishna* disappeared from this world, began *four thousand, eight hundred,* and *eighty four* years ago, that is according to our Chronologists, *seven hundred* and *forty-seven* before the flood; and the calculation of *M. Bailly,* but *four hundred* and *fifty-four* after the foundation of the *Indian* empire."[29] Five thousand years ago was India, according to Jones, a place with primitive, natural sexuality (marked by the natural deviance of women). It was time-linked to the epic battles of the *Mahabharata.* It is no accident that Kalidasa's *Sakuntala* was the first text translated from

Sanskrit by Jones. In contrast, Jones glosses Hindustan as a space for Muslim misogyny and violence against women. Hindustan existed in the time he was actively shaping, as a colonial translator, into British India.

Jones's "The Hindu Wife" inaugurates a gruesome fixing of the chronology of the past by colonial historians, philologists, administrators, and theorists. The notion of the five thousand years demonstrated the sharp rebuke of Hindustan by the colonial regimes of the early modern world. The subcontinent was a land without history, a primitive people without agency, whose present was shaped by foreign invaders. Jones sets the stage for future research to frame the history of "India" as differentiated from the Muslim "Hindustan." One can peruse the index of the *Asiatick Researches* of Bengal where "of the Hindu(s)" is the most common appellation. These articles and papers provide trenchant examples of how Indian antiquity—its five-thousand-years-ness—determined the capacity of historical research and interpretation. Jones, and his colonial compatriots in Calcutta, gave pride of place to Buddhist, Jain, and Vedic texts—and it was in that particular archive that a pre-Hindustan history of India was sought.

Jones, in 1791, said that he came to India "having an eager desire to know the real state of this empire before the conquest of it by the Savages of the North."[30] The decay, the darkness of Muslim rule in the subcontinent came into relief when Jones presented the first "Chronology of the Hindus" in 1788. Jones attempted to create an Indian chronology with the genealogical tables of Hindu kings taken from Sanskrit texts such as the *Manusmriti* and *Vishnupurana*. The only way to introduce historical time into the Indian past, Jones argued, was through its intersection with Alexander's campaigns—for which, he believed, there existed a verifiable chronology.

Following up on Jones, Captain Francis Wilford used the *Vishnupurana* and published "On the Chronology of the Hindus" in *Asiatick Researches* in 1798. Wilford linked Alexander's sojourn in India to the Hindu king Chandragupta Maurya: "In the *Vishnu-purāna* we read, unto *Nanda* shall be born nine sons; Cotilya, his minister shall destroy them, and place *Chandra-Gupta* on the throne."[31] Identifying the third-century BCE Chandragupta with Sandrocottus from the Greek sources allowed for the chronology of India to finally be fixed by history. This is perhaps the most celebrated moment in colonial historical thinking about India's role in world history.

From the *Vishnupurana,* cross-checked with "real" Greek histories, was then taken the chronology for the first significant political dynasty of India: "After the family of Nanda, Mauryas shall lord over the earth. This Kautilya shall install the Maurya king Chandra Gupta on the throne. He shall have a son by name Vindusāra, whose son shall be Aso-kavardana, whose son shall be Sujasas, whose son shall be Sangata, whose son shall be Salisuka, whose son shall be Vrihadratha. These Maurya kings shall reign for one hundred and seventy-three years."[32]

Asokavardana, that is Ashoka, made Chandragupta and this political lineage the most important for ancient India for the early historians of British India. Additionally, it also introduced Kautilya, the minister for Chandragupta, as the kingmaker, the most consequential adviser, parallel to Aristotle for Alexander.

Alongside the discovery of a dateable chronology was the discovery of the first political dynasty and theory of India—Chandragupta and his adviser Kautilya; Kautilya's political theory text called *Arthasastra;* and Chandragupta's grandson and ascendant king Ashoka. It is in these same pages of *Asiatick Researches* that we get an account of these discoveries, which shaped the discourse about the Golden Age of India. By the mid-nineteenth century Ashoka would be the hallmark of India's Golden Age: an India ruled by an Indian, a globalist India before Hindustan. His symbols and his edicts—terms of governorship carved into stone and installed across the subcontinent, which were "discovered" in the twentieth century—quickly became an enduring originary myth for the nationalist imagination. The material traces of Ashoka's edicts gave the twentieth century a generative map of an "Indian" subcontinent. The road to the cultural significance of Ashoka was, however, paved by philologists and archaeologists who took Ashoka as their object of study.

In the very first issue of the *Asiatick Researches* in 1797 two articles were published that begin the modern age of Ashoka in the twentieth century: The first was a report of Buddhist antiquities by Jonathan Duncan, and the second was a discussion of a trace of the inscription from the "Staff of Firuz Shah" by Antoine Polier.[33] Duncan came across the artifacts because workers digging for bricks (for Jagat Singh of Benares) found a sarcophagus with remains of two buried individuals.[34] The discovery of these Buddhist ruins provided the spark for colonial expansion into excavating the Golden Age of India. After Duncan's report, two major archaeological digs were undertaken by Colonel Colin Mackenzie and Colonel Alexander Cunningham in 1815 and 1835. These digs revealed the presence of an undecipherable script, which Polier had also reported on the "Staff of Firuz Shah" in Delhi. After Cunningham's excavation results were published, the matter of deciphering some of the inscriptions became more urgent. Finally, in 1837, James Prinsep, working at the *Asiatick Researches,* reconstituted the script, now known as Brahmi.

It was in the early twentieth century that Ashokan sites were excavated. Friedrich Oscar Oertel, in 1905, undertook a new excavation based on Cunningham's plans. He exhumed the capital from the western wall of the shrine. His description carries an admixture of glory and ruin, comparative gestures to Greece, and the supremacy of the Golden Age to anything produced in the last thousand years:

> The capital measures 7′ in height. It was originally one piece of stone but is now broken across just above the bell. As the photograph shows, it is surmounted by four magnificent lions standing back to back and in their middle was a large stone wheel, the sacred *dharmacakra* symbol. . . .
>
> The upper part of the capital is supported by an elegantly shaped Persepolitan bell-shaped member. The lion and other animal figures are wonderfully life-like and the carving of every detail is perfect. Altogether this capital is undoubtedly the finest piece of sculpture of its kind so far discovered in India. When looking at it and comparing it with later productions of animal sculpture in India, one fully realises Fergusson's verdict that *Indian art is written in decay.*[35]

The Sarnath capital, as this excavation came to be known, established the visual vocabulary for an "ancient" and triumphant "Golden Age" before the Muslim conquests and the "decay" that came after. Ashoka's edicts, found and cataloged across the subcontinent, constituted a map of "finds" that gave ancient India a geography and an ethics of awareness, nonviolence, and tolerance as opposed to the darkly violent Muslim kings.

In 1905, as the Sarnath capital was being excavated, the last missing piece of the Golden Age of Chandragupta was "found." A pandit brought to the Mysore Government Oriental Library a full manuscript of a text that had only previously been glimpsed through other texts: the *Arthasastra*. This "treatise on success" was immediately hailed as that long-lost source for political theory dating back to Chandragupta and his adviser.[36] Though the text, as extant, dates to between 1 BCE and 1 CE, it became linked in historical and political imagination to the third-century BCE Chandragupta.[37] With this colonial "discovery," the *Arthasastra* became the basis of political theory for pre-Hindustan India and Hindu kingship, with Kautilya emerging as an *avant la lettre* Machiavelli. Like the Ashokan edicts, *Arthasastra* gave a glimpse of political order in the full light of Hindu magnificence. It provided an idealized structure for a Hindu polity, a way for the Hindu king to exist within the hierarchies of kings, and the ethics of governance for a political geography. It cemented the divide between Hindustan and India.

The discovery of Ashoka allowed for the chronologies in scholarly texts, created in the early twentieth century, to "naturally" be organized around clusters of Hindu polities, such as the Gupta, the Rashtrakuta, the Kalyana Chalukyas, the Yadavas of Devagiri, the Chola, the Vijayanagar, and so on.[38] Each of these names encompassed a temporality of rule (seventy years to three hundred) of kings carefully culled from texts, epigraphs, and inscriptions. Historians would organize these polities into a hierarchy to illustrate the stagnant and fixed nature of those five thousand years: some were raja, some *rajaraja*, some *maharajadhiraja*, Ashoka was the *cakravartin* (wheel-turning monarch) who conquered the four quarters of the world (*digvijaya*).[39] He came at the beginning and, after him, was the decline.

Alongside the philologists and the archaeologists, the colonial historians were also invested in the divide between the timeless, history-less Hindus and the foreignness of Muslims. For the historians, the epic, or puranic, time gave no semblance of a working world-historical chronology. In 1817 James Mill cemented the notion of India versus Hindustan in his *The History of British India*—the first being aboriginal and native, the second foreign and barbaric; one Hindu, the other Muslim.[40] Unlike Jones, Mill had no patience for Sanskrit mythologies or poems. He quoted Edward Gibbon on Arabia's ancient past as indicative of his thinking on Indian pasts, "I am ignorant, and I am careless, of the blind mythology of the Barbarians."[41] He divided his book into two volumes: "Of the Hindus" and "The Mahomedans." The volume on Hindus had nothing to do with history. Instead it had three subsections: "Art," "Literature," and "General Reflections."[42] Following Mill, Mountstuart Elphinstone likewise opened his 1841 *History of India's Hindus* ("as the rudest of nations") with: "No *date* of a public event can be fixed before the invasion of Alexander; and no *connected* relation of the national transaction can be attempted until after the Mahometan conquest."[43]

With the discovery of Ashoka and the *Arthasastra,* ancient Indian *history* finally had a pronounced teleology outside of Muslim conquest. In 1919 Vincent Smith arranged history thus in his *The Oxford History of India: From the Earliest Times to the End of 1911:* the Ancient, Hindu, Muhammadan, and British periods. Part 2 of this volume is titled, "Hindu India from the Beginning of the Maurya Dynasty in 322 BCE to the Seventh Century AC," and begins with "Chandragupta Maurya, the first historical emperor of India, and his institutions."[44] This was the raw power, the inexorable logic, in the primitive claim of first arrival, of discovery, of first contact.

The paradigm of five thousand years covered two dimensions. First, it invoked a Golden Age for Indic pasts that gave form to not only the colonial episteme but to the postcolonial nationalist rendition. Second, and equally important, it cast the Muslim rulers of Hindustan as "Oriental despots."

The chronologies of Jones and Wilford led to the caustic histories of Mill, Elphinstone, Smith, and others through the mid-nineteenth century and onward. Against the natural chronology of the ancient Hindu king Ashoka was set a chronology of foreign invaders that defined the "degradation" of the subcontinent in the present: the conquest by Muhammad bin Qasim in 712 of Sindh, the invasions by Sebuktigin and Mahmud in 990 from Ghazni to Sindh and Gujarat, the conquest by Muhammad bin Sam in 1200 of Delhi, the arrival of Zahiruddin Babur in 1526. In the European imagination, the so-called invading Muslims brought already formed theories of kingship and their own chronologies to the subcontinent: from the Prophet (d. 632) to the first political state in Medina, to the figure of the *amir ul mu-minin* (commander of the faithful) to the institution of the Caliphate in Damascus and then in Baghdad, to the 'Abbasid, the Buyid, the Seljuq, the Ghaznavid, the Gurid, and the Mughal polities. They created themselves as sultan, shah, *shahanshah* in the subcontinent as foreign rulers. Thus, for the European imagination, Muslim political history was always outside, to be located in the Arab world, not in the subcontinent.

The entire history of Muslims, in the European imagination, is understood as one of "conquest" epitomized in the motif of the "sword of Islam."[45] A very early reaction, such as the one from Patriarch Sophronius of Jerusalem in 634, illustrates this point: "We do not see the twisting, flaming sword, but rather the sword of the Saracens, beastly and barbarous, which truly is filled with every diabolic savagery."[46] The sword is present in Dante Alighieri's *Inferno* (1320); in Walter Raleigh's *The Life and Death of Mahomet, the Conquest of Spaine together with the Rysing and Ruine of the Sarazen Empire* (1637); in Thomas Carlyle's "The Hero as Prophet" (1840).[47] Modern scholarship on early Islam has as well foregrounded the "conquest paradigm"—examples range from Philip K. Hitti's *Origins of Islamic State* (1917), to H. A. R. Gibb's *The Arab Conquests in Central Asia* (1923).

The paradigm of Muslim conquest creates an originary myth for all Muslim polities, that they are direct descendants of the earliest period and their "homeland" is in Islam's foundational geography—the desert. Any Muslim polity can be understood through a host of concepts Europeans used to describe the earliest period of Islam, such as "tribe," "raids," "nomadism," and so on. This has had the anachronistic effect of freezing Islam as a "religion of the desert" even as it, as has any other ideological or intellectual tradition, mutated, developed, matured, and flourished far from its denotive place of birth.[48]

Where Jones shaped the philological study of the five thousand years of India, the magistrate, collector, and later secretary to the Government of India in the Foreign Office, Henry Miers Elliot (1808–1853), established the archival study of "Muhammadan India" as the Dark

Ages. He epitomized the general colonial understanding of Muslims as invaders in India:

> Scarcely had the false prophet expired, when his followers and disciples, issuing from their naked deserts, where they had hitherto robbed their neighbours and quarrelled amongst themselves, hastened to convert their hereditary feuds into the spirit of unanimity and brotherly love. . . . The conquest of Persia was a mere prelude to further extension in the east; and though a more difficult and inhospitable country, as well as internal dissensions, checked their progress for some years afterwards, yet it was not in the nature of things to be expected, that they should long delay their attacks upon the rich and idolatrous country of India, which offered so tempting a bait to their cupidity and zeal.[49]

These Muslim invaders met the Hindu kings whom Savarkar and other nationalists had cast as resisters.

Elliot spearheaded a truly monumental project for the nineteenth century—the acquisition and excerpted renderings of Persian histories. He remained unconvinced that the Muslim chronology added actual knowledge to Indian pasts: "It must be understood, then, that this Index has not been constructed on account of any intrinsic value in the Histories themselves. Indeed, it is almost a misnomer to style them Histories. They can scarcely claim to rank higher than Annals. . . . If the artificial definition of Dionysius be correct, that 'History is Philosophy teaching by examples,' then there is no Native Indian Historian; and few have even approached to so high a standard."[50] The India-Hindustan division operated within the five-thousand-years paradigm. If Hindu kings were located in the *Bharatavarsha*, then the origins of Muslim kings were in the Prophet's Medina and the earliest Muslim conquests, as Elliot noted in 1853.

The notion of Mahmud Ghazni as a foreign invader was critical to this idea of the Dark Age of Muslim despotic rule. There was, however, an irony in the dual configuration of Ashoka as representative of the Golden Age and Mahmud Ghazni as herald of the Dark Age. British archaeologists, for instance, located three Ashokan edicts in Kandahar and three in Laghman (both locations are now in Afghanistan). The inscriptions were in Greek, Aramaic, or bilingual Greek and Aramaic. Archaeologists generally accepted that these marked the territorial reach of Ashokan governance—part of Ashokan's imperial rule—where his edicts performed the work of publicly proclaiming his vision for his polity: "And the king abstains from (killing) living beings, and other men and those who (are) huntsmen and fishermen of the king have desisted from hunting."[51] Ashoka's Laghman is about forty miles from Kabul and a hundred miles from Ghazni. It was from Ghazni that the European prototypical representative of the so-called Muslim invader came.

Mahmud (r. 998–1030), who ruled from Ghazni, Kabul, and Lahore was, to British historiography, the very epitome of the foreign Muslim invader. In 1776, Edward Gibbon introduced him as the first "sultan" on a holy war: "But the principal source of his [Mahmud's] fame and riches was the holy war which he waged against the Gentoos of Hindostan. In this foreign narrative I may not consume a page; and a volume would scarcely suffice to recapitulate the battles and sieges of his twelve expeditions. Never was the Musulman hero dismayed by the inclemency of the seasons, the height of the mountains, the breadth of the rivers, the barrenness of the desert, the multitudes of the enemy, or the formidable array of their elephants of war."[52] Almost seventy years later, Elphinstone rewrote that passage in his 1841 *History of India* as: "[To Mahmud] . . . the undiscovered regions of India presented a wider field for romantic enterprise. The great extent of that favoured country, the rumours of its accumulated treasures, the fertility of the soil, and the peculiarity of its productions, raised it into a land of fable, in which the surrounding nations might indulge their imaginations without control."[53] Elphinstone also reaffirmed that Mahmud military excursions to Lahore, Sindh, and Gujarat were for the purpose of plunder. The "seventeen raids" motif began its life first as the "twelve raids of Mahmud of Ghazni" in Gibbon and in Elphinstone, who cited the authority of Barthélemy d'Herbelot, Alexander Dow, and Silvestre de Sacy—all of whom wrote about the polity that emerged in Ghazni and asserted itself as a successor state to the 'Abbasid. It was Elliot who "corrected" the figure of the twelve raids of Mahmud to the now-mythical "seven-teen raids of Mahmud Ghaznavi on India." Elliot also framed Mahmud as driven by avarice and characterized Mahmud's Hindu adversaries as naturally weak and docile: "It was to have been expected that Mahmúd, after establishing himself on the throne of Ghazní, would have embraced the first opportunity of invading India; for while yet a prince, he had seen how easily the hardy warriors of Zábulistán had overcome the more effeminate sons of India."[54]

Elliot's seventeen raids that Mahmud waged on India would become totemic—W. W. Hunter reproduced it in *A Brief History of the Indian Peoples* (1880), and Vincent Smith added the number to his *The Oxford History of India*. By 1920, everyone taking the Indian Civil Services Exam would reflect on the seventeen raids of Mahmud: Ashoka was the perfect Indian King; Mahmud, the perfect Muslim invader.

If British colonial historiography recognized that Ghazni, Kabul, and Laghman were part of Ashokan Indian territory, then Mahmud's "plundering" would not qualify as one from "outside" nor differ in form or ideology from other polities of Mahmud's contemporaries, including his rival Shahis or the Gurjara-Prathiharas. Hence it is the explicit framing of Mahmud as Muslim that explains his foreignness, not the territory from which he staged his "raids."

The paradigmatic five thousand years of the colonial episteme was premised on a Golden Age of India that had its zenith in the age of Ashoka and that declined as a result of Muslim invaders, epitomized by Mahmud Ghazni. This India was to be differentiated from the Hindu-stan of the colonial present on the basis of customary practices that made the people of India remain in a state of so-called primitivity, produced through subjugation by Muslims.

AN INTELLECTUAL GEOGRAPHY
FOR HINDUSTAN

Having sketched out some of the contours of the colonial episteme, we turn to the critical question: What would it mean to write a history of Hindustan outside of the paradigm of foreign Muslim invaders and the stagnant five thousand years of a subcontinental past? Arabic and Persian histories were culled in colonial historiography for acts of violence, held up as representations of Muslim estrangement from the people of the subcontinent. To unthink the colonial interpretation of these histories then requires looking anew. Indeed, when one reads the histories of Hindustan in Arabic or Persian, one finds a radically different story than the despotic history glossed by the colonial historian. In this second section, I begin a reconstructive project, reading the Arabic and Persian accounts to understand a different modality for thinking about Hindustan. This imagination of Hindustan begins to take shape in a geography that stretches from the Deccan to Gujarat, to Sindh, and to Kashmir in an intellectual genealogy of Hindustani historians who wrote from the ninth and tenth centuries through the seventeenth century, in the time of Firishta.

In Chapter 1, I introduced Firishta's Deccan as constituted by the Indian Ocean world. It is a key pivot for the intellectual geography of Hindustan—incorporating the coastlines of Sindh, Gujarat, the Deccan, and Kerala. The Arab principalities of Sindh—most prominently the Habari (854–1010)—came into existence in the mid-eighth century and lasted until the mid-eleventh century. They were city-states built around Mansura, Uch, Multan, and Khambhat and have been only sparsely considered in historiography.[55] These were the earliest Muslim political entities in Hindustan. They inhabited a geography that had long been a circuit of land and sea trade routes, coastal and up-river marketplaces and settlements—connecting ports in Aden, Muscat, Bahrain, Dammam, and Siraf to Sindh and Gujarat with ports like Daybul, Diu, Thane, Surat, Khambhat, and farther down to the Kerala and Karnatak coastlines.

Some of the rulers in these polities marked some aspects of their political allegiance to caliphs in Baghdad, but they had deeper and resonant political ties to rulers in Deogir, Ujjain, and Gwalior. Their nearly five hundred years of political existence testify to their political and social success. The Arabic travel and merchant accounts from the ninth and tenth centuries help us conceptualize this mercantile geography. They orient us toward a past that need not be understood reductively as a violent encounter between two alien civilizations. The Arabic histories rendered Hindustan as *al-Sind wa'l Hind*—"Sindh and Hind," on either side of the river Indus—or as a cognate pair *bilad al-Sind wa'l Hind* (the places of Sindh and Hind). By the early eleventh century, *al-Hind wa'l Sind* was simply "Hind" or "Hindustan." In these accounts, I wish to highlight divergent traditions, ways of thinking that do not fit the colonial paradigms. Again, my aim is not to be exhaustive but to be suggestive, even indexical.

Take for example, Ahmad ibn Yahya Baladhuri's history *Futuh al-Buldan,* written in Baghdad in the mid-ninth century. In it is the account of a Raja Jai Singh, in Sindh, who received a letter from the Umayyad caliph 'Umar ibn 'Abdul 'Aziz (r. 717–720). Upon gaining the caliphate in Damascus, 'Aziz had sent numerous letters to the polities in Sindh and Hind, writes Baladhuri, "inviting them to Islam." Baladhuri, in a mode of praise, writes that these subcontinental monarchs were already aware of 'Aziz as a pious, ascetic, and just king. Hence, upon receiving the letter, they readily accepted and converted to his faith, changing their names to Muslim names.[56] Baladhuri presents the logic of political claim to a space that was decidedly not "conquest" but rather a preponderance of amity based on notions of mutually recognizable good—the dharmic ideals of asceticism, piety, and service. It is certainly a triumphalist conversion narrative, but the recognition of piety as a source for political legitimacy is noteworthy.

Another conversion narrative is contained in the early tenth-century Indian Ocean–centered text *Kitab 'Aja'ib al-Hind.* It is attributed to Buzurg ibn Shaharyar and opens with an account of a "King of Hind," located in Kashmir. The raja writes to the governor of the city of Mansura in Sindh—again during the caliphate of 'Aziz, asking for the "laws of Islam in the language of Hind."[57] The text narrates that the governor called upon a man of Iraqi descent who had grown up in Hind and spoke various languages of the land. Upon the governor's request, the man wrote, in the local language, an ode that set out the necessary rules and principles of Islam.

The poem was dispatched to the raja, who was very pleased with it, and asked that the poet himself be sent to his court. The poet went and lived in Kashmir for three years. Upon his return, he was asked to describe what had happened to him. He explained that, by the time of his departure from Kashmir, the king had already converted to Islam but had not publicly acknowledged it for the fear of losing the right to govern his country. The account continues:

> He further reported that the king had requested an exegesis on the Qur'an in the language of Hind [*hindiya*], which he was in the process of providing—when he reached the chapter of *Ya-Sin* and quoted Allah: "Say: He will give life to them Who brought them into existence at first, and He is cognizant of all creation." As he was explaining the verse, the king, who was sitting on a throne of immense wealth and beauty, rose up and walked on plain ground—ground that was wet from having been sprinkled—and he put his cheek on that earth and wept, such that his face was covered in mud. He said to me: "He is truly the One to be Worshipped, the First, the Ancient, the one Alone." After that, he had a room built, which he explained was for the purpose of contemplation in matters of polity. Instead he prayed there in secret. The poet reported that the king granted him six hundred *mann* of gold.[58]

This rendering of an encounter does not begin with a conquest but rather persuasion and a revelation. It showcases the poet, who was born in Sindh, of Iraqi descent, who was already at home with the languages and customs of Sindh. Here lies the movement of ideas and people across polities, the recognition of political sovereignty of the powerful Kashmiri king, the desire to create meaningful relationships between the Muslim city-state and Kashmir, the recognition that the political act of conversion is separate and distinct from the spiritual act of conversion. It also foregrounds the ways in which ideas move across texts—the rendering of the Qur'an into a poetic Hindi language and further as an oral exegesis. The encounter here is of language, poetics, and textual practices rather than of polities (though they clearly frame the project). There is an intimacy of living together and an attention to the nuances of political subjectivity that demonstrates long histories of coexistence.

Pointedly, conversion is not the only form of encounter. The direct interface between the Arab king and the Hindustani king becomes a subject of great interest in the early Arabic accounts. In these accounts we learn of extended correspondences between kings where nothing was valued more highly than the knowledge contained in a book. In these accounts the encounter between the Arab world and Hindustan is one not of conquest and subjugation but of intellectual exchange. For example, in Ahmad bin 'Ali ibn Zubayr's *Kitab al-Hadaya wa al-Tuhaf*, which dates to the eleventh century, there are lists of gifts exchanged between the courts in Iraq and Hind. Among the gifts mentioned are a diamond-encrusted mechanical she-camel that could move on its own and in whose belly were pearls of great value; a stick made of emerald; vast quantities of *'ud*, sandalwood, and ambergris; elephants; idols of silver or gold; and water buffalos. In addition to this gift exchange, I want to highlight a set of letters exchanged between Baghdad and polities in Hind, which are also reproduced by Zubayr. They demonstrate ways in which the littoral Indian Ocean world was connected in an economy of exchange at the courtly level.[59]

The first letter is from Dahmi, a king in Hind, to the caliph Harun Rashid (d. 833) and is reproduced in full by Zubayr. The letter was written in gold ink on the bark of a fragrant tree. Zubayr reports that the courier was a ranked, previously enslaved person from Sindh—a woman who was over ten feet tall "with hair so long that it touched the ground when she walked, of great beauty; with four braids on her head arranged like a crown; with eyelashes as long as an index finger, such that when she blinked they touched her cheeks; with teeth so white that they seemed like lightning between her lips; with firm breasts and eight bellyfolds."[60] The gifts that accompanied her were equally larger than life: a goblet made of ruby and filled with large pearls; a carpet made from the skin of a snake so large that it could swallow an elephant; small rugs made from the feathers of the mythic *samandal*, the lizard that can live in fire; large quantities of aloe wood and camphor.

The letter itself is much less fantastical than the description of the courier and her gifts. Dahmi begins by describing the excellence of the palace in which he lives, his polity, the land he governs, and then pivots to God's praise:

> It has not escaped us that when we made mention of the grandeur of our ancestors and our current greatness, all that will

vanish. Indeed, we should have begun this letter by mentioning God. Yet we think his name as too exalted with which to begin a letter. God's name should only be used in places of worship and prayers. We received word of your erudition and we have not seen any other ruler with such qualities. We are with you for friendship and love of knowledge. Therefore we open this correspondence with a search for useful knowledge by sending you the translation of a book "The Cream of Intellect." When you read it, you will discover that this is an appropriate title for it. We are also sending you some gifts but we know that they are much too inferior to one of your rank. Yet we request that you ignore our shortcomings and accept them (if God wills).[61]

The explicit privileging of knowledge—the book—over riches is the most noteworthy aspect in this letter. The significance of translation is again underlined, as it was in the earlier account of the raja of Kashmir—there the Qur'an was being translated into Hindustani script and here a text from Hind is being translated into Arabic.

The caliph replies to this letter with his own gifts. He dispatches the letter with a courier mounted on a horse with a saddle studded with carnelian, carrying ambergris, onyx, other fabric from Yemen and Egypt. The caliph's reply addresses Dahmi with a Muslim greeting, even though he was a non-Muslim, as a sign of respect. The caliph affirms Dahmi's faith without challenging it. He then continues on the theme of growing a relationship through the exchange of knowledge:

We offer you a gift of our love, which is the best gift to exchange between friends. We are sending you a book "An Anthology of the Cores of Intellect and Garden of Rare Minds," which is translated from Arabic. After reading this translation you will realize the virtue of this gift. You will also realize that the name [of the book] is apt. We accompany this gift with other gifts, which do not rise to your excellence. It is indeed true that if kings exchange gifts according to their standings, their treasuries would soon exhaust themselves. Yet, this exchange happens as tokens of goodwill among mutual relations.[62]

At both ends of the relationship there is awareness and recognition of the other's polity, religion, and customs. The letters emphasize that books, representing knowledge, are "self-evident" demonstrations of their worth. The books, and the letters for that matter, are indicative of the already existing infrastructures of exchange: the capacity to create translations, to send and receive messages and goods, and to understand what is of value, culturally and intellectually.

These exchanges document processes of transmutation and transculturation, of ideas and people across geographies. The Hindustani also looks different in these Arabic sources than what the colonial episteme projected—as an antagonist of the Muslim invaders. Unsurprisingly, Hindustan possesses history in these accounts: political history, intellectual history.

In the ninth- and tenth-century Indian Ocean texts, there is also the often-cited King Balhara of Hind, who is portrayed as a strong and wise king of a polity based in Gujarat, or the Deccan region. Firishta would later call attention to this king, in order to demonstrate the recognized history of exchanges between Hindu and Muslim kings in Hindustan to his audience. Perhaps the quintessential account of Balhara is in Sirafi's *Akhbar al-Sin wa al Hind* (ca. 851):

> The Balhara is the noblest of the Indians [Hindi], all of whom acknowledge his nobility. Although each one of the kings in India [Hind] rules independently, they all acknowledge his superior rank, and when his envoys arrive at the courts of any of the other kings, they make obeisance to them as a mark of honor to Balhara. He is a king who distributes payments to his troops as the Arabs do, and he owns many horses and elephants and possesses great wealth. . . . The people of Balhara's kingdom assert that their ruler's lengthy reigns and long lives on the throne are due entirely to their fondness for the Arabs. None of the other rulers show the Arabs such affection as does Balhara, and his people share his fondness for them.[63]

Balhara is a totemic figure. Balhara's support for Arab merchants and his status among the other kings are indicative of the attention paid to the political climate in the littoral regions in these texts. There are numerous other descriptions of other kings in India and descriptions of their qualities: They do not drink alcohol or have sexual relationships outside of their sanctioned marriages; they have excellent law and order in their lands such that no merchant is robbed; they organize debates and dialogues between Muslims and non-Muslims in which matters of theological importance are considered; they allow for the construction of mosques, and colonies of homes for Muslims; they provide employment and stipends to Muslims who live in their lands; their daughters are allowed to become rulers on their own accord and they are supported by the armies; they honor and protect treaties and pacts with other rulers, including the Muslim caliph.

The accounts of the kings of Hindustan in Arabic and Persian histories help us populate the world of an Indian Ocean milieu. That population consisted of merchants, travelers, enslaved or bonded persons, and women who traveled alone of all faiths. These glimpsed intersecting lives are not fictions of merchants and traders. A series of epitaphs on the graves of merchants from thirteenth- and fourteenth-century Khambhat, Gujarat, document genealogies back to Irbil, to Hamdan, to Tbilisi, all of whom had been living, and dying, in Hindustan for four or six generations.[64] The actual contents of these texts, fortified by the evidence of the material remains of the people who lived in Hindustan, undermine the colonial assertion that there was nothing within Arabic and Persian histories to account for the people of Hindustan. Having glimpsed the contours of the lived life of the Indian Ocean as found in Arabic and Persian texts, we can better contextualize why Mahmud Ghazni incorporated Saivite symbols of the Hindu Shahi rulers of Kabul and Kashmir on his coins and why Hindustani mints put Arabic legends on their own coins.[65]

Let me now expand the contours of the intellectual geography that shaped Firishta and his history—from the Indian Ocean world north to Kashmir, west to Sindh and Kabul. The intellectual geography of Hindustan that comes into focus in Firishta's history emerges in and around city-states that ranged from Kashmir to the Deccan. Firishta cites histories written by historians from these city-states dating back to the tenth through the twelfth centuries. By the early twelfth century, elite literary families were settling in Lahore and Multan. Uch, farther south, was another key site that emerges in the late twelfth and early thirteenth centuries as a major node in this intellectual geography—one that overlaps with the geographies of the mercantile Indian Ocean world, the literary "Persianate" world, as well of the epic worlds of the *Puranas.*

In these various ways of imagining the geographies of the subcontinent, this intellectual geography encompasses the network of texts, citational practices, archives, schools, royal patronage, and scholarly communities that shaped the writing of history. This intellectual geography intersects with, and is informed by, centers of power both political and sacral. The scholars in an intellectual geography are administrators, advisers, military commanders, poets, historians, religious leaders, or saints. What makes them a community—and the reason there is an attendant "geography"—is that they are embedded in institutions that cohere across political systems and for generations. Firishta proclaims his own membership in this intellectual geography.

For Firishta's Hindustan, the intellectual geography has cities such as Ghazni, Kabul, Peshawar, Srinagar, Lahore, Uch, Thatta, Agra, Awadh, Patna, Jaunpur, Dhaka, Gulbarga, Golkonda, Bijapur, Chitor, Ujjain, Ahmedabad, and Surat, to name the most prominent ones from the tenth to the seventeenth centuries. At times, these sites were centers of political dynasties, at times mercantile and trade nodes, often with monumental architecture. We cannot, in any analytical way, divide the histories of these cities along the lines of ideologies—there is no Hindu period followed by a Muslim period. These are significant urban and urbane centers where political power rested. The intellectual geography of Hindustan was formed *through* these cities as much as it was formed *by* them.

For Firishta, this intellectual geography is grounded in the works of seven centuries of Hindustani historians and poets. In Ghazni were gathered prominent poets such as Abu'l Qasim Firdausi (d. 1025), Abu'l Qasim Ḥasan bin Aḥmad 'Unsari (d. 1041), Abu'l Hasan 'Ali bin Julug Farrukhi (d. 1039), Manuchehri Damghani (d. 1041), Muhammad ibn 'Abd-al Jabbar 'Utbi (d. ca. 1040), and Abu Rayhan Biruni (d. ca. 1051). 'Utbi's *Kitab al-Yamini* is a primary account of the Ghazni polity, describing the splendor of the city under Mahmud's construction projects. Mahmud created a mosque to rival the grand mosques of Nishapur or Damascus. He had artisans and workers from Hindustan who incorporated wood, marble, frescoes, and idols taken from his various conquered cities and reconstituted them into walls, murals, and columns. He also created a school with a faculty and stipends for students.[66] The *Shahnama,* which Firdausi dedicated to Mahmud, was a monumental book of kings that would shape the very foundations of verse, history, and poetics for centuries to come. Hindustan, the geography and its rulers, are an important part of the *Shahnama.* Biruni's *Kitab tahqiq ma li'l-Hind* (Book of researches on Hind) would herald anew the study of the history, mathematical sciences, and religion of Hindustan in Arabic and Persian.[67] The historian Baihaqi (d. 1077), under Mas'ud, would imagine a philosophy of history for the realm. These Hindustani intellectuals and their texts did not disappear even as the polities and eras that surrounded them vanished. They are continuously read, copied, and cited through to the nineteenth century in an unbroken chain of use and commentaries. This is the intellectual geography in which Firishta bases his own history.

As we will encounter these texts and intellectuals over the course of this book, it is appropriate here to introduce them with some detail. The first three historians were all attached to the city-state in Uch. Minhaj Siraj Juzjani (c. 1190–1260) was a historian, jurist, poet, and educator who served in Uch and then later in Delhi. He came from a prominent intellectual class with close (patronage and marital) ties to the ruling elite in Ghazni and Ghur. His grandfather, father (born in Lahore), and other relatives had served for courts in Ghazni, Ghur, and Lahore as jurists, theologians, and diplomats. These are the relationships and histories that allowed for this scribal class to move, largely unmolested, across political contestations. Juzjani came to Uch in 1227 and was made the principal of the school Madrasa-i Firuzi. He was later employed by Shamusuddin Iltutmish (r. 1229–1236) as a scholar at court in Delhi—charged with giving weekly addresses from the threshold of the Royal Chambers. Juzjani spent forty years in the service of Delhi sultans and, during this time, produced the massive work of history *Tabaqat-i Nasiri*—a descriptive genealogical history of Muslim rulers from Adam to his present.

Muhammad 'Awfi (ca. 1170–1230) came to be in Uch in the early 1220s— he had earlier worked as a jurist in Samarkand, Bukhara, and then moved to Khambhat in Gujarat. He worked as a jurist, first in Uch and later in Delhi. 'Awfi began to translate sections from Arabic of Muhassin ibn 'Ali Tanukhi's tenth-century *Kitab al-Faraj ba'd al-Shidda* (Book of deliverance after hardships) and dedicated it to Qabacha, the ruler in Uch.[68] Tanukhi's text represented a popular example of the *adab* (belles lettres) genre, which contained anecdotes of travelers facing wild animals or robbers, and of officials facing execution, penury, or a capricious ruler. 'Awfi next wrote his own composition of the genre of traveler accounts in *Jawami al-Hikayat wa Lawam-i' al-Riwayat* (Collection of anecdotes and illustration of stories) incorporating into the Arabic canon stories from Gujarat, Uch, and Multan. 'Awfi links Arabic literary tradition to the contours of Hindustan's landscape; stories that moved between the iconic Baghdad and the everyday Uch.

In 1216, at the age of fifty-eight, 'Ali Kufi, a recent migrant to Uch, decided to create "a book of exceptional beauty and grace" that would provide a history of Muslim polities in Sindh.[69] Kufi inscribed a history of the Brahman Chach's rule over Sindh prior to the first Muslim campaigns in Sindh and linked these two polities intimately through both political theory and legal frameworks. The *Chachnama* modeled a world of politics that was grounded in Hindustan, linking Uch to Baghdad.[70]

Iltutmish established Delhi as the capital of his Hindustani polity in 1228. He founded a series of colleges, most importantly the *madrasa-i nasiriyya*, to one of which Juzjani was appointed as principal. At Delhi a series of historians gathered to write about the history of Hindustan. Hasan Nizami's *Taj al-Ma'athir* was commissioned by Qutbuddin Aybak, the governor in Delhi, around 1210. Similarly, Fakhr-i Mudabbir Mubarakshah, who grew up in Multan and moved between Peshawar, Lahore, and Delhi, dedicated his *Adab al-Harb wa al-Shuja'a* to Iltutmish. The life and career of Amir Khusrau highlights the intellectual breadth of Delhi in the late thirteenth century.[71] Khusrau was born in Patiali in Uttar Pradesh in 1253 and died in Delhi in 1325. He authored major works in history, poetry, epics, and romance utilizing Arabic, Persian, Turkish, and Hindustani. Khusrau was employed by a series of sultans during his career as a diplomat and historian. The historian Ziauddin Barani's family also had served as functionaries in the city of Delhi. He himself worked for Muhammad bin Tughluq (r. 1324–1351), producing his grand history of *Tarikh-i Firuz Shahi* around 1357. The sack of Delhi in 1398 by Timur produced the last great work of history that I want to draw into this conversation. Shams Siraj 'Afif's *Tarikh-i Firuz Shahi,* which was completed in 1399, gives a history of Firuz Shah Tughluq (r. 1351–1388).

Zahiruddin Babur's (1483–1530) defeat of Ibrahim Lodhi in 1526 established the polity commonly known as the Mughals in Delhi. Babur was himself a learned man whose interest in libraries, scholars, and historical and poetical works is abundantly clear in his memoir, *Tuzuk,* which he wrote throughout his life. It was translated into Persian from Chaghatai as *Baburnama* by the order of his grandson Jalaluddin Akbar (1542–1605). The Mughal kings of Hindustan inscribed their own life stories, but within their dominion the practices of historical writing also flourished. One of the most prominent was the historian Abu'l Fazl (1551–1602), who was a courtier, and later chief minister, with Akbar. Abu'l Fazl wrote *Akbarnama,* a history of the Mughal rulers, along with an attendant geography and documentation of Hindustan labeled *A'in-i Akbari.* Another prominent historian was Khwaja Nizamuddin Ahmad. His father had been employed by Babur, and Akbar appointed him to the governorship in Gujarat. Ahmad's *Tabaqat-i Akbar Shahi* (1593) was a history of nobility and kings in Hindustan, modeled after Juzjani's *Tabaqat.*

From Delhi we move down to the Deccan. 'Abd ul-Mulk 'Isami dedicated his verse history *Futuh-us-Salatin* (1350) to the new Bhamani polity in the Deccan. His ancestors had been in service of the sultans at Delhi and his grandfather was required to move to the Deccan to the newly appointed capital of Daultabad by Muhammad Tughluq. 'Isami's history extends the geography of Hindustan into the Deccan. By the time of Timur's sack of Delhi in 1398, the multiple polities in Gujarat and Deccan had become new centers for learning and knowledge production. The Deccan plateau saw a series of planned urban sites emerge from the fifteenth century onward—Firuzabad, Bijapur, and Nauraspur, among others. The Deccan from the mid-fourteenth century onward saw a number of polities with a series of Hindustani kings who patronized Arabic, Persian, and Dakhani literature and arts. Mahmud Gawan, in 1472, built a madrasa in Bidar with a massive library. These settlements, and such patronage, rivaled the intellectual networks growing alongside the West-East corridor—from Delhi to Jaunpur to Dhaka.

From the eleventh century onward, this Hindustani network of scholars produced a cohesive account of their world and their past. They connected their works to the previous generation, paid homage to the historians that came before, while reinventing the forms and content of history writing for their own social and political milieus. While the account above has focused largely on historians and histories, the intellectual network comprised, just as abundantly, poets, hagiographers, advisers, and entertainers.

I will use one last illustration to argue for the cohesiveness of an intellectual milieu in Hindustan, stepping slightly away from the "historical" to the register of the poetic, and turn to Qutban Suhravardi's 1503 *Mirigavati*, which was dedicated to Husain Shah Sharqi (1458–1505), the ruler of Jaunpur in Bihar. While my project is based almost exclusively on histories, it is worthwhile to note that Hindustani intellectual traditions were embedded in polysemic genres and forms. Qutban's *Mirigavati*, written in Awadhi, combines Persian, Arabic, and Sanskrit epics with its own Sufi gloss. The love story unfolds in a mythical landscape with a geography that maps fully onto that of the Himalayas, the Ganges, and the plains. Here is how the poet Qutban describes his work:

> First, this was a Hindavī story,
> then some poets told it in Turkī.
> Then I opened up its multiple meanings:
> asceticism, love, and valor are its *rasas*.
> When it was the year 1503,
> I composed this tale in caupāīs.
> If you read its six languages without a wise man,
> evening will fall and you'll still be reading!
> The Sign of the Lion was the auspicious constellation.
> There are many meanings in this tale; use your wit and
>   you'll understand.[72]

The interplay of languages and interpreters—literally those who are wise and thus can guide you—can be easily read as a barely shaded comment on gnostic knowledge, in this case, Sufic. Yet, a more powerful reading is the one that hints at the social world surrounding this text. Even a minor court, such as that of Husain Shah Sharqi, had the capacity to create a network of intellectuals within which epics could be rendered anew; thus the confidence of Qutban that he could open up new meanings to romances dating back to the *Mahabharata* or the *Thousand and One Nights.* This too is part of the intellectual network of Hindustan. We can place the *Mirigavati* alongside much more well-known examples, such as the movement of advice texts, including the *Arthasastra, Hitopadesa,* and *Pancatantra,* from Sanskrit into Pahlavi, then Arabic, as *Kalila wa Dimna,* and into Persian as *Anvar-i Suhayli.* Scholars have long cited such translations as evidence of specific nodes of intertheological exchanges. My point is that we ought to consider these texts as existing simultaneously in the intellectual geography of Hindustan rather than read them as siloed from each other along Hindu and Muslim lines. In fact, the vast corpus of nearly 300 million Sanskrit and Prakrit manuscripts extant in contemporary India dates from the Muslim medieval period. That is to say, these texts were copied, recopied, and archived between the thirteenth and the nineteenth centuries in Kashmir, Lahore, Benares, Gujarat, and Rajasthan.[73]

The Hindustan that I have tried to sketch here as an intellectual geography is the first necessary context for understanding the history of Firishta. The world of the Deccan is both connected to the Indian Ocean circuits that I have sketched using Arabic sources and the city-states that are represented by the Persian histories produced in Uch or Delhi. The immediate milieu of Firishta under the ʿAdil Shahi was a continuation of this polyphonic Hindustan where the exchange of knowledge, letters, and histories was foundational.

Muhammad Qasim Firishta dedicated his *Tarikh* as *Gulshan-i Ibrahim,* to Ibrahim ʿAdil Shah II (1580–1627). He also titled it *Naurasnama.* The courts of the Deccan, where Firishta or Wajhi or many other Persian poets produced their works, signaled such interpellations of literary and historical genealogies. In 1599 Ibrahim founded a new capital, Nauraspur—"city of *nauras,*" *nau* meaning "new" or "ninth" and *ras* meaning "juice / flavor" or "mood / melody," from the aesthetic theory of *rasa.*[74] Ibrahim was a musician and also composed a book of music, the

Kitab-i Nauras, around 1582.[75] The book is written in Dakhani, with a vocabulary that draws on Brajbhasa, Awadhi, Rajasthani, Punjabi, Sanskrit, Arabic, and Persian. The book takes the seventeen major melodies and assembles a collection of fifty-nine songs, plus some standalone couplets. The songs pay homage to gods, goddesses, saints, and a landscape of Hindustan:

> Saraswati and Ganesh you are my mother, my father
> you are crystal glasses
> Ibrahim was a nobody, covered in dirt
> you gave him fortune and now he has fame.[76]

Ibrahim celebrates the Sufi saint Makhdum Gisu Daraz, the Ganges, Shiva, Indra, and the Himalayas. His songs exclaim the form of beauty in Karnatak, in the Deccan; the salty water of the Indian Ocean; the sweet water of the river Saraswati.

Muhammad Quli Qutb Shah (1580–1612) founded the city of Hyderabad in 1591. At his court, Asadullah Wajhi wrote his *Qutb Mushtari* in 1609 also, like Ibrahim's work, in Dakhani. It is a romance about the prince of Golcanda, who falls in love with a fairy in his dream and eventually sets off on a quest to locate her in far-off Bengal, combating demons, dragons, and attaining spiritual enlightenment along the way. The romance was named after Muhammad Quli Qutb Shah's wife, the Queen Bhagmati. Wajhi evokes the same Hindustani world that Qutban created in the *Mirigavati* in Jaunpur. These texts thus share both registers of meaning-making and audiences that had a common conceptual universe across the subcontinent.

In Hindavi, from which both Hindi and Urdu emerge, the word for "tomorrow" and "yesterday" is the same—*kal.*[77] To be sure, *kal* is a whimsical way of thinking about the presence of present in the past and in the future. Yet it does gesture toward an impetus to think about time as more than linear. The interest in locating the Muslim-or-Hindu-ness in the deep past is a contest about the future of the subcontinent in material ways. The majoritarian politics that has come to the fore in the last decade is predicated on finding historical roots for imagined trauma. Such is the burden of the past for the subcontinent that, whether it is the name of the city Allahabad or the claim for the existence of a temple underneath a mosque, history writing has the power to sanction retributive violence in the present.

This chapter has demonstrated how the colonial episteme organized time and subjecthood to construct the idea of the five thousand years of India. The problem of five thousand years was a historiography that forced a singular imaginary of the subcontinent through a Golden Age within which a progressive history, or rather the lack thereof, was plotted. Against this Golden Age, to make apparent its decline, was the figure of the conquering Muslim invader. This invader appeared in the early eighth century and received new avatars in the eleventh, thirteenth, and sixteenth centuries from Ghazni, from Ghur, from Kabul, and from Lahore. This invader was distinguished not only by his Muslimness—and concomitant qualities of brutality, avarice, and hedonism—but also ethnically and linguistically.

My effort here in exhuming colonial historiography is to rethink the role of historical writing in Arabic and Persian for the second millennium. These histories were collected and rendered into English in slices by Elliot and others under the analytical assumption that they lacked a philosophy of history and that they were beholden to power in such a way as to render them full of superfluous and biased information. Reframing the second millennium as Hindustani—rather than "Muslim"— allows us to step away from the historiographic blockades to investigating the past.[78] We can break the affinities of recognition that collapse the India of the present with an India of Ashoka, treating the Muslim medieval as demonized, elided, or ignored; put up as the literal Dark Age between the Golden Ancient Age and the Modern. We can thus speak of history, and we can look to an archive of historical writings from which the concept of Hindustan emerged, took shape, and dominated the political imagination.

In re-enlivening the concept of Hindustan, this chapter sets up the work for the chapters that follow. In the next three chapters, I utilize both European archives of their encounter in the subcontinent and Firishta's archive of Arabic and Persian histories, sketched above as the intellectual geography of Hindustan. Each of the chapters ends with a close reading of Firishta's *Tarikh* and his world of Hindustan.

3

AN ARCHIVE FOR HINDUSTAN

HOW TO WRITE THE HISTORY OF HINDUSTAN? This book is
intended as a simultaneous history of Hindustan as a concept and its
erasure, a genealogy of political thought that persisted and that seems
to have vanished without a trace. It does require a lexical shift—from
secondary sources to archives—and an analytical shift—from origins
to belonging. In forming an intellectual geography of Hindustan,
historians created a corpus of thought intricately involved with the
production of history. This historiography was a distinct tradition in
itself. In these histories, written from the ninth century to the seventeenth century, we find rich accounts featuring protagonists and
antagonists, violence, and descriptions of power and grandeur. A remarkable feature of these histories is that they are self-consciously written
for future historians. We also find a carefully crafted philosophy of history and get a sense of the role of the ethical historian in telling the past.
It is this gesture that concerns us the most here. For if the idea of
Hindustan has a history, it is nurtured in the belief that Hindustan
has a future—a future that is nourished in these particular works of
historical imagination.

On the other hand, colonial historiography organized this expanse
of time solely through the question of political power—reduced, simply,
to the Muslim period. This illogical division of time according to political power made natural the division of Muslim kings versus Hindu
kings. It posited an unanimity to hundreds of years of history linking

the Arab kings of Sindh and Gujarat to the Ghazni and Ghuri warlords, to the sultans of Delhi and Bijapur, to the *Shahanshah* of Agra. Hostages in this "Muslim" geography, then, were the "Hindu kings," the rajas and *rajarajas* of Chitor, Jaipur, Bengal, or Vijayanagar.

Colonial histories overdetermine a specific understanding of *why* history was written during this period, for *whom*, about *which people*. Colonial material practices of collection, archiving, cataloging, excerption, and analysis introduced Muslim historiography into the domain of the European science of history along a narrow, predefined analytical frame. Such processes of knowledge-making mean that there cannot be a simple act of accessing a precolonial history of Hindustan without going through the intellectual edifice created by British India and its histories of the subcontinent.

The early nineteenth-century renderings of Muslim texts into European languages occurred alongside a robust acquisition project. The collection of manuscripts from British India, as well as central and western Asia, meant the development of new toponomies and taxonomies for sorting "Muhammadan" knowledge. We already saw how William Jones instituted a scribal distinction that linked "native" India to texts in the Devanagari script. The next step was initiated by Henry M. Elliot, who began the project for collecting an archive for the history of "Muhammadan India" through the assemblage, extraction, and translation of historical writings in Persian, for which he provided his own interpretative gloss. Elliot's particular practice of creating an archive and annotation of Muslim historical writings had a profound impact on how the history of Hindustan came to be written.

In this chapter, I am concerned with the articulation of the work of history expressed by historians in Firishta's archive. What were the reasons they gave for their works? What ethics and principles governed their work of history writing? As these histories were cited by Firishta, they constituted his literal archive for thinking not only about Hindustan but about the act of history writing itself. I take examples from Firishta's comprehensive history of Hindustan to see how his predecessors influenced his history writing and how, conversely, Firishta distinguished himself from the historians who came before. The writing of history and the writing of the history of Hindustan, this chapter will demonstrate, were one and the same act.

But before we get to Firishta's Hindustan, let us first work through what was "Muhammadan India" in the works of historians of colonial British India. Next, we turn to the historians that are cited by Firishta as his archive. Firishta read, utilized, and expanded the histories of these authors; he cites them throughout his work as evidence or when he agrees or disagrees with them. Why did those earlier historians choose to write their histories, and what guided their methods, what purpose did they imagine their histories would serve? These questions have a bearing on how Firishta imagined his task, and, subsequently, on how we are to think and interpret Firishta's history as a history of Hindustan. Some of the most prominent, and repeated, historians cited by Firishta are Baihaqi (d. 1040), Juzjani (d. 1260), Barani (d. 1367), Mir Khwand (d. 1498), Nizamuddin (d. 1594), and Abu'l Fazl (d. 1602), alongside epics and histories in Sanskrit such as the *Ramayana*, the *Mahabharata*, Ratnakara's *Haravijaya*, and Kalhana's *Rajatarangani*. There is a specific logic of the craft of history writing that unites these texts and the ways in which they lend their materials to be used, and reused, by successive generations. These historians deliberately create a sense of their belonging to an intellectual geography.

Ibrahim 'Adil Shah II, Firishta's patron, asked him to write the first total, comprehensive history of Hindustan. He told Firishta that no such comprehensive account existed, "Since the histories of the kings of Hindustan do not exist in one single volume . . . you should grab the pen and you grid yourself to write a book with such qualities; a book in plain language without artifice and lies."[1] It was with this mandate that Firishta set out to compile an archive of all of the histories that had come before him, all of the accounts of the different parts that would constitute the whole of Hindustan. In the archive available to him was a vast expanse of materials dating from the ninth to the seventeenth centuries that contained a remarkable array of histories about polity and space. Firishta inherited this archive, consisting of the work of historians of Hindustan who shared ethical and philosophical concerns. It is with this same archive that we can write a history of Hindustan.

AN ARCHIVE FOR MUHAMMADAN INDIA

As previously discussed, the paradigm of the five thousand years, with its attendant Golden Age, had posited an India that was timeless, devoid of historical change—a conceptualization that cemented itself as the very notion of a lack of history itself. In contrast to "native" India was the Muslim invader from Arabia. Unlike the India that was being "discovered" by the colonial historians and philologists, Islam was a known and understood entity—famously "born in history." Yet, in the context of the British colonial conquest of India, the ways in which Muslims wrote their history was a point debated and considered by the colonial administrators.

The British colonial project of creating a history for Muhammadan India emerged alongside European notions about history writing, and the development of the field of the philosophy of history. In this project, the question of how to properly see the worth and utility of Muslim histories had to be interrogated. Alexander Dow had dedicated his eighteenth-century rendition of Firishta's *Tarikh* as one suitable for an emperor who had to assemble and understand a newly acquired colony. Jones, James Mill, and the early British philologists and historians held similar views on the utility of acquiring, reading, or understanding Muslim histories. Such rationales, however, were beginning to shift.

In 1835, the historian and politician Thomas Babington Macaulay robustly argued against the teaching of Arabic and Sanskrit to the "inhabitants of the British territories." Macaulay was specifically critical of the British East India Company's practices of teaching "native" languages at the colleges established by the company in Calcutta and Delhi. When he visited Calcutta in 1835, he presented his "Minute on Education," where he dismissed all historical knowledge produced in the Indian colony: "When we pass from works of imagination to works in which facts are recorded and general principles investigated, the superiority of the Europeans becomes absolutely immeasurable. It is, I believe, no exaggeration to say that all the historical information which has been collected from all the books written in the Sanscrit language is less valuable than what may be found in the most paltry abridgments used at preparatory schools in England."[2] Macaulay was against the company's funding of the teaching of Arabic and Sanskrit, the practice of printing texts in those languages, and translations or studies of texts from these languages. Macaulay proclaims, "It is confessed that [the Sanskrit and Arabic] language is barren of useful knowledge. We are to teach it because it is fruitful of monstrous superstitions. We are to teach false history, false astronomy, false medicine, because we find them in company with a false religion."[3]

Such wholesale rejection of all knowledge produced in the colony was moderated by other officials of the empire. The work and career of Aloys Sprenger (1813–1893), an employee of the British East India Company in British India in the mid-nineteenth century, offers a singular perspective on the colonial debate on the utility of Muslim histories for the colonial project.[4] Sprenger not only provided an answer to Macaulay's critique but demonstrated the necessity of understanding the histories written in Arabic and Persian for the British colonial project. He first launched his argument in 1841, appended to his translation of one formidable source for the history of Hindustan—the tenth-century history by Mas'udi (d. ca. 956), a direct source for Firishta's *Tarikh*.

Sprenger dedicated his translation to his patron, the Earl of Munster, George Augustus Frederick FitzClarence, who was the first president of the Royal Asiatic Society. FitzClarence was exactly the right patron for Sprenger. In 1819, FitzClarence had published the memoir of his travels from Egypt to British India. FitzClarence had carried with him Dow's *Hindostan* to orient his wanderings.[5] FitzClarence was eager to solicit more translations of Arabic and Persian histories that would enliven the deep past—histories he felt would connect British India to colonial Egypt. Sprenger's translation was funded and published by the earl in 1841, at a moment when the pressure of expanding the colonial territories was deeply felt and with it a concomitant increase in the pursuit of knowledge of Muslim pasts.

Aloys Sprenger began the prologue of his translation of Mas'udi's *Muruj al-Dhahab* with a comparative claim equating Mas'udi with the best of the Greek historians: "If it is for these merits that Herodotus has acquired the name of Father of History, and of the greatest of all Historians, el-Mas'údí has a just claim to be called the Herodotus of Arabs."[6] The merits Mas'udi possessed, according to Sprenger, were that Mas'udi examined the history of other people without prejudice, that Mas'udi insisted on writing only verifiable facts, that Mas'udi relied on his first-hand experience and travel to collect materials for his history, and that Mas'udi took as his central concern for his history the need to illustrate the character of a nation and a people.

Sprenger acknowledged Macaulay's critique, "the usefulness of Oriental studies has been questioned by a class of men whose opinions deserve respect," and granted "that these Oriental texts enslaved [Oriental] minds rather than freeing them."[7] To respond to Macaulay, Sprenger asserted the Romantic position—following in the footsteps of Goethe, Voltaire, and Silvestre de Sacy—that ancient India was the origin for Greek philosophy, art, and sciences. These histories, Sprenger argued, might not be suitable for the colonized subjects, but they were *necessary* for the colonizing agent.

Historians such as Mas'udi or Firishta were critical, Sprenger argued, because the places and peoples described in their histories, were now the dominion of the British Empire. The recognition of Mas'udi as a historian, and the translation of his tenth-century Arabic history into English, was thus a critical step for the functioning of the British Empire. Sprenger performed, in his translator's introduction, a philological study to demonstrate characteristics of various races (Arab, Persian, Indian, Tatar) who now lived in British colonies. He performed an analysis of particular verb endings to posit how a particular race—the Arab—was prone to conquering and another—the Indian—was prone to being conquered. The evidence, the "facts" for this racialized knowledge, Sprenger posited, came from Muslim historians such as Mas'udi. Thus, against Macaulay's pragmatic dismissal of "Oriental" histories, Sprenger offered a utilitarian defense.

Some fifteen years after his publication of the translation, after spending years working in the colonial administration of British India, Sprenger returned to the themes from his translation of 1841. He restated his assessment that the compiling of facts from history was necessary for both governance and for the European philosophy of history and that such facts were sparse in the historical corpus of the colonized East. He articulated this in the preface to a catalog of manuscripts he had acquired from British India, Egypt, and Syria: "I admit that the literature of the

East has very little intrinsic value. . . . It contains few facts, if any, in astronomy, medicine, mathematics, natural history, or any other science, which are new to us. . . . Nevertheless it deserves to be cultivated."[8] The "nevertheless" was the practical, utilitarian side of the colonial knowledge project—one that needed specific and sustained data from Muslim pasts to organize the practice of colonial governance.

Sprenger offered that the natives of the colonized East themselves had no intellectual capacity to reflect on their past: "Oriental nations are no longer able to take care of their own literary treasures. This is not owing to a want of veneration for them but to apathy and imbecility."[9] Sprenger's acquisition and collection impulse was driven by his perception that manuscript libraries had been abandoned and neglected. While the Muslims were unwilling and indifferent to seeing the value of their own histories, these manuscripts had much to offer European thought: "A complete knowledge of the habits, life and literature of Asia appears to me to be at the present juncture a most important desideratum for Europe; not only will it complete the *philosophy of history* which ought to be founded exclusively on facts, but it will smooth the path to that connexion between the East and West, which is inevitable and is proceeding in much more rapid strides than it is usually supposed."[10] These manuscripts were thus to serve as additional materials to render complete a European project of history writing that needed facts from a global perspective.

Sprenger listed a total of 1,972 manuscripts in his personal collection. Of these, Sprenger cataloged some 370 manuscripts in the "Geography and History" and "Genealogy and Biography" sections. He had taken these from the libraries in Awadh and Rampur. He had taken several volumes of Tabari; Ballami's Persian translation of Tabari; two sets of Mas'udi and an additional excerpted version; universal histories of Mir Khwand and Khawandmir; histories of Ghazni to Delhi by Baihaqi, 'Utbi, Juzjani, Barani, and 'Afif; Mughal histories of Abu'l Fazl, and Nizamuddin; and a complete manuscript of Firishta.[11]

How did Sprenger "acquire" these manuscripts? He claimed to have purchased them in the process of collecting and cataloging manuscripts for the British East India Company. Sprenger had gone to British India to begin his career as the principal at Delhi College and an agent of the

BEIC in 1845. In 1846, he was appointed as an extra assistant "for the purpose of cataloging the extensive collection of works in Arabic, Persian and Hindustani literature in the king of Oudh's libraries."[12] Sprenger spent eighteen months on this task and examined ten thousand manuscripts in that collection, from which he published a catalog of about a thousand focused on Persian poetry. Sprenger's personal collecting efforts came from this access to and survey of "native libraries."

The acquisitions from Hindustan rose dramatically after Britain quelled the Uprising of 1857 and looted the various houses of nobility as well as Mughal libraries. These acquisitions are listed in the various catalogs published in the second half of the nineteenth century: William H. Morley's *A Descriptive Catalogue of the Historical Manuscripts in the Arabic and Persian Languages at the Royal Asiatic Society* (1854), Wilhelm Pertsch's *Verzeichniss der persischen Handschriften der königlichen Bibliothek zu Berlin* (1888), Charles Rieu's *Catalogue of Persian Manuscripts at the British Library* (1879), Eduard Sachau's *Catalogue of Persian, Turkish, Hindustani, and Pushtu Manuscripts in the Bodleian Library* (1889), E. G. Browne's *Handlist of the Muhammadan Manuscripts* (1900), and Edgar Blochet's *Catalogue des manuscrits persans de la Bibliothèque nationale* (1905), to list a few prominent examples.

Sprenger was asked to begin the process of acquisition and cataloging of Arabic and Persian manuscripts by Henry M. Elliot, then foreign secretary to the government of British India. By 1846, Elliot was already involved in putting together a bibliographic index of critical texts concerning histories of Muhammadan India. In an essay contained with the index prepared for his collected manuscripts, Elliot points out that chronologies created by "natives" were mostly fabricated, full of mistakes, misreadings, misquotations, misappropriations, and in general "fairy tales and fictions" under the "name of History."[13]

Elliot's aim, in publishing the bibliography and in asking Sprenger as well as other political agents of the company to acquire Arabic and Persian manuscripts and have "native subjects" prepare excerpted translations was to demonstrate the liberal value of the British Empire: "When we see the withering effects of the tyranny and capriciousness of a despot, we shall learn to estimate more fully the value of a balanced constitution. When we see the miseries which are entailed on the present and future generations by disputed claims to the Crown, we shall more than ever value the principle of a regulated succession, subject to no challenge or controversy. In no country have these miseries been greater than in India."[14] For Elliot, Muslim history, like the Muslim despot, was a site of revulsion, of horror, and a demonstration that the British were there to "fulfill our high destiny as the Rulers of India."[15]

Elliot's primary concern was to locate the archive for writing a "true" history of Muhammadan India. He planned to first collect a vast archive of Arabic and Persian histories, and then to have substantial excerpts from each translated into English. These excerpts would then serve as raw materials for the British project of history writing. Elliot's collection, and translation project, was the singular most profound colonial project for knowledge production until the mid-nineteenth century. Elliot's project, *The History of India: As Told by Its Own Historians: The Muhammadan Period,* was published only posthumously, in eight volumes, from 1867 to 1877. It needs to be stressed that the significance of Elliot's project is matched only by the Great Trigonometric Survey of British India, and the census of the late nineteenth century.

Alongside colonial officers like Sprenger, Elliot also relied on an array of Hindustani historians and libraries: Munshi Maulabakhsh compiled a set of seven volumes for Elliot, in which he summarized or gave extracts from 325 Persian histories of Hindustan; excerpts from an additional 351 Persian histories were provided by other scholars. Elliot also solicited listings and catalogs from private and public archives across British India—from Tonk, Cawnpore, Thatta, Lucknow, Delhi, Hyderabad, Benares, and Carnatic—totaling roughly 15,081 Persian histories.[16] It is from this list of fifteen thousand histories that Elliot selected 231 Persian histories for his *Bibliographical Index,* from which his translation project would emerge.

He then deputized political agents, an extensive list of officers, including Sprenger, to "collect" from the archives of Muslim royal houses the manuscripts for writing the history of Muhammadan India.[17] His own personal library, at the time of his death, had 222 manuscripts. The British Museum in 1878 *purchased* a further total of 458 manuscripts from Elliot's larger estate.[18]

Among these thousands of histories, the highest praise Elliot afforded to a work of history on Hindustan was to Firishta's *Tarikh*: "This work is by common consent, and not undeservedly, considered superior to all the other general Histories of India."[19] The index even begins with a short notice of "selected works for deposit in our College Libraries, exhibiting a series necessary for a full understanding of the history of Muhammedan India."[20] Firishta's history is the first title on that list.

Firishta had entered the European archive through Dow's 1768 rendition. Remarkably, Elliot even credits Dow's translation of Firishta with spurring the very study of Persian in Europe, "It is to be remembered, that this was one of the first works translated by an Englishman from Persian, that its publication gave an impulse to the study of that language."[21] Firishta had entered the European archive as a "historian's historian." As Elliot notes, "The value of the work commences from the Muhammadan period, the history of which he [Firishta] compiled from the best sources available."[22]

But Firishta, who is the key source for writing a history of Muhammadan India, also served a pivotal role in Europe's *acquisition* of manuscripts. In his *Tarikh,* Firishta lists some thirty works of history that informed his own history, ranging from composition in the early eleventh century to his contemporaries. Elliot recognized that the names of these historians and texts would be the ones needed to write the full history of Hindustan. These were the works of history that were systematically acquired, edited, translated in excerpts or in whole, and placed in the edifice of the colonial production of histories of Hindustan of the late nineteenth and twentieth centuries. The European historian was to categorize and catalog these histories in a particular taxonomy, a typology, and to determine the amount of "facts" or "history" contained therein. Firishta's bibliography thus becomes the founding bibliography for Elliot's history of Muhammadan India. Left out were those texts that Elliot categorized to be stories and romances—texts such as the *Mahabharata*—which were, however, used as histories by Firishta.

Yet colonial historiography was not the only approach to writing histories of the subcontinent. Clearly, Firishta's citation of his sources for history depended on his own notions of a theory for history. In order to see this archive of histories outside of an aggregate of historical fact as determined by colonial knowledge, we have to read anew Firishta and his archive of histories for Hindustan.

These histories require an examination from the vantage point of Firishta and the early seventeenth-century project of history writing for the Deccan. These histories are both works of individual agentive and creative thought and they form an intellectual geography of Hindustan. Firishta lists the names of these histories as a collective "under his gaze," writing that by incorporating their knowledge, his own work will become a "real currency that will ring true in all corners of the world."[23] What did Firishta understand of the task of history writing that he had inherited from the historians who had come before him? What ideas were present in this archive for writing a history of Hindustan? In order to understand *how* Firishta wrote his history, we have to return to his archive, to the theories of history writing that stretched from the eleventh to the seventeenth centuries.

The colonial historian and his effort to slice, fragment, and reformulate a history of the "Muhammadan Period" required an insistence that histories are mere collections of facts to be culled and assimilated into history by the expert European. Perhaps we ought to abandon this colonial tradition that masquerades as scholarship and exists only because the postcolonial states continue to harbor colonial prejudices incited by this episteme. In what follows, I read the Hindustani histories prior to Firishta and the ethical rationales they provided for the task of history in their works. In the last section I read Firishta to consider how he builds on and creates newness in his own task of history writing—focusing on the case of Mahmud Ghazni to examine the ways in which historians of Hindustan wrote a history of their past.

THE CASE FOR HISTORY

I have argued that Firishta saw himself as belonging to an intellectual geography within which was an explicit genealogy of historians. In listing his archive for the task of writing history, Firishta also stressed that he was "completing" histories from his past that appeared, to him,

to be unfinished, or lacking in scope or argument. It is this retrospec-
tive gaze by historians of Hindustan that foregrounds a community of
historians. In his preface, Firishta narrates the beginning of his project,
"[I] began to collect histories of Hindustan and reached out to all the
regions and corners for their histories but found not a single manuscript
that gave an account of all the events, all of the kings of Hindustan. The
only text that I found reasonably complete was the history of Nizamuddin Bakshi but it also missed events that had passed under these
unworthy eyes."[24] Firishta is here referring to Nizamuddin Ahmad's *Tabaqat-i Akbar Shahi,* which was completed around 1594 at the Mughal
ruler Jalaluddin Akbar's court. Ahmad's preface had stated that while
there are histories of specific regions, there is no one history of Hindustan, that realm under Akbar, the capital of which is Delhi.[25] Nizamuddin
is also clear that his history is particularly a history of Muslim rulers,
within four hundred years, of parts of Hindustan.[26] More critically, even
if Nizamuddin's history was arranged in nine sections, corresponding
to nine regional polities, it was addressed primarily as a history of regnal
kings, and not of the geography. Firishta's aim in completing the history of Nizamuddin was to write a history that flipped this structure—a
history of geographies within which polities appeared, and a history that
was not a history simply of Muslims. It is *this* impulse that makes Firishta's the first comprehensive history of Hindustan.[27]

   Like Firishta, Ahmad also cites a singular text from earlier historians
that he is in the process of bringing to completion. That text was the
thirteenth-century *Tabaqat-i Nasiri* of Juzjani. When we go look at what
Juzjani writes in his preface, he too pushes forward the claim that he is
completing a new task for history due to the existing, and insufficient,
example of the eleventh-century Baihaqi's *Tarikh.* Part of such invocations is a rhetorical act of displacement, one that asks the reader to constantly recall a genealogy in order to grasp the significance of words that
are now presented. More significant is that such gestures toward the desire for completing an ongoing historical narrative cement a kinship of
historians whose work is being emended and built upon, dismantled
and restitched. It is also an *open* project, one that invited the readers
or listeners of the histories to understand the architectures of knowl-

edge. The metaphors used by historians—of ornamentation, embroi-
dery, structure—explicitly allow the reader to imagine history writing
as a continuous and ongoing project. The work of history was thus always
understood as attaining its completion in the future.

To get a better sense of this genealogy of citations and its effect on
the work of history, let us turn to the historians that are cited by Firishta
as his archive. The first four historical works cited by Firishta belong to
the early thirteenth-century moment. The concern they all share is in
their choice to write their histories in Persian rather than Arabic. In 1206,
Jurfadiqani renders 'Utbi's *Tarikh-i Yamini* into Persian. He is advised
to do so by the Ghurid minister on the stated grounds that "it is com-
mendable that a more commonly regarded Persian register through
which Turk and Tajik folks can directly benefit . . . I may bring this bride
to the world."[28] Muhammad 'Awfi, in 1224, rendered into Persian and
expanded the archive of Arabic traveler accounts in *Kitab Faraj ba'd
Shidda.* He dedicated it to Qabacha in Uch as a beautifully adored bride,
hidden behind the Arabic script and now revealed to the eyes of the
learned Persian betrothed.[29] The metaphor of a work of history as a "new
bride" highlights both the beginning of a new relationship and the beauty
of the work presented, but also that there is an understanding of a "union"
between Arabic and Persian. 'Awfi's contemporary 'Ali Kufi concluded
his history of Sindh, the *Chachnama,* with: "It was behind the veil of
Arabic and devoid of the decoration and beauty of Persian . . . for the
Persian speakers no one adorned this bride . . . or dressed her with gar-
ments of exquisite language, justice, and wisdom."[30]

These histories should not be understood as translations but as new
renderings of text with a deliberately constructed sense of shared ethics.
Yet, the historians do make a specific claim to translation, that too at a
moment when the political power in Hindustan was itself transitioning
and new forms of social and political structure were emerging.[31] The
metaphorical language of translation was a key way in which these historians advanced an argument for the significance of their histories.
Alongside the ornamented bride, there are also echoes of the literary
presence of the *Jatakamala* genre from the ninth and tenth centuries in
these early histories—they contain numerous metaphors of pearls and

jewels on a string. Hasan Nizami, in his *Taj al-Ma'athir,* completed around 1220, laments:

> To pierce pearls is my task, but why do it
> for there are no customers. Refined speech was my habit,
> but why do it
> there is none worthy of praise left.[32]

Abu'l Fazl Baihaqi worked as a scribe and secretary for eight successive rulers, beginning with Mahmud Ghazni.[33] Only the last five chapters of his history, now labeled as *Tarikh-i Baihaqi,* have survived. Hence, we do not have a usual opening section of dedication and prefatory remarks to consult. However, one consequential section, that discussing the rule of Baihaqi's greatest patron, Mas'ud son of Mahmud, includes Baihaqi's thoughts on the work of history writing.

Baihaqi begins by noting his own inadequacy in writing a history of any magnitude compared to his peers. His peers, he writes, were "riding horses [of intellect and craft]," while, in metaphoric comparison, he was "on foot and with a limp."[34] Yet, his more capable peers, he regretfully adds, were busy with statecraft and did not have time to research accounts of the past or record the present. Meanwhile, those who were eyewitnesses to history are dying. There was thus a crisis that confronts both history and memory and that prompts the "inadequate" Baihaqi to take up this difficult task of writing history.

It is for such reasons, Baihaqi writes, that he studied the histories that were written before his time by employees of other rulers and found in them "additions or subtractions or embellishments" making them ill-suited for the present monarch.[35] Baihaqi, then, declares his own specific reason for writing his history, "my desire is to build a foundation for history and upon it a grand structure such that its notoriety would last to the end of times."[36] Baihaqi elaborates that he has in his mind a future audience, not simply one of nobility or elite monarchs, but of future historians who would benefit from the careful work he is doing. He creates a link between the histories he consumed, which contained embellishments or elisions, and the one that he is structuring on a grand scale, to be read by future historians.

Baihaqi also differentiates between the task of writing history and the work of being a historian:

> I have read in the Histories of the Kings of 'Ajam translated by Ibn Muquffa' that their greatest and most capable kings had the wisest sages attend on them all day and night until the moment of sleep. These men would point out to them that which was good and that which was reprehensible among the events of the day. When the king was stirred by an ill passion and became wrathful and spilled the blood of notable families, they would illustrate the good and bad consequences and inform him with stories and reports of past kings, cautioning him to stay on the right path.[37]

Baihaqi draws a distinction between the historian and his product, the work of history itself: The work, or the narrative of history, was meant to serve future generations, while the historian himself served the present. This distinction is a particular insight that is worth underscoring. The relationship of the text to political power, in other words, is not a direct relationship. It is the historian who serves the monarch, but the text produced has its audience in the future outside of the intent of the patron or the historian. This difference allows the historian to be far more clear-sighted in the writing of history without fear of either reprisal or the temptation of reward.

Baihaqi underscores this line of thought in various places. After providing an anecdote regarding the mishandling of secret letters in faraway Baghdad and far removed from the present, he concludes:

> Those who are wise will recognize the significance of these two stories. Both stories are now at an end and we can return to history. The aim of narrating these stories is to make history beautiful. It is also that one who is brave, talented, wise, and finds employment with the king and uses his intellect and strategies to slowly move up from the ranks that he enters. . . . The values of books, stories, and accounts of the past [lies in that] people read them and choose what is of utility and discard what is irrelevant. May God Guide Their Fortune.[38]

The utility of historians, according to Baihaqi, lies in being an intellectual class that can act *upon* political power as a retardant for any excesses and an accelerant for its kindness and generosity. This intellectual class was, like Baihaqi, in direct service to the political regime and needed such manuals for thinking and being. Akin to the manuals of codes of conduct of princes that emerged in the tenth and eleventh centuries in Arabic—from Sanskrit and Greek roots—it appears that Baihaqi's task was to train specific historians to inform nobility. His other aim, and the purpose for which he was writing his history, was to create a monumental text that would survive time itself and become a foundation for that future, much like the histories of Baihaqi's own past were functioning for him.

Baihaqi's history was indeed a model for future historians, such as Juzjani. Juzjani was a jurist, a poet, a historian, and someone deeply familiar with the elite families and concerns of thirteenth-century Hindustan. His great-grandfather was a scholar employed at the court of Ghazni, and his grandfather, based in Lahore, was a jurist of such repute that, when he visited Baghdad, he was given a robe by the caliph. Juzjani himself began his career in Ghur and was headed to Uch in the hopes of getting employment with Nasiruddin Qabacha. He suffered a mishap on the way, as he was jailed for forty days in Sistan for refusing a warlord's offer of employment and trying to leave the city without permission. He got out of jail by writing a laudatory poem for the warlord, and by having allies make appeals on his behalf. Upon release, he made his way straight to Multan and, from there, to Uch around 1227.

His career at Uch was off to a good start—he was appointed the principal of the central college—but Uch soon fell to Iltutmish, and Delhi became the political center for Hindustan. Juzjani entered Iltutmish's service, giving Friday sermons, accompanying the army toward Bengal, and later, serving as a judge and jurist. He spent forty years in the service of Delhi sultans and, during this time, produced the massive work of history *Tabaqat-i Nasiri*.

In his preface, Juzjani narrates that after being appointed to a position at the court and at the judiciary in Hindustan, he saw "a book from the past in which the possessor of knowledges had written for the benefit of coming generations, histories of the prophets, caliphs, and their descendants. All this knowledge was organized as books during the reign of the descendants of Sebuktagin at Ghazni in which a flower was picked from every garden and a drop from every ocean."[39] The spatial metaphor of gardens and oceans, which lends diversity to the narrative, was chosen carefully. Juzjani's text was both a history of Muslim kings rising to power in Delhi and a full geography of the world of Hindustan imagined within the framework of a universal history.

Juzjani sought and incorporated all prior histories for his own text, but with the idea that he must improve upon them: "A desire came to this weak self to augment that history of prophets with all of the rulers of Arabia and 'Ajam from the beginning to the end, such that every royal household is illuminated by its forefathers and descendants. When I depart this temporary abode [of life], those who read this book will send me their prayer of benediction. If there are mistakes, they will hide them."[40] Juzjani deliberately placed himself among an intellectual geography by agreeing to finish the task of a previous history.

Juzjani's *Tabaqat* is arranged along noble and ruling family lines and genealogies of descent, segmented according to specific places in which these rulers came to power. This structure of genealogical descent in Juzjani's history is constructed almost as a material structure—something like the Qutb Minar at Delhi that Iltutmish was constructing—wherein the forms and logic of power was oriented for the gaze of the reader. As in a physical monument, which is understood to be the work of generations to come, Juzjani is arguing that even if there are mistakes in his history, they will be corrected by those who follow him. In other words, his history would be completed by other historians, just as he completed the work of those historians who came before him.

There are two significant aspects to Juzjani's theory of history writing. Juzjani recounted that he wrote only what was in "credible books of history."[41] He does not provide a listing of such source materials in his preface, but each of his chapters and sections leads with the name of the text that he is drawing upon—a list of some dozen titles. In addition to previous histories, much of Juzjani's historical reporting depends both

on him as a witness and on the oral histories that he collects. He underscores his methods in the concluding verse of his preface:

What I heard, I wrote
the ear is the truth behind duplication
When they see a mistake, the kind are forgiving
for they have rank, intellect, and awareness
Whoever reaches a high station
to them patience is honey
Their habit conceals
mistakes made in the path to knowledge
Remember Minhaj in your prayers
Even if he is silent in the cage [grave].[42]

Juzjani privileges the listening ear and the seeing eye of the narrating
historian but also emphasizes the fallibility of the act of interpreting
texts. The dichotomy laid out by Baihaqi between history as text and historian as subject is much starker here. Juzjani is aware that his interpretative choices could be "mistakes" and begs those who have rank to for-
give him. He understands that his errors could be seen as rebukes to
political power, yet he is willing to take the risk.

Juzjani meant for his history to be a continuous task, undertaken by
others after him. Ziauddin Barani was the historian who took up that
task, almost a hundred years later. Barani, like Juzjani, came from a
long line of intellectuals and bureaucrats who had served the polities of
Ghur, Lahore, and Delhi.[43] He served Muhammad Tughluq for nearly
twenty years, ending in 1351. Barani's history *Tarikh-i Firuz Shahi* is
dedicated to Muhammad Tughluq's successor, and he began it, by his
own count, some ninety-five years after Juzjani's *Tabaqat-i Nasiri*.[44]

Barani begins his preface with the statement that it is God who has
left the annals and reports of prophets and sultans, quoting from the
Qur'an that "we record what they have sent before and their footprint"
and that "we relate to you the best of stories" from the parable of Joseph.[45]
Barani then asserts that the science of history is equal to the exegetical,
juridical, and the commentarial and gnostic sciences. History, he pro-

poses, is the knowledge of events and records of prophets and kings, as well as of notables and state dignitaries.

In his prefatory remarks, Barani presents the reader with seven statements regarding the science of history. The first reclaims the Qur'an as history, and the second underlines that any practitioner of the science of prophetic tradition is also a historian. The next five points regard the beneficial qualities of history: knowing history makes one wise and gives one superior judgment (such as Aristotle, the adviser of Alexander, or Barzawayh, the adviser of Khusrau I); knowing history makes the rulers and governors calmly face calamities and difficulties, for they can use history to predict the outcome; knowing the history of the prophets gives sustenance to those facing trials and tribulations; knowing history gives one the incentive to be good and to do good, for through history one knows the evil ends of those who practice evil; and finally, knowing history makes the writer of history beholden to truth, for the writer understands that "truth is indeed the foundation of history."[46]

Barani's case for history is built around an ethics that is derived from God and the Prophet. However, ethics is not merely that which pertains to the cultivation of the self. Rather it forms a social contract between ruler and ruled, with the historian markedly participating in the rule-making process. Barani's constellation of ethics is easily grasped from his citations from the Qur'an and his invocation of Greek and Sassanid advisers alongside the caliphs from early Islam. This is a broadly ecumenical concern, though with some clear boundary-making.

Historians, Barani contends, should be of superior birth, and superior character. Histories written by those of "ill religions or who follow the paths of ill faith" will be filled with untruths that may not be apparent to the reader.[47] Thus, only the righteous should be allowed to write history. Barani's historical method is thus tied intimately to the birth and rank of the historian and to the "correct" faith and practice of this elite cadre. Barani's central recommendation is that the good deeds of kings recounted in exemplary histories be written by men of good character. These histories were not solely meant for the king. Barani insists that they must be read out loud to assemblages of notables and rulers, in order to provide insight from the past and to shape ethical behavior in the present.

Barani cites as his own guides for history this set of works: Ibn Ishaq's *Sira* of the Prophet, Ibn Waqidi's *Kitab Tarikh wa al-Maghazi,* Firdausi's *Shahnama,* Baihaqi's *Tarikh,* 'Utbi's *Tarikh-i Yamini,* Hasan Nizami's *Taj al-Ma'athir,* 'Awfi's *Jawami al-Hikayat,* and Juzjani's *Tabaqat-i Nasiri.* Barani explicitly states his wish to update the history of Juzjani and make it current to his own time. He does not wish to rewrite the history Juzjani provided, for he does not consider himself able to match his superiors in history writing. Barani ends his preface by declaring, "If they [readers] declare it history, they will find accounts of kings and sultans, but if they look for rules of governance, they will not find it lacking, and if they look for advice and council, they will find more here than other books."[48] Barani is certain that his history will serve as a model for future work but ends with a lament—"If I say that there is no other book in the world like mine / But there is no scholar left in this world, who will believe me?"[49]

Two centuries after Barani, at the end of the fifteenth century, Mir Khwand also put forward the argument that history was first and foremost a project of ethics. Muhammad ibn Khwandshah Mir Khwand was based in Herat, and his history of the world, *Rawzat al-Safa,* is one of the key texts for Firishta. Khwand, like his predecessors, imagined his work as a garden, and his task as that of an assembler of an aesthetically pleasing work of natural beauty. His history is intended as both a model for building a universal history as well as a theory for thinking about history. After getting the commission for the work, Khwand describes his intentions to write a book that would "never be superseded by pens of other scribes nor disappear in the ravages of time."[50] To do this, Khwand begins with a prolegomenon on the ten qualities of history, the five necessary qualities for historians, and why those in political power require the services of historians.

The first quality is that humans gain knowledge through their experience—sight, sound, touch—but that no one can live and see everything, so one is dependent on written records of the experiences of others and "there is no other science that approaches history in that regard."[51] Second, history is a science that promotes energy and clears away rust from the senses. Third, it is studied with ease and in abundance. Fourth, it develops the faculties of critique and allows one to separate "truth from falsehood."[52] Fifth, there are three different types of intellect gained from experience: that of predicting whether good or ill will come from an action, that of distinguishing between the act and the actor, and that of knowing the past and understanding the causes of misery or prosperity.

Sixth, by reading works of history from the past, one learns from those whose wisdom far exceeds one's contemporaries, "when one reads a history, one has the experiences of many intelligent persons at his disposal and may prevent calamity or illuminate his affairs and put them to a fair end."[53] Seventh, knowledge of history produces in one a robust intellect. Eighth, knowledge of history is comforting when one is struck by tragedy; one knows from history that worse has happened in the past, and one will eventually survive the tragedy. Ninth, knowledge of the history of the world allows one to know about the prophets and exalted figures who have lived in its various parts. Tenth, the just and pious rulers have in history, lessons and guidance that can prevent a ruler from becoming a tyrant.

Finally, Mir Khwand discusses the qualities necessary for a historian, which he claims is a profession full of danger, for it exposes the author to political machinations and even assassination. The first quality is that the historian should be of "sound belief" and "pure sect," otherwise he would either insert impurity into history or not be able to discern the impurities introduced in the past (such as in the accounts of the life of the Prophet).[54] The second quality needed is that the historian should write the "full" picture of the past—the good and the bad. Third, the historian should neither exaggerate the good nor minimize the bad and seek a path of moderation at all times. Fourth, the historian should write as if the whole world, high and low, is the historian's audience and should make his work such that all can understand it. Fifth, a historian should be known to be trustworthy and dependable such that his work is taken as an extension of his personality.

Mir Khwand goes on to address specifically the rulers and kings whom, he writes, "are most at the mercy of history." First, their actions, good and evil, have consequences in the world, and they, thus, need to learn critical lessons from how rulers acted in the past. Second, careful study of the science of history makes them better rulers, for accounts of great deeds in the past will give them the impetus to also reach for excellence. Third, their daily lives are full of necessary stress and diversions and the study of history exhilarates the mind. Mir Khwand also defends history here from the claim that it propagates lies or inventions, and says that even if this were so, histories can still be read to create the faculty of discernment in the minds of rulers.[55]

With this portrait of the ideal historian, Khwand lists the historians who wrote in Arabic—most prominently Tabari, Mas'udi, and 'Utbi—and those who wrote in Persian—Firdausi, Baihaqi, and Juzjani—totaling some forty historians. Mir Khwand makes a point of noting that this archive represents sources he had directly consulted for the writing of his own universal history, and reaffirms that the reader of his work will see Mir Khwand citing these sources in their appropriate places.[56] Mir Khwand's articulation of the work of history thus combines many of the registers already encountered in the work of previous historians, and much that, as we will see, would go on to inform Firishta.

Abu'l Fazl's *Akbarnama* is one of the greatest histories of the age. Abu'l Fazl was the chief adviser and official during the reign of Jalaluddin Akbar (1556–1605), and *Akbarnama* gives the history of Akbar's rule until 1602 CE. Abu'l Fazl is keen to insist that his role as a historian is not to be a sycophant to his emperor, and, at numerous places in his mammoth history, he stresses the nobility of the task that he has undertaken. Although it is clear that Abu'l Fazl saw the primary task of his history to elucidate the (near) divine right of Akbar's rule, it is still instructive to register his sustained thoughts on the normative and ethical work of history writing.[57] With that caveat, Abu'l Fazl's most lucid engagement with the task of history comes at the conclusion of his account of the year 1572.

Abu'l Fazl details how he prepared himself for the task of writing Akbar's history, once commanded to do so. This required training himself: "I refrained from listening to old tales of hobgoblins [for] . . . in that state of certain splendor the castle of narrative history appeared to be in ruins."[58] The historian, according to Abu'l Fazl, would be someone who avoids "worthless potsherds," "fantasy-worshipping potheads," "evil-natured, greedy persons and foolish blatherers."[59] He cautions that

"many people of all descriptions have fallen into great and eternal calamity by reading hoary, misleading books . . . instead of the unique
pearl of understanding."[60] How then did the hesitant Abu'l Fazl proceed with all these dangers and lies surrounding him? In the long tradition of historians, he too claims a divine inspiration:

> A heavenly notion gave a slap to my wayward psyche and began
> to give advice in an unspoken language. "Son of Mubarak," it
> said, "when you have been given such standing in the realm of
> right-thinking, what are you thinking of? Why are your eyes
> opened to nothing but faults? . . . Possessing no talent in the rhe-
> torical craft, the common herd rise up in vengeance against
> anything they do not comprehend and sully their tongues and
> hearts with criticism. Will you, like them, tread the path of
> ignorance and superficiality? Were it not for the light of nar-
> rative history, how could so many lamps of knowledge have
> been lit?"[61]

The divine voice gave Abu'l Fazl a new way of thinking about history.
He learned that history was a path to gain enlightenment, that it gave a
glimpse of worldly beauty. The history Abu'l Fazl would write would not
use poetry to embellish, would not rely on quotations nor "elaborate introductory passages, allusions, enigmas, and encomia."[62] Instead, Abu'l
Fazl would write for the "cognizant truth-singers" who would understand the true (and hidden) meanings that his history contained.

A central motif that emerges from this study of historians, from Juzjani to Abu'l Fazl, is the requirement of cultivating a personal ethics in
thinking about one's political world. These historians, and their works,
form a series of cohesive arguments for the role of history in public and
intellectual life. Each is a rung in a ladder that demands that the historian climb to ever-greater heights and observe the past and the future.
It is this shared ethic, this reliance on historians past and conversations
with historians present, that creates a philosophy of history for Hindustan. It is with this understanding of what history meant to the historians that informed Firishta that we can now turn to his own history.

A CONTRAPUNTAL HISTORY
OF HINDUSTAN

Seen from the vantage point of Firishta, there is a substantial body of writing that constitutes a living archive for writing a history of Hindustan. We can see a coherent inter-referentiality, a clear sense of development of a theory and a practice of doing history and deliberate ways in which the logic of history is made apparent to future generations. The historian in this intellectual geography of Hindustan sees himself as an ethical servant of the governing elite but also beholden to future generations. While he served the governing ruler, he was not in a subservient position. The historian sees as his audience a future reader who will judge his work on the grounds of truthfulness and critical approach to understanding power. As Firishta launches his own project to write a complete history of Hindustan, rather than a history of royal lineages, these ideas of history writing must have directly influenced his thinking.

To approach Firishta through the lens of the historians who preceded him is already to dismantle the claims of colonial historiography where these histories are mere repositories of facts that can only be gleaned by the European historian. What I want to foreground is that Firishta was deliberately participating in a comity of historians whose works informed Firishta's interpretation of history. From within such particular viewpoints of thinking about history, Firishta aimed to produce a new mode for historical thinking.

Firishta's preface, like the prefaces of the works before his gaze, drips with humility, recognizing his shortcomings and handicaps while confronting the monumental nature of the task ahead:

> In my youth, my worthless ears would often hear whispers from
> the sky that if the heavens have this manifest beauty and if the
> world is so carefully crafted; if recognizing the order of the uni-
> verse is to praise the Creator, then it is incumbent upon one to
> write such a book that will contain the doings of Muslim kings
> and the conditions of the Elders of Faith such that the internal
> and external conditions of the country of Hindustan are re-
> vealed as being sustained by these fundamental groups.[63]

What is this prompt from a disembodied voice to write a history of the great kings of Hindustan? The whispered command to write a history that Firishta hears is a command from the archive. Firishta is gesturing to canonical literary and historical works, including Firdausi's *Shahnama*. Firdausi admits to a "prompt from heaven," which gave him a desire for composing a worthy text for the right patron. In constructing parallels between his work and Firdausi, Firishta notes that he too searched for a proper patron before embarking on writing a "new" history of Hindustan.

Firishta was perhaps born in Ahmadnagar decades before 1570 CE.[64] His father, Ghulam Ali Hindu Shah, came to Ahmadnagar from Astarabad. It was while in Ahmadnagar that Firishta heard the whispers prompting him to write a history. Firishta searched for a patron for whom he might fulfill the whispered command but found none until, in 1589, he moved to Bijapur to the court of Ibrahim 'Adil Shah II. Ibrahim "recognized his literary talent" and commissioned from Firishta a history "carefully placing pearls and jewels on a string of all of the great rulers of Hindustan."[65] Again, the garland here is a deliberately deployed literary device; a nod to a specific aesthetic project that governs Firishta's work. Firishta is acknowledging historians such as 'Awfi, Kufi, and Nizami, who also deployed this motif of carefully placed pearls.

Now with both a heavenly mandate and an earthly patron, Firishta took up the task of amassing the jewels of history and putting them in a wondrous and beautiful order—a necklace, a garland—something so new that it could only be called *Naurasnama* (the newest flavor). With Ibrahim's Nauraspur and his *Kitab-i Nauras,* there was certainly a palatable energy for newness around the 'Adil Shahi court. Firishta's contemporaries at the court were consuming the ninth- and tenth-century Kashmiri works on aesthetics circulating in the Deccan, such as *Samaya Matrika,* and composing new epics in a new language, Dakhani. Firishta's impetus for a new universal history certainly incorporated the newness of his new age, of the new millennium (in the Hijri calendar), of a new city, of a new aesthetic.

Firishta declared in his preface to have written a history such that "the Zulaikhas of the time will call it a second Yusuf." This is a reference to the Qur'anic story of Yusuf (Joseph) as well as to one of the most influential romances, Jami's *Yusuf Zulaykha* (1483). Firishta is calling attention to the significance and worth of his history by comparing it to the Persian classic and a sacral account. This is a reference previously invoked by Fakhr-i Mudabbir and Nizami.

In order to understand the project of his work of history, it is useful to think about the analogy to the story of Joseph. The story of Yusuf in the Qur'an is recounted in the twelfth chapter. The Qur'an labels it the "best of stories," of which the world was as yet unaware. Recall that Barani had also prefaced his work with this call to the Qur'an's endorsement of narrative and history. The story of Joseph is a familiar one from the biblical and Hebraic tradition, though the Qur'anic narration is a distinct one.

This "best of stories" begins with a dream that Yusuf narrates to his father, the prophet Ya'qub: "O father, I have seen in a dream eleven stars and the sun and the moon prostrating to me."[66] It is a prophetic dream. Ya'qub cautions Yusuf from telling the dream to his brothers, saying, "This is about how your Lord will choose you and teach you the interpretation of narratives and complete His favor upon you."[67] At the end of Yusuf's adventures, Yusuf interprets the dream as his becoming a king and a prophet.[68] Between the prophecy and its fulfillment, for this best of stories, the life of Yusuf is narrated through a series of hardships and tests. The Qur'anic story emphasizes Yusuf's capacity to persevere based on his work and his belief in God.[69] From this "best of stories" emerges a figure of enduring fascination, with many romances casting characters like Yusuf in annotated stories of the past.

What is important from Firishta's perspective is that Yusuf is also a storyteller, an interpreter, one who narrates the past using testimony and material evidence, guiding the listener and the reader to the meaning behind the riddle. To Firishta, Yusuf seems a model of the task of the historian—an interpreter and a prophet of the future. To Firishta, a work of history was an opportunity to interpret the past for the present and to prophesize the future.

The lives of prophets were long a part of the genre of history known as *Qisas al Anbiya'* (Tales of the prophets).[70] Yusuf was a figure that historians of Hindustan consistently turned toward in order to clarify their works of history. Yusuf's story was not received via scripture alone.

More likely sources were the *Yusuf Zulaykha* romances written by Firdausi, Saʿadi, Rumi, and certainly Jami.[71] *Yusuf Zulaykha* was also available in Dakhani and Sanskrit for Firishta and his peers.[72]

Firishta's readers would have had a clear understanding of how his claim that his history is "a second Yusuf" was meant to be understood. Firishta is saying that his history is beautiful; that, at first glance, one would fall in love with it and contemplate it; that it is blessed and beatified from God; that it performs acts of prophetic interpretation on both its own present and the future that lies in front of it. This is an indexical relationship that Firishta created between his history and the "best of stories" from the Qur'an, an intellectual geography of Hindustan that included historians but also the great poets of romances and epics.

While he likens his task to that of Yusuf, Firishta begins his "best of stories" by opening his historical account with the *Mahabharata*. This is remarkable on two grounds. The first is that Firishta is breaking from the understood forms of historical writing of his predecessors. All of the Arabic and Persian historiography that preceded him began history with the creation of the world by God, the creation of Adam and his descent to Earth, and continued to Noah's flood, which reset Qur'anic time into historical time. The classic example is in Tabari's *Tarikh,* which goes on, after Noah, to describe the Hebrew Prophets and Patriarchs, the various kingdoms and kings who predated Muhammad in greater western Asia. For Tabari, and for much of the historical tradition that followed him, Qur'anic time—highlighted by the accounts of the lives of prophets—ends with the last prophet, Muhammad. All of this history is understood as a source of distress and the decline of humanity into spiritual, social, and political darkness—the *jahiliyya*—which Muhammad's birth in Mecca and his subsequent migration to Medina brings to an end.

After Tabari, other historians such as Masʿudi, Baihaqi, ʿUtbi, Juzjani, and others would follow roughly the same chronology. Even if they also drew upon Prakrit or Sanskrit texts—such as the *Pancatantra*—they did not shift the temporal regime set by the Qur'an. They did not bring into their histories cosmologies that differed from their own as part of their accounts. The most radical break in this tradition was in ʿAli Kufi's *Chachnama,* which began its historical account with the political rule of a Brahmin ruler, Chach, in Sindh. However, with the exception of *Chachnama,* the conventions of historical writing in Arabic or Persian maintained a singular emphasis on Qur'anic temporality until Firishta. It should be noted that, while these histories adhere to Qur'anic time, they depict people of all faiths in the polities of Hindustan—much like *Chachnama.*

Firishta labels the prolegomena of his history "The Beliefs of the People of Hind and the Accounts of the Appearance of Islam in their Land." He begins, "Among them there is no other book more significant and reliable than the *Mahabharata.*"[73] Firishta goes on to describe the text as having more than a hundred thousand verses and that it was translated from the Hindi script into Persian during Akbar's reign. He is referring here to the rendering of *Mahabharata* into Persian from Sanskrit ordered by Jalaluddin Akbar in 1582. That project was undertaken by a series of scholars of Persian, and Sanskrit—Badayuni, Thanesari, Mulla Shiri, Naqib Khan, Deva Misra, Satavadhana, Madhusadhana Misra, Chaturbhuja, and Shaikh Bhavan. These scholars created a Persian rendition of *Mahabharata* that was given the title of *Razmnama* by Akbar.[74] The historian Abu'l Fazl, Akbar's chief minister, wrote an introduction to this completed work in 1587.[75]

In order to see the significance of Firishta's engagement with the *Mahabharata,* it is important to flesh out what his contemporaries thought about the text. While renderings of Sanskrit texts into Persian had a long and storied history before Akbar, there was a renewed emphasis at Akbar's court on creating new versions and having them reproduced for the wider nobility. Abu'l Fazl's introduction to the *Razmnama* gives us a good indication of the motivations and framework around such projects. Abu'l Fazl frames the rendering as motivated by Akbar's direct orders. Akbar sought harmony between the "nation of Muhammad, Jews and Hindus" by making available their "authentic books" in clear and easy-to-understand renditions.[76]

The *Mahabharata,* Abu'l Fazl declares, is a "work of wise sages" and "covers many principles, including the smaller issues and beliefs, of the Brahmins of Hind" and there is "no other book more comprehensive, voluminous" than this.[77] Those who foment or display hostility toward other sects, Abu'l Fazl cautions, deliberately use texts of religion that are

inaccessible behind different scripts. Hence: "It was desired by the detailed reason [of Akbar] that the *Mahabharata,* which is filled with most
valuable things connected with religion, be translated so that those who
display hostility may refrain from doing so and may seek after the truth.
[This means] Those Muslims who have not perused the pages of their
heavenly and religious books and have not cast their wondering eyes on
the different histories of the world, such as that of Khatain [Cathay] or
Hindiyan [Hindustani]."[78] Abu'l Fazl suggests that there is history in the
Mahabharata. Abu'l Fazl's own work of history, the monumental *Akbarnama,* contained a summary and discussion of the *Mahabharata,* but
he does not open the work with it. Instead, Abu'l Fazl places the text as
contributing to ancient pasts and coming from the perspective of believers from whom polytheists can also learn. The importance of the
work, for Abu'l Fazl, lies in the way it can open up common pathways
into sacral understandings of the past.

Firishta, in contrast, reads the *Mahabharata* as a work of history. For
example, when he concludes his summary account, he proclaims, "God
be praised, such an account of marvels and wonders is not contained in
any history of the seven climes except for this book from Hindustan."[79]
This is followed by Firishta's explanation as to why the *Mahabharata* was
composed by Viyasa. Firishta calls Viyasa an eyewitness to the history
of the war. Firishta argues that Viyasa not only witnessed the events but
also made his narrative useful with wise anecdotes and aphorisms for
his readers to ruminate upon, thus providing an ethics for the reader.

In naming his work *Nauras Bustan Kalam-i Qadim* (A new bouquet
of ancient knowledge), Firishta signaled to his readers his intent to in-
vent something new beyond the patterns established by his fellow historians. His opening differs immediately from theirs by calling the
Mahabharata a historical text. Recall here Dow's admonishment and
condemnation of Firishta for considering the *Mahabharata* a work of
history. Dow considered the *Mahabharata* as nothing more than poetry.
Firishta, however, holds the *Mahabharata* in high regard—he can
imagine multiple cosmologies and temporalities in a contrapuntal register for his own history.

In beginning his history of Hindustan with the *Mahabharata,* Firishta
disrupts the standard placement of Qur'anic time with dharmic time.

Firishta now faces the challenge of reconciling two temporal regimes. Thus, his first concern is to establish a chronology. Firishta is summarizing his knowledge of the *Mahabharata* (from the *Razmnama*), but he also mentions speaking to Brahmins at various times, as sources for his history. In his restatement of the *Mahabharata* and its conception of time, he introduces the concept of chronology according to the Brahmins of Hindustan, that one full circle of time takes 4,320,000 years and comprises four ages: *satyug, tretayug, dvaparayug,* and *kalyug.* Firishta describes these ages thus: the duration of *satyug* was 1,720,000 years, and a human life span in that age was of 100,000 years. Satyug was the age of full righteousness, that is, all human beings in that age were just and righteous. *Tretayug* was 1,296,000 years, in that age three-fourths of human beings were righteous beings, and their life spans were 10,000 years. *Dvaparayug* lasted 864,000 years, with half the population on the right path, and human life spans ran to a thousand years. Finally, *kalyug* lasts for 432,000 years, only a third of human beings are righteous, and their life spans are a mere one hundred years long. Thus, Firishta notes, his present and the world of Islam itself was 40,688 years into the *kalyug.*

After accounting for time in the *Mahabharata,* Firishta turns toward explaining its intersection with that of the Muslim understanding of time. Firishta begins by first narrating an account he read in a "trustworthy" book, "A man questioned 'Ali [the cousin and son-in-law of the Prophet and the most revered figure in Shi'a Islam], 'Who was there thirty thousand years before Adam?' 'Ali replied it was Adam. The man inquired this thirty times and fell silent after getting the same reply. 'Ali then said, 'If you had asked me this thirty-thousand times who was there before Adam, I would have replied the same.'"[80] This gnostic account, where Adam was always the first, Firishta writes, allows one to conceive of the creation of the Earth as having an unknowable beginning as far as dating is concerned. Adam is always the first in whatever time schema that is at play, and, for this reason, "the sayings of the people of Hind do not appear to be without merit" for Muslims. He then makes an effort to reconcile the two temporalities by placing the lives of Adam and Noah within *dvaparayug.* This is possible because Adam and Noah, Muslims believe, had life spans nearing a thousand years, which was also the life span of human beings generally in that age. Finally, he calculates the time of the Prophet's migration within the *kalyug*. What emerges from reading Firishta is a serious effort to intertwine the time from the Qur'an with the continuously unfolding time of the *Mahabharata*. It is only after this summary of the *Mahabharata* that the true import of Firishta's narrative beginning reveals itself.

Firishta notices that there is a great variety of belief in Hindustan: Some people do not believe Adam was the beginning of the world; some do not believe Noah's flood reached Hindustan; some do not believe the world will persist after the end of a full cycle.[81] In order to reconcile these disparities, Firishta subtly changes the definition afforded to gods, granting that figures from the *Mahabharata* were indeed real and existed but that they were not human like Adam—as in, they were not "made of clay." With his "research and investigation," Firishta concludes that Hindustan, like the other regions of the world, was populated by human beings who descended solely from Adam seven thousand years ago, allowing the gods of the *Mahabharata* to occupy a parallel temporality. This allows for dual and, perhaps, overlapping possibilities of existence, the simultaneity of the times of the *Mahabharata* and the Qur'an.

The "human" world, Firishta argues, was repopulated after Noah's flood. Noah's son was Ham, whose sons were Hind, Sind, Jaish, Faranj, Hurmuz, Buya—each of whom settled cities with their names in the world.[82] Firishta provides a novel account of the foundation of these cities, mixing the stories from the *Mahabharata*, Firdawsi's *Shahnama*, and the Qur'an. In following the history of Noah's sons who moved into Hindustan, Firishta consistently highlights the great kings of Hindustan, descended from Noah, who founded the major cities, including Bijapur in the Deccan. Firishta is able to provide a genealogy for the places in Hindustan that are neither Muslim nor Hindu but contrapuntally intertwined.[83] Firishta ends this introductory chapter with a very brief account of the coming of Islam to Hindustan, with Kabul acting as the western limit of Hindustan.

Firishta's opening gives clarity to his concerns as a historian, his method, and the philosophy governing his narrative. He asserts that the *Mahabharata* is a work of history, written at the behest of a court and by Viyasa, an eyewitness to the events.[84] In his interpretation of time and gods in the *Mahabharata*, Firishta relies on ʿAli to present his argument. He places figures such as Krishna from the *Mahabharata* and Rustum from the *Shahnama* as larger-than-life figures in Hindustan's geography. Firishta constructs a temporality for his history that incorporates the *Mahabharata* and thus opens up newer spaces for interpretation of past figures and polities.

This has consequences for the ways in which Firishta narrates figures from his past, and the ways in which he reads or renarrates historical sources. Remember Sprenger had posited that the only value of Firishta or other Persian histories was to use them to assemble a repository of facts for the purposes of colonial governance. By returning to Firishta, we see radically different possibilities. First, Firishta is building on a long tradition of a theory for history. Second, Firishta is deliberately expanding the notion of history and creating a new paradigm for thinking about Hindustan. Firishta's history is thus no static accumulation or repository of facts without synthesis or analysis. His history of Hindustan mandates a reading that considers his philosophy of what it means to think historically, spatially, and ethnographically. It is only in this reading that we may understand how Firishta approached his past.

In order to flesh out the contours of how Firishta approached the work of history, I turn to examine a particular instance from his history, where he reads his archive and interprets the past to make his own argument. The instance I highlight is the account of Mahmud Ghazni (d. 1030)— the prototypical "Muslim invader" for the colonial episteme.[85] Mahmud was the subject and the object of a vast array of historical and poetical works. As mentioned earlier, his court featured luminaries such as Firdausi, Farrukhi, ʿUnsari, Biruni, and ʿUtbi, among others. The literary and historical work produced at Ghazni set the tone for not only the forms and contours of Muslim polities in Hindustan but also influenced the development of history writing in subsequent centuries.

It is this tradition that forms Firishta's intellectual geography. Looking at the past from Firishta's perspective highlights the availability and circulation of the major texts from the previous six hundred years. As this chapter has argued, the histories produced in Hindustan were aware of, and responding to, each other across time and space. The awareness that this was a "canon" of histories changes our perception of how to read them. How did Firishta deal with the availability of multiple sources, of competing pictures of the past? What interpretative choices did Firishta make, as a historian, in accordance with, or against, a then canonical understanding of Mahmud?

Firishta titles his first section "Account of the Sultans of Lahore popularly known as the Ghaznavi Sultans," which formally acknowledges the geography of Hindustan to encompass Lahore and Ghazni. Firishta structures his chapter in two parts—first comes a political history of events, and then he narrates anecdotes, dreams, and remembrances of the principal actors of the chapter. The main sources for Firishta for his history of Sebuktagin (d. 997) and his son Mahmud are ones that Firishta understands as contemporary to Mahmud. The earliest histories are eleventh-century Gardizi and 'Utbi and then the thirteenth- and fourteenth-century historians Juzjani, 'Awfi, and Mir Khwand. Throughout his account of Mahmud, Firishta relies heavily on 'Awfi and Mir Khwand, from whom he takes numerous stories, anecdotes, and quotations. What we see operating in this micro-episode is Firishta's method and how Firishta takes in and recasts his predecessors' histories to shift both the meaning and the agency of past actors. As in his privileging of the *Mahabharata*, Firishta plays out the themes of his contrapuntal history by interpolating actors, victors, and conquered into a sustained understanding of Mahmud.

After narrating the family and political history of Sebuktagin, Firishta recounts Sebuktagin's decision to advance his army against the polytheists of Hindustan. In 977, Sebuktagin conquered a few forts "where Islam had made no pathways," constructed "mosques in places," and collected vast riches, returning victorious to Ghazni.[86] Sebuktagin's actions, Firishta writes, alarmed Jaipal, son of Istpal, who "was Brahmin by birth and whose polity extended Sirhand to Multan to Kashmir" and who worried that his hereditary polity would be taken "by these outsiders."[87] Sebuktagin and Jaipal clashed near Multan. The war raged for days, and Firishta calls attention to the bravery and skill of the young Mahmud in combat.

The battle was so evenly balanced, Firishta writes, that "one could not differentiate between the victorious and the defeated."[88] In that balance, an unspecified group approached the young Mahmud and told him that near Jaipal's camp was a natural spring with the miraculous power that, should any impurity be thrown into it, the gods will be angered, the skies will darken, and snow and thunderstorms will appear. Mahmud ordered that manure or other impurities be immediately thrown into the spring. As foretold, an immediate darkness engulfed the battleground, "a bright day became like the darkest night," and such a cold wind blew that mules and horses perished from it.[89] Frightened by the calamitous shift in weather, Jaipal's warriors lost their courage and appealed to him to surrender to this heavenly foe. Jaipal was thus forced to appeal for peace, which Sebuktagin accepted.

To get at Firishta's method here, we have to first look at what Firishta's sources were telling him, and then consider his own addition to this account of the past. The earliest version of the clash between Sebuktagin and Jaipal is in 'Utbi's *Tarikh-i Yamini,* which describes the conflict. However, in 'Utbi's narration, it was the young Mahmud himself who already held the knowledge that polluting the spring would bring about darkness over the land.[90] The later historian, Juzjani, only mentions that Sebuktagin defeated Jaipal, and gives no details about the pitched battle nor of any heavenly intervention. 'Awfi's *Jawami al Hikayat* also describes this battle in an anecdote, with interesting differences. In 'Awfi, the information that there is a sacred spring in the vicinity of the battleground is conveyed to the young Mahmud by an old woman. When Mahmud pollutes the spring, it brings about the snowstorm and a victory for Sebuktagin.[91]

The earliest account, from 'Utbi, is the easiest to interpret. It is an homage to the young Mahmud. It demonstrates the sacral reach of a young Mahmud, who can turn even the natural world of Hindustan against the polytheists. In 'Awfi, the story invites reflection: Mahmud is not the holder of knowledge, rather, the knowledge is held by an old woman of Hindustan. 'Awfi places his anecdote in the section titled "On the Chemical Properties of Natural Objects," thereby drawing attention not to Mahmud's sacral power but to the natural world and its mysteries. In Juzjani, whose emphasis is on tracing the descent of power from the Ghuri sultans of Lahore and Uch, the Ghaznavi stage is of little direct importance. Juzjani simply states the outcome of the event—the victory of Sebuktagin without any elaboration.

In Firishta's recounting of this history, some critical changes were made to the narrative. The motif of "cooperation"—often a means to invoke divine intervention—shapes Firishta's narrative. Thus, Firishta's account of this first battle is a unique reconfiguration of this historical event: The Muslim army and the Hindu army are portrayed as equals, the landscape has sacral elements that cause divine intervention, and those inhabitants who live around the battlegrounds, an unspecified group, have a stake in halting wars on them. While the markers of religious difference foreground this particular incident—Sebuktagin intends to build mosques from place to place—Firishta does not spell out which sacral power was offended by the pollution of the spring. Unlike 'Utbi, Firishta takes the glory and agency away from Mahmud and gives it to the people of Hindustan—they are the ones who knew about the spring, and their intervention stops the bloodshed.

Juzjani, in his account, had endowed Mahmud's birth with divine significance—at the occasion of his birth, an idol in Waihind fell over and smashed into bits. Mahmud, Juzjani writes, "converted thousands of temples into mosques, and conquered many cities of Hindustan and defeated many rajas of Hind."[92] However, Juzjani, writing two hundred years after Mahmud's time, does not delve much into Mahmud's history. The only battle of Mahmud that Juzjani describes is the one at Somnath, in Gujarat. Juzjani writes that Mahmud "brought back 'manat' the idol from Somnath and divided it into four parts: one part was placed in the central mosque in Ghazna, one in the palace, and two were sent to Mecca and Medina."[93]

Juzjani narrates miracles associated with Mahmud's journey back from Somnath. As Mahmud and his army are trying to cross the desert between Gujarat and Sindh, they get lost. A local man offers to show Mahmud's troops a path. However, he deliberately leads them astray such that the army is hopelessly lost in the desert without enough water or food. Mahmud asks the guide to explain himself. He replies that he was "giving up his life to avenge the calamity hurled [by Mahmud] upon the idol of Somnath and now [I] have made you and your army adrift in the desert so you die from lack of water."[94] Enraged, Mahmud has the guide put to death. That night, Mahmud goes out in the desert and weeps and prays for guidance. Then Mahmud sees a light appear in the north, and instructs his troops to march toward the light. By daybreak, they reach water and, thence, return to Ghazni. In the Juzjani account, Mahmud is able to ask for direct intervention from the divine.

Juzjani's portrait of Mahmud undergoes a marked shift in Firishta. Unlike Juzjani's account, Firishta describes battles at Ghur, Multan, Tanesar, Nindona, Khawarzam, Qanauj, Mathura, Nar'ain, Lahore, and Balkh—a long history of clashes—before Mahmud gets to Somnath. In these events, Mahmud is presented as focused on building alliances where possible and destroying temples only when necessary. 'Awfi and Mir Khwand are the most-cited historians in this section, but Firishta changes the meaning and import of many of the events narrated in the section—changes that amount to a recalibration of the ways in which Mahmud can be seen as a person, and as a warrior.

An example of Firishta's shifting depiction of Mahmud is an event from 1021. After his taking power in Lahore, Mahmud heads toward Raja Nanda of Gawaliar. After a short siege by Mahmud, Nanda asks for peace with an offering of thirty-five elephants. Mahmud counters and asks for three hundred elephants. Nanda agrees but, Firishta writes: "As a test, he [Nanda] released the three hundred elephants without any riders, but Mahmud's troops are able to corral the elephants, impressing Nanda. Nanda then writes, in the language of Hind, a couplet for Mahmud. Mahmud shows this couplet to the 'literati of Hindi, Arabic and Persian' at his court and 'they unanimously praised it.'"[95] Duly impressed by Nanda, Mahmud consults his advisers and then grants the governorship of fifteen forts, including Kalinjar, to Nanda. This is certainly not a simplistic portrayal of an idol smasher who conquers and despotically rules, which was to become the dominant understanding of Mahmud in later European historiography. Firishta highlights Mahmud as responding as much to a literary exchange as to a stalemate in warfare. When we turn to Firishta's account of Somnath, we again see that it does not simply hew to what previous historians had reported. Firishta keeps the skeletal framework from Juzjani—Mahmud's arrival in Somnath, the taking of the deity (in parts) to Ghazni, and being lost on the way home requiring divine intervention—but greatly transforms it.

In Firishta, Mahmud decides to campaign to Somnath only after he heard reports that all of the other deities of Hindustan are subservient to the one in Somnath. When his troops reach Somnath, the battle is so intense that Mahmud gives up hope. Again, remember that Firishta's history of Mahmud started with this same motif of an equally balanced battle. In despair, Mahmud pleads for divine intercession. He holds the robe of the Sufi shaykh Abu'l Hasan Khurqani, which had been gifted to him, and begs for intercession. As a result of this special plea, the Muslim army wins the fort. When Mahmud sees the idol of Somnath with his own eyes, he is immediately compelled to strike it with his own hand and breaks the face of the idol.[96] Mahmud then orders that the idol be broken into four pieces—one for the central mosque in Ghazni, one for his palace, and two for Mecca and Medina.

Upon hearing the order, Firishta writes, the caretakers of the temple plead with Mahmud to spare further destruction of the idol and to instead take from them a substantial annual tax. Mahmud consults with his advisers; they agree with the caretakers' plea. Firishta writes that Mahmud's advisers told him that he should leave the idol alone and accept the tax, for by destroying the idol, "neither will the practice of idol worship end here nor will it benefit us. Instead, this sum of money will benefit many poor of Ghazni."[97] Mahmud, however, responds with a stunning articulation of his paradoxical approach to power: "What you say is correct, but if I follow your advice, I will be known to posterity as 'Idol seller' and not an 'Idol smasher.'"[98]

Firishta documents this difference of opinion, registered six hundred years prior—between Mahmud's advisers, who are making a mutually beneficial case, and Mahmud's personal convictions as an iconoclast. Firishta is certainly clear that Mahmud makes the choice not based on what is good for either the people of Somnath nor for the people of Ghazni but on what he imagines the judgment of posterity would be on him.

On the journey back from Somnath, Mahmud is beset with increasing difficulties: A rival raja's army comes to rescue Somnath; another city rises up in rebellion against Mahmud, and the local governor barely manages to quell it. Finally, on the journey back, Mahmud is confronted by the self-sacrificing guide, who leads his troops into the desert, and Mahmud has to pray again for the intercessions of the Sufi. The Sufi admonishes Mahmud for letting his piety slip.

In Firishta's account, Mahmud's destruction of Somnath renders him a complicated, even contemplative, figure. The repeated divine intervention of a Sufi master as well as Mahmud's alliances with the local elite contest the simplistic iconoclasm that surrounds other depictions of his actions at Somnath. In Firishta's contrapuntal history, Mahmud becomes a lone iconoclast, a singular figure worried about his position in history, rather than a glorified representative of all Muslims. He is keen to build relationships with rajas as much as he has advisers who do not see the wisdom in iconoclasm for the sake of Islam.

Juzjani ends the life of Mahmud by proclaiming how his rule extended east across "all of 'Ajam—Khurasan, Khawarzam, Tabaristan, Iraq, Nimruz, Fars, Ghur, Tukharistan, Turkistan," and that he died after visiting Baghdad and getting a title from the caliph.[99] Juzjani celebrates Mahmud as a conqueror and ties him to the caliphate. Firishta again differs when he comes to close the chapter on Mahmud.

Firishta writes that after Mahmud's campaign against Saljuq in Turkmenistan, he grew ill from either anemia or tuberculosis. Two days before his death he commanded that all of the treasures he had collected over his life be gathered in the compound so that it resembled a garden. Mahmud sat "looking at them with covetous eyes and with audible gasps cried and cried and then ordered them to be put back in the treasury."[100] Firishta's reckoning of Mahmud continues across several anecdotes where Mahmud is shown to be covetous, hasty, and often of two minds. He is no paragon of virtue nor an ideal of kingship—instead, much of the time, he is described by Firishta as harming his own nobility. Unlike Juzjani, there is no attempt by Firishta to connect Mahmud's reign to that of Baghdad or to glorify his memory in any way.

Mahmud's history allows Firishta to highlight a theme to which he repeatedly circles back: the necessity of listening to advisers, of showing kindness to civilians, of resolutions through pacts instead of wars. Firishta highlights Mahmud's flaws as an individual as well as a king. Mahmud, to Firishta, is brave, capricious, and attentive to the judgment of history. Firishta leans into that judgment to show that Mahmud's iconoclasm is no longer a point to celebrate. Rather his zeal and personal drive is a story of caution. According to Firishta, what is lacking from Mahmud is a sense of promoting the greater good of those he governs.

What we learn from examining Firishta's treatment of Mahmud is that the life of Mahmud serves as an illustration to the imbricated history Firishta is sketching, where piety does not lie with Muslim rulers alone.

The past, to Firishta, is a repository from which new ethical registers can be opened up. His history always has agents and protagonists who act according to their personal foibles and predilections and not due to grand forces of ideology or religion.

Firishta's mandate was to write the first comprehensive history of Hindustan. He does so by assembling an archive of histories that could span the whole geography of Hindustan, written in Persian and Arabic from the ninth to the seventeenth centuries, to which he adds histories of the places and peoples of Hindustan from epics like the *Mahabharata* and *Shahnama*. This history was not simply an amalgamation of facts, as argued by Sprenger and Elliot. Instead, Firishta's history was a novel interpretation of the histories that had come before him. It reflected a long genealogy of historians interested in the practice and ethics of history writing. Their accounts provide an intellectual geography that reaches across the many places of Hindustan. It is to these places of Hindustan that we now turn.

4

THE PLACES IN HINDUSTAN

WHERE WAS HINDUSTAN? The nineteenth-century colonial obsession of carving out the territory of the subcontinent into domains of political control and resource extraction, of treaties and recognitions of indirect rule, remains starkly clear in the themes of the histories they produced, the archives they assembled, and the people they enslaved. The colonial episteme organized Hindustan under the rubric of politics, extracting the Mughal administrative vocabulary to transfer land management. It delimited sacred spaces: temples from mosques, shrines from cemeteries. It defined public and private places, rural and urban places. Through the census, they began to carve out the Muslim-majority and Hindu-majority places. With the logic of political rule the marker of Hindustan, the space of the subcontinent was fractured into particular territorial claims and slowly the pink hue of the British East India Company maps crept up to swallow all of the subcontinent. All of the complex ways of being in space, belonging to a place, were reduced to a cartographic certainty of control. The map emerged as the most robust truth, the ontologically secure representation of what was British India. The other ways of description, the relations between people and place, were grimly wiped out. By the end of the nineteenth century, there was no Hindustan to be located on any map, and no text, no monument, could stand and attest to its once-there-ness.

It is thus uncanny to read Firishta. His history is organized as a geography of a Hindustan that stretched from west to east, north to south, with the Deccan at the center. He notes at the beginning that when prompted to write a history, he looked to gather "the histories of various kings and countries of Hindustan."[1] Unlike many of his predecessors and contemporaries, his history is not organized as a genealogy of kings, but around the vast spaces that make up Hindustan. Firishta is not writing for a court that claims ownership of Hindustan, but a universal history that he clearly imagines to be constituted through his location, the Deccan. While he is in conversation with imperial Mughal histories, and with an intellectual genealogy that came before him, he is most committed to his own expertise in depicting the whole of Hindustan's historical geography. As shown in Chapter 3, Firishta develops a philosophy of history that incorporates and extends the history and geographies from the *Mahabharata* to the *Shahnama*.

Firishta's history is organized in a particular spatial order. The text has a prologue, twelve chapters, and a short conclusion. Each of the twelve chapters tells us of polities in a particular geography in the vast subcontinent. Firishta starts with polities in the Northwest, moves to the southern center, travels up to the eastern shores, and returns again to the South by the ocean—Lahore, Delhi, the Deccan, Gujarat, Malwa, Khandesh, Bengal, Multan, Sindh, Kashmir, Malabar. He expresses his love for this geography in the conclusion, titled "An Account of Conditions of the Heaven-Representing Hindustan," where he narrates the diversity and expansiveness of this geography.

Firishta's Hindustan is constituted first by multiple dominions, and then by cities. He gives specific origins to these dominions, providing a notion of sacral and political power in these spaces, and their relationships to each other. Hindustan already had an extensive corpus of historical narratives for each of the "regions," imagined as polities or cities. Firishta relied on such histories and accounts for his own work—citing and using pre-existing regional histories for some of these spaces, but Firishta makes an effort to organize such pre-existing spaces into discrete historical places.[2] He gives each of these spaces a chronology, an ethics, a set of actors, and multiple stories in order to assimilate these spaces into a unified history of Hindustan. The places described in time and across geography, collectively, make up Firishta's Hindustan. Firishta's invention was to give this Hindustan a universal history that reflected a diversity of cosmological political claims.

Firishta's Hindustan had a deep past and an immediate political present. The present, in the early seventeenth century, was the dominant Mughal imperium toward which European embassies, merchants, missionaries, and travelers were flocking. The Mughals, of course, had adopted and used the label of the kings of Hindustan since Babur in the early sixteenth century. This identification, paradoxically, did not shrink the conceptual boundaries of Hindustan to the political boundaries of the Mughal dominion. That Firishta was writing a history of Hindustan in the Deccan, outside of Mughal rule, specifically means that Hindustan was greater than the Mughal court. Firishta's Hindustan reflected the broader political and cultural landscape of the subcontinent that was firmly present in the seventeenth century.

The making of the subcontinent as Hindustan is a political and cultural process stretching across nearly a millennium. It happened in textual representations, in legal and liturgical forms, in titular conventions; it was deployed and used by a wide variety of the people of the subcontinent. Firishta had inherited the idea of a multi-polity Hindustan with the Deccan holding a prominent position. Firishta quotes a chronogram composed by his father, Ghulam Ali Hindushah, in a year when three kings of Hindustan died, which gives us a sense of how Hindustan was imagined in the sixteenth century:

> Three kings expired at one time
> By these just kings, Hind was a place of peace
> One, Mahmud the king of kings of Gujarat
> who was as young as his fortune
> Second, Islam Shah [Suri] the sultan of Delhi
> In Hindustan, he was the master of felicity
> Third was Nizam Shah Bahri [Ahmednagar]
> Who held the royal insignia of the country of Deccan
> Why do you ask me of the date of the death of these
>   three kings?
> It was "Fall of the Kings." (961 AH / 1553–1554)[3]

The three kings, in Delhi, in Gujarat, and in the Deccan, all belong to places within Hindustan.

Today in the subcontinent, Hindustan is colloquially understood as a synecdoche for a particular set of customary practices tied to north Indian languages, or as an attitude toward interfaith relations and social decorum—"the Hindustani civilization" (*Ganga-Yamuni tahzib*). Yet today's colloquial understanding is not the history of Hindustan as a political and historical entity that endured for centuries. The Hindustan evoked in the titles of kings or in histories and treatises was a geographic, social, and cultural construct. That Hindustan created a public, an affect, a desire, a set of characteristics—in territory and in the individual self. It is that particular history of Hindustan as a political geography that is erased analytically by the substitution of "India" to represent the medieval and early modern subcontinent.

The erasure of Hindustan as a political concept began with the European arrival to the subcontinent. India, the East Indies, or Indostan was, of course, known to Europeans; the quest for it, its imagined riches, propelled both Christopher Columbus and Vasco de Gama. This India of wonders and wealth was a space that attracted Portuguese settlements and Dutch factories. It was where the Jesuit missionaries and priests flocked—to the land of a small band of Christians, the reputed followers of St. Thomas the Apostle, living among "faithless" people. It was India, whose ports like Diu, and Surat, were to be controlled or burned down.

Throughout the sixteenth and early seventeenth centuries, the imagined riches and curiosities, the miracles and mystiques persisted despite repeated and extensive encounters of Europeans with the subcontinent. The European project engaged in its own task of describing the geography of Hindustan, breaking it down, extracting riches, and finally surveying and mapping it back into a whole, finally named, British India. The maps of British India, deemed scientific, framed the subcontinent solely in relation to its land as an expanding colonial project.

I begin this chapter with the ways in which Hindustan was seen by European—largely English—visitors. They labeled Hindustan the "East Indies" or "Grand Mogor"—sometimes "Hindoostan"—but ultimately "British India." My interest, in this first section, is to present what the

British saw as their experience and knowledge of the geography of the subcontinent. In essence, the British military conquests of subcontinental territories were intimately tied to the cartographic representations of the subcontinent. I then move to some of the key historians who wrote about the space of Hindustan prior to the seventeenth century. In these histories, we find a Hindustan that is the center of the world, a heavenly geography. The third section focuses on Firishta's history and examines his engagement with the space of Hindustan. I focus on Firishta's novel use of multiple cosmologies and histories to discuss the natural and political landscape.

COUNTRIES OF THE MUGHALS

A series of transitions was taking place in the sixteenth century in the ways in which the subcontinent was perceived by Europeans: from the earliest sources of information in Greek to Latinate Roman accounts of "Peninsula Indiæ," to the Portuguese, Dutch, French, and English renderings. The first transition came with the introduction of the eyewitness traveler, the first-person testimonial, the European sailor, merchant, diplomat, or missionary who physically traverses the landscape of the subcontinent and describes it in detail for the audiences in the metropole.

The earliest European gaze saw the subcontinent as a series of political forms, divided between Muhammadans and Gentiles, and with Akbar—the one possessing the most wealth, the most power—as a key ruler. This is in contrast to the ways in which the European colonial gaze had described the Americas as *terra nullius*.[4] Collected in the compendiums of Richard Hakluyt's *The Principal Navigations, Voyages and Discoveries of the English Nation* (1598) and its successor, Samuel Purchas's *Hakluyt Posthumous, or Purchas His Pilgrims* (first edition 1613, fourth completed edition 1626), are scores of authors and travelers whose accounts describe the lands and peoples of the "East Indies" or the "Grand Mogols." Hakluyt's text contained both English accounts and others translated from Portuguese, Italian, and German in order to give a territory to the colonizable worlds. In these early accounts, the geography of the subcontinent begins at its sea limit, and it is described from the port cities inland. The information provided (or noted) tends to favor travel routes, market details, customs of trade, and natural and artisanal products—everything from diamonds and pepper to ivory bangles. The places described—Goa most frequently, but also Daman, Calicut, Vijaya-nagar, and Bijapur—are first noted for their markets and then for their political realm, and finally for their, often termed barbaric, customs.

An exemplar of the myriad ways of imagining the subcontinent is in Hakluyt's account of M. Ralph Fitch, a merchant who travels, with M. John Newberie, from London to "all the kingdome of Zelabdim Echebar the great Mogor" and back between 1583 and 1591.[5] Fitch's itinerary re-flects what would have been a typical route for a merchant in the late sixteenth century who traveled from London to the subcontinent and back. We see the port of entry (Gujarat on the Indian Ocean) as well as the main cities and regions traversed within the subcontinent. The itin-erary moves from the western shores into the Deccan plain, up to the Gangetic plains, follows the Ganges river to Bengal, goes up to Burma, then back down via Orissa to Cochin and to Ceylon (Sri Lanka) before returning to the starting point of Goa. The route he takes is: London, Tripoli, Aleppo, Birra, Babylon, Felugia, Basora (Basra), Ormus (Hormuz), Diu, Daman, Basaim (Vasai), Tana (Thana), Chaul, Goa, Bellergan (Bel-gaum), Bisapor (Bijapur), Gulconda, Masulipatam, Servidore, Bellapore (Balapur), Barrampore (Burhanpur), Mandoway (Mandogarh), Ugini (Ujjain), Serringe (Sironji), Agra, Fatepore, Prage (Allahabad), Bannaras, Patenaw (Patna), Tanda, Cacchegate, Hugeli, Angeli, Satagam (Satgaon), Bottia, Chatigan (Chittagong), Bacola, Serrapore (Serampur), Cosmin, Medon, Dela, Cirion (Syriam), Macao, Pegu, Jamahey, Malaca, Cosmin, Cochin, Ceylon, Cochin, Goa, Chaul, Ormus, Basora, Babylon, Mosul, Medin, Orfa (Urfa), Birra, Aleppo, Tripoli, and London.

In Fitch's travels, the triangle of the subcontinent, starting from Diu, is formed, in order of appearance, by the political "countreys" of the Por-tuguese, the Adil Shahi (Hidalcan), the country of Zelabdim Echebar (Jalaluddin Akbar) out to Bengal, and Burma, where there are many countries ruled by "Gentiles."[6] At each stop on his itinerary, Fitch dis-cusses the political rule, the wondrous elements, and the material or mercantile resources. The entry for Bijapur gives us a good sense of this political geography:

> One of the first towns which we came unto, is called Bellergan, where there is a great market kept of Diamonds, Rubies, Saphires, and many other soft stones. From Bellergan we went to Bisapor which is a very great town where the king doeth keep his court. He hath many Gentiles in his court and they be great idolaters. And they have their idols standing in the Woods, which they call Pagodes. Some be like a Cow, some like a Monkey, some like Buffaloes, some like peacockes, and some like the devil. Here be very many elephants which they go to war with. Here they have good store of gold and silver: their houses are of stone very fair and high. From hence we went for Gulconda, the king whereof is called Cutup de lashach [Abdullah Qutb Shah]. Here and in the kingdom of Hidalcan ['Adil Shah], and in the country of the king of Deccan be the Diamonds found of the old water. It is a very fair town, pleasant, with fair houses of brick and timber, it aboundeth with great store of fruits and fresh water. Here the men and the women do go with a cloth bound about their middles without any more apparel. We found it here very hot.[7]

What Fitch notes, or annotates, are deities and riches—a template of seeing wonders and marvels in the landscape of Hindustan. When Fitch enters the Mughal realm, he announces its grandeurs, and presents Akbar as one among the great kings:

> From thence we went to Agra passing many rivers, which by reason of the rain were so swollen, that we waded and swam of-tentimes for our lives. Agra is a very great city and populous, built with stone, having fair and large streets, with a fair river running by it, which falleth into the gulf of Bengala. It hath a fair castle and a strong with a very fair ditch. Here be many Moores and Gentiles, the king is called Zelabdim Echebar [Akbar]: the people for the most part call him The great Mogor.[8]

Just a short while after Fitch, William Hawkins landed in Surat in 1605, traveled to Agra, and left for England in 1608. His account is included in the *Hakluytus Posthmus or Purchas His Pilgrimes* by Samuel Purchas in 1625. Hawkins ends with "a brief discourse of the strength, wealth and government, with some customs of the Great Mogol."[9] For Hawkins, political power defines the geography of the subcontinent. In other words, his was an account principally of Mughal dominions. For him, Hindustan was the kingdom of the Mughals, with Agra at its center: "The compass of his country is two years travel with *Carrauan,* to say, from *Candahar* to *Agra,* from *Soughtare* to *Agra,* from *Tatta* in *Sinde* to *Agra. Agra* is in a manner in the heart of all his Kingdomes."[10]

In contrast to Fitch, Hawkins's geography centers around the Mughal court—Agra is the "heart," a space labeled as "Great Mogol." The accounts of the Mughal king, built on the wide success and circulation of Hakluyt and Purchas, add to the immediate urgency and luster of one of the most significant political journeys to the subcontinent: Thomas Roe's embassy to Jahangir's court in 1615. To his narrative account of the Mughal realms, Roe added a geographical note on the "Mogul's territories." Roe reported that he gathered the information about the "Seuerall Kingdomes and Prouinces Subiect to the Great Mogoll Sha-Selim Gehangier [Jahangir]" from "the Kings Register."[11]

Roe begins his listing of the countries from the Northwest: Candahar, Tata (Thatta), Buckar (Bhakkar), Multan, Haagickan, Cabull (Kabul), Kyshmier (Kashmir), Bankish, Atack, Kakares, Pen-Jab (Punjab), Jenba, Peitan, Nakarkutt, Syba, Jesvall, Delly (Delhi), Meuat (Mewat), Sanball, Bakar (Bikaner), Agra, Jenupar, Bando, Patna, Gor, Bengala, Roch, Vdeza, Kanduana, Kualiar (Gwalior), Ckandes (Khandesh), Malva, Berar, Guzratt, Sorett, Naruar, and Chytor (Chitor). Agra is the "hart of the Mogolles territorye," and the road from Lahore to Agra is "one of the great woorkes and woonders of the world."[12] For the British, the Mughal imperium became the central object of attention, and their political realms were properly situated and understood as part of the "East Indies."

The first transition in the European narratives, such as those of Fitch above, is that the "first-person" account of their travels in the subcontinent begins to take priority over the abstract geographies from Greek or Roman sources. While many of these accounts continue to reference the Latinate canon—the import of wonders and marvels and the modes of description—the newness comes from the very personhood of the writer. His authority derives from his experiences "walking the landscape," "speaking to the people," and "seeing the place."

The second transition was the inclusion of local knowledge, first incorporated as oral reports, and then more authoritatively as "translations" from local sources. Roe introduced this convention by linking to the authority of the Mughal king himself in using the "King's Register" for his listing of the dominions. The "King's Register" would later be understood as Abu'l Fazl's *A'in-i Akbari* (ca. 1595). This was a compendium of places, customs, and traditions of Hindustan that was appended to Abu'l Fazl's history of the Mughal kings *Akbarnama*. The *A'in* had been rendered into English, in bits and pieces, by Francis Gladwin since 1777, and it was finally published in 1783. By then, the descriptions of place names and spaces from Roe's account were canonical.

The colonial efforts at mapmaking relied on these two foundations: the colonial agent who walked, described, and wrote the subcontinent; and sources of geographical information that could be translated and rendered into cartographies. In the European imagination, the geography of the whole of Hindustan began to be the geography of colonial dominions and their relationship to the Mughal polity. Roe's account was the basis for the first British map of Hindustan, produced by William Baffin, in 1619, "A Description of East India conteyninge th'Empire of the Great Mogoll." The map is labeled "Indolstani." The map reproduced almost all of the territories and kingdoms mentioned by Roe, but with the Deccan—while represented—as an empty space. The authority of Roe's account and Baffin's map became enshrined in the public imagination with their inclusion in the influential and widely circulating *Purchas His Pilgrimes*. With Baffin's map, the efforts of colonial mapmakers became focused on seeking more travel accounts and further translations of Sanskrit or Persian texts in order to construct better and more detailed maps of the subcontinent.

The map emerged in the early seventeenth century as, analytically, the most powerful instrument of colonization. It was a representative medium, and an aspirational visual, for European power in the subcontinent. The cartouche, the colorization, the "filled in" spaces as well as the *terra nullius*, were ideological tools for the enactment of European territorial expansion. The map was among the first and most vital instruments of colonialism.[13]

Louis Delarochette's 1788 map "Hind, Hindoostan, or India"—published by William Faden—captures the many modes of British representation of the subcontinent at a pivotal moment in time. The map bears the legend "Tu Regere Imperio Populos Brittanne Memento" (You, O Britain, govern the nations with your power, remember this), adapted from Virgil's plea to the Romans in the *Aeneid*.[14] It carries a note for how to think spatially about the subcontinent: "NB. Hindoostan is comprehended under Two General Divisions viz. Hindoostan (proper) to the North of the River Nerbudda and Decan to the South of that River."[15]

The equivalence drawn in the cartouche between "Hind, Hindoostan, or India" gestures to the many textual traditions that are feeding the spatial representation. The map's "Advertisement" carries the texts being used: "For the new and interesting particulars with which This Map is enriched, especially in the Northern Parts, we are chiefly indebted to the Geographical Description of Father Joseph Tieffenthaller, Apostolic Missionary in India, and to the Curious Draft of the Ganges and Gagra by Mons. Anquetil du Perron."[16] Not mentioned or cited in the copy are the Arabic and Persian historical texts inscribed into the very fabric of the territory: "Attock R. According to the Ayin Acbarri," "Minhaûareh afterwards al Mansura according to Abu Rihan al Biruni," and so on. The Jesuit missionary Joseph Tieffenthaller's account was translated by M. Jean Bernoulli in 1786 alongside the works of Anquetil du Perron and James Rennell on the description of "l'Indoustan."[17]

Baffin's map based on Roe's account, and Delarochette's map based on Tieffenthaller and du Perron's accounts represent a flattened visualization of a territory that comes with a godlike perspective. Yet, there is another crucial act of knowing that goes missing from the text to the map: the specific ordering of the geography of Hindustan from textual sources like Fitch's itinerary or Roe's geography—an ordering that, in text, had created a specific path through which to traverse the territory. Tieffenthaller, though coming a hundred and fifty years after Roe, maintains the specific order in which he walks the subcontinent: Kaboul,

Kandahar, Cachemire, Lahor, Moultan, Tatta, Delhi, Agra, l'Elhabad, d'Oude, d'Adjmer, Malva, Barar, Chandess, Guzarate, Behar, Bengale, d'Oressa, d'Aurengabad, Bhalagate, Safarabad ou de Bedor, d'Hederabad, and Bedjapour. This particular ordering, like Roe's, begins from the Northwest, goes south to Sindh, then to the Gangetic plains, back to western Ghats, then to Bengal, and finally to the Deccan. The ordering privileges one particular form of thinking about the subcontinent—the Mughal perspective.

The movements of the travelers from Europe to the subcontinent—from Fitch onward—were shaped by the sea and the vagaries of those controlling passages across the subcontinent. The maps produced from those textual renderings of place could not incorporate the ordering, but they did incorporate the particular biases, the gaze that looked for wonder or marvel or horror. Delarouchette labels "the Beels a Wild Nation of Robbers," "Village of Robbers," "Bhoodie where they adore a Serpent," "the Khands a wild people," "Rettenpour Wild People," "subterraneous caves out of which issue Fire, Wind, and Water," the "Diamond Mines," and much else in translating the accounts of Tieffenthaller and du Perron into the cartographic.[18]

In the 1780s, the effort to create a cartographic representation of British India to match the empire that was emerging in the territory was in full swing. James Rennell was appointed surveyor-general in Bengal by Robert Clive and created the Bengal Atlas, which served as the basis of British administration. He also published the first general map of Hindoostan in 1782, with revisions in 1788 and 1791.[19] He would go on to publish a history of his mapmaking endeavor. Rennell's *Memoir of a Map of Hindoostan or the Mogul Empire,* published in 1788, was dedicated to Joseph Banks, colonialist and president of the Royal Society and African Society, and labeled an "attempt to improve the geography of India, and the Neighboring Countries."[20]

British India is ascendant and hegemonic in Rennell's account: "The Mogul empire was now become merely nominal: and the emperors must in future be regarded as of no political consequence."[21] Rennell introduces the space of the subcontinent thusly: "Hindoostan, has by the people of modern Europe, been understood to mean the tract situated between the rivers Ganges and Indus, on the east and west; the Thibetian and Tartarian mountains, on the north; and the sea on the south."[22] This, he argues, is "a lax sense," and for the subcontinent "it may be necessary to distinguish the northern part of it, by the name of Hindustan *proper.*"[23]

To define this Hindustan, Rennell looks to the works of history: "There is no known history of Hindoostan (that rests on the foundation of Hindoo materials or records) extant, before the period of the Mahomedan conquests: for either the Hindoos kept no regular histories; or they were all destroyed, or secluded from common eyes by the Pundits."[24] Their histories, even if they had written them, would not amount to much, for they would have

> contained nothing more than that of Mahomedan conquests; that is, an account of the battles and massacres, an account of the subversion of (apparently) one of the mildest and most regular governments in the world, by the vilest and most unworthy of all conquerors: for such the Mohamedans undoubtedly were, considered either in respect to their intolerant principles; contempt of learning, and science, habitual sloth; or their imperious treatment of women: to whose lot, in civilized societies, it chiefly falls to form the minds of the rising generations of both sexes; as far as early lessons of virtue and morality may be supposed to influence them.[25]

As already argued, Rennell's portrayal of the Muslim conquerors as despotic rulers and the invocation of the plight of women were two emerging, and soon to be dominant, tropes within British depictions of subcontinental politics and society.

Yet, Rennell saw value in the Persian histories, for they still had a geography embedded in them that Rennell could cull for his scientific mapping project. In order to do so, Rennell turns to Firishta:

> It is chiefly to Persian pens that we are indebted for that portion of Indian history, which we possess. The celebrated Mahomed Ferishta, early in the 17th century, compiled a history of Hindoostan, from various materials; much of which, in the idea

of Col. Dow (who gave a translation to the world, about 20 years
ago) were collected from Persian authors.[26]

While Rennell praises Firishta and uses him extensively for resolving
place names, his cartouche confirms his prejudicial eye toward the
Muslim rulers and their knowledge systems. It depicts Brahmins bowing
and presenting an envelope labeled "Shafter" (Shastra) to Brittannia.[27]

Rennell relies specifically on Firishta for the history of the Maratha
polity with which the British East India Company was engaged in active warfare at that time. Firishta was one among several key sources
used by Rennell to make his map. The war itself was one key source of
information for the map. Rennell credits the "war with Hyder Ally and
Tipoo Sultan," which provided information through "the marches of different armies."[28] There was also the information from *Ayin Acbaree*
(*'Ain-i Akbari*) through an earlier, piecemeal rendering by Boughton
Rouse and then by Francis Gladwin. Then there were the letters from
various military attachés and travelers such as du Perron. Despite these
sources, much of middle of the subcontinent and some of the Northwest
is empty in Rennell's map—labeled "little known to Europeans," while
the parts colored in pink are denoted as "British Possessions."[29]

British colonialism, after sketching out the various countries of the
Mughals, turned swiftly to marking out the cartography of British India.
The Persian sources—from Abu'l Fazl to Firishta—that had played a
significant role from the sixteenth to the late eighteenth centuries,
vanished by the early decades of the nineteenth century. No longer were
histories of Hindustan required for their place-names or facts. Their
accounts were replaced by the data collected by the colonial geographer
(and his "native help") on the ground in the science of the "Great Trigonometric Survey."

FROM BORDERLAND TO HOMELAND

Hindustan was more than a territory—it was the very notion of land,
people, and place that created political rule. Mas'udi's description of
Hind in *Muruj al-Dhahab* from the late tenth century is one beginning

for charting out the shape and scope of Hindustan. He names "Balhara" as the king of Hind, one among the many other kings of the world, like the kings of Zanj or Tabaristan, and describes the territories under the control of Muslims in Multan and Mansura. Mas'udi begins with a description of the rivers that flow from Kashmir or Ghazni down to the Indian Ocean in Sindh.[30] To the north, Mas'udi places Kashmir as a natural frontier inaccessible to armies due to the mountains and with only one mountain pass that can be shut with a single gate. Beyond that gate, Mas'udi writes, are sixty to seventy thousand towns and cities. The kings of Qanauj and Hind are described as being at war; each with four armies for their four cardinal directions, and each army engaged in war at each frontier.

He describes a state of constant conflict in Hindustan where, paradoxically, a million villages coexist. He describes the city-state of Multan as a "Muslim frontier"—one of the largest polities.[31] Multan's richness comes from an extensive Indian Ocean trade and the tax that the Muslim governor imposed on the pilgrims who came from across Hind and Sindh to the Sun temple of Multan: his "greatest revenue came from Qumuri 'ud [agarwood], which was worth a hundred dinars for a *mun*."[32]

In Mas'udi's depiction of Multan, two geographies collide. One is the segmented, four-cornered political geography of warring armies, and the other is the moving, linked geography of people and objects. The Qumuri 'ud is agarwood (or aloeswood) from the southernmost tip of the subcontinent, Kanyakumari in Tamil Nadu, which came through the port cities of Gujarat. Multan, with its golden idol and Muslim governor, was a node on a sacral route that incorporated the smells of the Indian Ocean. Mas'udi narrates that the idol acted as both a beacon for the faithful and also protection for the Muslim governor of the city-state against warring neighbors: "whenever the polytheists march against Multan, the Muslims threaten to break the idol and the armies stop."[33] The detente is what defines the borderlands of Hindustan—a space with overlapping political regimes, networks of mobility that intersect across borderlines and the ever-present violence.

The early second millennium sources, written in the subcontinent, extend this imagination of Hindustan as a borderland space from Mas'udi. Many of the authors of texts written in the eleventh through thirteenth centuries were born and raised in the borderlands themselves. Their texts maintain this delicate balance of networks of mobility and growth with the threat and emergence of military violence.

When they write of their personal histories or the histories of the cities in the borderlands, they write with an intimacy and the fact of belonging. In their invocations, as we will soon see, the borderland spaces are simultaneously unsettled, politically volatile, yet full of potential and with deep historical resonances. The newness here is the imagined resolution of political change. The cities of Uch, Multan, and Lahore—moving up the river—become borderland cities always in anticipation of the next ruler.

Farther afield from the Indian Ocean world, at Mahmud's court in Ghazni, Hindustan has a different shape. In Firdausi's *Shahnama* of the eleventh century, Hindustan is seen as a place adjoining Iran and part of the same political and cultural world. Firdausi, describing his first gaze upon Mahmud, asks

> Is this the sky or moon? Throne or crown?
> Are these stars before us or soldiers?
> replied: "He is the king of Rum and Hind
> King from Qanauj to the river Sind."[34]

Hindustan is a constant presence in the *Shahnama*—prominently featured, certainly, in the adventures of Alexander but also in those of Behram Gur, Khusrau Pervez, and others.

Some of the other leading poets at Mahmud's court, 'Unsari and Farrukhi Sistani, also wrote praises of Mahmud, with Hindustan, the land and the mountains, prominently cited as belonging to his armies.[35] This we can assume as the first layer in the making of Hindustan—as a borderlands space that followed the Indus River to the port cities on the Indian Ocean, including Gujarat. Standing in Lahore, the poets could see the plains stretching toward Multan and the desert beyond but no more. Hindustan is part of Mahmud's polity, but it requires elaboration.

Gardizi's *Zain al-Akhbar* (ca. 1050) contains an account of the peoples and places of Hindustan. Gardizi details various spells and powers that the people of Hindustan possess, including the knowledge of mathematics, astrology, and numerology. All of this wonder is "produced within cities" found in the "territory of Qandahar toward Kashmir" and other towns in the "territory of Ganges such as Jalandhar."[36] He asserts that the city of Jalandhar (Punjab) has a king who can live to be 250 years of age due to his skills in healing. He describes that farther to the east is Kamrut (Assam), where musicians make otherworldly music; there is the birth-place of Buddha at Saravast, and the town of Ujjain, which holds many treasured books of wisdom.[37]

Fakhr-i Mudabbir Mubarakshah (ca. 1157–1236) recounted that his father was known as the teacher of the rulers of the cities of Ghazni and Lahore. Mubarakshah also wrote major works on genealogy and morals in Lahore. The two works, taken together, crystalize the twinned nature of Hindustan at the time—*Shajara-i Ansab* (Tree of descents) and *Adab al-Harb wa al Shuja'a* (The etiquette of war and bravery). In *Ansab,* which he dedicated to the Delhi ruler Iltutmish, he traced his own descent back to Caliph Abu Bakr in early Islam, thus producing another network of filiation that moved Lahore and (by extension) Hindustan closer to Arabia. In *Adab,* Hindustan is the place that gave chess to the world; whose kings are akin to the kings of Rome or Arabia. When discussing the battle formations of various armies in a comparative format, Mubarakshah highlights the similarities and distinctions between the armies of Hindustan and those in Arabia and 'Ajam.[38]

The place-making of Hindustan in Persian texts, by the early thir-teenth century, whether in the littoral regions of Sindh and Gujarat or the land-locked cities of Ghazni and Lahore, detailed a knowledge of the physical geography of the subcontinent. Beyond mere description of place names, these texts domesticated subcontinental territory within a Muslim ecosystem. They also reformulated histories of encounters as histories of belonging. The temples, and the circuits of pilgrimage as-sociated with them, constituted a form of territoriality. The political con-testations between various polities were carefully placed within a bor-derlands space, bracketed, peopled, and well understood. Hindustan was not *res nullius*—a place simply of warfare and in need of conquering. It was instead a place of political and social interdependence and growth of city-states across the peninsula.

Starting in the eighth century, a series of city-states emerged along the Indus River Basin and the western shores of the subcontinent with a Muslim mercantile and / or political presence. By the tenth century, polities linked the city-states of Ghazni and Ghur to Lahore and Multan and Uch, with the Indus and its tributaries providing the necessary link between Indian Ocean traffic and the land-locked interiors of the North-west. There was a decisive shift in the early thirteenth century with the establishment at Delhi of a new polity lead by Iltutmish. With the move from the Indus to the Ganges, the flow of Delhi's political power, sym-bolically and materially, shifted to the Deccan and to the eastern and southern subcontinent. Hindustan, in Persian histories, became a polity centered in Delhi, Bengal, and the Deccan, with its world defined by the spaces within the triangle. New cities were built, becoming nodes in a network that linked almost the entirety of the subcontinent by the early seventeenth century.

The role of Juzjani's *Tabaqat-i Nasiri* in making Hindustan a concept is critical to understand, for it is Juzjani who begins to map the intel-lectual geography of kings that came before. Juzjani sees his history as presenting generations of kings in a connected world geography. He be-gins with praise of Iltutmish, who is given the "throne and crown of the countries of Hindustan" by the grace of God.[39] Juzjani was taken in by Iltutmish when he subdued Qabacha and Uch. After taking Gwalior, on December 12, 1232, Iltutmish appointed Juzjani as "Judge, Orator, Imam, Adjudicator, and care-taker of all matters of Law."[40] Juzjani explains that after his appointment to the post of chief judge of Hindustan, he encountered a book of history that he decided to update. Juzjani wished to create a fuller portrait of kingship. His method of getting to such a world history was via his conception of linked geographies: starting from the Himyarites of Yemen to the polities in Iran, to the rulers of Ghur, Ghazni, and Hindustan.[41]

Juzjani reframes Hindustan to make it central to the concerns of the Delhi polity. His history begins with the account of the expulsion of Adam, Eve, Iblis (Satan), and the Peacock and the Snake from Heaven. Adam, literally cast down from Heaven, lands in Sarandip (Sri Lanka), Eve lands in Jeddah, the Peacock lands in Hindustan, the Snake lands in Isfahan and Iblis in islands in the ocean—this is clearly an Indian Ocean originary myth for humanity itself.[42]

Juzjani says that the wonders of numbers and even mathematics were bestowed upon Adam, and it is his progeny that filled to capacity Hijaz (the Arabian peninsula), Syria, Iraq, Hind, Sindh, and Ethiopia. This is Juzjani's constellation of world geography in which Hindustan is enmeshed. After Noah's flood, Hindustan is given to Noah's son Ham to populate. Even Sulaiman (Soloman) has a mountain near Multan that he routinely visited on his flying carpet.[43] As Juzjani continues his history, he places Hindustan under each layer of kingly authority—whether the pre-Muslim Persian heroes and kings or the Muslim polities based in Damascus and Baghdad. In his re-accounting of these various polities, the cities of Hindustan remain those of the Indian Ocean littoral—most prominently Lahore, Multan, and Uch, which rise up again and again as the forts are conquered from one polity by another.

Juzjani labels his twentieth chapter the "Account of Sultans of Hindustan who were Mu'izzi." These are the rulers who "sat on the thrones of the various countries of Hindustan . . . and with their rule the signs of Muhammad's faith were made apparent across Hindustan and may it be thus written until eternity."[44] It is at this point that Hindustan's geography expands, for Juzjani, as Mu'izzi's political power expands. The first among the sultans is Qutbuddin Mu'izz. In describing Mu'izz's conquests, Juzjani sketches the journey from the Northwest to the sea: from Meerut to Delhi to Benares to Nahraval until "he conquered other kings of Hindustan, such that he reached the eastern regions of China."[45] Juzjani describes the literal march from Delhi to the Bay of Bengal naming cities and polities that form the network of Hindustan. The rulers, portrayed as enemies, are named. Otherwise, this account from Juzjani has no other details.

As the narrative progresses toward the thirteenth century, and to his own experiences, Juzjani begins to add both geographic and ethnographic details. In his account of Muhammad Bakhtiyar Khilji, he describes Khilji's decision to conquer Tibet, after taking Laknauti, with an assembled army of ten thousand troops. A guide led Khilji to the town Mardan Kot, where he provided this history: "In ancient times, when

King Garshasp returned from China, he came toward Kamrud and laid
the foundation of this city. A large river flows through it and is called
Bunkmati. When this river enters Hindustan, they call it 'Samandar' in
the language of Hindawi [Hindustani]. It is thrice the size, width, and
spread of the Ganga [the Ganges]."[46] Juzjani turns the borderlands into
the familiar and domesticated, bringing it into history. He links a far
eastern town to a warrior king familiar to all due to his role in Firdausi's *Shahnama*, where Garshasp's is a prominent and familiar story. Yet,
he does it more strikingly by linking the river to the Ganges, giving a
sense of the scale of the river and also its Hindustani name—Samandar
(generically "the sea").

At Iltutmish's death, in 1236, Juzjani memorializes him by providing
a set of lists. He begins with a list of governors, appointed by Iltutmish,
arranged by territory. Next, he provides an extensive list of Iltutmish's
territorial domain.[47] This reckoning at Iltutmish's death gives us a finer
glimpse of the territories encompassed within Hindustan. The polity of
Iltutmish is well within the geography of Hindustan but is not comprehensive of it. Hence, Juzjani lists individually which cities, forts, and regions entered Iltutmish's domain in Hindustan. Nested within the conquests of Iltutmish, violence is an integral part of territorial claim.

Iltutmish's conquests in Malwa, as described by Juzjani, demonstrate
the ways in which the violence of warfare reshaped the city:

> In 1231, the army of Islam left for the country of Malwa and
> seized the city of Bhailsa and took the three-hundred-year-old
> temple, as tall as five hundred *guz* [roughly three hundred me-
> ters] and sent it to the capital. From there they went to Ujjain
> city and made the temple of Mahakal Deo [Mahakaleshwar
> Jyotirlinga] unusable. One thousand and two hundred years ago,
> Bikramjit [Vikramaditya II] was the king of Ujjain city. The his-
> torians of Hindwan begin writing history from his rule. Some
> idols in his name, and the iron pillar of Mahakal, were also taken
> to the Delhi capital.[48]

The violence here is specific to remaking the territory. First, there is the
invocation of both material history (the three-hundred-year-old temple)

and the originary regnal moment (the rule of Vikramaditya II) from which the writing of Hindustani history commences. The dismantling of the temple and the taking of the stones, the Ashokan pillar, and other spoils to build structures in Delhi—practically and materially remakes the topography of Malwa and Ujjain.

For Juzjani, the city is made and unmade by the political power that gives it shape. Hence, he describes the material ways of transforming from one set of sacral and political power to another set. The violence attendant to warfare does not annihilate. It reshapes, reforms the territory. It reroutes the pilgrims, as well as the elites who participate in political power. These two strands of making Hindustan—a familiarizing and domestication of the territory within Persian and Muslim cosmologies and the re-forming of sacral and political nodes through military violence—dominate the historical renderings of Muslim polities from Iltutmish onward.

Khusrau's works—both his poetry and histories—are an exemplary space for thinking through these two dimensions of making Hindustan. Khusrau is well recognized within Hindustani or Hindavi poetics and lauded for his "nativist" turns.[49] Khusrau's *Khaza'in al-Futuh* details seventeen years of Sultan ʿAlauddin Khilji's wars from Delhi to the Deccan and then to Warangal up to 1305. Khusrau finished the text in 1311. It is composed in nearly two hundred paragraph-length compositions often headlined as *nisbat* (in relation to).

Khaza'in al-Futuh is concerned primarily with the advances of the Delhi forces across the Deccan to South India. Khusrau begins with an acknowledgment that his is a treasury of conquests from Deogir to the capture of Warangal and the wiping out of Hindustani polities.[50] It is the account, he writes, of this "caliph of his age," ʿAlauddin Khilji, who is "Muhammad in name, Abu Bakr in truth, ʿUmar in justice."[51] Khusrau calls Khilji like ʿUthman in bringing into a volume the words of God, and like ʿAli in opening the gates of knowledge in the City of Islam, Delhi.

According to Khusrau, the conquests of Khilji grew like spring from Lakhnauti to Malwa, and he grew as a tree in the "grounds of Karra by the banks of Ganges, with branches that gave such a wide shadow that he reached the rank of 'Shadow of God.'"[52] The territory of northern

India and the ideas of divine Muslim kingship are intricately sewn to-gether in this opening by Khusrau. The Muslim political idea of the ca-liph as a shadow of God is manifested as a tree, with roots next to the Ganges, and the shadow spread across the territory. Khusrau imagines political rule as a tree—an organic representation of kingship—naturally planted in the territory. Khusrau re-uses the trope of rootedness of po-litical power even when speaking about Khilji's opponents—such as the Raja of Deogir, Ram Deo, who is "a tree of noble lineages in that ful-some garden of Deogir who had never faced harsh winds but he was plucked out of the ground with force and again planted such that it was a free standing tree."[53] The plucking out, and replanting, is the power of Khilji, who defeats and then reinstates Ram Deo.

Describing political power through natural metaphors was one tech-nique for visualizing Hindustan for Khusrau. Another was to represent the built material environment in anthropomorphic terms—as humans. Again, in the early sections praising Khilji, he writes about Khilji's ef-forts to renew, rebuild, and reconstruct old mosques, whose columns and walls "were kneeling or prostrating themselves [as in prayer]."[54] When Khilji planned to build a tower double the size and grandeur of the Qutb Minar, "seekers for stones were sent to all sides, some clawed the breasts of hills to shreds as one does to a lover's shirt. Others, with a determi-nation like steel, fight the ancient stones of the idol houses. Where they found a temple that had bowed at his waist in prayer, with their strong argumentative speech they took the foundations of unbelief from its heart until the temple prostrated in gratitude."[55] Khusrau's depiction of material buildings as personified believers, engaged in the act of prayer, allows an equivalence between the old mosques and the old temples, which both highlights and undercuts the difference in belief.

As in Juzjani, violence is a living presence in Khusrau. As in Juzjani, warfare plays a specific role in making legible the process of transfor-mation from one polity to the next. Khusrau relies heavily on metaphors and similes to portray the effects of political violence, such as in the opening accounts of Khilji's defeats of the "Mughal polytheists" (Mon-gols), where the battleground, covered with cut up bodies of the Mughals, resembles a chessboard.[56] Khusrau, however, cautions about reading vio-lence literally through the similes he uses, and clarifies: "Blood is not clean and cannot make clean; it is the sword that makes clean, after a victory, their blood [the polytheists] as well—but what is meant [here] is not blood [itself]."[57] That is, Khusrau is cautioning against reading him literally.

Khusrau regularly shapes the geography of Hindustan via parallels to Arabia and West Asia. The temple of Somnath was "made to bow" to Ka'bah in Mecca.[58] When Khilji fords the mighty Narmada River, Khusrau describes the army as being so skilled that they could have easily "forded across the Nile of Egypt and Tigris of Baghdad."[59]

Khilji, after taking Gujarat, turns toward Malwa, where Khusrau says the landholding elites came to subject themselves to his governance until "there was no insolent polytheist left in the cities of Hind."[60] Khilji takes "the country of Malwa, whose expanse could not be measured by the mathematicians with sight" and appointed to it a governor who would then bring about the conquest of the fort of Mandu.[61] Governance and conquest, shadow and light, are continuously at play in Khusrau's detailing of the lands of Hindustan.

Khusrau ends his account with an apology for writing such a short narrative of only some selected clashes of Khilji: "May this history wander every city, night and day, until the Day of Judgment. The reason for its brevity and reliance on just a few clashes is that the imperial commands are being issued throughout the lands; to spread the Truth that victory will soon bring terror-inducing command from mountain to mountain [east to west]."[62] That is, in essence, this specific account of a Delhi army's wars across the Deccan to Warangal is only part of a larger world of Hindustan. For Khusrau, in *Khaza'in al-Futuh,* Khilji's polity in Hindustan was still a meager portion of the actual territory of the subcontinent.

During the early fourteenth century, the precise place of the Muslim political, social, and cultural role in Hindustan was an actively formative project. In 1318, Khusrau produced *Nuh Sipihr* (Nine skies), as a metered poem with rhyming couplets. Much of the account concerns the wars of Qutbuddin Mubarak Shah Khilji (r. 1316–1320), to whom the poem is dedicated. The overarching theme is Qutbuddin Shah's battles to Deogir, but it intersects with other events, such as the construction of the palace and public mosque in Delhi, and descriptions of hunting, advice to the nobility, and so on. The third "sky" is dedicated to Hindustan, its prominence, a heaven on Earth, a place with the finest fruits and flowers, with the highest forms of logic, philosophy, and language, and, most significantly, a home for Muslims. With *Nuh Sipihr,* Hindustan goes from being a borderland to a homeland. How Khusrau portrays this process helps us position the ways in which Hindustan operates in the fourteenth and later centuries. The most interesting aspect of Khusrau's proclamations on Hindustan is that he builds it as a "logical" argument against those who question him about the centrality of the conceptual territory of Hindustan

To Khusrau, Hindustan is Heaven. In the section entitled "Sound Logical Reasons for Why the Country of Hind Is Heaven," Khusrau begins by proclaiming that Saturn is the ruling planet of Hindustan and the source of all his information.[63] The reason Khusrau speaks for Hindustan is because he is himself of this land, born and raised—"[it is] my parent, my nourisher, my nation."[64] He is also tired of being told by those in "Rum or Khurasan or Khatan" that his land is of no consequence because here there is no prominent poetry.[65] Khusrau presents *Nuh Sipihr* as poetry whose excellence will demonstrate that Hindustan is a land worthy of being called Heaven. Khusrau is clear that, as a born and bred Hindustani, he can call on particularly Hindustani reason to shape his argument because, "wisdom, logic, philosophy, artistry / All these have their own shape in Hind."[66] Hindustan is not only a place, it is also a unique place.

Khusrau provides seven arguments, based on logic and reason, in support of his assertion that Hindustan is Heaven itself. The first argument is that Hindustan's climate matches Heaven's climate, which is why when Adam was expelled from Heaven and he landed in Hindustan, he was able to easily acclimate himself, for it suited him perfectly. If God had put him down in Khurasan, Arabia, or China, Adam would have left within a few hours, for he would not have tolerated the heat or the cold. Hence Hindustan has the perfect, moderate climate, like in Heaven.[67]

The second argument is that God also expelled the Peacock from Heaven and the Peacock exists only in Hindustan—for it can smell the winds of Heaven there.[68] Third is that while the Snake was also expelled from Heaven, and does exist in multiple places in the world, Hindustan is the only place where it does not bite unless provoked—for it feels most at home. Fourth is that Adam, before traveling to meet Eve (in Jeddah) where he expelled his bowels—full of Heavenly food—he remained fasting until he had found new edible food that matched the heavenly cuisine. This was only in Hindustan.[69] Fifth is that the Prophet Muhammad proclaimed that the winds from Hindustan are akin to that of Heaven, and this also explains why fruits and flowers are in bloom all year long.[70] Sixth is that the polytheists are supposed to get their Heaven on this Earth (as opposed to Muslims who will only get to Heaven after dying), and the polytheists live and flourish in Hindustan.[71] Seventh is that the righteous caliph now lives and breathes in Hindustan, which is thus the natural seat of Muslim power in the world.[72]

Compared to the project of Juzjani, Khusrau's reframing of the subcontinent within Muslim cosmology is both more precise and far more expansive. It is, specifically, an argument from a Hindustani who takes for granted that he was born and nurtured as a Muslim in Hindustan. Khusrau's representation of Hindustan as Heaven allows him to demonstrate how he perceives of himself—a Muslim in his homeland of Hindustan, which is the only place on Earth worth living.

Khusrau's next concern, and one that connects back to the question of poetics, is that of the languages of Hindustan. In the section entitled "The Reasons for the Supremacy of the Languages of Hind, in Their pleasant Vocabulary, over Persian or Turkish," Khusrau lays out the relationship between language and territory while making a case for the superiority of Hindustani languages over all others.[73] Khusrau argues there are three languages that are worthy of universal acclaim—Arabic, Persian, and Sanskrit.[74] The first is Arabic—a universal language, for it is the one in which Qur'an is written. Arabic and Sanskrit are universal as well as languages in which Heavenly speech can be recorded. Persian is universal because it is spoken around the world and by the most diverse communities.[75] There are other languages, but they are not universal, for they are restricted to their sites of origin. When languages move, Khusrau writes, they do so only when they have the support of kings and merchants.[76] Khusrau believes that one should privilege the language they are born with—and as Khusrau was born in Hindustan, it is imperative that he speak in his own language over Persian or Turkish.[77]

In the countries of Hindustan, Khusrau notes, there are regional languages, but there is one language that cuts across all regions:

> Sindhi and Lahori and Kashmiri and Kubr
> Dhur Samandari and Tilingi and Gujjari
> Ma'abri and Ghuri and Bengal and Awadhi
> are spoken in Delhi and in frontiers around
> These are all languages of Hind from times ancient
> For all commoners alike they are useful
> Yet, one other language
> is crucial to know for all Brahmins
> Since old ages, it is called Sanskrit
> Though the common folks are not attuned to its rules
> The Brahmin knows but all Brahmins
> do not understand the depths of this speech
> It is like Arabic in its complexity
> its grammar, vocabulary, appreciation and poetics.[78]

There is a particular order in which Khusrau presents the geography of language in Hindustan. Sindhi, Lahori, and Kashmiri are in the Northwest. Then along the western coastlines—Gujjari in Gujarat, Tilingi (Telugu) in the Deccan, and Dhur Samandari (Kannada) in Karnataka (present-day Halebidu), Tamil in Ma'abri, and then along the Ganges to the eastern coast, where Awadhi, Gauri, and Bengali live. These regional languages are local and popular vernaculars. They are spoken by the commoners as opposed to the universal language, Sanskrit, known only to a select few Brahmins.

Khusrau endorses the validity and importance of Sanskrit—comparing it to both Arabic and later Persian—and deems it the only language in which one could write a proper praise and salutation of one's own ruler.[79] The languages of Hindustan provide a distinct geography for the subcontinent, and the fact that these various languages are spoken and understood within Delhi and its environs also gives a centrality to the political power in the subcontinent.

Khusrau's demonstration of Hindustan as a homeland moves along with the next section, concerning the birds and animals of Hindustan, which have superior, if not humanlike, intelligence—such as the fabled parrot, the mynah, the peacock, among many others that "if I account the qualities of every bird / in ten and two registers I could not finish writing."[80] Khusrau narrates the qualities of these birds, the monkey, the horse, the deer, the elephant, and other animals. All of these animals demonstrate the natural wonders of Hindustan. They are proof of the ways in which a unique environment, given by God, has permeated life on the subcontinent—the literal Heaven on earth. Like his previous sections, this section also ends with praise for the current ruler, Qutb Shah, and how these birds and animals, especially the elephant, make Qutb Shah the true king of the world. Thus, Khusrau's Hindustan is peopled with remarkably rich languages, multiple polities, animals, flora and fauna of wonder. It is a place that can clearly be called Heaven, and one that Khusrau can wholly claim to be the site of his belonging.

Khusrau's contemporary, Barani, takes a different tack in creating the place of Hindustan in his *Tarikh-i Firuz Shahi*. Barani, writing in 1357, recounts a history that begins roughly where Juzjani stopped (1260s) and extends to the first few years of the reign of Firuz Shah Tughluq (r. 1309–1388). Barani depicts Ghiyathuddin Balban (r. 1266–1287) as proclaiming Hindustan, not as a place for conquest but for long-term governance. Ghiyathuddin is asked by his nobility why he is not leading expeditions to "Malwa or Ujjain or Gujarat" like his predecessors Qutbuddin 'Aibak or Iltutmish. Ghiyathuddin replies that he is cognizant of the threat the Mongols pose on his eastern borders: "Hulagu, the son of Chinghiz with plentiful armies has captured Iraq and is established in Baghdad. These cursed people have heard much about the wealth and prosperity of Hindustan and in their hearts is the hope to plunder and destroy Hindustan. Lahore, that is the frontier of our polity, is attacked and plundered almost yearly. . . . If they hear that I am far away [from Delhi] with my army, busy in other countries, they would come destroy Delhi and all."[81] Barani situates Ghiyathuddin's reticence to engage in warfare in Hindustan as a result of threats outside of Hindustan that could encroach upon his own polity. Ghiyathuddin would rather attend to his current domains and "hold them securely with governors who are kingly and with wise and competent advisers."[82] For Ghiyathuddin, the threats at Hindustan's frontier are due to "the renown of Hindustan from the elephant and the horse. One elephant is equivalent to five hundred cavalry," which is also what sustains his own polity: "I granted the region of Sindh to my oldest son and from there arrive Baharji and Tatari horses to the Capital. . . . I have given Lakhnauti and Bangala to my younger son and he has full control over it for years. Elephants for my stable come from there."[83] Ghiyathuddin is convinced that it is "more important to secure and keep firm the polity then to add the polity of others and which one cannot hold firm."[84]

Barani, in providing this history, is presenting a landscape of Hindustan under a wise king, who is attuned to both the dangers of overextending one's own polity as well as the threats posed from outside of Hindustan. Much of his history concerns the rule of Muhammad bin Tughluq, from 1325 to 1351, during which Barani was employed as a historian. Barani sees Hindustan as a body politic that needs a healthy and just ruler. The motif of the illness in the body politic is as significant for Barani as Khusrau's emphasis on naturalized language to think about political formations. A healthy and just king comes to Hindustan with the ascension of Firuz Shah to the throne in 1351.

With Firuz Shah, "worry fled the populace and peace and tranquility took hold," Barani writes.[85] Barani introduces Firuz Shah as the "unanimous choice of the royalty, the dignitaries, and the eminent of the polities of Hind and Sindh."[86] Firuz Shah was "beseeched" to take the throne by "the scholars, the learned, the governors, the commanders, the elite, the commoners, the troops, the merchants, the children, the adults, the elderly, the Muslim, the Hindus, the horse-riders, the infantry, the bonded men and women."[87] This public acclaim for Firuz Shah underscores Barani's belief that a just polity is formed via the consent of everyday people in Hindustan.

The territory of Firuz Shah's domain in Hindustan is inscribed by Barani in the next section, in which Firuz Shah's prominent buildings, forts, and cities are mentioned. The key for the prosperity of a polity, for Barani, is the prosperity of all the people in Hindustan. Public good lies in the urbanization efforts of Firuz Shah, as he writes in one of the last sections of the history, titled "Section Six: Account of Canal Excavations

for Public Good in Deserts and Uncultivated Lands Where People Would
Die from Thirst and Animals and Birds Would Also Perish from Thirst":

> Only God knows, in the passage of time, how many thousand
> villages will come up on the banks of these canals and how
> many kinds of harvests and delicacies will be grown. . . . Since
> the time that Hindustan has been populated, due to the lack of
> water, people have to continuously move themselves and their
> domesticated animals from place to place, looking for water. . . .
> Now, after this development under the benevolence of Firuz
> Shah, they can establish their own villages and build houses and
> their children and women will live under secure roofs.[88]

Barani provides a glimpse here of how Hindustan, a place inhabited long
before Muslim polities emerged, was now the home for all faiths and
peoples, including Muslims. For him, these settled villages, with their
proper houses, will yield to judiciously appointed mayors and governors,
and soon they will be cultivating wheat grain and sugar, and Delhi's
markets will call for their yields, and the region will prosper—all under
the justice-giving kingship of Firuz Shah in Hindustan.

The idea of a populated and prosperous Hindustan took firm root
during the fourteenth century. The histories that emerge after Barani attest to this. Shams Siraj 'Afif's *Tarikh-i Firuz Shahi,* which was completed in 1399, finishes the narrative account that Barani had begun and,
in it, the countries of Hindustan make explicit appearance as the king
moves toward the borders of Bengal or Sindh or Telangana.[89] The contours of political rule and the idea of a settled and prosperous Hindustan are intertwined.

A HOME IN THE WORLD

Hindustan had been a home for Muslims for centuries, and the historians of Muslim polities reflected that understanding in their works. Zahiruddin Babur, in 1526, was explicitly aware of the borders that separated him from Hindustan. He was well aware of the history of Muslim

polities in Hindustan as well as the historians who had written these histories. After defeating Ibrahim Lodhi, Babur pronounces himself *badshah-i Hindustan*.[90] Then he writes a synopsis of the political history of Muslim polities in Hindustan in which he directly references Juzjani's *Tabaqat*:

> From the time of the Prophet to this day, only three kings from this side [Central Asia] have ruled over Hindustan. Sultan Mahmud and his progeny, who ruled various countries in Hindustan for a long time. Second Sultan Shihabuddin Ghuri and his slaves and followers for many years ruled here. Third is my rule. My rule is unlike those rules. Though Sultan Mahmud conquered Hindustan, he remained on the throne of Khurasan. . . .
>
> There was not a single *badshah* in Hindustan, only rajas who ruled their own countries. Next, while Sultan Shihabuddin Ghuri did not control Khurasan, his brother Ghiyathuddin Ghuri possessed it. In the *Tabaqat-i Nasiri* it is recorded that once he led an army of 120,000 armored troops into Hindustan and his opponents were rajas and rayas [rulers]. The entirety of Hindustan did not belong to any one person.[91]

Babur believed that the control of Khurasan meant that kings like Mahmud or Shihabuddin were not rulers *in* Hindustan. Babur saw himself as the first ruler in Hindustan who had arrived from Central Asia. Babur was acquainted with the histories of Hindustan and acknowledges the many centuries of Muslim political rule.

Since he is new to the territory, he sees it with new eyes: "The countries of Hindustan are vast, abundant and full of people. To the east and south, and to the west also, it is surrounded by ocean. The edge of the North is a mountain range that connects the mountains of Hindukush and Kafiristan and the mountains of Kashmir. To the northwest are Kabul, Ghazni, and Kandahar. The capital of all Hindustan is Delhi."[92] Clearly the Hindustan that Babur is describing here is the entire subcontinent. Babur then describes the history of Muslim rule over the five central regions of Delhi—Jaunpur, Gujarat, the Deccan, Malwa, and Bengal.

Next, he turns toward the "other realms and areas of Hindustan where [there are] many raja and ray, some are obedient and others are strong and do not obey the Muslim kings."[93] He lists the raja of Vijayanagar, who possesses a great polity and army, with another great king, Rana Sanga of Chittor. He demarcates the Indus as crossing into Hindustan, after which Hindustan has its unique geography, cities, birds, animals, fruits, and peoples. This Hindustan has large settled populations in Lahore, Sirhind, Sambhal, Multan, Thatta, and Agra, which he finds "unpleasant," for they lack planned canals and gardens.

By 1600, Abu'l Fazl, as a historian of the reign of Babur's grandson Jalaluddin Akbar, can speak with great love about "Hind from which he [Abu'l Fazl] had descended."[94] For Abu'l Fazl, Delhi is the implicit center of Hindustan, just as Hindustan is the explicit domain of the Mughals. Abu'l Fazl quotes Humayun at Delhi:

> The emperor enjoyed himself in the capital Delhi and occupied himself with ordering administrative affairs. He turned his attention to improvement of the realm, reducing enemies to naught and subduing other realms. Repeatedly he said, "We shall make several capitals and endeavor to bring order to Hindustan. We shall see to it that Delhi, Agra, Jaunpur, Mandu, Lahore, Kannauj, some other places that are appropriate, and every place with a contingent under the command of a farsighted, subject-nurturing, just and intelligent person will not be in need of reinforcement by other troops, and we will not keep more than twelve thousand horse-men in the imperial train."[95]

Already, Humayun is envisioning a network of capitals that stretch only Mughal administrative power—pointedly not military power—across Hindustan. In Abu'l Fazl's *A'in-i Akbari*—part of his *Akbarnama*—a section is devoted to "Conditions of Hindustan" and is in marked contrast to the account of Babur: "It was for long an unfulfilled desire of my wanting heart to tell the geography of this land and present the knowledge gathered from Hindustan-born intellectuals and historians."[96] Abu'l Fazl mentions an unnamed book that becomes one of his sources, and though he clarifies that he does not understand Sanskrit, he had important works translated at great expense and effort.

Abu'l Fazl describes Hindustan as being surrounded by the ocean on the east, west, and south and includes "Sarandip (Sri Lanka), Aceh, Malaca and many hundreds of islands."[97] It is a vast plain that is "unparalleled" for the temperate nature of its climate and its inhabitants.[98] It is populous, and one cannot travel any distance without encountering "villages and towns filled with people, manicured greenery and heart-capturing gardens."[99]

Like Khusrau, Abu'l Fazl links languages to various parts of Hindustan: "There are numerous languages spoken in Hindustan. Those that are related to each other are countless. Those which are distinct are in the following regions: Delhi, Bengal, Multan, Marwar, Telangana, Maratha, Karnataka, between Sindh, Kabul and Kandahar, Baluchistan and Kashmir."[100] Abu'l Fazl's list shifts Delhi to the center of the map, then moves east, and circles back to the Northwest in a clockwise fashion, whereas Khusrau's geography of languages had moved from the Northwest in a counterclockwise fashion.

Abu'l Fazl introduces the conceptual world of Hindustan by first expanding on the Brahmanical cosmology—their account of the stars, planetary movements, distribution of time. After the astronomical details, he describes the spatial understanding of the known universe—citing the unnamed text in Sanskrit. This world is placed among seven islands and seven oceans, and Hindustan is placed on Jambudvip.[101] Abu'l Fazl uses Jambudvip to link Brahmanical cosmology to Greek cosmology and discusses the Greek sciences, further linking to Ptolemy and the theory of seven climes. What follows is an extended table of the known cities, regions, and islands of the world listed according to the climes—Hindustan's nearly 150 sites being in the second and third climes.[102] For Abu'l Fazl, Hindustan is also a place of a singular polity.

This long history of writing and being in Hindustan had a massive impact on Firishta's text. As stated earlier, the most visible marker of change from previous and contemporaneous histories was that Firishta radically altered the subject of history writing. His is the first history of Hindustan itself. The various parts of Hindustan divide the text into dis-

tinct chapters. They are arranged in a unique order, are given a teleology, clusters of kings and key personalities, and then events. In this
way, Firishta advances the conceptual space of Hindustan that began
with Juzjani and Khusrau. Where Abu'l Fazl, as Firishta's contemporary,
privileges the life of the monarchs over the place of Hindustan, Firishta
is keen to do otherwise.

Firishta provides, in the introduction to his history, the origins and
significance of the making of place in Hindustan. Firishta had begun
his history with a contrapuntal framing of human origin stories from
the Qur'an to the *Mahabharata*. Firishta resolved the problem of temporal cohesion by linking Hindu origins with Muslim origins and cal-
culating that, from Adam to his present, only seven thousand years had
passed. This restitching of time was done by first positing an agreement
between believers and nonbelievers—"The Hindus believe that the world
began with a clay-made Adam"—and then stressing that, in the Hindu
cosmology, many thousands of Adams would have come and gone over
the period of 800,000 years.[103] However, it is the flood, during the life of
Noah, that syncs up Hindu time and Muslim time—"After the flood,
Noah sent his three sons, Sam, Japheth, and Ham, to populate the four
corners of the world."[104]

Firishta provides an expansive list of patrilineal descent, sons from
Noah who spread out across the world to seed populations and estab-
lish cities, like the descendants of Sam, the eldest, who became the
nations of Arabia, Iraq, Syria, and Iran. Hindustan was populated by
Ham and his descendants, Hind, Sindh, Habash, Afranj, Hormuz, and
Buia—who all laid the foundation of cities after their own names. From
Hind came four sons who established the regions of Purab, Bang
(Bengal), Dakan (Deccan), and Nahrwal. Dakan had the sons Marhat,
Kanhar, Talang; Sindh had sons Thatta and Multan; Nahrwal had sons
Bahraich, Kunbaj, and Malraj, and so on.[105]

Originating from Noah were not only populations, regions, and cities
but political and social entities. Purab's sons would be administrators
and from them came the first king of Hindustan. Kishan, Firishta warns,
is not Krishna the avatar of Vishnu, but a raja who was elected by the
people of Hindustan to govern for his wisdom and bravery. Kishan had
a brilliant minister named Brahmin, son of Bang, who was the son of

Hind, whose inventions included metallurgy and writing.[106] Thus, Firishta inserts a direct lineage of Brahmin administrative elite into the standard mythic origins.

The Deccan is the place from which Firishta organizes the defense of Hindustan against the Persian kings—most notably Rustum. Firishta's narrative of kings who are descendants of Maharaj—Malchand, Kishavraj, Munir Rai, and Suraj Rai—links them all to the illustrious kings of Persia from the *Shahnama,* which would be known by heart to any reader of his text. His narrative expertly intertwines the *Mahabharata* and *Shahnama* cosmologies. Firishta describes that it is from this particular admixture that Hindus began worshipping idols, as sun worship came from Iran during the rule of Suraj Rai. Sun worship caught on, and then a Brahmin invented the notion of creating gold and silver representations of ancestors as a way of worshipping them.[107]

This history of inventions—regions, cities, idol worship, mathematics, music, taming of elephants—theorized within Firishta's frame is thus a history for both Muslims and Hindus in Hindustan. The cities were founded by sons of Hind, and their sons created the tools of governance, of social and cultural cohesion. The sons ruled for hundreds of years (though their ages dwindled in duration with each successive generation) and created the territory of Hindustan. They did so explicitly by creating agreements and warring with Persian kings—including Alexander—and their actions within and toward the borderlands gave the territory of Hindustan a distinct history. Firishta's priorities remained to keep the history focused on the Deccan. After a string of sons and founders of cities in the Northeast, he writes that one should not forget that "Deccan too has seen glorious kings such as Gulchand, who founded Gulbarga and Muchand, who founded Miraj and Bijaychand, who founded Vijayanagar and made it the capital of the Deccan."[108]

Firishta's history of Hindustan continues in an unbroken chain as sons proliferate and kings create new constellations of power. After Suraj came Behraj, then Kidar, than Shankal, then Kecchwa, then Jay Chand, then Raja Dehlu, then Raja Fur (who was the grandest king Hindustan had ever seen), then Sisarchand, then Juna, then Karyanchand, then Bikramjit, during whose reign calendars were invented. Firishta dates Bikramjit to 1668 years before his present and links his time to that of

Ardeshir I and Shahpur I, the Sassanid monarchs. Before the dawn of Islam in Arabia, Maldeo was the last ruler of Hindustan who could unite its various regions under his rule. After his death, there were no more kings of consequence, as Firishta puts it. This is what the Muslims find as they establish polities in Sindh, or even later when Mahmud comes from Ghazni. A series of small polities ruled by individual rulers made up the whole of Hindustan.

Firishta's history is the first history of Hindustan as a concept, an idea, and a place that contains multitudes of faiths and polities. Firishta is providing a unified history of Hindustan, stretching back through Noah and Adam to the Indra. His emphasis is also on the Deccan as the center of Hindustan.[109] The rulers of the Deccan are the inheritors of the whole history of Hindustan, even as they remain politically and formally a smaller power compared to the Mughals.

The histories of particular regions given by Firishta reflect the same emphasis. Firishta's second section is the history of the sultans of Delhi. Throughout the section, Firishta cites histories such as *Tarikh-i Alfi, Tabaqat-i Nasiri, Jawami' ul-Hikayat, Rauzat-al Safa,* and Nizamuddin's *Tabaqat* to narrate a political history of the sultans and rajas of Delhi: "It would be proper to account the history of the rulers of Delhi and the foundation of this city."[110] Firishta reminds his readers that he had explained in his preface the ways in which time is divided by the wise intellects of Hindustan. He cites, again, the Persian translation of the *Mahabharata* to reconcile the existence of prophets in each distinct age and the ways in which it dovetails with the timeline from the Qur'an.

This time around, Firishta's recounting of the *Mahabharata* story serves a different purpose. Here, he is interested in highlighting the presence of the Deccan in the story of Delhi—such as when the Pandavas came to the Deccan in exile or when Bikramjit became the ruler of the Deccan and united all of Hindustan under one polity. Eventually, the Rajput inherit the polity of Bikramjit and control many countries. The city of Delhi, Firishta narrates, was founded by Vadputa Rajput in the early tenth century in the environs of Indraprastha, and it was named Delhi because the soil was so soft that an iron stake could not remain upright.[111]

The political history of Delhi presented by Firishta tells stories embedded in the landscape of Hindustan. Firishta focuses on stories, legends, origin myths, and marvels that make Delhi's past come alive, such as the episode where Iltutmish decides to build a water reservoir, Haus-i Shamsi in Delhi. Iltutmish is unsure where to build the reservoir until one day, in passing, he sees a likely place and thinks that it might be suitable. However, "that very night, the Prophet, seated on a horse, appeared to him in a dream. He inquired from Iltutmish: what do you desire? Iltutmish replied 'Oh Prophet of God, I wish to build a water reservoir.' The Prophet replied, 'Build it here,' and his horse struck the earth with the hoof and water sprouted from the ground."[112] When Iltutmish visited the site upon waking up, indicated in his dream by the Prophet, he found it drenched with water.

Firishta includes this story to demonstrate Iltutmish's religiosity and, in this event, the Prophet's own guidance to the Hindustani ruler. Yet it also goes alongside the many instances where Firishta is eager to document Muslim rulers as builders of new structures for the public good and welfare. At the end of his account of Firuz Shah Tughluq (d. 1388), Firishta lists all of the structures he built for public welfare: "fifty dams, forty mosques, thirty colleges, twenty monasteries for Sufis, a hundred palaces, five hospitals, a hundred graveyards, ten bathhouses, a hundred and fifty wells, and a hundred bridges and countless public gardens."[113]

Firishta's overarching vision remains focused on the bigger Hindustan, even as he narrates the comings and goings of kings in Delhi. He reminds the reader that Delhi was the place from

> where once Bikramjit had ruled all of Hindustan, these sultans of Lahore and Delhi could only be master of smaller dominions. . . . By the year eight hundred and fifty [1447], Sultan 'Alauddin had left for Badaun and enjoyed its environment and did not wish to return to Delhi. . . . In those days, all of Hindustan was captured by warring kings. In Deccan, Gujarat and Malwa and Jaunpur and Bengal were all different kings; Punjab and Diplapur, and Sirhind to Panipat, Bahlul ruled with his coteries; from Mehruli to Sarai Laddu that is in the suburbs of

Delhi, was Ahmad Khan Miwati; from Sunbhal to Khwaja Khizr Passway behind Delhi was ruled by Dirya Khan Lodi; Eisa Khan the Turk was in Kaul; in Rabery was Qutb Khan Afghan; Rai Partap was in Patiala and Bhungaon district; in Bayana Daud Khan was proclaiming his independence. 'Alauddin could only claim the capital of Delhi and some surrounding districts.[114]

The many polities of Hindustan face a change when Babur's armies take Delhi in 1526. Firishta quotes extensively from the *Baburnama,* underlining Babur's exceptional claim for leadership over all of Hindustan. However, factional rule was still very much the case. Firishta points out: "Since the people of Hindustan were frightened of the Mughal rule and politics, every one began to cement their own polity wherever they were and vowed to resist Firdaus Makani [Babur]."[115] It is notable that even as Firishta recognizes the supremacy of Mughal rule, he makes room in his narrative to highlight those particular actions of the preceding era, when the wider public good was apparent.

Firishta reports that after Babur's death, Humayun was caught in an internecine conflict with his brothers, and one of the Afghan warlords of Hindustan, Sher Shah Suri, claimed Delhi. Firishta memorializes his rule through the works of social welfare and good governance:

> Sher Shah spent fifteen years as a commander and governor and five years as a ruler over Hindustan. He was an extremely intelligent, wise, and patient ruler who left many traces of his good governance. Such as a road that extended from Bengal and Sunargaon to the river Indus, and which was one thousand and five hundred *kos* [around 2,900 miles] and at each *kos* was a rest house [in Hindustani *dak-choki,* "news post"], a public watering well, and a mosque. The imam and caretaker of the mosque were given stipends from the chancery. The rest house had two doors to distribute wine and food, one for Muslims and one for non-Muslims. Every rest house also had two fresh horses so that news from Bengal could reach Delhi every day. At both sides of the road he planted trees such as *jambolan* and mango so people could eat the fruits and rest in their shade. . . . During his reign,

there was such peace that travelers could rest in ease with their belongings in any wilderness or jungle.[116]

The sons of Sher Shah Suri were unwilling to keep the same priorities of the public welfare and public good, thus becoming unjust rulers, which gave Humayun, son of Babur, the opportunity to reclaim Hindustan. Firishta consistently insists on highlighting the ways in which justice and welfare of the common subject was visible across all polities in Hindustan.

Finally, Firishta turns to the Deccan. The narrative arc of Firishta's entire history has been leading up to this region and its stories. In the Deccan landscape, Firishta narrates the geography of cities through their founders. Thus, the third section of Firishta is titled "The Account of Sultans of the Deccan," and Firishta divides the history of the Deccan into six "gardens," which are, in fact, cities: the first is the Bahmani polity and the founding of Gulbarga and Ahmadabad Bidar, then the 'Adil Shahi polity and the founding of Bijapur, then the Nizamshahi polity and the founding of Ahmadnagar, then the Qutbshahi and the founding of Hyderabad, then the fifth on the polity at Berar, and finally the sixth about the rulers at Bidar.

Firishta describes the establishment of Muslim polities in the Deccan through the account of 'Alauddin Hasan Gangoi (known as 'Alauddin Bahman Shah), who declares his independence from Delhi in 1347 at Gulbarga. He sets up the governance of the new polity with close ties to the local Brahmin elite. Firishta writes: "It is well known that before ['Alauddin Hasan Gangoi] the Brahmins did not hold any rank or employment with the Muslim sultans, instead busying themselves with the craft of astrology, geometry, and mathematics . . . and the first from the group of Brahmins to enter employment in a Muslim polity was Kango Pandit and from then to the present of year one thousand seventeen [1617], unlike all other countries of Hindustan, the offices of epistolary in the Deccan are under the Brahmins."[117] Firishta also provides an origin for the polity created in the Deccan by 'Alauddin Hasan Gangoi. Even in this originary myth, a Brahmin astrologer, Gangu, who had employed 'Alauddin, was the one who prophesized that he would one day become a ruler. Firishta quotes the authority of "historians" that 'Alauddin's

Brahmin employer used the stars to predict that 'Alauddin would one day reach great heights. It is perhaps on this basis that Firishta calls 'Alauddin Hasan by the name Gangoi. Alongside the prophecy of the Brahmin astrologer, verified by historians, Firishta also includes a prophecy from the great Chishti Sufi Nizamuddin Auliya. Nizamuddin gave 'Alauddin a four-cornered piece of bread and said, "this is the parasol of kingship, which with great effort and in a long while, will unfurl on you in the Deccan."[118]

With these two prophecies happening in the early life of 'Alauddin, Firishta assesses the various auguries that shaped his rise to the Bahmani polity in the Deccan, and his conquests in Telangana, Karnataka, and Gujarat. Firishta is keen to point out that he is no mere panegyrist and quotes a number of popular histories, including an anonymously authored tract he personally found in the royal library during his employment in Ahmadnagar, which made the case that 'Alauddin was the descendant of the Persian kings Kayan and Behram Gur. Firishta rejects all such formulations as the works of flattery by poets, hagiographers, and sycophants.[119]

The Deccan is thus a polity created by a lowly servant of a Brahmin, divined by both Brahmanical astrology and Sufi prophecy, and one that ought not to be understood in exogenous kingship lineages. It is thus that the exceptional nature of Deccan is set up by Firishta, from his history of the very first Muslim polity.

The role of prophecy in the making of the kings of the Deccan continues in Firishta's history. When Ahmad Shah I becomes ruler on September 22, 1422, he also acquires the throne after a prophecy by the Sufi shaykh Gisu Daraz.[120] Ahmad Shah I is the ruler who lays the foundation for the new city of Bidar at a site that he declares to be the "actual center of the polity of Deccan and for its water and air the finest place in Hindustan."[121] Firishta inserts his own concurrent opinion: "The writer of these pages, I have seen all the major cities of Hindustan, and in artistry and pleasure nothing matches the landscape here. The earth is vermillion and even in the monsoon there is never any mud."[122]

While Firishta is keen to highlight the intercession of divine powers in the making of kings, in the winning of battles, and in the foundation of cities, that divine will is imbricated with the personality, the character, and the vision of the kings themselves. Bidar's foundation is driven by Ahmad Shah I and his realization that it is the place to create a new capital—the textual and contextual confirmation of his decision comes only after that fact. It is also this focus on individual actions that gives Firishta's history the liberty to chart the rise and fall of dynasties without ascribing a set pattern to them.

After Bidar, Firishta moves to the history of Bijapur's 'Adil Shahi rulers. It is the story of Yusuf 'Adil Shah that Firishta invokes to begin the history of the polity of 'Adil Shahi. The story Firishta provides bears a striking resemblance to the story of Yusuf from the Qur'an. This Yusuf is brother of the Ottoman sultan Murad II (d. 1451). The sultan is advised to kill his siblings in order to reduce any claims on the throne. However, Yusuf is the favorite son of their mother, and she is able to secret him away to Iraq. Eventually, he ends up in Shiraz, and there the prophet Khizr comes to him in a dream and tells him to let go of his desire to return to his home and to see his friends and family again. Instead he should head to Hindustan, where both worldly and otherworldly glory will be his.[123]

This directive by Khizr—the immortal prophet, long held to be a caretaker of the traveling and the forgotten—is enough to propel Yusuf to Hindustan. He arrives to the port city of Mustafabad (Dabil) in 1461, and there meets an old man who offers him a glass of sweet cold drink. As soon as Yusuf drinks from the glass, the old man vanishes. This confirms to Yusuf that the old man was Khizr himself. Now doubly certain that his fortune is in the Deccan, Yusuf, then only seventeen years old, heads to Bidar. The rest of the account is resplendent with Yusuf's skills and the ways and means through which he becomes the independent ruler of Bijapur. Firishta details the myriad twists and turns in the fortune of Yusuf's descendants and the ways in which they deal with the Vijayanagar polity, the Portuguese, the Dutch, and the Mughals.

It is to fulfill his allegiance to Khizr, Firishta writes, that Yusuf declares to an assembled crowd in 1502 that he wishes to propagate the Shi'i faith in his polity. Firishta notes that this was a political gesture that would link Yusuf's polity to the Safavid in Iran. Firishta records that Yusuf was the first to make the Twelver faith official in Hindustan and that he did so with such cleverness that "everyone prayed in their own

mosques and all worshipped in their own way [without conflict] such
that the notables of faith and scholars of religion bit their fingers in
amazement at this miracle of toleration."[124]

Ibrahim 'Adil Shah restored the Sunni faith, expelled Safavid advisers,
and made Dakhani the language of official correspondences instead of
Persian.[125] He also hired contingents of troops and commanders of East
African descent. His son, 'Ali Adil Shah, reversed the proclamation of
state faith back to Shi'i and offered his political allegiance to the Vijayanagar polity. As Firishta narrates this history, he cites more and more
from contemporary sources—such as using the chronogram of his own
father, Ghulam 'Ali Astarabadi, to cite the death of Ramaraja in 1564.[126]
Ramaraja's son, Ibrahim 'Adil Shah II, is the one who commissions
Firishta to write a new history: "Since the histories of the kings of Hindustan do not exist in one single volume, and the book written by Nizamuddin Ahmed Bakshi has such little research and description of the
Deccan, you should grab the pen and you gird yourself to write a book
with such qualities; a book in plain language without artifice and lies."[127]

After the 'Adil Shahi, Firishta moves to the Nizam Shahi, which, like
the previous polities discussed, begins with Ahmad Nizam and his
decision to create a new capital city, the city of Ahmadabad, in 1494. In
three years, Ahmadabad rivaled Baghdad or Cairo.[128] Ahmad Nizam's
son, Burhan Nizam Shah I, would ascend the throne, and became Shi'a.
Scholars from Deccan, Iraq, or Shiraz made their way to Ahmadabad.[129]
Burhan Nizam Shah created mosques and colleges in order to facilitate
the work of scholarship. The Nizam Shahi, like the 'Adil Shah, also engage in the building of new fort sites and new markets—implanting a
specific materiality to the Deccan soil.

The Qutb Shahi of the Deccan follow the account of the Nizam Shahi.
Again, Firishta dedicates much of his attention to Muhammad Quli
Qutb Shah, who comes into power in 1580. In the early days of his reign,
Quli Qutb Shah falls in love with a woman, Baghmati (whom Firishta
calls "scandalous"). When Quli Qutb Shah builds a new capital that in
"all of Hindustan, whether East, or West, or South or North, would have
no rival in its high artistry and beauty," he names that city Baghnagar—
after Baghmati.[130] Firishta writes that eventually the king "regretted that
name and began to call the city Hyderabad, but the populace continued

to call it Baghnagar."[131] Firishta describes that the markets of this city, "as compared to all other cities in Hindustan, are clean and well organized. The air is excellent and the city suits both the travelers and the residents."[132]

Firishta ends the major part of his history—the history of Deccan sultans as founders of cities—with another panoramic view of Hindustan. Again, like his beginning, he ends by citing from the histories and stories of the inhabitants of Hindustan: "It is written in the books of the people of Hind that there are three contiguous countries that resemble each other in their climate and their specific customs: Tiling and Dang and Bang. The country of Telangana is this very country [Deccan], which is located in southern Hindustan. It is under the reign of the Qutb Shahi sultans. Bang is Bengal, and Dang is the area between these two countries. No Muslim has ever ruled over that area."[133] What Firishta provides is an embedded history of Hindustan in which the birth of new polities, cities, and practices all contribute to an existing territorial, historical, and historiographic structure. Firishta extends the vision of Hindustan that began four hundred years prior and moors it to a mythic past that he conjures from theology as much as history. Firishta's account of Hindustan and his description of its composite structure remain populated, rich, and full of life. There is no terra incognita in Hindustan—not for any of the historians, not for figures such as Babur, and certainly not for Firishta. The world of Hindustan is populated by friends, foes, family, lovers, languages, and the material past.

5

THE PEOPLES IN HINDUSTAN

WHO LIVED IN HINDUSTAN? Firishta's account of the life and rule of Mahmud I Begarha (1458–1511) in Gujarat provides a handy synopsis. This was a world where elite political figures, nobility, rajas, and sultans were engaged in a contest taking place in city streets and agrarian fields. As Firishta opens the account with Mahmud I coming to the throne at the age of fourteen, the reader encounters a whole host of characters: a rebellious landed elite, a cabal of commanders and courtiers, thirty thousand rebel troops, a transgender palace guard, the Nizam Shahi sultan, the raja of Malwa, the raja of Junagarh, a mediator, a butcher, an unjust governor, the Prophet (in a dream), Rajput bandits, a drunk elephant, groups of bandits and highway robbers, a community of animist pirates, four thousand Baluchi bandits, a scholar from Samarkand and his family, a raja of an island who attacked that scholar from Samarkand, the population of the island massacred by Mahmud, the governor of Khambhat, the rebellious elite of Ahmadabad, the people of Malabar, the Rajput raja of Baroda, a group of merchants who attacked the raja of Abu, a rebel Bahmani commander who took control of ports in Gujarat, a rebel commander of Gujarat who fled to Malwa, a rebel commander of Gujarat who went to Khandesh, rebellious commanders in Ahmadabad, Portuguese ships and troops at Chaul, a rebel commander in Thanesar, a rebel commander in Burhanpur, the Sultan of Delhi, a Sufi saint in Patan, and an ambassadorial mission from the Shah of Iran.[1]

Firishta's abiding interest in telling regional histories of Hindustan was in narrating the many diverse types of people who lived there. It is through the people of Gujarat that Firishta outlines his theory of the necessity of a just king in his treatment of the rule of Mahmud I. Firishta tells of Mahmud I as being constantly in battles. The people who live in his cities are unhappy due to the turmoil, lack of public safety on major roads and river passages, and the constant attacks by the rivals of Mahmud I. Firishta criticizes Mahmud I for ignoring the needs of his subjects; he only singles out for praise particular episodes when Mahmud I works to improve the conditions of his people.

Across his monumental history, Firishta provides numerous descriptions of the peoples in Hindustan. In doing so, he is concerned with constituting them as a coherent populace, in order to highlight the duties and responsibilities of the ruler to his public. The populace of Hindustan was diverse, with many faiths, political allegiances, and social hierarchies. Not one community, nor people, are introduced or described by Firishta in terms of their "otherness," nor does he remark that one faith supersedes another. In Firishta's telling, the Brahmins, or caretakers, of temples are akin to the ulama and religious scholars of the mosques; the rajas and ranas are framed as sultans; the nobles hold proud lineages for generations in Hindustan.

In recounting the history of Gujarat, one of the most prominent polities of Hindustan in the late fifteenth and early sixteenth centuries, Firishta focuses on one of its most important kings. The events of Mahmud I's life were significant in the history of Gujarat, and this is why Firishta's history gives prominence and detail to it. Gujarat itself was an important part of Hindustan, and Firishta's history collects all known histories of Gujarat in order to do justice to this region. In Firishta's comprehensive history, Hindustan is best understood through detailed narratives from each of its parts. The parts have their own particular history, and that history is made by individuals, both prominent and subaltern. The task of the synthetic historian, Firishta contends, is to highlight individuals who acted ethically and justly toward their peoples. The historian has the responsibility to judge and assess the actions of the rulers who came before toward their subjects.

At the same moment that Firishta was composing his history, Portuguese and English observers were also narrating their encounters with the subcontinent. These European histories overlap and diverge from Firishta in important ways. We have already seen how the territorial subcontinent was imagined peculiarly as the Mughal dominion and, from there, as the Estado da Índia and British India by Europeans. The accounts of Thomas Roe and James Rennell relied on histories such as that of Abu'l Fazl and Firishta to "fill in" the spaces about the subcontinent, but these European historians also made drastic changes according to their imperial desires.

The peopling of Hindustan was treated similarly in the European imagination. Where Firishta describes a dynamic and diverse populace that requires a just ruler, the European gaze is starkly different. It fixates on extended and extensive ethnographic descriptions of the "inherent oppression" of Hindus at the hands of Muslims in the subcontinent and the enslavement of Hindu peoples to custom. From Firishta, we see Hindustan as an eminently hospitable space—heavenly—with excellent weather, climate, access through water to the hinterland, and political structures that were already open and accommodating to a diverse population. In contrast, from the earliest European texts of the Portuguese, we see a subcontinent that is inhospitable, where Muslim violence was rampant, unpredictable, despotic, and the Hindu populace was oppressed, unchanging in their "customs."

The first section of this chapter features pivotal histories of the Portuguese and English encounter with the subcontinent. I begin with the earliest Portuguese accounts, which stage a civilizational clash between Christians and Muslims, one they imagined as dating back to the Crusades and as happening in their own times in Europe as the Reconquista, displaced onto the peoples of the subcontinent. I then trace extensive descriptions of social practices that represent the enslavement of the peoples of the subcontinent to "custom": from immolation to sexual excess, to the deleterious effects of the climate on their bodies. In the second section, I turn to the earliest Arabic accounts, Persian and Sanskrit inscriptions, and histories leading up to Firishta to illustrate the centrality of the concept of just rule for managing political relationships in Hindustan. Finally, I turn to Firishta, whose history reveals the diversity of peoples in Hindustan—from complex relationships between kings and their successors to conflict across polities and communities.

A CRUSADES FOR INDIA

The Portuguese "discovered" an "India" that was already known to them, even if they did not know how to get there. In order to take a closer look at who lived in the "discovered" Indias, we can turn to the Portuguese history of the "discovery and conquest" of Indias by Fernão Castanheda, written in 1552.[2] It was translated into English by Nicholas Lichefeld in 1582. It was known and consulted by Richard Hakluyt in 1599 and cited by Samuel Purchas in the first edition of *Purchas His Pilgrimage* in 1613.[3]

Castanheda claimed distinction for his history on the grounds that he had experienced this past directly, as well as learned from a deep study of the histories in the Indias as well as in Portugal.[4] Castanheda made a case in his prologue, in a letter addressed to King João III, "the king of Portingale, and of the Algarues, &c," that his account was a true and unbiased history. It was based, he wrote, on his personal experience in the Indias, where he "gave my self greatly in reading of ancient Histories, and having seen and read a great part thereof, did then immediately procure to know and with all diligence did my best endeavour to understand what had been done in the Discouery of the Indias, and in the Conquest of the same, by the Portugues."[5] The Indias, described by Castanheda, would have felt deeply familiar to King João III. Castanheda's history presented the groups who peopled this world and its riches: the antagonist Muslims; the poor, destitute, and violent "natives"; their wealth of gold or natural resources; and their fellow Christians.[6]

In Castanheda's history, the Muslims are a constant and ever-present threat for the Portuguese, who are forever in an entrenched struggle against these "heretics." The Muslims live along the East African shores and know how to sail across the Indian Ocean. The Muslims are the only guides the Portuguese have to the subcontinent. Yet, their "untrustworthiness" can only be confronted with Portuguese violence, demonstrated in the case of "Ilha da Açoutado" (Island of the flogged-one), named thusly because "the Moorish pilot of Mozambique was here severely whipped by order of the general, for having falsely said that these islands were part of the continent [Hindustan]."[7]

The threat of violence, and violence itself, overshadows each encounter. Muslim ports and islands in East Africa are attacked, people are speared and captured and enslaved as sailors and guides. As the Portuguese move from Malindi to Mombasa, they seek the aid of those of the "Indias" to help them navigate. From Malindi they are given an enslaved person, "a pilot, whose name in Guzarate [Gujarati] was Canaca [Canaqua]."[8] Navigated by the pilot, the ships eventually reach the vicinity of Calicut, where they encounter "people [who] came all naked, their members were covered, with little pieces of linen cloth."[9] Such depiction of the people of Hindustan, as unclothed, and slovenly in their appearance is rampant in Castanheda.

As Castanheda proceeds to describe the "Indias" and "second Indias," he gives a history of the people who lived there, and how Muslims first came to Hindustan: "This Province of Malabar was in the old time governed altogether by one king, who made his abode in the City of Conlan, and in the last king's days of this land (whose name was Sarana Perimal, and died six hundred years ago) the Mouro [Moor] of Mecca discovered the Indias, and came to the Province of Malabar, the inhabitants whereof then were *Gentiles,* and the king himself was a Gentile."[10] Once discovered, Malabar's rulers and their rich resources are quickly dominated by the Muslims. Castanheda describes this domination of Muslim merchants in Malabar and how they controlled all the trade and economy. The text overflows with the list of coveted objects and tradable goods:

> the greatest and richest fairs or markets of all the Indias, finding there all the Spices, Drugs, Nutmegs, and all other things that could be wished, as all kinds of precious stones, pearls, & seeds of pearl, Musk, Saunders, Aguila, fine Dishes of earth, Laker, gilted Coffers, and all the fine things of the China, Gold, Amber, Wax, Ivory, fine and course cotton, as well white as dyed in colors, much raw silk, & silk twisted, and all kinde of linen cloth

of silk, and gold, and cloth of gold, and cloth of tissue, cham-
lets, grain, scarlets, carpets of silk, Copper, Quicksilver, Ver-
milion, Allome, Corals, Rose waters, and all kind of Conserves,
so that there is no kind of Merchandise of all the world, which
could be demanded, but it should be found there.[11]

Though all these riches are controlled by Muslim merchants, it is also
one of the Muslims who steps forth to greet the Portuguese. Vasco da
Gama's men immediately encounter a man from Tunis who speaks Portuguese. He is named Bontaibo, and he greets the captain with "Good
luck, good luck, many Rubies, many Emeralds thou art bound to give
great thanks to God, for that he hath brought you where there is all kinds
and sorts of spices, stones, and all the riches of the world."[12] Two strands
of Castanheda overlap again. Like the Muslim sailor who brought the Portuguese ships to Calicut, here was another Muslim "informant" who
predicted to the Portuguese the riches of the world that are promised
by God. Castanheda underscores the righteousness of discovery, because
the riches are promised to the Christians by their own adversary. The
"new" discovery has been familiar all along.

The shock of recognition from Bontaibo's ability to speak Portuguese
does not erase the continuity of imagining Muslims as enemies. When
Vasco da Gama is in the city to meet the Calicut ruler, he learns that the
Muslims, "enemies to the Captain general," were actively conspiring
against him.[13] The cause was this same Bontaibo, the friendly Muslim
who had greeted Vasco da Gama. Bontaibo had told his fellow Muslim
merchants that the Portuguese would strip them of their share of the
profits. These Muslims were now filling the ears of the ruler of Calicut
against the Portuguese. Castanheda imagines the conversations of the
plotting Muslims for his readers. What he asserts is that the Muslim
traders were looking to kill the newly arrived Portuguese in order to
monopolize the trade:

That we being Christians and once come to settle a Trade in Calicut, their commodity then would fall of the price they were
at, and so would abate the most part of their gains. About this
they layed their heads together, to work all means they could

possible with the king, to take the Captain general prisoner, and to command his ships to be taken also, and to kill all our men, and this the rather, for that in no wise they should return to Portingale, to carry news of Calicut.[14]

This simmering threat leads Vasco da Gama to depart from Calicut.

The next contingent of ships that arrived in Calicut from Lisbon in 1500 came with fully hostile intentions. The Portuguese proceeded to speak to the king in Malabar but only after taking hostage some of the local sailors who had boarded their ships. In retaliation, there was an attack on the Christian fortification in Calicut, and the death of fifty-three Christians. The Portuguese response is described in a news missive from 1505:

> In the meantime the Captain was sick, and having heard the news, waited a day to see whether the [Malabar] King would make any amends for this incident. And seeing that the King was not concerned over it, he ordered that ten large ships [belonging to the Muslim traders] that were there be captured and, having unloaded their cargoes, they found three elephants which they ate later on, because of a dearth of provisions.
>
> He slew the greatest part of the people, and the rest whom he made prisoner he ordered to be burned in sight of the city. The following night, he had all ships drawn near the land, and at dawn he began bombarding the city, which did not have any wall and which was greatly damaged, so much so that the King was forced to abandon his palaces.[15]

There was a war in the waters around Calicut. The Portuguese captured ten ships of the Muslim traders, slaughtered all on board, and even slaughtered and ate three elephants. In the Portuguese narration, this struggle was not against the King of Calicut, but against the Muslims for the domination of the people of Calicut; itself a part of the long history of the Crusades.

One of the sources for Castanheda was Duarte Barbosa, whose *Livro* was composed around 1516.[16] Duarte Barbosa, like Castanheda, had lived in the subcontinent. Barbosa provides the account that Castanheda reproduced of Malabar's history. His rendition connects the presence of Muslims not only to the present domination of trade but to the ways in which Muslim contact had fermented political discord in the Indias. Barbosa writes: "They say that in the ancient days there was a heathen King whose name was Cirimay Pirençal, a very mighty Lord. And after the Moors of Mecca had discovered India they began to voyage towards it for the sake of the pepper ... and they had discussions with the King himself and he with them, that in the end they converted him to the sect of the abominable Mafamede [Muhammad]."[17] The conversion, Barbosa recounts, resulted in the king leaving his people and migrating to Mecca, sowing behind him political discord. It was this first conversion of a king to Islam that led to the domination of trade by the Muslims.

The history of the peoples of the Indias, given by Portuguese historians, imagines a subcontinent where the "natives" were long under the thrall of the "foreign" Muslims. One of Firishta's Portuguese contemporaries who wrote of the Portuguese history in the subcontinent was Luís Vaz de Camões (ca. 1524–1580). Camões gave an account of Vasco da Gama's voyage in his *Lusíadas* (ca. 1572). In his account, written some fifty years after Barbosa's and Castanheda's, conversion and chaos are the central themes. Camões's Canto Seven begins with a clarion call to Christians to confront Islam, a task that he bemoans his fellow Europeans are not paying attention to—the Germans and the English are complacent, Jerusalem is under Muslim control, and the terror of the [Ottoman] Turks is fast approaching Europe itself. The Iberian peninsula is already in a steep conflict between the Christians and the Muslims.

It is with his description of a global Muslim-Christian conflict that Camões opens the account of Vasco da Gama's arrival to the Indias.[18] Camões speaks directly to his reader, representing Vasco da Gama and his sailors as ignorant of the historical encounter that is unfolding around them. Camões has already introduced the Canto using strong anti-Muslim polemics. He describes the Indias as peopled with religious anarchists and known enemies of Christianity. The encounter with the subcontinent, in other words, is no encounter with the new. Rather, it is merely another stage on which the struggle between Islam and Christianity plays out.

At shore, the sailors are greeted by a familiar stranger—a "Mouro" (Moor) who speaks in fluent Castilian. The Muslim, here named Monçaide, or Monsayeed, is asked for an account about the land "[Indias] and all its ways."[19] This Muslim, an enemy of Christianity, but a friend in language, begins with divine approval, it must be God who has guided the Portuguese to a land so far.[20]

Monçaide responds to the Portuguese request to tell the history of Calicut by providing the origins of Muslims in the Indias. Malabar was, Camões writes in the voice of Monçaide, a land with one faith [idolatry] from ancient times who lived in harmony until all was fractured by the invasion of the "culto Mahomético."[21] The invasion led to the conversion of the "native" king. The Muslims convinced the ruler, Saramá Perimal, to give up his kingdom and sail to the land of the Prophet. As he left, he divided his kingdom, and since then, political chaos has reigned in the subcontinent.

In Camões's account, this king's conversion was the first act that Christians had to undo. They had to reunite the subcontinent under one faith and one rule. Camões sees the Christian Portuguese as having arrived in this land in order to resolve this conflict. The conversion to a heretic fate had doomed the Indias, and the Portuguese, as the gloried combatants of Islam, were now stepping into the history of Indias. Again, Camões couches this description in the voice of Monçaide. The Muslim is a familiar "informer" for Camões's narrative, like Bontaibo in earlier accounts, as the Muslim is made to translate between the Christian world and this "new" land. In Camões's words, Monçaide describes the people as content to be naked, with a religion composed of fables and legends, who are divided into castes (*casta*) that prohibit touching between the "Naires" and the "Poleás."[22] The Muslim explains marriage practices, where the Naires share wives among the husband's family and their "indulgences" in matters of love.[23] Camões's history of Malabar is a history of Christian struggle with Islam in which a new population enters as representative of a place of unbelievers. The history is thus a history of a people of Indias.

For Camões, the Portuguese burden to rule and govern the subcontinent is universally welcomed by the non-Muslims of Calicut. Camões describes Vasco da Gama meeting one of the Brahmin advisers of the king, Catual. Catual, like Monçaide, greets the arrival of the Portuguese as an omen for a world conquest that is coming:

> Other conquests are fast approaching
> To eclipse those you are looking on;
> Fresh legends will be carved here
> By strange people yet to appear,
> for so the pattern of coming years
> Has been deciphered by our wisest seers.
> And their mystic science declares
> Further that no human resistance
> Can prevail against such forces,
> For man is powerless before destiny;
> But the newcomers' sheer excellence
> In war and peace will be such, they say,
> Even the vanquished will feel no disgrace,
> Having been overcome by such a race.[24]

Camões posits that the failure of the people of Indias to accept the benign and well-meaning Portuguese conquerors was the work of an "Ismaelite." This prophecy of a benign, welcoming conquest that the true inhabitants of Indias would embrace faced hurdles from a familiar enemy: the Muslims.

Bacchus appears in a dream as Muhammad to a different adviser to the king, a Muslim "soothsayer," and warns him to resist these newcomers: "While they are still weak in number / Oppose them in every way you can."[25] The Muslim then begins a conspiracy against the Portuguese by bribing the Brahmin advisers and corrupting their advice to the king. Thus, in this account, the moment of encounter between Vasco da Gama and people of Calicut is hostage to the malicious intent of Muslims and a new portal into the struggle between Christianity and Islam. Where Castanheda had Bontaibo turn the polity against the Portuguese, Camões has this unnamed adviser play the same role. The end result is nonetheless the same: Vasco da Gama departs Calicut having secured assurances of trade, and India is the newest venue for the struggle between religions.

These Portuguese histories of the sixteenth century imagined the Muslims in the Indias as their foremost rivals—in faith and in trade. Thus, the "Mours," or "Ismaelite," versus the "Gentoos" was the primary division, the marker of difference, rendering the peoples encountered into the dominant and subordinate, the outsiders and the insiders. Those not marked as Muslims were given further markings as "Indian Christians," "Gentios," the "Baniyas" or "Naiyers."[26] These early histories describe the Indias through the rupture caused by the Muslim domination.

A development occurs in the seventeenth century in European histories contemporary to Firishta. The ethnological description becomes dominant, and the Muslim interlocuter gives way to the Muslim despotic ruler. Foreignness and violence remain a critical part of the narrative, but the histories now present the Indias through "stories" about social and cultural practices and rituals. As we saw in Chapter 4, the landscape is split into an itinerary. In the accounts of travel along the itinerary, the European historian can sketch characters of "natives," describe conversations with "despots," and present a moral case for colonial expansion.

The violence that marked the Portuguese histories continued with the Muslim despot as the principal actor for enacting that violence. The ethnographic gaze focused its attention on a particular victim: the Hindu woman. Violence on, and toward, the Hindustani woman floods these narratives. These stories define either the brutality of the Muslim ruler or of "social custom," a critical concept used to frame the timelessness of social practice in the subcontinent. Later, the British East India Company would argue that, as the Muslim ruler must be a target for annihilation and removal, so too should the customary practices in which the Hindu woman is a victim be removed.

THE HINDU WIFE

The European had long visualized "India" through Greek and Latin accounts. In its annals of wonders of "India" is the body of the Indian woman as the physical representation of customary practice.

No customary practice received more attention than the act of immolation.[27] These accounts simultaneously produce revulsion and fascination in the reader. The account of Strabo of Amaseia (ca. 64 BCE–21 CE), in his *Geography,* makes this relationship clear:

> Aristobulus mentions some novel and unusual customs at Taxila: those who by reason of poverty are unable to marry off their daughters, lead them forth to the market-place in the flower of their age to the sound of both trumpets and drums (precisely the instruments used to signal the call to battle), thus assembling a crowd; and to any man who comes forward they first expose her rear parts up to the shoulders and then her front parts, and if she pleases him, and at the same time allows herself to be persuaded, on approved terms, he marries her; and the dead are thrown out to be devoured by vultures; and to have several wives is a custom common also to others. And he further says that he heard that among certain tribes wives are glad to be burned up along with their deceased husbands, and that those who would not submit to it were held in disgrace.[28]

The sexual marketplace and the funeral pyre are discursively linked. The citations to Strabo, Diodorus of Sicily, Plutarch, and other authors of antiquity abound in the English travel narratives. As such, the propensity of these authors to "witness" violence against women in Hindustan— either because of their excessive sexuality or because of the death of their husbands—is remarkably consistent.

In an early sixteenth-century Portuguese account, Barbosa provided a template for describing the immolation of a woman whose husband had perished. In his *Livro* he narrates the polity of Vijayanagar through their customary practices. Particularly "this abominable practice of burning is so customary, and is held in such honour among them, that when the King dies four or five hundred women burn themselves with him in this way."[29] Barbosa describes the woman going to the pyre thus: "[She] attires herself very richly with all the jewels she possess, then distributes to her sons, relatives and friends all the property that remains."[30] The violence of a woman performing ritual prayers, or sitting

with equanimity, while fire consumed her, demonstrated her nonhu-
manity, her lack of feeling pain, her devotion to her "heathen" belief to
the European reader.

By the time the English merchant Nicholas Withington arrived in
Surat in 1612, he was actively *seeking* the woman burning on a pyre.
Withington was one of the English merchants who traveled from Gujarat to Sindh in the early seventeenth century. His narrative was excerpted, and made popular, in the compendium *Purchas His Pilgrimes*
in 1625.[31] Withington sets off from Ahmadabad in Gujarat to Thatta in
Sindh in 1613, in order to meet an English ship. He describes cities as he
observes them: Amadavar (Ahmadabad) is a "chief City of Guzerat [Gu-
jarat], near as great as London, walled with a strong wall, situated in the
Plain by the River side, store of Merchants Moores, Christians, Hea-
thens."[32] The city is described both through its materiality (a strong
wall) and through the religious diversity of the people in it.

On his journey, he describes encountering a village that consists entirely of women who make their living through dance performances and
sleeping with men. Note the sedimentation over time of the trope of
sexual excess to describe the Hindustani woman, from Strabo to Withington. This is "Callwalla, a pretty Village, which Ecbar [Akbar] gave to
a company of women, and their posterity for ever, to bring up their
children in dancing, &c, they did this in our Caravan, every man giving
them somewhat; and then they openly asked if any wanted a bed-
fellow."[33] Purchas appends the label "A Towne of common women" to
this passage in order to make the point of sexual deviance clear to the
readers. Where Withington's travelogue makes itself familiar by linking
Ahmadabad to London, Purchas makes the wondrous sexual deviance
familiar by labeling the women as "common," a euphemism for "prosti-
tute" in early modern England. Withington particularly notes that this
village was endowed by the Mughal emperor himself. Akbar, who had
only conquered Gujarat in 1573, is representative of the despotic power
of the Muslims. Withington is linking an "immoral" activity to the
highest authority in the realm, making of it a state practice that will be
redolent in future renderings of Muslim despotism.

As he traverses the land, Withington describes Sindh, and the city of
Thatta, through its people: "Inhabitants of Sinda are most Razbootches

[Rajputs], Banians, and Boloches: in Cities and great Townes, the Governors are Mogols [Mughal]. The Country people are rude, naked from the waist upwards, with Turbans contrary to the Mogoll [Mughal] fashion."[34]

After describing the Rajputs as strong, and "willing to die," he describes the "burning of Rajput wives." It is notable that, in describing women immolating, Withington moves across places (from Thatta to Surat) to give the account a wide geographic expanse. Importantly, he highlights his own testimony by declaring that he has seen many such immolations, before describing the "first" such event that he "witnessed" as an exemplar:

> When the Rajput dies, his wife accompanies his body going to be burned, in her best array, accompanied with her friends and kindred, and Music, and the fire being made at the place appointed, compasses the same twice or thrice, bewailing first her husbands death, and then rejoicing that she shall now live with him again, after which, embracing her friends, she lastly sits down on the top of the pile, and dry flicks, taking her husbands head in her lap, and bids them put fire, which done, her friends throw oil and other sweet perfumes on her, she enduring the fire with admirable patience, loose and not bound.
>
> I have seen many, first in Surat the woman but ten years old and a Virgin, he a Soldier slain in war, from whence his clothes and Turban were brought home. She would needs burn with his clothes; the Governor forbad her, which she took grievously, bidding them put to fire presently.[35]

Again, following Barbosa and others, Withington specifies the dress, the jewelry, the materials touching the body of the woman as carefully as he describes the act itself.

Witnessing the act of immolation as a dramatic narrative device is a pervasive feature of the many European observations of the peoples of the Indias.[36] It was considered to be such a ubiquitous practice that Samuel Johnson's 1759 compilation of world travel accounts, *The World Display'd*, quoted Claude-Marie Guyon in support of this notion: "A very ingenious Author of great reputation takes notice that there are none of the almost infinite number of travellers who have passed through India, who do not mention the abominable custom of the women publickly burning themselves at the death of their husbands."[37] In the excess that is promised by the "infinite" lies the true import of the fact: a woman's immolation defines the timelessness of the Indias as much as the European man's eyewitnessing of the act defines their presence in Hindustan.

The traveler whose witnessing account was then quoted from in *The World Display'd* was one Johan Albrecht de Mandelslo, who witnesses an immolation in Khambhat. It is worth taking a moment to track the widespread use and reuse of Mandelslo's account in seventeenth- and eighteenth-century England. Mandelslo's account enters English via John Davies of Kidwelly, who published a rendering from German as "The Travels of John Albert de Mandelselo" in 1662. He credited the original text to Adam Olearius's publication. Both Olearius and Johan Albrecht de Mandelslo were part of an embassy sent by Frederick III, duke of Holstein-Gottorp, to Moscow and the shah of Persia from 1633 to 1639. Olearius, who was secretary to the embassy, published the account of the embassy in 1647, to which he appended a brief manuscript by Mandelslo.[38] A Dutch rendering of the full travelogue appeared in 1651, and a French rendition in 1659. Davies's second rendition came in 1669, and then another German edition followed in 1669.[39]

Mandelslo's testimony on immolation of women in India was a pivotal account for the English imagination in the late seventeenth century—its presence is attested to in the works of two major intellectuals, John Locke and John Dryden. John Locke in his 1676 *Essays on the Law of Nature* quoted Mandelslo's "eyewitness" account of the immolation of a woman as an example of a customary practice that can overcome even the natural law of the human drive for self-preservation. What, conceptually, is the immolation doing in these accounts? It is useful to quote from Locke to see the critical work that the event of immolation does for his philosophy:

> For among the Indians the weak and timid female sex dares to make light of dying and to hasten to rejoin departed husbands by passing through the flames and through the gate of

death. They allow the nuptial torches to be extinguished only in the flames of the funeral pyre, and they prefer to seek a new marriage-chamber in the grave itself. . . . Of this fact Mandelselo, in the recently published itinerary of Olearius, declares himself an *eye-witness*.

As he himself relates, he saw a beautiful young woman who after the death of her husband could not be prevailed upon, or restrained from murdering herself, by the advice, entreaties, and tears of her friends. At length, after an involuntary delay of six months, with the permission of the magistrate, she dressed as if for a wedding, triumphantly and with a joyous face ascended a pyre set up in the middle of the market-place, and cheerfully perished in the flames. *It would be tedious to describe further instances.*[40]

The main contours of the narrative of a European witnessing a woman's immolation in the subcontinent are all present in Locke's retelling: the overlap between wedding and funeral, the insistence on "will," the linkage between the marketplace and the pyre. There is also the recognition of its ubiquitous nature; Locke excusing himself from the unnecessary tedium of putting forth more than one example. In fact, if he had not named Mandelslo, one could easily have confused this account to have come from Withington. What the "single" event of immolation does for Locke is to simultaneously naturalize the basic human drive for survival while also demonstrating that the Hindu woman lacks that very fundamental trait for being human because of her enslavement to "custom."

John Dryden places the event of immolation at the heart of the Mughal imperium. Dryden's play *Aureng-Zebe: A Tragedy* appeared at the Royal Theatre in 1676. In the play, the character Melesinda willingly immolates after the death of the character Morat, the brother of Aurangzeb. The ritual is performed on the stage as a wedding ceremony:

A Procession of Priests, Slaves following, and last Melesinda in white.

Ind. Alas! what means this Pomp?

Aur. 'Tis the Procession of a Funeral Vow, Which cruel Laws to *Indian* Wives allow, When fatally their Virtue they approve; Chearful in flames, and Martyrs of their Love.

Ind. Oh my foreboding heart! th'event I fear; And see! sad Melesinda does appear.

Mel. You wrong my love; what grief do I betray? This is the Triumph of my Nuptial day.[41]

The audience in the Royal Theatre witnesses the immolation just as Aurangzeb and Indamora do on the stage. Dryden was drawing upon Davies's rendering of Mandelslo (they were contemporaries and both engaged in translation) in creating this scene for the English public.[42] Dryden transposed the act of immolation into a dramatic love triangle set in the Mughal household and sold it as a tragedy for the London public. Dryden's invention of immolation's centrality to all ritual (like Locke's designation of it as a customary practice) was no accident. It was widely understood that Dryden was relying on accounts from Hindustan in composing his portraits.[43]

Mandelslo's account had numerous instances in which the landscape of the subcontinent is marked specifically with sexual violence, sexual deviance, or oppression of women by the Muslim rulers. For instance, Mandelslo describes a story of incest, literally embedded in the ground as a mausoleum: "There is a Sepulchre, which they call *Betti-Chuit* [quite literally, daughter-fucker] that is to say, *thy daughters shame discovered.* There lies interr'd in it a rich Merchant, a Moor, named *Hajam Majom,* who [fell] in love with his own Daughter."[44] The Muslim merchant asks a Muslim judge if it is legal for him to "eat the fruits of a tree planted by himself."[45] The judge grants permission, and the Muslim merchant approaches his daughter. When she refuses him, "he ravished her. She complain'd to her Mother, who made so much noise about it, that the King Mahomet Begeran coming to hear thereof, ordered him to lose his head."[46]

Mandelslo revels in the special access that the European male had to women of the subcontinent—in the "noblest Gardens about the City," which were "planted by a beautiful and rich young Lady" and where "a man can seldom go to this Garden, but he shall find some young Women bathing themselves; they will not permit the Indians should see them, but suffered us to come in and speak to them."[47]

Mandelslo sensationally narrates the story of a Muslim despotic ruler who "murders" women, such as the governor of Ahmadabad, Gujarat—who "sent for twenty Women-dancers, who as soon as they were come into the room fell a singing and dancing."[48] They danced for two hours, and then the governor called for another troupe, but "the Servants brought word, that they were sick and could not come. This excuse being not taken, he sent out the same Servants, with express order to bring those Prostitutes away by force; but they returning the second time with the same excuse, he ordered they should be cudgell'd."[49]

The women then admitted that they had lied about their sickness and that they "were at a certain place, where they got Money at a more delightful and easier sport than dancing, and that they absolutely deny'd to come, saying, they knew well enough Governour would not pay them." Having heard this, he ordered them brought to his presence, and "they were no sooner entered into the Hall ere he ordered their heads to be struck off. They beg'd their lives with horrid cries and lamentations; but he would be obey'd, and caus'd the execution to be done in the room before all the Company, not one of the Lords then present daring to make the least intercession for those Wretches, who were eight in number."[50]

Mandelslo describes the "horrour of the Spectacle and the inhumanity of the Action," which the governor laughs off with "if I should not take this course, I should not be long Governor of Ahmadabad. For should I connive once at their disobedience, these Bete-Seioth, or Sons of Whores, would play the Masters, and drive me out of the City."[51]

Mandelslo relays another case of women's immolation in Khambhat. He saw a "not above twenty years of age woman whose Husband was a Rasboute [Rajput] and had been kill'd near Lahore, 200 leagues from Cambaya" and who wanted to put "her self to be burned alive."[52] While the Mughal governor prohibited such an "inhumane action," he eventually "permitted her to comply with the Laws of her own Religion."[53] She goes in a procession, distributing her "Rings and Bracelets." Mandelslo is eager to tell that he had a personal memento of this act. The woman had seen Mandelslo and "perceiv'd in my countenance that I pitied her, whence it came that she cast me one of her Bracelets, which I had the good hap to catch, shall keep, in remembrance of so extraordinary an Action."[54]

Mandelslo argues that women of the subcontinent experience early sexual maturity. He narrates it as a story of wonder and marvel: "They marry their Children very young, which is the less to be wondered at, inasmuch as it is very certain, that the Indians of both Sexes are capable of engendering much sooner than any other Nation." To this fact, Mandelslo provides a "story, which may seem fabulous" that in Agra was a "a Daughter, which at two years of age had Breasts as big as those of any Nurse." They tried to "remedy" this by "applying a hot Iron to her body by a Lock-smith," but he died as well as "all those that had been present at the said cure." At three the child had "what those of her Sex are not wont to have till twelve or thirteen" and at four "her Belly was so swollen as if she had been with child." This child was then "brought to bed of a Boy" at the age of six.[55]

There are these, and many other accounts, in Mandelslo, which present the women of the Indias through their capacity to experience and endure extreme violence. These are the earliest, and come to be some of the most influential, characterizations of the peoples of the Indias. Mandelslo's fabulations came to be known and widely accepted as truths about the enslavement and degradation of the "Gentiles" at the hands of the Muslim despots. The sexual excesses and social depravity in Mandelslo's text are repeated over and over in European travelogues, compilations, anthologies, and histories. There was indeed, as *The World Display'd* argued, a nearly infinite number of François Berniers, Niccoli Manuccis, Jean-Baptiste Taverniers, and Alexander Hamiltons, all narrators of violence meted out by and to the peoples of the subcontinent.

Robert Orme, the appointed "First Historiographer" of the British East India Company, had his *Historical Fragments of the Mogul Empire* published posthumously in 1805. His notes cite his "Authorities" and feature Bernier, Dow, Du Perron, Hamilton, Manucci, Purchas, and Firishta, all also cited in the writing of two essays, "A General Idea of the Government and Peoples of Indostan" and "Effeminacy of the Inhabitants of Indostan," in 1753. Orme's essays anticipate nineteenth-century English studies of the colonized people of British India. They provided the necessary framework and inspiration for the field of ethnology and historical geography that came to be identified with Henry Maine's *Village Communities* (1871), William Wilson Hunter's *A Brief History of the Indian Peoples* (1882), and Herbert Risley's *The People of India* (1908).

Orme's Indostan is a despotic place without control, much as in early sixteenth-century accounts: "If the subjects of a despotic power are every where miserable, the miseries of the people of Indostan are multiplied by the incapacity of the power to controul the vast extent of its dominion."[56] The chaos of political despotism, Orme offers, would expect us to "find throughout Indostan dreary plains, lands uncultivated, miserable villages thinly interspersed, desolated towns," but, in fact, it is a flourishing land. This flourishing is due to the "effects of the climate of Indostan," which has subverted the people from "the violences to which it is subject from the nature of the government."[57] Orme places the "Moors of Indostan" into two categories of people: "the descendants of the conquerors" and the "descendants of converted Gentoos—a miserable race, as none but the most miserable of Gentoo castes are capable of changing in their religion."[58]

The Gentoos Orme considers as "slaves" of a despotic state, much as the Portuguese had imagined the history of Calicut under Muslims. The Gentoos are characterized through their "commerce with public women," and the Moors as "addicted to drinking spirituous liquors."[59] Orme's further thesis on the peoples of Indostan as "effeminate" begins with an exultation to his audience to "read the description given by Diodorus, of the Indian woman who burnt herself with the corpse of her husband, in the army of Eumenes. She distributes her ornaments among her friends and relations . . . a mark of her desire to be remembered by them."[60]

Orme notes that it seemed to him that Diodorus's account "was wrote yesterday. It is not probable that any great changes can have been introduced amongst a people, who have preserved for two thousand years, a custom which so strongly revolts the first feelings of humanity."[61] This is the timelessness that envelops the people of British India. Orme is also, like Locke, defining the peoples of Hindustan through their "revolting" customary practice.

Orme's description of the effeminate Indian begins by putting the reader at the same shore where Vasco da Gama had encountered his false friend, the Muslim. "The sailor no sooner lands on the coast, than nature dictates to him the full result of this comparison; he brandishes his stick in sport, and puts fifty Indians to flight in a moment: confirmed in his contempt of a pusillanimity and an incapacity of resistance, suggested to him by their physiognomy and form, it is well if he recollects that the poor Indian is still a man."[62]

Orme relies on theories of climate—he cites Montesquieu—to demonstrate the history of the subcontinent as one of weakness, as one personified in the study of a woman's immolation, and in the gendering of the peoples as weak, abject, and "effeminate." It is a prominent feature of eighteenth-century thought when it came to thinking about the colonized subcontinent. The men are scarcely men, full of nervous energy, ill-equipped to perform hard labor, while the women of Indostan "are all, without exception, fit to be married before thirteen, and wrinkled before thirty."[63] The people of Hindustan are indolent, obtain their grain with minimal labor, remain "by choice almost naked."[64] These peoples living in the "softest of climates; having so few real wants; and receiving even the luxuries of other nations with little labour, from the fertility of their own soil," concludes Orme, "must become the most effeminate inhabitant of the globe; and this is the very point at which we now see him."[65]

The European production of a "discourse" on the race and moral character of the people of the Indias proliferated across Europe as theory. Immanuel Kant's 1775 lecture, printed as *Von den verschiedenen Racen der Menschen* (On the different races of human beings) serves as an apt coda to this section. Kant is interested in laying out his theory on the formation and significance of race as a world historical phenomenon. He distinguishes Indians, based on their clime, as having "cold hands" as a hereditary condition:

> I had indeed read somewhere that these Indians have the peculiarity of cold hands in very great heat and that this was supposed to be a fruit of their sobriety and moderation. When I had

the pleasure of speaking to the attentive and insightful traveler, Herr Eaton, who had been stationed as Dutch Consul and head of the Dutch office in Bassein, on his travel through Königsberg, he told me the following: when he had danced with the wife of a European consul in Surat, he had been surprised to feel sweaty and cold hands on her (the habit of gloves had not yet taken hold there), and since he expressed his astonishment to others, he received the answer that she had an Indian mother and this peculiarity was hereditary in them.[66]

It is unsurprising that Kant's reliance on a self-narrated experience comes from Surat and concerns the body of a woman who stands in for the race of all Indians. It is fitting also because the European will to narrate Hindustan embeds itself deep within the folds of rational, objective, and scientific persona. The ethnologists, ethnographers, and historians of the nineteenth century took a set of circulating theories of racial difference and made them conceptually coherent—integrating "customary practice," "sati," "Oriental despotism," and Indian "effeminacy" into a unified natural law for the peoples of the subcontinent.

In the section that follows, I turn to Hindustani histories to see how a lived reality of peoples of Hindustan was imagined, historicized, and written.

COMMONERS AND KINGS

The narratives of merchants and traders in the Indian Ocean world illuminate histories of Hindustan that do not fit within paradigmatic categories established by the European historians and philosophers of the early modern period. Let me begin with the earliest depictions of the peoples of Hindustan in Arabic merchant narratives from the ninth and tenth centuries. The ninth-century 'Aja'ib al-Hind and Akhbar al-Sin wa'l Hind, composed and compiled by merchants of the Indian Ocean, are meant to invoke the lives of communities along the western port cities. These accounts reveal shared cosmologies making the explicit claim that Muslims are native to Hindustan. They also reveal the central facets of everyday lives in the littoral region—that these are regulated communities with agreements, treaties, and governance across all communities.

The 'Aja'ib gives a history of asceticism in Hindustan by beginning in Sarandip (now Sri Lanka), where live the "Bikarji," who "love Muslims and meet with them with pleasure."[67] They are described as wearing small-patched clothing, having cremated ash rubbed on their bodies, having shaved heads and faces, and carrying a skull or bones around their necks or in their hands. The 'Aja'ib reports that when the wise of Sarandip learned of the emergence of the Prophet Muhammad, they sent someone to Medina to learn about his teaching. The traveler reached Medina only after the Prophet had passed away, during the caliphate of 'Umar Khattab. They turned back. The man perished in Makran on the way back, but his servant continued to Sarandip and reported all he had seen and heard, including the ascetic ways in which 'Umar lived—"he wears patched-up clothes and spends his nights in the mosque." The ascetics of Sarandip are so impressed by the stories of this just king that they begin to emulate his practices of wearing and living. This is a moment of recognition in the text. The Arab merchant account does not describe an encounter with an unknown, alien ritual practice. Rather, the story signifies the recognition by the Arab merchants of a commonality between a practice of asceticism of the people of Hindustan and their ruler in Arabia, who is himself an ascetic.

These very early Indian Ocean accounts see separate polities in Hindustan, with their own particular histories, and laws. While these accounts also highlight the wild abundance of wealth or the wondrous asceticism of yogis, they are nonetheless approaching Hindustan from a position of commensurability and not alterity. The Akhbar's section "Accounts of the Countries of Hind and China, and Their Rulers" begins:

> The people of Hind and China are united in their opinion that there are four greatest of kings in the world. They consider the first of these four to be the king of Arabs: it is a unanimous opinion among them, about which there is no disagreement, that of the four kings he is the mightiest, the richest in possessions, and the most resplendently fine in appearance, and that

he is the king of the great religion to which nothing is superior. The king of China counts himself next in importance after the king of the Arabs, then comes the king in Rome and finally Balharā, the king of those Indians who pierce their ears.[68]

The hierarchical distribution of powers, and the recognition of the superiority of the king and the religion of Arabs opens this account, but it is crucial to note that this recognition is not one that is premised on possession or conflict. Rather, the account goes on to provide details of other kings in Hindustan. The account of kings in Hindustan separates the rulers who are kind and accommodating to the Arab merchants—Balhara, Taqa, Dahmi—from those who are hostile—Jurz and Kashibin.[69] These kings, and their polities, exist outside of Arab or Muslim dominion, with their own politics, their own sense of community. The *Akhbar* is typical in such an understanding of Hindustan. The Arabic accounts are keen to highlight both the independence of the kings of Hindustan as well their attitude or interactions toward the Muslim community.

The concern with treatment of Arabs, the adherence to the question of law and order, compels us to read these Arabic accounts as nontriumphalist in nature. They are not asserting Muslim supremacy, or positing annihilation of other people. Rather, they are interested in understanding hierarchy as a mutually recognized difference. In Mas'udi's history, *Muruj al-Dhahab,* contemporaneous to the *Akhbar* and *'Aja'ib,* are numerous descriptions of other kings in Hindustan and their qualities. The kings of Hindustan do not drink alcohol or have sexual relationships outside of their sanctioned marriages. They have excellent law and order in their lands so that no merchant is robbed. The kings allow their daughters to become rulers of their own accord, and the women are supported by the armies. The kings honor and protect treaties and pacts with other rulers, including the Muslim caliph. Indeed, the kings organize debates and dialogues between Muslims and non-Muslims in which matters of theological importance are considered, and allow for the constructions of mosques and neighborhoods for Muslims. The kings provide employment and stipends to Muslims who live in their lands.[70]

Take another example from the *'Aja'ib.* A sailor arrives in a port and seeks debauched pleasure. He sees a beautifully carved idol in the shape of a woman, which he mistakes for a real woman. He lays with it and despoils it. A caretaker at the temple catches him and takes him to the governor of the city. The man confesses his crime. The king asks his advisers what the punishment ought to be for this crime. One says to have him trampled by elephants. Another says to have him cut to pieces. The king rejects them and says that since the sailor is an Arab, and they have treaties with the Arabs, they have to consult Abbas bin Mahan, who is the one in charge of the affairs of these Muslims. "Go ask him what is the penalty for one who has committed such desecration in their mosque." Abbas bin Mahan responds quickly that the punishment should be death. The king then had the sailor put to death. Shortly thereafter, Abbas bin Mahan leaves the port, fearing that the king will punish him as well for the transgression.[71]

The Hindustani king makes a direct equivalence between the mosque and the temple, an equivalence passed into the narrative, without comment. The king does not assert unilateral authority in punishing the sailor, instead he has the Muslim governor responsible for the merchants propose a punishment. The *Akhbar* mentions a similar arrangement between Muslims and a Chinese king: "Sulaymān the merchant reported that, in Khānfū, the meeting place of merchants, there was a Muslim man appointed by the ruler of China to settle cases arising between the Muslims who go to that region, and that the Chinese king would not have it otherwise."[72]

The Arabic accounts do refer to caste divisions and practices of immolation among the people of Hindustan, but they are nowhere as ubiquitous or predominant as in the later European histories. Even when narrated, the description of social practices and rituals does not overshadow the text as it does in the European accounts. The *Akhbar*'s description of immolation is in Sarandip after the death of the king: "In [Hind], all burn their dead in fire. Sarandip is the last of the islands, is part of the land of Hindustan. At times it also happens that, when a dead king is burned, his womenfolk enter the fire too and are burned alive with him; but if they wish, they do not do so."[73] This account is framed as the death of the king and the choice of his wives. It highlights not the act of immolation but the many rituals attendant to the king's body, including the burning of dead.

The *Akhbar* returns to the topic of immolation in a later section, "Some Reports of Hind." The immolation is carried out by a *man* and takes place in the polity of Balhara. The text provides a reason for his immolation, a belief in the movement of the souls after death: "There are people who burn themselves to death with fire. This stems from their belief in the transmigration of souls."[74] The account further notes that one who seeks to immolate must get permission from the king for the act. Here then is described intention and agency in the act of immolation. There is also a geographic distinction in the Arabic account, where this practice is unique to the region of Balhara.

From the earliest Arabic accounts of the Indian Ocean world, we now turn inland, up the River Indus to Multan, to see how this landscape of Hindustan is peopled. In the late twelfth century, we find a Hindustan where a Muslim poet is composing in Prakrit (Sanskrit vernacular) poetry from a classical genre of poetics—the messenger poems. The late twelfth-century message poem *Samdesarasaka,* by Abdulrahman, provides a glimpse into the world of travelers between Khambhat, Gujarat, and Multan, Sindh. The poem depicts a woman from Jaisalmir but living in Multan sending a message to her merchant husband in Khambhat.[75]

The poet Abdulrahman opens with a salutation to God, who created "the earth, the mountains and trees, stars in the sky, even the whole world, give to you enlightened, his blessing."[76] His opening cleverly calls attention to his own name, referencing the opening of the Qur'an in which the merciful God is also called Rahman.[77] The poet then identifies himself as belonging to a glorious line of poets, most significantly Kalidasa, author of the *Meghaduta*. Abdulrahman proclaims his work belongs to the common man, the merchant, the trader, and the farmer: "The magnificence of the skill of his own poetic craft, and the great extent of his learning, is published abroad among men by a weaver, declaimed with earnestness and sincere emotion: the Saṃdeśarāsaka. Knowing that, O enlightened ones, accord your indulgence for half a moment, and listen to a work that was composed in the thick letters of a ploughman."[78] Abdulrahman's poem gives the texture of everyday social life. The traveler in the poem names his hometown as Sāmora [halfway between Jaisalmer and Khambhat]: "The name of my town, lady of the lotus-petal eyes, is Sāmora, [a town] full of joy, O lady whose face is like the moon; a town enhanced with fortifications consisting of white turrets and walls; [there] no fool is to be found, but every person is a scholar."[79] This Hindustan is peopled with a poet, writing in Prakrit, who identifies himself with farmers. The poem's depiction of the city is one where everyone is a scholar in their own right. For Abdulrahman, the cities of Hindustan were filled with scholars, poets, and merchants.

Such thick depictions of peopled Hindustan abound as well in epigraphic records. In the environs of Delhi were located a series of inscriptions from the thirteenth century that attest to the peopled past of Hindustan. For instance, a thirty-one-line Sanskrit inscription originally affixed to a stepping well in the village of Palamba dates from 1276.[80] The inscription was commissioned by a city official named Uddhara from the city of Delhi but whose family came from Uch, "by the divine nectar of Sindhu (Indus) which removes all kinds of distress."[81] The inscription begins with a political history of the Hariyānaka region where Delhi is located. It informs us that "the land of Hariyānka was first enjoyed by the Tomaras and then by the Cauhānas. It is now ruled by the Śaka kings."[82] The "Śaka" are the Muslim rulers of Delhi: "First came Sāhabadīna, then Khudavadīna, master of the earth, Samusdīna, then Pherujsāhi, lord of the earth. After him Jalāldīna, and then was born king Maujadīna, [then] the glorious and noble king Alāvadīna, and Nasaradīna, the lord of the earth."[83] The Muslim polity sketched begins with Shihabuddin Ghuri and continues with Qutubuddin Aibak, Iltutmish, Razia Sultan, and so on. The inscription then gives a full political genealogy of rulers in which no distinction is made between Muslims and non-Muslims. The current ruler of Delhi, Ghiyathuddin Balban, is recognized and celebrated by Uddhara, a non-Muslim, who was his employee.

After the description of the political history and supremacy of Ghiyathuddin, the inscription describes the family of Uddara himself: his father Haripala, whose father [was] Yasoraja, whose father [was] Dallahara, whose father [was] Kipu, all of whom were residents of Uch; his mother Candi, daughter of Prithu, whose father was Harischandra, whose father was Utsahana, whose father was Sahadeva, whose father was Tola, whose father was Vyagarahara, whose father was Singha, whose father was Gaura.[84] These detailed family genealogies are preserved, the inscription notes, in a work named *Vamsavali*. The genealogies continue to be noted, spanning generations and good deeds. This is a lived history that connects Uch and Delhi. The last stanza notes that the inscription, a praise poem, has been composed by a "pandit Yogisvara of eternal fame."[85] From the inscription we get a rich understanding of the social world of Hindustan. Families that stretched across geographies, from Delhi to Uch, are understood in the same register as political lineages that stretched across the same space.

Another inscription, from a watering well near Delhi, dated to 1327, reflects these linked strands of family and political lineages. The "Naraina stone inscription" begins with a description of "this town of Ḍhillī covered with innumerable jewels, whence sin is expelled through the chanting of the Vedas by those who know the sacred lore."[86] This Delhi is ruled by "the famous king Mahammud Sāhi, the crest jewel of all the rulers of the earth, who by his personal bravery has crushed [his] enemies and is the powerful Sáka lord."[87] After describing the valor and might of Muhammad Tughluq, the inscription describes the family history of Sridhara, who had "the well dug for the propitiation of his ancestors" in the "village called Nāḍāyaṇa."[88] Looking back from Sridhara, a genealogy is traced: Sridhara and his brother Solhana were born to Prithvidhara, one of the sons of Srivara, who had two wives, Kallya and Gangadisri. Srivara and his brother Dullrabhadeva were born to Risada and his wife Rajasri. Risada and his brother Sudeva were born to Dhiradeva and his wife Dhani. Dhiradeva was one of nine sons to Damodara and Virada. Damodara was one of four famous sons born to Ratna and Gangasri. Ratna was the son of "a merchant named Govindadeva who made his abode in the Nāḍāyaṇa village and lived amidst friends and family."[89] These nine generations of merchants of Nāḍāyaṇa have their past inscribed into stone in order to preserve their memory as history.

Such family genealogies double as histories of how the political past was understood at the level of everyday life. It is probable that women and children as well as merchants and wayfarers stopping at these wells to quench their thirst or take a supply for home would not be able to read or understand the complex melding of gods and kings with fathers and mothers. Yet the stone inscription acts as a legible object outside of the capacity to "read" it, bearing the marks of a commemoration of lived history. It is a marker of being embedded in space and time—a grounding for a past that is composed of the people in the village. It reflects the daily lives of those who commissioned, composed, and carved these inscriptions as prosperous, abundant individuals remembering their ancestors and recognizing the generosity of the just kings.

These inscriptions reflect the people's understanding of the characteristics of a just ruler who nourishes his people. Such emphasis on a content populace is a central concern to the historians of the thirteenth century and later. The histories detail the ways in which a king ought to be trained and taught lessons from previous times in order to best serve his subjects. The historians mark popular discontent, riots, and rebellions as the breaking down of social order caused by unjust rulers. In sharp contrast to European histories, which posit a populace in the Indias under tyrannical absolutism, these histories of Hindustan present a deep commitment to the idea of public welfare.

Juzjani's history, *Tabaqat-i Nasiri,* written in Delhi, is contemporaneous to the Palamba inscription. Juzjani also gives a genealogy of rulers, nobles, and elites, and traverses the same geographies. He inscribes into memory a history of being Hindustani just as much as these contemporary and near-contemporary Sanskrit inscriptions from Delhi, which make clear the shared social agenda of a peopled past. *Tabaqat-i Nasiri* is also a repository of a history of the peoples as they existed under the political and social structures of Delhi. Descriptions of the lives and actions of nobility form the bulk of Juzjani's history, but he is unique in offering not only the accounts of those who won battles and rose to prominence but those who were lost and forgotten.

Juzjani highlights the actions of the governing elite that demonstrate their justice or commitment to public welfare. When he is posted to Lakhnauti in 1243, he remarks on the governance of the local noble, Ghiyathuddin 'Awaz Khilji, who constructs bridges and rest areas for the populace and protects the houses of merchants.[90] Even when Juzjani tells the history of his main patron, Iltutmish, he emphasizes that Iltutmish was generous and supportive of the ascetics and mendicants of Delhi. Iltutmish had this quality, Juzjani writes, because it was an ascetic who gave Iltutmish a prophecy that he would one day become a king.

In Juzjani's telling, Iltutmish had an abiding love and care for the down-trodden among his populace. Juzjani writes that Iltutmish told this story about his own childhood: When Iltutmish was young, he was given a small coin to fetch grapes from the market. On the way, he lost the coin and began to cry by the roadside. A holy man stopped, held his hand, and purchased the grapes for him, saying: "'Promise me that when you will possess countries and riches, you will respect the ascetics and holy.' I took that oath and all that I have received in possessions, it is the blessing of that holy man."[91] Such divine ordinances humanize rulers, emphasizing their humble beginnings and their ready encounters with the people, who are always encountered on roads, pathways, market-places, or sacral sites.

Iltutmish's death created a power vacuum in Delhi. He appointed his daughter, Razia Sultan, as his successor, for she was the most ethical of his children. However, after his death, there was a struggle among his children. The struggle for succession fractured the political alliances in the polity, creating vast turmoil across all levels. Razia Sultan was able to take Delhi after she made a direct public appeal, appearing in the Grand Mosque and proclaiming she had the proper right to rule. A popular uprising then installed her in power.[92] While she was able to rule for three years, her reign was beset with problems, as her ruling elite con-spired against her and the public.

Juzjani relates a major popular uprising against the ruling elite that happened in 1237, during Razia's reign. The culprit for the mass violence, according to Juzjani, was a popular marketplace preacher, a common "wise man" called "Nur Turk" by his followers.[93] Nur Turk's followers were scattered around Hindustan, in Gujarat, in Sindh, around Delhi, and by the banks of the Rivers Ganges and Yamuna. Nur Turk accused the elite of being too close to political power, of being sycophants and upholders of the status quo. Nur Turk directed his message to the "com-moners"; Juzjani, a member of the clergy, calls him and his followers heretics and sectarians.

On Saturday, March 13, 1237, a thousand of Nur Turk's followers, armed with swords, spears, and arrows, headed to the congregational mosque in Delhi in two groups. One group entered the mosque from the north gate, but the other, mistakenly, entered the school attached to the mosque. Once inside, both groups unsheathed their weapons and attacked the worshipers and students inside. Juzjani writes that, in this massacre, "many people perished, some by the spears of the heretics and some trampled underfoot in the chaos."[94] The residents of Delhi who lived nearby heard the commotion, armed themselves with weapons and armor, and went to the mosque to repel the Nur Turk faction. Even those who did not have weapons joined the resistance with stones and bricks. Juzjani informs us that, after a violent struggle, Nur Turk, and all of his followers, were defeated and killed.

The violence here, framed by Juzjani as emanating from commoners against the elite classes, gives us a glimpse of the tumultuous social and political world.[95] Materially, it shows the movement of ideas (including rumors and conspiracies), organization, and traffic connecting Delhi to places like Khambhat, Uch, or Malwa. It shows that the figure of the common man—the Sufi, the preacher, or the prophet—held immense political power among the populace, one that someone could wield in the face of an unjust ruling class. It further demonstrates that people would rise up against unjust political power.

Razia Sultan also faced multiple rebellions from her own elites, in Lahore and Multan, during her short reign of three years and six months as sultan. While trying to fight her opponents, she was captured by a contingent of military commanders near Bathinda (halfway to Delhi from Lahore) and imprisoned. In 1240, she was killed and buried in a field. The rebellion against her, Juzjani writes, was motivated by elite discontent: The elite were jealous of her relationship with a supervisor in the Royal Stables, Malik Jamaluddin Yaqut; they were upset that she was dressed in male battle attire; they were upset that she wore the headdress reserved for male nobility and went out in public, unwilling to seclude herself from the common populace.[96] The theme that cuts across the several reasons provided by Juzjani for the rebellion against Razia Sultan was the desire of the military and civic elite to maintain public decorum. Juzjani's account helps us catch a glimpse of a social world where concerns of decorum could motivate the organization of armies, as Razia's opponents did against her, and where even a preacher from the marketplace was able to assemble a mass armed militia to strike at the political order.

A populace that rises up against unjust practices of political power is also found in Barani's *Tarikh-i Firuz Shahi*. In his history, Barani relates the story of the career and actions of a young man named Hasan from Gujarat, who entered the service of Qutbuddin Khilji in Delhi in 1317. That young man was given the title "Khusrau Khan."[97] This "cunning and wicked" man, according to Barani, climbs higher and higher in the estimation of Qutbuddin.[98] Khusrau Khan was a controversial figure. Barani describes a series of accusations against Khusrau Khan, from homosexuality to being an apostate to Islam. Khusrau Khan is appointed the governorship of Gujarat, and he soon expands his portfolio over Ma'abar. The besotted Qutbuddin, Barani writes, is oblivious to Khusrau Khan's power grab.

Eventually, Khusrau Khan decides that he has enough support from Gujarat to depose Qutbuddin and become himself the sultan in Delhi. He thus plots and carries out the assassination of Qutbuddin in his own palace.[99] The Palace of a Thousand Pillars is now filled with Khusrau Khan's relatives and followers, commoners from Gujarat who installed a temple in the palace for their devotion.[100] Khusrau Khan rules for only four months. Ghiyathuddin Tughluq is able to create a coalition and defeat the insurrection. Yet, Barani is shaken by this episode, in which someone from a shepherding clan in Gujarat is able to rise to power in such a way as to assassinate even the sultan in his palace, to declare his own rule. For Barani, as for Juzjani, the people could be unruly and unhappy, and this was the greatest threat to a political ruler. This threat is why the histories of Juzjani and Barani provide elaborate theories of good governance for the kings of Hindustan, for when a king neglected to attend to the needs of the people, he lost the right to rule. When Khusrau Khan is defeated by Ghiyathuddin, Barani rejoices that the "hearts of the general populace" were lifted, for order had been restored.[101]

Like Juzjani and Barani, Firishta is deeply concerned with the relationship between the people and the ruling elites. As we saw at the beginning of this chapter, Firishta's history of Gujarat's Mahmud I Begarha has a rich cast of characters, peoples from all layers of social and political classes. Firishta's intent in recounting the many people of Gujarat is to make a usable history for good and bad governance. He assesses the actions of Mahmud I, distinguishing between those acts geared toward public good and those where Mahmud I engaged in warfare to the detriment of his people. The history of another region told by Firishta, Kashmir, gives us another opportunity to think about the relationship between just and unjust rule, rule that allows a people to prosper versus rule that causes pain and suffering among the people. In telling the history of Sultan Sikander of Kashmir in the early fifteenth century, Firishta describes the appointment of a newly converted Brahmin, Siabut, as Sikander's chief minister. Siabut launched a campaign of conversion or expulsion against the Hindus of Kashmir. Firishta writes that this caused immense pain for the community and many people left Kashmir, while many Hindus "for fear of the Minister and terror of the Sultan pretended to be Muslim."[102] After Sikander's death, in 1413, his young son 'Ali Shah comes to the throne, but the real power was still fully held by Siabut. Siabut continues his campaign of terror against "the Brahmins, of whom he was a member, who were told to become Muslim or be killed. In a short while, none were left in Kashmir."[103] After the death of Siabut and the removal of 'Ali Shah from power, the younger son of Sikander, Shahi Khan, becomes the ruler of Kashmir and takes the title of Zainul 'Abidin.

'Abidin was a different ruler than his father. Firishta contrasts the just practices of 'Abidin from his father and brother. 'Abidin was fluent in Persian, Hindi, and "Tibeti," and commissioned a translation of the *Mahabharata* into Persian and a history of Kashmir in Sanskrit, the *Rajatarangani*—a text consulted by Firishta for his history.[104] 'Abidin recalled back to Kashmir all those Brahmins who had fled the polity during the time of Sikander and gave them estates and freedom to practice their faith. He abolished the special tax on non-Muslims, and cow slaughter.[105] Those who had converted to Islam during Sikander's time, Firishta writes, returned to their original faith and faced no consequence from the Muslim religious clerics.

Firishta is unhesitatingly of the view that 'Abidin was a model ruler. He admires 'Abidin's appreciation for music and history and his patronage of the arts. Firishta asserts that 'Abidin had a firm commitment to justice. His policy of allowing non-Muslims freedom to practice their faith without compulsion is a necessary condition of rule for Firishta. Firishta anoints 'Abidin as a near-Solomonic figure, for correcting the wrongs of his father, for bringing justice to Kashmir. He shows that the populace that had fled, or was expelled, from Kashmir is able to return back to their homes and faiths and flourish under the just rule of 'Abidin.

It is the world of the Deccan itself that Firishta is able to describe in the greatest depth and with the most detail. Firishta had entered the service of Ibrahim 'Adil Shah II in 1589.[106] It was around 1593 that Firishta was given the commission to write in a single volume the history of all the countries of Hindustan.[107] Firishta narrates, at different places, how he traversed the Deccan to gather materials for his history. From the library of Nizam Shah in Ahmadnagar, he gathered the genealogy of Murtaza Nizam Shah I (r. 1565–1587).[108] From the library in Burhanpur, he found the history of Malik Raja Faruqi of Khandesh.[109] As a historian, Firishta is eager to describe the scholars with whom he crossed paths, like Khwaja 'Alauddin Mahmud Shirazi, whose acclaim as a scholar was so great that 'Ali Adil Shah had invited him to Hindustan, and his library and generosity Firishta acknowledges to his readers.[110]

Yet Firishta was also serving the 'Adil Shahi as a diplomat, and his description of the histories of various elite factions and power struggles in the Deccan is especially evocative in its details. Firishta describes a world with a diverse set of peoples vying for power and place. The Deccan elite were both Hindu and Muslim, they spoke and wrote in Dakhani, they came from around the ocean region and included the Persian elite, the Turkic elite, and the African elite. These various ruling elites were installed across the different polities of the Deccan including, before its fall, Vijayanagar.[111] The Mughal military forces and the Portuguese naval forces were also a constant presence. In Firishta's account of the world of the Deccan, we get snapshots of many parts of society: the elites who organized palace life, and the farmers and merchants who made up a lively city. The vibrant world of the Deccan was a place of diverse people, from skilled farmers attuned to the seasons and crop yields, to scholars and artists and elites contesting for power, to women caregivers, mothers, and queens. The Deccan region of Hindustan in Firishta's history comes to life in the stories of merchants and workers, animals and plants, and temples and mosques.

The relatively short section on the Qutb Shahi of Telangana demonstrates Firishta's eye for seeking out the stories of the peoples of Hindustan. He asserts that he composed these histories not from previously written histories, but from oral histories that he himself documented. Quli Qutb Shah came to power in 1512. He began his career as a teacher of mathematics and letter writer in the palace in Golkonda. As part of his job, he read petitions from unfortunate people who begged for relief from the rise of banditry in various areas of Telangana. He petitioned Muhammad Shah, the Bahmani sultan, to give him the job of responding to those petitions and restoring law in those districts. Once he was appointed, he hired a band of militia who intimately knew the geography and landscape to help him rid the districts of robbers and bandits. After his success, he was given the title "Master of the Sword and the Pen."[112]

The Qutb Shahi were, by and large, good rulers of Telangana, according to Firishta. Quli Qutb Shah was conciliatory toward the other Deccan rulers. He ruled his populace with compassion. He was assassinated in 1523 at the behest of his son, Jamshid, who was eager to become a king. Jamshid Qutb Shah was a tyrannical ruler, who, in his seven years, ruled with a short temper—he ordered people killed or imprisoned at the slightest affront.[113] His successor, Ibrahim, restored order in Telangana such that the dense forested parts of the country, previously dangerous for travelers and merchants, became so safe that a merchant could travel alone with his merchandise through them whether in day or night.[114]

In 1608, during the reign of Ibrahim's successor, Muhammad Quli Qutb Shah, a particular massacre of foreign merchants occurred in Baghnagar (Hyderabad). Firishta calls this episode the worst event to happen during the Qutb Shahi reign in Golkonda. The merchants, Firishta describes, were passing through the city at night and came across a palace that belonged to the king. It was only sporadically used and was locked and empty at this time. They broke the lock and entered the building in order to rest, prepare a meal, and eat. The royal guards, hearing of this, came and tried to evict the merchants. The merchants refused to budge and locked themselves inside the palace. The next morning the guards informed the king that his property had been seized by these merchants. The king was furious and told the guards to forcibly evict the merchants. The people of the city, whom Firishta notes just needed an excuse to turn violent, attacked the merchants with swords, killing many and destroying their belongings. When the king heard of this act, he was even more enraged. He was forced to send royal troops to subdue the populace. The people of Baghnagar, Firishta noted, killed nearly a hundred foreigners in the riots that followed.[115] Firishta praises Muhammad Quli Qutb Shah for maintaining law and order despite an unruly populace and for keeping peace with his brothers such that his kingdom was not riven by rival warfare.

Writing a history of Hindustan for Firishta meant writing a history of the many people of Hindustan. It also meant documenting the many encroaching threats that were beginning to disrupt the people of Hindustan. And no threat appears greater in his *Tarikh* than what he described as the war-mongering Europeans, who took territories and resources and fought among themselves in the Indian Ocean region, all the while acting cordial at the courts of the kings of Hindustan. According to Firishta, they put up a facade in the courts of Hindustan before the king, of cordial deference to political power and trade relationships. But these performances of European alliance before the king hid their true intent.

Firishta ends his comprehensive history of Hindustan where the Portuguese and English encounters had begun—in Malabar. His last section deals with Malabar, where, he writes, sea trade had always brought Jews and Christians to Hindustan. The raja of Malabar, Samari, meets a group of traders who were returning from visiting Adam's footprint in Sarandip and were shipwrecked in Kodungallur. Samari is intrigued by their message about equality. When they mention the Prophet's miracle of splitting the moon, he asks his own court's historians to check their records for any sightings of such an event. The historians come back with a positive answer, and Samari converts to Islam. Firishta details a few different accounts concerning whether Samari leaves Malabar to visit Mecca but concludes that the more important thing is that Muslims were allowed to build mosques and houses and to flourish in Malabar.[116] The Jews and Christians were jealous of the accommodations allowed to the Muslims, Firishta writes, but they remained silent and were helpless because the Brahmin rulers were supportive of the Muslim presence. Until 1495, everyone enjoyed peaceful relations, but then the sultans of

the Deccan became weak and allowed the ruler of Portugal to build fortifications on the shorelines of Malabar.[117]

Firishta bemoans the arrival of the *farang* (meaning the Europeans);
the wars that followed, in which the Deccan sultans were unable to come
to the aid of the Malabari kings; and the creation of Portuguese enclaves
along the coastlines. The ruler of Malabar repeatedly asked for help from
Muslim rulers in Hindustan. After stating that his ancestral home was
under attack, the king pleaded that what was most upsetting was that
the *farang* were harming the Muslims, and even though he was not a
Muslim, he had always supported them. He appealed that he was too
weak to resist the Portuguese alone, for they had wealth and troops far
exceeding his. He asked that the kings of Hindustan, and those of Muslim
countries elsewhere, come to his aid and repel the Europeans.

Firishta writes that the rulers of Cairo, Gujarat, and Bahman sent
ships and troops, and the Muslims won some skirmishes. By 1556, Firishta
describes that the "fear-inducing" Europeans had taken the ports of
Hormuz, Muscat, Sumatra, Malwa, Mangalore, and Bengal, all the way
to the frontier of China. Unlike the rulers of other parts of Hindustan,
Akbar did nothing, Firishta notes, but watch in silence. For Firishta, Mughal inaction was a severe setback for the people of Hindustan against
the Europeans. By the time of Jahangir, in 1610, the English *farang* had
been allowed to settle in Surat. The English and the Portuguese were now
living in Surat, as one of the peoples inhabiting Hindustan. Firishta describes that he is aware that the English are the enemies of the Portuguese and observe a different sect of Christianity, but though they fight
each other everywhere else, when in presence of Jahangir, they express
generosity toward each other.[118]

The peopling of Hindustan, according to Firishta, did not rest on the
difference of faith between Muslims and non-Muslims. His Hindustan
has no empty quarters or pockets of wonder and terror. Only intermit-
tently does he provide some sense of the marvels of the place: He says
there are magicians in Karnatak who eat the ashes of the dead in order
to cast spells, or he describes the story of a dog with such immense loyalty to his owner that when he died they built a tomb on his grave that
lasts to the present, or he tells the story of 'Abidin, who got so ill that all

hope was lost until a yogi came and offered to swap the illness to his own body and, in doing so, cured the ruler. Firishta, ever interested in medical marvels, considers the probability of disease being taken from one host to another. Yet, these are only a few instances in a massive corpus of text wherein the people of Hindustan are defined not by the marvelous, or solely by the alien nature of "customary" practices, but by the ordinary.

6

A HISTORY FOR HINDUSTAN

WHAT WAS THE AFTERLIFE OF FIRISHTA'S *TARIKH*? As I have argued throughout this book, Firishta's history was instrumental to a wide-ranging colonial project of history writing, as well as the creation of a European philosophy of history. However, Firishta's influence on the historiography of Hindustan is itself a significant history to uncover and understand. Just as Firishta had before him an intellectual geography to wander through, he acquired a prominent stature in later historiography, and his *Tarikh* became a model for synthetic histories of Hindustan, as well as source material for the many Persian and Urdu histories that emerged in the eighteenth and nineteenth centuries. Thus, we must begin to trace the many afterlives of Firishta's text by starting with its circulation, citation, and influence in Persian, and later Urdu, historiography.

It is worthwhile to briefly consider this output and recognize Firishta's importance and significance prior to his text being taken up by Alexander Dow and the British East India Company (BEIC). For example, Sujan Rai Bhandari's *Khulasat-ut-Tawarikh* is a synthetic or general history of Hindustan written around 1695. Bhandari's history is situated in Delhi. In this history, one sees a glimpse of the intellectual reach of Firishta's Hindustan. Bhandari begins by quoting the most prominent histories of Hindustan—the first is the "oldest history," the *Mahabharata*.[1] From there, Bhandari lists the *Ramayana*, the *Yogavasishta*, the

Singhasan-Battisi, the *Padmavat,* the *Rajabali,* and the *Rajatarangani,* all tales, epics, and histories of Hindustan, which he noted were translated into Persian or Hindi. Bhandari lists these before the Persian histories of 'Unsari, Barani, and the Mughal historians.[2] Next, Bhandari takes his cue from Firishta's last chapter, and opens his work with a long exegesis on the favorable qualities and characteristics of the land of Hindustan as a paradise, praising the physical beauty of its territories, its cities, villages, its fortifications and monuments, its mosques, and temples, its gardens and fields, its rivers and mountains:

> Every other country has a population less than [Hindustan]; in Hindustan the roads have bridges over rivers and streams; every river has boats; every [mile] is a watchtower, and ample accommodations for travelers where foodstuff, medicines, amenities are available to them. Every road is lined with fruit-bearing trees on both sides. There are sweet-water wells, lakes. The merchants, and sellers, walk in the shadow of trees, eating these abundant and free delicacies, with their goods, their women and their children, free of any fear of thieves or robbers. In the east of Hindustan is Bengal, in the south, Deccan, in the west, Thatta, and in the north, sky-kissing mountain.[3]

Bhandari goes on to describe the monsoons, the rains, the mangoes, the grapes, the sugarcane, the spinach, the roses, the elephants, the peacock, before he begins his history of the rulers of Hindustan beginning with Yudhishtira and the Pandavas, citing both the *Mahabharata* and the Persian version of Faizi. He introduces the various cities and regions of Hindustan (from Bengal to Kabul, from Kashmir to Malwa), with ethnographic and sacral details for each—noting where prominent Sufi shrines and temples existed and giving details about the pilgrims. Firishta is not mentioned by Bhandari in his prologue, but is certainly a model, as both histories begin not with the history of Adam and the Muslim cosmology but with the history of Hindustan, its epics and its pre-Muslim polities.[4] His accounts of pre-Mughal polities, his clean style of prose, his conversational tone, and frequent interjections of his own testimony are redolent of Firishta's *Tarikh.*

Khulasat-ut-Tawarikh foregrounds the shift in the practice of history writing that emerged in the seventeenth century. Firishta was explicit in his desire to offer a new mode or style for writing history in the beginning of the seventeenth century. He gave his work a specific Hindustani temporality by beginning with the summary account from the *Mahabharata*. He also foregrounded space and place, by speaking first of the various cities and their origins. In his narrative, Firishta interspersed political and social details, referring to common people as much as speaking about the rulers. By the end of the seventeenth century, a history such as *Khulasat-ut-Tawarikh* was confidently presenting itself as a summation of previous histories of Hindustan in a particular form—a text that envelops all of the space of Hindustan with a Hindustani flavor.

In the eighteenth century, a number of synthetic histories were composed in Persian. These histories focused on Hindustan and aimed to provide a sense of the history of the various constitutive parts of the subcontinent. They did so in a brisk, readable voice. Firishta's *Tarikh* was both a key source text as well as a model in prosody. Many of these texts called themselves "selected histories" or "excerpted histories" in order to highlight their attempts at being synthetic overviews of Hindustan's past. Some notable histories that mention their reliance on or cite from Firishta are Jagjivan Das Gujarati's *Muntakhab-ut-Tawarikh* (1708 / 9), Mirza Muhammad's *Jannat al-Firdaus* (1714 / 5), Muhammad Hasim's *Muntakhab-ul-Lubab* (1731), Lal Ram's *Tuhfat-ul-Hind* (1735), Rustam 'Ali's *Tarikh-i Hind* (1740 / 41), and Ghulam Basit's *Tarikh-i Mamalik-i Hind* (1782). As noted, a fair number of these texts are explicitly of the "history of Hindustan" genre.

Several works also compiled selections from Firishta's history, such as *Muntakhab az Tawarikh-i Firishta* (1827) and Ratan Singh's *Sultan-at-Tawarikh* (1851). Similarly, works based on Firishta also begin to appear in Urdu: *Tarikh-i Hindustan* (1782), Maulvi Alam Ali's *Zubdat-ut-Tawarikh* (1852), Ratanlal Mast's *Umdat-ut-Tawarikh* (1852), and Munshi Totaram Shayan's *Tilism-i Hind* (1874) were the most notable examples. In addition, Firishta's own text was printed, in lithograph, in Bombay in 1831–1832, with reprints from one of the largest printing presses in British India, Nawal Kishore Press, in 1864–1865, and other editions from Cawnpore in 1874 and 1884. The colonial state also went searching for

Firishta's manuscripts. It was through the efforts of Henry Miers Elliot in the 1840s that Firishta's manuscripts from 1633 and 1639—now at Staatsbibliothek zu Berlin and the British Library—were acquired. The East India House in London has a 1648 recension, while the Royal Asiatic Society Museum has the 1734 manuscript, owned by James Briggs. Another dozen manuscripts of Firishta, copied in the eighteenth century, are housed in Cambridge, Oxford, Edinburgh, and Paris. Thus, Firishta's *Tarikh* has had a rich and varied afterlife in Hindustan and in Europe. It inspires new work and has itself been summarized and excerpted. It has moved from Persian into English, French, German, and Urdu. It has been a remarkable career for a text that, compared to Abu'l Fazl's *Akbarnama,* is often understood as being written at the margins of political power.

The influence of Firishta on Persian histories of the eighteenth century is but one part of Firishta's afterlife. It was also taken up by the British East India Company and organized their projects of history writing, in English as well as in Persian. Hence, to fully grasp the circuits through which Firishta's history flourished, it is important to examine the constitutive role played by the BEIC's engagement with Firishta's history. The BEIC's efforts to narrativize the Mughal and other polities in the subcontinent was the impetus for producing histories of particular regions, of particular families, and particular cities. Such histories of the later seventeenth and the eighteenth centuries, produced at the behest of colonial officials, or written by men who were under colonial service, were particular histories of that time—a key example is Ghulam Husain Khan Tabatabai's history, *Siyar al-Mutakherin* (1781).[5] Historians like Tabatabai were asked by the BEIC to produce memoirs doubling as histories in order to explain and describe the rule of Mughal governance in Bengal, or northern British India. Firishta's text was an important primary source for such histories, as was his writing style and the tone of his history.

The story of the afterlife of Firishta's history begins properly inside his own text. Firishta was already part of a rapidly colonizing world, with the Portuguese, Dutch, and British presence in the subcontinent, and the last sections of his text grappled with this contemporary dilemma of dealing with the European forces. The history of Europe and the history of Hindustan are linked in Firishta's own text. Certainly, by the late eighteenth century, as Firishta's text is taken by Alexander Dow to London, this intertwining of Europe and Hindustan becomes a central pivot in this history, in this historiography, and the story that this book has told so far.

Firishta had ended his history by detailing the arrival of the Europeans—the Portuguese, Germans, French, English—and the responses of the Deccan and Mughal polities. There hangs a sense of doom in his text, both impossible to miss and difficult to pinpoint. Almost 150 years later, Dow already had access to numerous histories of Bengal and of Delhi, even to Abu'l Fazl's *Akbarnama*. Yet what he sought was a synthetic history of Hindustan. His aim was to present such a primary document to his king as a comprehensive vision for what the British forces—mercantile and military—could acquire of the subcontinent. This was the history he claimed to have discovered in Firishta. The promise of British India was simultaneously the deliverance of Hindustan to the king. In rendering some portion of Firishta's *Tarikh* into English, Dow marked the appearance of the English crown as a subcontinental polity—the birth of British India.

As Dow stated in his dedication of his *History of Hindostan* to King George III (r. 1760–1820), it was the success of British military forces that "laid open the East to researches of the curious," and Dow wanted his text to further that agenda.[6] Yet, the real crux of why Dow produced his rendition comes up when he writes, "In the history of Hindustan, now offered to your Majesty, the people of Great-Britain may see a striking contrast of their own condition; and whilst they feel for human nature suffering under despotism, exult at the same time, in that happy liberty, which they enjoy."[7] The history of Hindustan that Dow presented was a history that demonstrated a Muslim despotism that subjugated the Hindus. It would make clear to the British public their moral and ethical superiority over the forms of governance at present in the subcontinent. While the project was announced, advertised, circulated, and applauded as a "History of Hindustan," it was instead meant to herald the creation of British India.

Dow elaborates in the preface to his *History*, "The history now given to the public, presents us with a striking picture of the deplorable condition of a people subjected to arbitrary sway; and of the instability of empire itself, when it is founded neither upon laws, nor upon the opinions and attachments of mankind. Hindostan, in every age, was an ample field for private ambition, and for public tyranny."[8] In Dow's version of Firishta, Hindustan was less a geography to be explored or conquered and more a system of oppressive governance to be combatted and replaced. Markedly, it was not Firishta's text that would be the demonstration of this argued reality; it would be Dow's own essays appended to his rendition of Firishta's text. Dow would write three dissertations—one for his 1768 edition and two for his 1772 edition. These paratextual works would acquire immediate significance and would be widely cited. The essays made clear to the people of Great Britain how they were to read the history that they had purchased. It was the history of a ruin—a monument to a backward civilization that now faced a long operation of liberation and progress.

In his preface, Dow was explicit that there was less value in the quality of the history being presented, and more in the insights that he was offering as a soldier-scribe. In Dow's assessment, Firishta's history was an amalgamation or a synopsis of other histories—in other words, a derivative work. He writes, "The history of Casim Firishta being an abridgment of a variety of authors, who wrote distinct accounts of the different reigns of the Mahommedan Emperors of Hindostan, he, with a view to comprehend in a small compass, very material transaction, has crowded the events too much together, without interpreting them with those reflections which give spirit and elegance to works of this kind."[9] Dow argued for the utility and importance of the work for the purposes unique to the British crown and publics, while deliberately denying any inherent value in the work itself, or in Firishta's role as a historian. Following Dow, such notions of "derivations" would become ingrained in the historiographical assessment of Persian and Urdu histories of the early modern and modern periods. Almost all of the histories based on Firishta, noted above, that would appear in the eighteenth and nineteenth centuries are cataloged as derivative works in European libraries.

The claim for derivation also operated as proof of Dow's argument about Muslim despotism—and Hindustan as a land standing still under oppression. It was impossible to imagine that an "original" work could appear in such a place, let alone be authored by Muslims. Hence, the particular importance of Firishta's *Tarikh* to Dow's project was also tied to its so-called derivative nature. Once Dow had rejected any "spirit" to this work, the *Tarikh* was a compendium of historical facts and events, assembled by space and time, that could be taken and assessed by the soldier-scribe as raw materials for the invention of British India's past as a despotic Hindustan. Firishta's *Tarikh* enters Europe as a dissected, derivative text, carrying with it general and theoretical statements on the nature and character of the people and governance of the subcontinent. It was in that moment, in the late eighteenth century, that the projects of how to disassemble a historical text and how to govern a colonized subject were first unified. They would remain so, and a central pillar of colonial governance, throughout the British East India Company's (BEIC) rule, until 1857.

In what follows, I discuss the ways in which the three primary renderings of Firishta by BEIC soldier-scribes—those by Dow, Jonathan Scott, and John Briggs—treated the *Tarikh*. In their individual projects, as in the project of history writing under the BEIC in the late eighteenth century in general, Firishta was used as a structure onto which was grafted the project of forgetting Hindustan and creating British India. In the early nineteenth century, taking Firishta as a foundation, another generation of BEIC authors enacted a regime of amassments that collected the texts mentioned by Firishta, those they deemed to be derivative of his history, and other such materials for a history of "Mohammadan India." Lastly, I turn to the ways in which Hindustani intellectuals responded in the late nineteenth century to this archive and history by composing their own histories in Persian and Urdu and for whom Firishta emerged as key source material for new synthetic histories.

The project of writing a history of Hindustan in the eighteenth and nineteenth centuries is the central concern of this chapter. This book began by thinking about what happened to Hindustan—a place, a concept, a poly-vocal history that was seemingly vanished. I argued that it was in the work of history writing that this concept of Hindustan could best be examined—how it emerged, who wrote it and how, what constituted the geography and peoples in it. Firishta's was the history and the text that I argued could be used to illustrate the history of Hindustan.

It is indeed an exceptional text in that it takes as its central object the dominion of Hindustan and not any particular polity, ideology, or genealogy. Along the way, I have made the case for why Firishta was such a history and how Firishta incorporated the histories and stories that came before him into a new monumental structure. Since my aim here is to understand the history of Hindustan as a concept, Firishta is the most apt textual source material for that task.

In this final chapter, Firishta is both an inspiration for and a haunting of the project of history writing. His history acts as a document of a near-impossible past for a set of Hindustani historians of the nineteenth century. They looked to it as a key source but also as a conceptual model, the clearest articulation for a project of history writing that aimed to recognize and reassess the medieval history of the subcontinent. The historians of the late nineteenth century were writing after the formal end of the BEIC and with British India now a "Crown Jewel" for the empress in London. They saw in Firishta a model of dealing with power, both remote and immediate. Yet, the concept of Hindustan that was so clear and central to Firishta was already a dim memory by the end of the nineteenth century. It is no simple task to engage with Firishta without dealing with the memory of Hindustan: What happened to Firishta's *Tarikh* is, in many ways, intertwined with what happened to Hindustan.

THE CONQUEST OF HINDUSTAN

Lieutenant Colonel Alexander Dow liked to tell stories. There is one particularly striking story that he told to guests at a dinner party at his house in London, in 1769. At the dinner with Dow were Alexander Carlyle, a reverend and the narrator of the night's events, the philosopher David Hume, and the historian and poet James Macpherson—among others. Carlyle had just met Dow, but he knew of Dow's reputation as someone who had "translated well *The History of Hindostan*, and wrote tolerably well the *Tragedy of Zingis*."[10] Carlyle first describes Dow before narrating the story Dow told that night:

> Dow was a Scotch adventurer, who had been bred at the school
> of Dunbar, his father being in the Customs there, and had run
> away from his apprenticeship at Eyemouth, and found his way
> to the East Indies, where, having a turn for languages, which had
> been fostered by his education, he soon became such a master
> of the native tongue as to accelerate his perferment in the army,
> for he soon had the command of a regiment of sepoys. He was
> a sensible and knowing man, of very agreeable manners, and of
> a mild and gentle disposition.[11]

Carlyle is clearly marking Dow's competence in the "native tongue" as
the reason for his advancement in the BEIC's territorial and knowledge-
capturing campaigns.[12] Carlyle also notes Dow's "mild and gentle"
disposition—another way in which the intellectual classes of Britain ignored the violence of the BEIC's soldiers in the subcontinent. At that
moment, the company was expanding out of Bengal and toward Delhi,
which was ruled by the Maratha, while the Mughal king, Shah Alam II
(r. 1760–1806), was in exile at Allahabad, under company protection.
Carlyle describes Dow's story:

> As he was telling us that night, that, when he had the charge of
> the Great Mogul, with two regiments under his command, at
> Delhi, he was tempted to dethrone the monarch, and mount the
> throne in his stead, which he said he could easily have done:—
> when I asked him what prevented him from yielding to the
> temptation, he gave me this memorable answer, that it was re-
> flecting on what his old school fellows at Dunbar would think
> of him for being guilty of such an action.[13]

Dow's fabrication, of commanding Delhi in 1769 and of holding the very
emperor in his hands, such that he could conceivably become the emperor of Hindustan, ought to be seen as more than dinner table brag-
gadocio. Dow was keen to link himself, and his *History of Hindostan,* to
the body and polity of Mughal rulers. The title page of his 1768 rendition claimed to be "Translated from the Persian of Mahummud Casim

Ferishta of Delhi." The frontispiece of the edition was an engraving by Josiah Taylor, labeled "from an Original painting," of the Mughal king Shah Alam II. The caption read, "Shan [*sic*] allum the present Emperor of Hindostan."[14] In the second volume, Shah Alam II was replaced on the frontispiece by Jalaluddin Akbar as "Mahommed Akbar, Emperor of Hindostan; died A.D. 1604."[15]

There were two sets of displacements that Dow fabricated for his dinner companions. As the representative of the BEIC, he was interacting with Shah Alam II in Allahabad. Placing Shah Alam II at Delhi was Dow's first displacement. The second was moving Firishta hundreds of miles north and making of him a historian of Delhi, a city of great political significance to the British in 1769, rather than a historian from the Deccan, which was of little political value to the company. In these displacements, the cover title of Dow's *History* made explicit the nature of its significance and relevance to the readers: that this history concerned the Mughal emperor as the ruler of Hindustan and Delhi as the seat of Mughal power over Hindustan. The rendition of Dow aimed to center Firishta's *Tarikh* as a document relevant to the particular colonial needs of the Crown and the BEIC at that moment. Dow's misrepresentation—whether in the anecdote regarding his literal power over the emperor's life, and consequently his control over Hindustan, or in his claim to represent himself as the explicator of Hindustan's history—is instructive for understanding how he represented his acquisition and rendition of Firishta's *Tarikh*.

Dow's fabrication about having the Mughal emperor in his hands also calls into question his acquisition narrative of Firishta's history. In the first volume of his *History of Hindostan,* Dow writes how he came to learn about, and acquire, Firishta's history: "To translate some piece of history, was, by his teachers, recommended to him as a proper exercise in the Persian. The works of Mahummud Casim Firishta of Delhi, who flourished in the reign of Jehangire, about the beginning of the seventeenth century, was *put into his hands* for that purpose."[16] Once Dow has identified the history, he seeks to procure further histories directly from the Mughal emperor. So, he provides in his preface, the letter he wrote, in Persian, to the Mughal king, asking for additional histories of Hindustan to be provided to him, but, Dow notes with sorrow, that he had to leave Calcutta before he was able to get a reply.

In his 1772 continuation of *The History of Hindostan,* Dow had acquired more histories from which he "draws his information" and notes specifically that the originals are, at this moment, *in his hands.*"[17] There is a running motif in Dow—from the emperor's life being held in his hands, to the manuscript of Firishta being placed in his hands, to the further histories of Hindustan that he has in his hands. The fantastic link offered between the history of Hindustan and the emperor in colonial hands, allowed colonizers to hold Hindustan in their hands. A version of this motif of history being literally placed in the hands of the European historian is also visualized in James Rennell's cartouche for his 1782 "Map of Hindoostan," where a pundit, mid-supplication, presents an envelope labeled "Shashtar" (crudely, "law") to the personification of Britain. The same fantasy that prompted Carlyle to acknowledge the "mild and gentle" nature of Dow was also the willfully romantic self-imagination where the violent military colonization of Hindustan was actually the subservient colonized offering themselves, and their knowledges, to the bare hands of the colonizer.

A key to Dow's rendition of Firishta is his commitment that the chief task of his history is to serve the British reading public, not simply as a fount of information about the colony but to inform a conviction regarding their moral superiority. In 1768, the same year that he published his *History of Hindostan,* Dow also published a rendition of Shaikh 'Inayatallah Kanbu's romance *Bahar-i Danish* (Springtime of wisdom) from 1651, which he introduced as being of service to the women of Britain by marking out the deprivations women suffer under Muslim rule:

> The severity with which our author treats the fair sex stands in need of an apology. The British ladies will, no doubt, see with pleasure, how superior their own virtue is to that of the fair sex in India, though the latter are immured within harams and guarded by the watchful eyes of eunuchs. There is a strange perversity in human nature: it rises up in arms against all restraint;

and perhaps the best guardian of the chastity of wives is un-
bounded confidence from the husbands.[18]

Where the audience for the *History of Hindostan* was the king and the
political elite who could see the ways in which Muslim despotism had
taken hold over Hindustan, the audience here is the "fair sex" that can
witness the "perversity" of Muslim households. Prefiguring William
Jones's "Hindu Wife," Dow is keen to pinpoint the domestic incarcera-
tion of Indian women by the despotic Muslim, which results in their
sexual deviance. Dow contrasts this with British women, who enjoy the
confidence of their husbands and, as a result, remain chaste. Dow demonstrates the deviance of Indian women using the titillating stories narrated
in the romance between the prince Jahandar Shah and princess Bahravar
Banu. In all of his works, Dow insists on the necessity of the British colonial effort to civilize and govern the subcontinent and argues for the creation of British India by highlighting the despotism of Muslim rulers.

Dow returned to Bengal in 1769. In 1772, he published his next install-
ment of *The History of Hindostan,* with one of his appendices focused
on his "plan for restoring that Kingdom to its former Prosperity and
Splendor." What had robbed that kingdom of its splendor? In March 1771
it was reported in *The Gentleman's Magazine* that "two million" had perished from widespread famine and pestilence as a consequence of the
British East India Company's revenue schema.[19] The magazine ruefully
noted that "the manufacturers are all at a stand for want of workmen;
and it is impossible for proper investments to be made to Europe for two
or three years to come."[20] In 1772, Dow argued that property reform was
key to pivoting away from the economic crisis facing the BEIC. His appendix was meant to provide a way in which the BEIC's governance of
Bengal could be streamlined and the farmers become taxable subjects.
Dow's appendix was a massive success in shaping BEIC policies.[21] He became a protegé of William Murray, the first earl of Mansfield, who was
the lord chief justice of England. By 1775, Dow was promoted to the rank
of lieutenant colonel and given the task of being the commissary
general—with control over all military expenditures. In the midst of the
wars and famine in Bengal, Dow's *History* was, itself, an instrument of
domination.

It is fruitful to compare Dow's "bringing" of Firishta to London with another soldier-scribe's similar attempt to bring Firishta to Paris. Jean Baptiste Joseph Gentil (1726–1799), who was employed in the Awadh state from 1752 until 1774, also was commissioning works of history and maps of Hindustan for the French king, Louis XVI. He himself produced a rendering of A'in-i Akbari, *Essai sur l'Indoustan, ou Empire Mogol, d'après l'Ayyn-Akbéri* (1769) and associated maps he had commissioned. He also presented to Louis XVI a simplified rendition of Firishta, *Abrégé historique des souverains de l'Indoustan ou Empire Mogol* (1772–1775), whose folio pages were accompanied with illustration made by the Awadhi artists.[22] These works, despite some attention to the maps and architectural drawings, failed to draw any audience or circulation.[23] They were markedly unadorned by the dissertations and essays Dow had appended to his rendition. Instead, their line art adornments relegated them to relative obscurity, even as Dow's rendition was quickly translated into French and German. Gentil's Firishta, silent in the European record, brings into stark relief the power of Dow's essays and appendices in making his *History* the foundational document that it became.

The appendices Dow wrote to *The History of Hindostan* were critical to the success of his books and his career. Ranajit Guha, in 1963, commented on their importance in his discussion of Dow, noting that, "We owe the beginnings of Indological studies to this body of literature which, with all its curious mixture of the erudite and the polemical, still must be recognized as being among the first intellectual attempts in modern times to explore the East. To explore the East was above all to study the nature of oriental despotism."[24] The essays of Dow, while appended physically and formally to Firishta's history, were also connected to that history at a granular level. The argument Dow put forth in his appendices over three volumes of his *The History of Hindostan* proceeded in a comprehensive manner to present the analytic lens as well the necessary conclusions that the reader should acquire before reading the rendered Firishta. This was Dow's case for *why* Firishta was needed as a text.

Take Dow's claim that Firishta's history was a mere abridgment of histories that had come before Firishta, and that it was a derivative work. The intellectual framework for that assessment was not Dow's full grasp of Persian histories written before Firishta, rather it was his conviction that, in the sphere of despotism, there was no possibility of fresh thought, of new perspectives, of a self-aware history. Firishta was derivate precisely because it was a text produced under Muslim despotic rule by a Muslim. It was a text heralded by an "imbecile" and "declining" empire whose inhabitants "permit themselves to be transferred from one tyrant to another, without murmuring."[25]

As a military commander, Dow was frank that the British project in the subcontinent was a militaristic and imperial one. Their rule over Bengal was "an absolute conquest," and he proclaimed that "the sword is our tenure."[26] Similarly, the history of Hindustan that Dow was presenting through Firishta was a history of conquest by the swords of Muslim invaders over the subcontinent. The key distinction between the Muslim rulers and the British was that, where the Muslim rulers were despotic, the British were wise and liberal. This was the reason that Firishta's text was an exemplar, for "Hindostan, in every age, was an ample field for private ambition, and for public tyranny. . . . An arbitrary government can inflict the most sudden miseries, so, when in the hands of good men, it can administer the most expeditious relief to the subject."[27]

That the despotically ruled Hindustan was a place of misery was just as certain to Dow as the truth that the good governance of the British could alleviate in "a few years . . . the misfortunes of half an age of tyranny."[28] The way to changing the condition of the Hindu subjects of Hindustan, was in changing the basic condition of despotism itself; as Dow put it, "All the lands in India are considered as the property of the King."[29] The British East India Company had already displaced the Mughal sovereign, but it now faced a governance problem of how to change the ruling infrastructure. Dow offered his solution in his appendix to *The History of Hindostan*. He argued that it was necessary for the company to introduce the rule of property ownership for the inhabitants of Bengal: "To give them property would bind them with stronger ties to our interest; and make them more our subjects; or, if the British nation prefers the name—more our slaves."[30] The former subjects of a despotic Muslim, Dow proposed, would easily become the new "slaves" of the British.

Dow's prefatory essays were intricately tied to the text he rendered from Firishta. To the first volume of his *History* in 1768, he appended a "dissertation concerning the customs, manners, language, religion and philosophy of the Hindoos." Dow noted that this essay was a response to J. Z. Holwell's 1765 work on the religion of the "Gentoos."[31] In doing so, Dow faithfully replicates Firishta's own opening to his *Tarikh*. Dow took the impetus to write this essay from Firishta's *Tarikh,* which also opens with a long section taken from the *Mahabharata*. In his essay, Dow provides a synopsis of Vedic thought from what he claims is a "general idea of the doctrine" gathered "through the medium of Persian language, and through the vulgar tongue of the Hindoos."[32] Dow assembles a curious amalgamation of named texts—such as "Bedang Shaster" or "Dirm Shaster"—alongside his conversations with "pandits," in order to buttress his account as an informed one.

There are two significant ways in which Dow's appendix overlaps with Firishta's opening chapter. Dow discusses a "digression" of how Faizi came to learn Sanskrit. Faizi's rendering of the *Mahabharata* opens Firishta's first chapter. Second, Dow concludes his survey of Vedic thought by addressing polytheism and its comparison to monotheism, much as Firishta had done. Dow asserts that Brahmanical polytheism was, in actuality, much like the monotheism that organized the Christian and Muslim cosmologies. Dow concludes that the many gods worshipped by the "more ignorant Hindoos" were merely allegorical and that "the unity of God was always a fundamental tenet of the uncorrupted faith of the more learned Brahmins."[33] Another parallel he draws, that "subaltern divinities do exist, in the same manner, that Christians believe in Angels," was also similar to Firishta.[34]

This first appendix of Dow was disentangled from his *History* soon after publication. Claude-François Bergier published a French translation in 1769. It was read and commented upon by Voltaire, and it continued to circulate into the nineteenth century, often with additional texts attached.[35] However, even as an orphaned text, it retained an intimate relation to the *History* from which it was taken. The insights Dow had established in his essay were dependent on his reading of Firishta, just as much as on his time as a military officer in Bengal.

The first volume of *The History of Hindostan* published by Dow in 1768 had three parts. The first part was an abridged version of Firishta's first chapter on the *Mahabharata*. Dow titled that section, "The History of Hindoos, before the First Invasion of Hindostan, by the Mahomedans." The second part was titled, "The History of the Empire of Ghizni," replacing Firishta's "Sultans of Lahore," and the third part was titled, "The History of the Empire of Delhi, from the Accession of Cuttub to the Throne, to the Invasion of Timur." Dow removed the histories of place that had organized Firishta and began his parts directly as genealogies of invaders. The second volume covered "The History of Hindostan from the Invasion of Tamerlane, to the Final Conquest of that Country, by Sultan Baber; Being a Period of One Hundred and Thirty Years," in part four and "The History of the Life of Humaioon, the Son of Baber" in part five. Part six covered the reign of the Mughal king Akbar. After that, Dow appended another section, titled "From Its Decline in the Reign of Mahummud Shaw down to the Present Times," which concluded the volume with the history of the Mughal Empire to his present.

What was a history of the constitutive places of Hindustan, in Firishta, would become a history of polities centered eventually on Delhi in Dow's rendition. Dow's rendering was not a form of translation, but rather a strategic excision and replacement of Firishta's content. This cutting apart and suturing of Firishta as a history of conquest allowed Dow to make clear the deep linkage between his colonizing aims and Firishta's work. A reader opening the second volume, in 1768, would have read an appendix titled "The Decline of the Mogul Empire." In 1772, the third volume would open with an appendix titled "A Dissertation on the Origin and Nature of Despotism in Hindostan." These late and declining Mughals were the exemplary Muslim despots. Dow described them as being born in the sunshine of a court, brought up in the bosom of luxury, and "shut up in the haram from infancy" under the care "of eunuchs, a race of men more effeminate than those whom they guard," such that there was no wonder that the princes of the East become "voluptuous and degenerate" in a few generations.[36]

In Dow's estimation, Hindustan's splintering into regional kingdoms was due to two factors: the first was that the "Hindoos, or the followers of the Brahmin faith, [though in] number far superior to the Mahommedans in Hindostan [and] mild, humane, obedient, and industrious, [are] of all nations on earth the most easily conquered and governed."[37] The second factor for the political fragmentation was not only the innate nature of Brahmin "effeminacy" and compliance. It was also the decline in the mettle of the Muslim rulers, and not the work of any "foreign arms."[38] Thus Dow was careful to keep the imperial aspirations of the BEIC out of his analysis. As that volume drew up to 1764, Dow remarked that this present state of Hindustan was such that "virtue had fled from the land; no principle of honor, patriotism, or loyalty, remained; great abilities produced nothing but great crimes."[39] This was the Hindustan, Dow argued, that was to be restored to its former glory by the British East India Company—purely as a selfless act of rescuing the dominated Brahmins from their despotic Muslim rulers. Thus, the first appendix of the third volume begins by defining and elaborating this true cause of the decline; that of Muslim despotism.

Dow's assertions would not have been able to rise to the level of canonical truth had they been unattached to this singular work of scholarship and argued intimacy with Mughal power. Firishta's text was the key to making Dow's assessment of Hindustan as a land bereft of virtue and of Mughals as effeminate rulers a well-considered fact (Robert Orme's own assessment of Hindustan as a land of effeminacy comes in 1782).[40] Dow begins his depiction of despotism from the land, which yielded abundant resources, and those resources were simply accumulated by the passive peoples of the land. If the nature of the land gave a passive character to the native Hindu inhabitants, Dow argued that the nature of Islam gave the conquering Muslim his violence and tyranny: "The seeds of despotism, which the nature of the climate and fertility of the soil of India, were, as has been observed, reared to perfect growth by the Mahommedan faith."[41] Where the Mughals were tyrannical, Dow found the Maratha state to be the only virtuous power in Hindustan: "When their armies carry destruction and death into the territories of Mahomedans, all is quiet, happy, and regular at home. No robbery is dreaded, no imposition or obstruction from the officers of government, no protection necessary but the shade.... This is no ideal picture of happiness. The Author of the Dissertation, who travelled lately into the country of Maharattors, avers, from experience, the truth of his observations."[42] To be perfectly clear, Dow was not condemning "Oriental" despotism but specifically "Muslim" despotism—which is why the textual history of Firishta, and his personal observations of the deposed Mughal ruler and the Maratha polity, were in intricate relationship with each other. For Dow, Firishta provided a deep historical diagnosis of the decline of Muslim power, while Dow's political experience provided ethnographic truths to understand the contemporary world in the subcontinent.

Dow appended his social and political diagnostics and a manifesto for future governance to his rendering of Firishta. In doing so, Dow also manufactured the formal project for writing British India—isolating the Muslim despot, segmenting Persian histories as source materials for the story of decay and conquest, and constructing the political intervention of the soldier-scribe in the conquest of knowledge about Hindustan. Dow's project resonated with Robert Orme and William Jones, who crystallized the notions introduced by Dow into social scientific disciplinary truths within the fields of history and philology. Orme followed Dow in 1782, with his *Historical Fragments of the Mogul Empire of the Morattoes, and of the English Concerns in Indostan, from the Year 1659,* creating a fuller historiographic picture of the effeminate and conquered peoples of Hindustan.

However, Firishta's *Tarikh* was not yet exhausted as a source for the colonial project. In fact, as shown above, Dow had barely scratched the surface of the text. Thus, rendering a more complete text of Firishta into English would become a major strain of work for BEIC soldier-scribes. The first to take up the project was Captain Jonathan Scott. Scott was appointed as Governor General Warren Hastings's personal tutor for Persian in 1783 and was one of the founding members of Jones's Asiatic Society of Bengal. In 1794, Scott published his own rendition as *Ferishta's History of Dekkan from the First Mahummedan Conquests,* with another volume comprising "The History of Bengal" to 1780. Where Dow had dedicated his work to the king, Scott dedicated his rendition to the directors of the BEIC, noting his was an "attempt to add to the publick stock of Hindoostan History."[43]

Scott, like Dow, extracts from Firishta one specific locale for his rendition. Dow had taken from Firishta the history of the Muslim conquest of Delhi, while Scott focuses on the parts of Firishta's text where the author was himself a witness to the events. Scott corrects Dow's deliberate error and calls Firishta a historian of the Deccan: "Ferishta, author of the history now offered to the public in an English dress, is one of the most esteemed writers of Hindoostan, and was of noble rank, and high in the office at the court of Ibrahim Adil Shaw, of Beejapore, one of the sultans of Dekkan."[44] Scott also added a veneer of historicism by declaring that his objective was to collate only "eyewitness" accounts of Hindustan's past.[45]

In essence, Scott's *Ferishta's History* is a gloss on Firishta's Deccan sections of his larger history. Scott provides copious footnotes on each page, addressing the ways in which Firishta narrates the history of the Deccan as well as the relevance it has for British governance. Hence, he constantly "updates" the information—substituting Firishta's place names with contemporary and current ones, adding geographic or historical materials from other sources to complement Firishta, and, most importantly, demonstrating the relevance of this history to the colonial project. Take the example where Scott writes about the treatment of prisoners of war. Scott footnotes the following sentence, "From that time to this, it had been the general custom in Dekkan to spare the lives of prisoners in war, and not to shed the blood of an enemy's unarmed subjects."[46] Scott's footnote makes the following gloss, "It might have been so when Ferishta wrote, but modern warriors have too often stained their victories with unnecessary slaughter, especially Tippoo Saheb; for which he has been punished by our arms."[47] Here Scott marks out the BEIC attempt to conquer Tipu Sultan's Mysore polity as justice for the sultan's claimed violence over Hindustan's civilians.

The next major rendition of Firishta into English comes thirty-plus years after Scott's. It was to be a central achievement of General John Briggs to render Firishta fully in English—combining the ways in which Dow had used the text as a base structure and the ways in which Scott updated the text with contemporary information. Briggs served in the BEIC and became one of several young soldier-scribes attached to the Resident of Pune, Mountstuart Elphinstone, who was later the author of the influential *The History of India*. Briggs published his *History of the Rise of the Mahomedan Power in India, Till the Year A.D. 1612. Translated from the Original Persian of Mahomed Kasim Ferishta* in four volumes in 1829. While praising Dow as "one of the earliest and most indefatigable of our Oriental scholars," Briggs calls attention to his own version for improving on Dow's lack of access to maps and the excerpted manner in which Dow chose to render Firishta.[48] Briggs would make the claim that his was a complete rendition that had the benefit of the colonial machinery of mapping and native services. He sees the text as one to be dissected, excerpted, added to, and fortified. He lauds his "secretary," Mir Khairat 'Ali Khan, whose labors in traveling and noting down inscriptions allowed Briggs to present his Firishta text with material annotation.[49] Briggs's Firishta expands the ways in which Scott annotated the text. In his footnotes, Briggs performs the role of the philologist, the ethnographer, and the colonial administrator.

Briggs approaches Firishta's history, which covers "the extensive regions over which the historian passes," as a history of "tracing the movements of numerous armies of many different kingdoms, marching and countermarching over a region as extensive as Europe."[50] That is, he makes of Firishta's history a book of conquests that explains "Mohamedan Power" over the subcontinent. Briggs's formulation of Firishta's history as a conquest history re-territorializes the text in a different key—what had been a coherent space of the subcontinent is now the march of an army. Briggs, like Dow and Scott, is himself a military officer, engaged directly in the conquest of the subcontinent. His interpretation of Firishta is consistent with the history and effort of the BEIC's engagement with this text. He too sees Firishta as an organizing history for the medieval period—exemplifying the period of Muslim despotism.

The renditions of Dow and Scott and the manuscripts of Firishta gave material shape to the production of histories of the subcontinent. Dow and Scott were used directly as source materials by the likes of Edward Gibbon, Thomas Maurice, and James Mill for their synthetic histories. These historians were content to remain ignorant of any direct knowledge of the colony of British India and did not feel the need to learn "Oriental" languages either. These renditions, from Persian into English, served as ample raw materials from which to construct their histories. Thomas Maurice's 1795 *The History of Hindostan* was one of the earliest such synthetic histories of Asia, which attempted to cover the "history of Hindostan as the history of Asia itself, and of the human race in their infant state."[51] More famous, for reasons of both acclaim and circulation, was James Mill's 1817 *The History of British India*. In these British synthetic histories, the history of the subcontinent was temporally divided into the ancient Hindu period, the medieval Muslim period, and contemporary liberal British rule. The appendices and glosses of Dow and Scott were critical in fulfilling this act of historical suturing.

The soldier-scribes of British India were not content with providing sources for the metropolitan historians. They were also quick to write synthetic histories of their own. An early adapter was Major David Price, who was present at the fall of Srirangapatna and the killing of Tipu Sultan, in 1799. Price was the "prize agent" after the BEIC's capture of Tipu Sultan's palace. He was responsible for cataloging and distributing Tipu Sultan's possessions—including the libraries that the sultan had inherited and acquired from the Deccan. Price himself acquired a "collection" of manuscripts and objects from his war campaigns. He used his collection to begin writing a general history. In 1821, he published a three-volume history, *Chronological Retrospect, or Memoirs of the Principal Events of Mahommedan History*, which attempted to produce a timeline of events from the birth of the Prophet Muhammad to Emperor Akbar, arranged according to the Islamic calendar.[52] His history also made the critical claim of adding to, and improving, Firishta's history—with a range of later Persian histories as well as Price's own personal experience in the colony. After his death in 1835, his estate, consisting of nearly a hundred Persian manuscripts, among them a folio of Firishta, went to the Royal Asiatic Society in London.[53]

However, the most significant, and influential, of the soldier-scribe histories, was undoubtedly Governor Mountstuart Elphinstone's *The History of India: The Hindu and Mahometan Periods*, published in 1841. Elphinstone (1779–1859), who rose through the military ranks to end his career in India as the governor of the Bombay Presidency, was one of the founders of the Royal Geographic Society in London. Elphinstone, like Price, would marshal his personal experience as the crucible for narrating the subcontinental past to imperial audiences. Elphinstone framed his *History* as a corrective to James Mill's popular history, which was written without immediate and personal knowledge of British India.

His history would indeed displace Mill and become a valorized text for Victorian England.[54] Despite his critique of Mill, Elphinstone was committed to the colonial understanding of cleaving subcontinental history into Hindu antiquity and the Muslim medieval periods. He popularized the Muslim medieval with the new appellation "Mohammadan India" in order to distinguish it as the immediate precursor of "British India." It was due to Elphinstone that Firishta emerged as the principal historian for Mohammadan India. Like Briggs, who was under his command, Elphinstone relied heavily on Firishta. Elphinstone called Firishta his "principal dependence" for writing his *History,* and a historian "much superior to most of his class in Asia."[55] Elphinstone not only set the mark for Elliot's effort at cataloging and excerpting, his bifurcated Indian history was translated into Marathi and Gujarati in 1862 and into Urdu in 1866. It became one of the most important single-volume British histories of India.

The work of writing history for the colonial empire, initiated by Dow, had focused on providing, in English, primary source documents for the history of Hindustan. Those primary sources were appended with an analytic rubric that determined its reception and the modes within which it would circulate. Scott and Briggs were some of the key contributors in that project. Colonial educational institutions, such as Fort William College and the Asiatic Society of Bengal, were institutional bulwarks and repositories for such acquisition and translation projects, such as those by Francis Gladwin or Charles Stewart. The BEIC's conquest of the Marathas in Delhi in 1801, of the Talpurs in Thatta in 1843, and of the Sikhs in Lahore in 1849, while being important markers in the history of nineteenth-century colonial expansion, were also key moments in colonial historiography. Each of these conquests furnished new archives and collections for the soldier-scribes to amass. The leader for much of this project of amassment was Henry Miers Elliot, who worked in the Foreign Office—Elliot was the chief negotiating agent in Lahore for the BEIC, for instance.

Elliot's project to compile "A Complete History of Mohammadan India" was also organized around Firishta's history. He noted that Firishta was the most widely circulated work of history in British India, and maybe the most circulated work, period: "The history of Ferishta is universally known in India—at least by name, and there are few large towns without a copy. If we add to these works labelled 'Naurasnāma' and 'Tārikh-i-Ibrāhīmī' which few of the present ignorant generation know to be same as Ferishta's history, we shall find that it is probably more common than any secular work of equal size in this country."[56] Elliot launched an amassment project for collecting manuscripts in Persian and Hindustani of the Muslim medieval. In his 1849 call to acquire manuscripts, published as *Kitab-i Misbah at-Talibin,* Elliot listed 220 titles that he deemed necessary and added instructions for other titles to be suggested.[57] This call was sent to the scholars of Persian in Lahore, Delhi, Thatta, Hyderabad, and Calcutta. Dow, Scott, Price, Briggs, and Elphinstone had all acquired manuscripts, but Elliot launched a subcontinent-wide regime of colonial amassments. For this effort he recruited entire classes of colonial military and salaried bureaucracy as collectors, catalogers, and translators. He also expanded his efforts to incorporate in a systematic fashion Hindustani scholars and secretaries. It was through Elliot's efforts that the work of philology gained popularity in nineteenth-century Delhi. This colonial rendition and amassment effort erupted into a furor after the colonial suppression of the 1857 revolt.

HISTORY AFTER DESTRUCTION

On September 22, 1857, some ninety years after Dow enthralled his dinner companions with a story about holding the life of the Mughal emperor in Delhi in his hand, Captain William Hodson did hold the life of Emperor Bahadur Shah Zafar (1775–1862) in his hands. Hodson was part of General Wilson's British troops who had just recaptured Delhi from sepoy revolutionaries. The uprising against the British East India Company had started on May 10, 1857, and was led by sepoys in the company's army. At the moment of the uprising, the British were convinced that the Mughal emperor and his family were the instigators. Thus, as soon as Delhi, the seat of Mughal power, was recaptured, the British were keen to arrest or kill the Mughal family. Hodson shot and killed two of the emperor's sons, Mirza Mughal and Mirza Khizr Sultan, and a grandson, Mirza Abu Bakr. A total of thirty Mughal princes were executed by the British. The last Mughal emperor was put on trial and sentenced to death. He was then exiled to Rangoon, where he died in 1862.[58]

The idea of Hindustan as a polity had already become a dim memory by the time the sepoys had risen up against their colonizing officers in 1857. The literal killing of the future heirs to the Mughal throne enacted a grim foreclosure of any possible future for it. The period after 1857 is labeled "Direct Rule" or "The Raj," by scholars. Queen Victoria took on the title of the "Empress of India." The BEIC was discarded, and the role of managing and civilizing the subcontinent was taken up by the British Parliament. It is certainly appropriate to recognize the systems of rendition and amassment that ended the idea of Hindustan and established "British India," but it is essential to underscore that the British conquest of Hindustan was done by shedding Hindustani blood. When the Hindustani in Delhi—those who had lived through and experienced the British razing of Delhi—turned to the task of history writing, they wrote from this trauma. As generations of historians have now documented, during the raj, the dynamic between colonial power and knowledge about the colony underwent a shift toward new forms of surveillance and control—with the emergence of the investigative, the enumerative, the cartographic, the museological, and the historiographic strategies of colonial governance and hegemony.[59] By the end of the nineteenth century, the Hindustani historians of the medieval period would conform to the new formal requirements of the social sciences—and many did so with great conviction—but writing the history of Hindustan as a colonized subject would not be so easy to navigate.

What is the past that remains visible after the annihilation of one's present? The British had brought the Mughal polity to an end, after having ended nearly a dozen other polities over the course of the previous one hundred years. The present—as well as the immediate past— gave testimony to colonial domination, and to the annihilation of whatever systems of world-making or knowledge formation that had come before the colonial powers.[60] The past that constituted Hindustan was— assuredly and forever—closed to any project of rehabilitation. To the British researchers, the medieval period became a linguistic or archaeological specialization, a project of antiquarian meaning-making, devoid of any life. They turned to it, as philologists or historians, in order to dissect and autopsy. Yet, what was this period to the Hindustani researcher? Was it a temporal subjunctive? An almost limitless archive of past events, persons, and institutions that could be re-rendered as romance, nostalgia, or utopia? This is the key concern in exploring the histories produced in the nineteenth century on Hindustan. How are we to understand this massive production?

In the second half of this chapter, I turn my focus to the Muslim intellectuals who, largely in the wake of 1857, undertook intellectual projects concerning the history of Hindustan. They self-consciously understood their project to be a continuation of Firishta and the Persian histories of the subcontinent, while also responding to the colonial sciences of history and philology. This was a generation of scholars who began to write histories of Muslims, of Islam, and of Hindustan in Urdu and in Arabic; who wrote critical introductions to Persian historical works; who published scholarly and popular histories; and who took on the intellectual task of grappling with the past and present of colonial knowledge machinery.

Beginning with Sayyid Ahmad Khan, there were a host of historians, storytellers, religious scholars, journalists, and anti-colonial activists: Abdul Halim Hali, Shibli Nu'mani, 'Abdul Halim Sharar, Muhammad Hussain Azad, Syed Hashmi Faridabadi, Hasrat Mohani, and Syed Sulaiman Nadvi, to mention the most prominent.[61] These intellectuals did not share the same understanding of the past or diagnose their colonial condition along similar lines. Some turned toward a history of Muslim origins to bypass the medieval period entirely and link the subcontinent to Arabia and early Islam, others turned to historical romances, others to histories of religious orders as a way of reconceptualizing the colonized subjects' relationship to the subcontinent.

I will bookend my analysis with the work of two of these well-known figures—Sayyid Ahmad Khan (1817–1898), who wrote his works on history before 1857, and Muhammad Zaka'ullah (1832–1910), who wrote his after 1857. I read Sayyid Ahmad's work in conversation with the philological projects of colonial officers such as Briggs (or James Todd), and that of Zaka'ullah as a response to the synthetic histories of Elphinstone. In 1897, Zaka'ullah produced a nine-volume, six-thousand-page-plus

Tarikh-i Hindustan that would certainly be one of the last works to bear the title of "History of Hindustan." I focus on Sayyid Ahmad and Zaka'ullah for two reasons, one historical and the other historiographic. The first reason is that these authors wrote some of the earliest responses to the colonial histories of the medieval period. The work they produced, and the community of intellectuals they inspired, shaped much of the intellectual horizon of twentieth-century anti-colonial and nationalist movements. The historiographic reason is that, in works of secondary scholarship, these histories written in Persian or Urdu have remained largely ignored, as disciplinary or as intellectual history. While the Bengali and Marathi intellectuals of the late nineteenth and early twentieth centuries are, rightfully, recognized for their contributions to the rise of disciplinary history in the subcontinent, such is not the case with historians writing in Persian or Urdu during the same period.

These histories have remained quarantined from the broad understandings of how the twentieth century was shaped by colonial knowledge systems.[62] They have been called derivative, mere translations from English or French; simply positivist, without a robust theory of history; written by amateur historians; and so on.[63] Yet, in looking closely at the historical production of Sayyid Ahmad and Zaka'ullah, one can see contrasting philosophies of history and the ways in which 1857 impacted these intellectuals. Their writings also clarify the continuing importance of Firishta, specifically in organizing the political thought of Hindustan in the nineteenth century.

Sayyid Ahmad Khan is perhaps most well known as the founder and intellectual forebear of the Muhammadan Anglo-Oriental College, later Aligarh Muslim University. Founded in 1875, it was the first institution for higher learning focused exclusively on Muslim men. Sayyid Ahmad was born in 1817 into a family with several generations of employment at the Mughal court and more recent employment with the BEIC. He entered service with the BEIC as a court recorder in Delhi and, in 1841, was promoted to the rank of sub-judge. He was in Bijnor, in 1857, when the uprising occurred. By the time he reached his family in late September, he found his cousins and an uncle shot and killed by the British, and his mother hiding in a horse stable. She passed away almost immediately, from the tribulations of the siege.[64]

Nearly all of Sayyid Ahmad's historical writing dates from before 1857. The first work was the Persian *Jam-i Jam* (1840). He gave his date of composition as 1839 in a chronogram that refers to this work as "the cup of Jamshed" (*Jam-i Jam*), which held the elixir to immortality and the mirror of Alexander (*a'ina-i* Iskandar), able to reflect the whole world. *Jam-i Jam* was a chronological ledger of the rulers and princes of Delhi from Amir Timur's sack of Delhi in 1399 to the last Mughal emperor, Bahadur Shah Zafar. The ledger had sixteen columns: Father's name, Mother's name, *qaum* (community), date of birth, coronation site, age at time of coronation, year of coronation (in a chronogram), duration of rule, coinage, life span, year of death, chronogram of year of death, title after death, burial site, and conditions (aftermath).[65] There were forty-three entries in the ledger. Sayyid Ahmad described his methodology and philosophy for this work in an appendix at the end. He wanted to provide a reliable dating framework, and citations, for anyone undertaking the task of writing medieval history. He described his labor and effort in having to comb through almost thirty histories, page by page, and assembling family genealogies from poetry compendiums. The first of his key sources for making this chronology was Firishta's *Tarikh*.

Sayyid Ahmad was hopeful that his effort to cross-check and summarize basic and needed details for the task of history writing would be useful for anyone wishing to write a history of Delhi. In itself, this was a new gesture that was aimed at shifting the role of the historian away from the specialized secretarial and salaried classes and toward a common public person. At the time of this composition, Sayyid Ahmad was himself a young man—twenty-two years old—who proudly claimed in the preface that his family had begun to work for Jalaluddin Akbar in Delhi and had always been a part of the governing elite. Now, Sayyid Ahmad was continuing this tradition by participating in governing with the new BEIC rulers. He was also in conversation with Henry M. Elliot and his efforts to identify and catalog historical manuscripts. Elliot had acquired a copy of *Jam-i Jam* and praised its "useful tables," which were made by consulting "excellent authorities."[66]

More importantly, *Jam-i Jam* represents an effort to incorporate newer forms of historical research into the established formal structures for writing history in Persian in the early nineteenth century. *Jam-i Jam* was a lithographed text, meant for reproduction and distribution. Formally, it is not a visual genealogical chart, nor is it a narrative in the *tabaqat* genre. The "ledger" form was already being used by the colonial state to collect data—most specifically by Elliot, who sent instructions to scholars and archivists to construct their responses to his queries in the form of ledgers. *Jam-i Jam* was also a source-critical text, even if the apparatus was invisible to the reader. Sayyid Ahmad was reconciling the various dates across different historical sources. A key insight here is the inclusion of chronograms and coin inscriptions that acted as primary source evidence for each column. While Sayyid Ahmad does not cite the sources for each of the ledger items, his work was in parallel to the chronologies being produced by British researchers at the Royal Asiatic Society in Bengal.

In 1852, Sayyid Ahmad updated his chronological table with a new title, *Silsilat-ul-Muluk*.[67] He expanded the chronology to include all of the kings of Delhi, starting with Yudhishtira and ending with Queen Victoria. He again cites Firishta as the first source for his list "Kings of Delhi." Like Firishta, he introduces the *Mahabharata* and its chronology. In order to create a chronological parity between the two cosmologies, Sayyid Ahmad argues that the key event that links time between the Brahmanical and Muslim cosmologies is Noah's Flood. He discusses the various accounts from Muslim, Jewish, and Christian sources about the extent of the Flood. Sayyid Ahmad is skeptical that the Brahmanical epics predate the Flood. Yet, he includes the Persian versions of the *Mahabharata, Bhagavad Gita,* and some family histories he had collected. In his table, Yudhishtira is 1450 years before Jesus Christ—meaning that the time of the *Mahabharata* is cosmologically legible within Islamic time.

Sayyid Ahmad's early interests in history were particularly focused on the history of Delhi. He wanted to present Delhi as a lived-in and inhabited place, recognize the elite structures of social and political power attached to the Mughal court, and argue for the continuity of Delhi's significance to British India. In 1847, he published *Asar-us-Sanadid,* in Urdu, with the hope "[to write] a wondrous map and marvelous anthology, shaped by this reed-pen with the aid of heavenly thought, in which are described the remaining buildings of the capital of Shahjahanabad [Delhi] and the houses within that city and the condition of the Royal Fort, and to register the customs and rituals of the inhabitants of the city."[68] This material and ethnographic portrait of the notable—architecturally and socially—aspects of Delhi was done by walking the city, copying the inscriptions mounted on built structures (including gravestones), and consulting the now burgeoning data produced by colonial archaeological efforts. To this material, Sayyid Ahmad added his consultation of manuscripts of historical work.

On formal grounds, *Asar-us-Sanadid* resembled the works of colonial soldier-scribes, especially in their efforts to understand the ancient past of major cities in British India.[69] However, in contrast to the colonial historiography, which was focused on the pre-Muslim past of Delhi and articulating a history of Muslim arrival, Sayyid Ahmad Khan offered a lived history of his contemporaries in Delhi; one in which the houses and households gave testimony to the richness of the past two hundred years. In his text, he included sketches of monuments and of various buildings as well as biographies of individuals and families. *Asar* was well received. Arthur Austin Roberts, the collector of Delhi, presented it to the Royal Asiatic Society. Sayyid Ahmad Khan was encouraged by him, and by Aloys Sprenger, to produce an expanded edition. In 1852, Sayyid Ahmad published this revised and enlarged edition, which now incorporated the idea of Delhi within the framework of the *Mahabharata*, using the chronology of kings of Delhi from Yudhishtira that he had created. Similarly, he added buildings and forts that placed Delhi within the history of Hindustan.[70]

Sayyid Ahmad Khan's *Asar* is remarkably innovative as a major text in Urdu, and one that writes back into the colonial record the people who lived in Delhi. It is a major intervention in the ways in which colonial archaeological efforts were digging for the pre-Muslim past in the cities of British India. It formally demonstrated the existence of a community surrounding architectural or archaeological remains—this was no Delhi as a ruin of the Mughal imperium. That this was a conscious effort is made clear in the two critical editions of histories created by Sayyid Ahmad during the same period. In 1855, he published a critical edition of Abu'l Fazl's *A'in-i Akbari*. In itself, this was a major philological achievement. Yet, Sayyid Ahmad introduced a significant formal change:

He commissioned pencil sketches of the clothing, various artisanal techniques, forms of agriculture, weapons, instruments of cooking, flora, and fauna described in the *A'in,* alongside maps of the various sections of Hindustan and the world. The sketches were made from observing contemporary practices and botanical gardens. This work of the history of Hindustan was no mere philological exercise in collating manuscripts and erasing errors—it became a document of a living Hindustan. Sayyid Ahmad Khan also published critical editions of the Persian manuscripts of Barani's *Tarikh-i Firuz Shahi* in 1862 and of *Tuzuk-i Jahangiri* in 1864.

These critical editions, even though in conversation with Elliot, were markedly different than Elliot's project. The colonial soldier-scribes were invested in creating an archive for writing the history of the Muslim medieval. The manuscripts amassed were dissected into chunks useful for such a project, then translated, with the manuscripts themselves stowed away in Europe. In contrast, Sayyid Ahmad Khan's critical editions were meant to reintroduce the Persian texts to the Urdu- and Persian-reading public by having them printed as lithographs. Sayyid Ahmad also invested his own money in getting the colonial histories translated into Urdu—such that both the primary source material and the colonial scholarship were available to the researcher. In 1866, Sayyid Ahmad's "Scientific Society" had translated into Urdu Elphinstone's *History of India* as *Tarikh-i Hindustan.*[71] This translation, alongside other histories written by French and English authors, spurred much of the historiography in Urdu in the last decades of the nineteenth century.

While Sayyid Ahmad Khan's historical work pales in significance to his later career, it still marks a critical phase in the history being sketched in this book.[72] It shows one of the earliest responses to the colonial project of rendition and amassment within the colony. It also inaugurates and prefigures the role of disciplinary sciences—history and philology—for Muslim intellectuals. The three major strands of historiography in Urdu that developed after 1857, led by Shibli Nu'mani, Zaka'ullah, and 'Abdul Halim Sharar, were distinct in many ways, but they remained inspired by Sayyid Ahmad's innovations in enlarging the domain of reading and writing history. All three of these authors aimed to popularize the Muslim past. They did so by simultaneously producing works in various genres, varied forms of publishing, diverse institutions and organizations, and writing in Urdu, Arabic, or Persian.

Shibli Nu'mani (1857–1914) focused his work on Islam's early period and linking the history of Muslims in the subcontinent to the history of early Islam. In his *al-Farooq* (1898), a history of the second caliph of early Islam, 'Umar bin Khattab, Nu'mani cites the need to adopt the methodology of German historian Leopold von Ranke. Following Ranke, Nu'mani declared that a historian should avoid poetic excess and attempt to present the ideas that motivate the past, and drive history. A modern work of history, Nu'mani wrote "should be an account of the cultural, social, ethical and religious" events of a particular period and that "the cause and the chain of effect must be traced in recounting all events."[73] Like Sayyid Ahmad, Nu'mani read widely and engaged with the European historical tradition. He particularly wanted to respond to, and correct, the histories of Muhammad and early Islam written by Edward Gibbon, Thomas Carlyle, and Louis Sédillot.

'Abdul Halim Sharar (1860–1926) gained much of his acclaim from being a major publisher and editor. He wrote immensely popular serialized historical romances, of which he eventually produced some twenty-five. In introducing his first historical novel, *Mulk-ul-Aziz Virginia* (1888), he declared that his project of historical writing was inspired by Walter Scott:

> Up to this time in Urdu, with as many original novels as have been written, none have attempted anything based on any historical events and they have only made use of fantastical stories. . . . But, in this novel, great care has been taken so that history will not in any way leave our grasp. For this reason, the difference between this novel and other original Urdu novels is basically the same difference between the truth and lies. I do not claim that everything written in it is true, but there is also no doubt that whoever looks at this novel will become intimately familiar with this particular part of history.[74]

Sayyid Ahmad Khan was keen on expanding the tools available to the public for writing histories, and Sharar's project was to expand historical consciousness and bring to the people a sense of different places and history in a passionate and imaginative form.[75] The same spirit engaged the dozen histories Sharar wrote, which focused on early Islam and Muslim history in Spain, Syria, and Arabia. The only history he wrote that focused on Hindustan was his history of Muslim arrival in Sindh, *Tarikh-i Sindh*, serialized in his journal, *Dil Gudaz*, in 1906. The history of Sindh, Sharar noted, "must be strange for the readers to see [as they were asked to] leave aside all of Hindustan and focus on an unknown region of the country."[76] Yet, Sharar argued that Sindh was a critical region to study because it had suffered the most historiographic injustices by the colonial regime. Sharar introduced this history as his response to the work of Elliot and Elphinstone. However, even though he uses the materials made available by colonial historians, he denounces them at multiple occasions for being simplistic, ideological, and dismissive of histories written in Arabic. Here, for example, he criticizes Elliot and Elphinstone—as well as Firishta—for not being source critical and taking an account from the *Chachnama*, a thirteenth-century history of Sindh, at face value:

> This account, found only in the *Chachnama*, became so popular in eastern and Persian histories that nearly every author reported it. It is even found in Firishta—an author who can be relied upon for his strenuous research. English historians, who rely only on Persian histories, have also reproduced this account. Elphinstone writes in his history that "all Muslim historians support this." The History of Elphinstone was taught for decades in courses, and this account was so dearly propagated by the English historians that every child in Hindustan can recite it.[77]

Sharar strongly disagrees with such a reading. However, leaving aside Sharar's interpretative act, it is more significant to note that he fully engages with colonial historians, and adopts the formal aspects of European historical science—citation of previous scholarship, footnotes with page numbers and annotative gloss, description of archival access, source criticism in his work. As a serialized history, *Tarikh-i Sindh* would reach a broad swath of the Urdu-reading public and shape their ideas about the early history of Muslims, formally and thematically.

Sayyid Ahmad, Nu'mani, and Sharar created and shaped historical consciousness for the Hindustani public in the late nineteenth century. Their works are important interventions into what was until then a purely colonial project of writing history. At the same time, it is remarkably clear that in the post-1857 world, Hindustan, as a political space, was barely visible. While all of these scholars referred to the inhabitants of the subcontinent as Hindustani, they were in conversation with, or working on, projects that were pan-Asian or pan-Islamic. Their textual worlds are almost explicitly confined to the hyperlocal (Delhi, Aligarh, Lucknow) and the global (London, Cairo, Istanbul, Beirut).[78]

Yet, before we turn the last page on this story of Hindustan, there is one final monumental history to take into account. This is the ten-volume *Tarikh-i Hindustan* published in 1897, which was written by Muhammad Zaka'ullah. In the words of Charles Freer Andrews, who wrote a biography of Zaka'ullah in 1929, "He was the last relic in Delhi of an age that has now passed away."[79] He was born in 1832 and, at age twelve, joined Delhi College. He was trained in Arabic and Persian by Imam Bakhsh Sahbai (who was killed by the British in 1857) and by Ramchandra, in mathematics. In 1851, Zaka'ullah was appointed teacher of mathematics at Delhi College. For the next thirty-five years, he worked as a professor of mathematics for the British state and in 1887 retired and joined Sayyid Ahmad Khan's Mohammadan Oriental College at Aligarh. Zaka'ullah had joined Sayyid Ahmad Khan's Scientific Society in 1866.

Over the course of his life, Zaka'ullah wrote more than 150 books—both original compositions and translations into Urdu from English. He focused on mathematics, history, and medicine. In addition to his *Tarikh-i Hindustan*, Zaka'ullah wrote a five-volume history of the colonial beginnings of British India, a biography of Viceroy Lord Curzon and one of Queen Victoria, a series of books on ethics, women's education, and more.[80] Zaka'ullah tended to write in simple Urdu prose, but his texts would often intersperse quoted material and his own voice in the same sentence, making it difficult to decipher his authorial voice. While he would cite his source materials, and quote the authors, he did not use footnotes. In his writing style, he did harken to an age that had passed, and Andrews also quotes him as lamenting the fact that his writings were all in Urdu, and thus doomed to irrelevance:

> Sometimes, in moments of despondency, during his later years, he would tell me how he felt that his own life work of Urdu adaptation and translation, for the use of schools, had been altogether wasted. . . . Then he would point to the number of volumes he had written, which were lying idle on the shelves, with no one to take down and read them. He would say that they would only moulder into dust, and his name and his effort would be forgotten: the tide had gone against him, and he had not been able to turn it back in the other direction.[81]

In contrast to the works of Sayyid Ahmad Khan, Nuʿmani, and Sharar, whose body of work continues to be studied and republished and circulated, Zakaʾullah was never republished after the initial run.[82] Later scholarship, as pointed out above, found him lacking as a historian. He was determined to be not "objective, detached, or reflective" with respect to the colonial state or colonial officials, and, for the pre-British Muslim rulers, he "shows more emotion in his approach to his subject than the scientific detachment he preached."[83] The accusation that a history written in Persian or Urdu was unobjective, beholden to political power, or being derivative is, after all, a perennial feature of colonial historical sciences. Recall Dow's judgment against Firishta. Whether Zakaʾullah, or the larger community of writers in Urdu in the last quarter of the nineteenth century, rise to some notion of "objective" historical scholarship is tangential to the question of how they were engaged with the historical scholarship being produced and circulated around them—at the same time—by British researchers.

In sketching the intellectual history of Hindustan, Zakaʾullah's engagement with the projects of Elliot and Elphinstone allows us to see how he reinterpreted the domain and dominion of Hindustan. It is undoubtedly the case that his massive history was used for the creation of numerous pedagogical textbooks in Urdu well into the twentieth century.

Yet the medieval historians of the nationalist, anti-colonial, period had little use for such synthetic works. Zaka'ullah's *Tarikh-i Hindustan* was destined to be an orphaned text. Yet, the materiality of *Tarikh-i Hindustan* remains a visual argument—a monument, an excess, that is meant to stand alongside Elliot's posthumously published multi-thousand-page, eight-volume *The History of India, as Told by Its Own Historians.*

Zaka'ullah lists his sources in the beginning of each volume. He gives the individual titles and then adds that "these books are in my possession."[84] In addition, he cites Elliot's and Dowson's compilation, and Elphinstone, as well as articles from the journal of the Royal Asiatic Society. Firishta is his primary source in the first four volumes. His citation of Persian histories for the seventeenth and eighteenth centuries is extensive, including manuscripts he had consulted from private collections. For each source, he adds a note concerning whether the account is as a participant and eyewitness or not. He opens his first volume with a sixty-five-page prolegomenon on the nature and meaning of history as an ancient and modern science. In this introduction, he discusses the works of historians—from Baihaqi and Barani to Ibn Khaldun—and then European historians—from Bacon to Hegel to Carlyle—and whether Eastern languages and religions face an epistemic challenge when it comes to the task of history writing. Zaka'ullah's prolegomenon on the notion of history and his idea of Hindustan are intertwined. The prolegomenon is the most visible attempt, in *Tarikh-i Hindustan*, to synthesize, at an intellectual level, the intellectual genealogy of Hindustan with the histories of British India as well as the geography of Hindustan with the story of Muslim origins in the subcontinent—the latter being causally linked to the former.

Consider first Zaka'ullah's definition of history and his engagement with Elliot and Elphinstone. Zaka'ullah argues that "the key to history is science."[85] By science here, he explicitly parallels the efforts to create theorems from observations that can provide rules and laws governing social and cultural actions—the key outputs of his heroes, Keppler and Newton. Zaka'ullah models his case on history as a social science on Hegel, and begins with the declaration that Hindus have no history, and that "poets are born before historians."[86] The Muslims, he writes, enter into the art of history writing in order to document the life of the Prophet

Muhammad. He then provides extensive translations from Mas'udi, Baihaqi, Barani, and Ibn Khaldun on the role of the historian for Muslim societies. Yet, he argues that much of the historical production of the pre-Mughal period shared a fundamental flaw in that the historians rarely, if ever, gave a sense of the social worlds, the inequities, and the violence that shaped their times. The historians of the later medieval period, Zaka'ullah adds, did allow a glimpse of these issues, but much of those histories are not read in a scientific manner by his contemporary scholars.[87]

Zaka'ullah is critical of European scholars who do not learn "Eastern" languages and rely on imperfect or partial translations, done by Elliot, for their history writing.[88] While he appreciates Elliot's project for bringing to light the source materials for the medieval period, he argues that it also had inherent biases and led to the prejudiced output in the synthetic histories, like Elphinstone's. These colonial histories, Zaka'ullah believes, have encoded prejudice against the Muslims by selective usage of historical evidence and an anti-Muslim thrust to all of their work. In contrast to the work of colonial historians, Zaka'ullah reads European historians writing on Europe's past with genuine admiration. He cites Voltaire, Hume, Macaulay, J. S. Mill, and even Freud. Their works provide, for Zaka'ullah, a methodology for his own writing of the history of the medieval period of the subcontinent. In his own *Tarikh-i Hindustan,* he wants to follow the practice of Thomas Carlyle or Herbert Spencer and produce a work that is not mere antiquarianism, but a critical history of his own past. Drawing on Europeans' writing on their own past, Zaka'ullah argues that Hindustani historians of the medieval periods read widely and critically the Persian histories, incorporate sources in Hindustani and Braj, and also use the testimonies and travelogues provided by Europeans about Hindustan. This would, Zaka'ullah suggests, provide a wider base for the task of reconstructing the medieval period with attention to the social and cultural milieu.

The task of the Hindustani historian, Zaka'ullah argues, is to develop an understanding of the "ideology" that governed each of their past epochs. The work of history is to highlight the patterns of intellectual thought and provide keys to future imaginations. In Zaka'ullah's analysis, the Muslim rulers of the eighteenth century had deposited Hindustan into a tyranny from which the British rescued them by establishing the rule of law and social welfare.[89] The task of his history was to furnish a new vocabulary—a scientific one—for understanding the past and envisioning the future.

The future for Zaka'ullah was best reflected in the transition from Hindustan to British India. Hindustan was a territory upon which Muslim rulers had ruled with laws and ideals that were not meant to provide for the welfare of the people of Hindustan. Hence, it was important that the ideals of Islam and the rule of law of British India be brought into conversation by historians. Zaka'ullah's history of Hindustan begins with the history of Islam in the world. He narrates first the period of early Islam, followed by brief accounts of all the Muslim rulers in Asia and in Europe. His account of Hindustan begins with the history of Sindh as the first site of a Muslim polity in Hindustan, and only then does it pivot to documenting the histories of the various regions of Hindustan. Where Firishta had spatially organized Hindustan with the Deccan at its center, and Abu'l Fazl with Agra at the heart, Zaka'ullah's Hindustan is both spatially and ideologically translocal.

For Zaka'ullah, the only Hindustan that was visible was the one that was tied to Muslim polities. Where Firishta had begun his *Tarikh* with a long discourse from the *Mahabharata,* Zaka'ullah's *Tarikh-i Hindustan* only accounts for the history of Muslim prophets. Indeed, Dow was the first to reject Firishta's claim that the *Mahabharata* was a text of history, and Elliot and Elphinstone further partitioned the epic "Ancient Hindu period" from the "Mohammadan period." Zaka'ullah naturalized these colonial claims and distinctions. Even with all of his critique of colonial historians, Zaka'ullah's *Tarikh* was not conceptually different from that of Elphinstone. Even though Zaka'ullah was attentive to society outside of elite power structures, the world of non-Muslim subjects of Muslim polities remains silent and absent. Zaka'ullah wrote elsewhere about the solidarities between Hindu and Muslim cultures in Delhi, but as a work of history, his *Tarikh-i Hindustan* was devoted to the world of Muslims alone.

In the works of Sayyid Ahmad Khan, Nu'mani, and Sharar, the idea of Hindustan glimmered at the edge as a social reality. For them, there was a Hindustani self, and a Hindustani subject to be reformed, and educated. They were invested in the debates about language and script—the tearing up of Urdu and Hindi—and they were keen to provide social mobility to the Muslim middle and upper classes.[90] In Zaka'ullah, Hindustan was a critical reality, but only in the past. It was in the domain of history writing that the question of Hindustan was an important one for Zaka'ullah. It is clear, from the way he disregards the particularities of how Firishta had organized Hindustan, that Hindustan had no political valence in Zaka'ullah's British India. Zaka'ullah was invested in a historiography for a particularly Muslim past. While he was critical of both European and Muslim historical sciences, the valences of his present political order with British India reigning over the subcontinent were beyond question.

By the end of the nineteenth century, Firishta's *Tarikh* and Hindustan were both vestiges of a ruined past. Muslim historians embarking on the task of adapting history as a social science could only see Firishta as raw material for their new scientific studies in history. In that, the colonial project of restating the Muslim medieval period as an interruption in "five thousand years" of the Hindu Brahmanical past came to be held as true by these intellectuals as well. The pivot toward writing a history of Islam rather a history of Hindustan, in Urdu, would emerge forcefully in the early decades of the twentieth century. Just as the British colonial order eliminated Hindustan as a concept over the course of the long nineteenth century, it also gave birth to the "Muslim World" that flourished and took root in the early twentieth century.[91] The Muslim intellectuals in Hindustan were very much involved in the translocal project of a global community (*umma*), specifically to stop the British divestment of the Ottoman sultan as a caliph after World War I.[92]

The long nineteenth century, from Alexander Dow's *History of Hindostan* to Zaka'ullah's *Tarikh-i Hindustan,* coincided with the dominance of British colonial regimes over the subcontinent, the emergence of a European philosophy of history, and the creation of new social sciences, including disciplinary history. The histories and historians of the subcontinent were the nominative and denotive subjects of these colonial forces over this period. Firishta's *Tarikh* was the putative text and the demonstrative paratext throughout this expanding project. The late nineteenth-century Muslim historians were constructing new origins and finding space for their community in their current colonial order. Firishta's history was as well a crucial tool for their project of writing synthetic, universal histories that were usable for the colonized subjects.

In the anti-colonial struggle of the early twentieth century, the concept of "Hindustan" was reborn and rearticulated: It would emerge in the debates on Hindustani as a language, in the articulation of a Hindustan that is a homeland for Hindus alone, in the nostalgia for a long-lost Hindustani culture, in the rallying cry for a free Hindustan. Largely forgotten in popular memory, however, is the *history* of histories in which Hindustan was an archive, a space, and a belonging for diverse peoples.

7

AFTERWORD

The "India" that colonial powers made was filled with clichéd natives, invented temporalities, and religious antagonisms presumed to be factual and true. In contrast, "Hindustan" was made to be figurative, a place of false harmonies, limited geographies, and forgotten languages. The philologists asserted the supremacy of texts such as the *Manusmriti* to contextualize "custom" and law. Colonial historians sidelined Persian histories as demonstrative solely of Muslim despotism. None of this went unchallenged.

A generation of Hindustani medieval historians wrestled with this colonial episteme in the history departments of Calcutta, Allahabad, Aligarh, Lahore, Baroda, Hyderabad, Deccan (later, Pune), and Delhi. To name and recognize a few: Jivanji Jamshedji Modi (1854–1933), Ghulam Yazdani (1885–1963), Iswari Prasad Upadhyaya (1888–1986), Tara Chand (1888–1973), Surendra Nath Sen (1890–1959), Haroon Khan Sherwani (1891–1980), Shafa'at Ahmad Khan (1893–1947), Mohammad Habib (1895–1971), Beni Prasad (1895–1945), Umar Muhammad Daudpota (1896–1958), Syed Hasan Askari (1901–1990), Kunwar Muhammad Ashraf (1903–1962), Shaikh Chand Hussain (1907–1982), Athar Mubarakpuri (1916–1996), Ram Sharan Sharma (1919–2011), Syed Nurul Hasan (1921–1993), Banarsi Prasad Saxena (active ca. 1930–1970), and Ram Prasad Tripathi (d. 1983).

This comity of historians had to contend with the ways in which the colonial knowledge paradigm had shaped the study of the medieval. This was no mere task of historiography—for these historians were simultaneously engaged in wrestling with the condition of coloniality and the rising tide of self-determination and nationalism. They sought to understand the ethical burden that the historian faced in the task of writing history for the future. In making critical editions, translations, and studies of historians like Baihaqi, Juzjani, Barani, Khusrau, Abu'l Fazl, and Firishta, they were also joining an intellectual genealogy that gave explicit voice to the place and people of Hindustan.

The partitioning of the subcontinent in 1947 was based on anticolonial politicians and intellectuals—from Muhammad Ali Jinnah to Bhimrao Ramji Ambedkar to Vinayak Damodar Savarkar—internalizing the colonial argument about Muslim foreignness and considering the past five hundred years of the subcontinent as representative of despotism and decay. The historians of the medieval critically grappled with this question of Muslim belonging, of assessing whether Muslim rulers were oppressors and tyrants. With clarity, they foresaw the arc of history tilting the subcontinent toward violence. With rising alarm, they sought to establish ethical ways of thinking and writing history that would combat the rising rancor and separatism in British India.

One of the most searing examples of a historian confronting a despairing unfolding reality is the address given by Shafa'at Ahmad Khan at the inauguration of the first national gathering of Hindustani historians. The Indian History Congress began in Pune in July 1935 as the "All India Modern History Conference," a collective of historians studying the medieval and modern period.[1] Shafa'at Ahmad Khan, the chair of the history department at Allahabad, was elected president of the session. The Indian History Congress would go on to meet annually, in Allahabad in 1938, Calcutta in 1939, and Lahore in 1940. The tenth session was held in Bombay December 26–28, 1947.

Shafa'at Ahmad Khan, in his inaugural presidential address to the assembled historians, cautioned that "history has not yet attained the status of an exact science," that it was neither Euclidean nor Newtonian, and, in fact, "the Hegelian conception of history, when applied to the concrete facts of Indian development, will make moral shipwreck of most traditions and ideals."[2] Shafa'at Ahmad Khan was less convinced that European sciences, or even colonial rule, would be the necessary salve for healing the subcontinent into a utopia. In fact, he saw grave dangers ahead, based on the recent histories of "perverted sectionalism," as he put it. These histories were creating "a gross prejudice," one that historians could not ignore or fail to confront.

He spoke about the great moral calamity facing the subcontinent and how quickly the narratives of separation would move from books to the market: "I have been watching the onset of this disease for some years and I can no longer remain silent. It has a far-reaching effect on the future of our entire political structure, for the ideas that take root in the formative and impressionable years of youth are difficult to dislodge, and the prejudices of worthless history text-books are imported into the Council Chamber, the market place and the public platform."[3] With the future of the political structure at stake, Shafa'at Ahmad Khan asked his fellow historians to "decide on the launching of a campaign that will clear up the miasma of suspicion, insinuation and downright untruth, which is served up as history to the virile and hardy youth of India."[4] He wanted the historians to reject any "fixed idea" (namely, Muslim outsider-ness to the subcontinent) and not to "devote years to the elaboration of our curious prejudices and sub-conscious impulses."[5] Instead, he argued that the Indian historian ought to take the "slow but difficult task of conscientious and honest investigation of elusive material." He imagined a critical role for the gathered historians. He asked them to function as a guild, to "perform the function of an Academy and regulate the standards [of historical writing] with strenuous vigilance and scrupulous honesty."[6] The prejudices in the marketplace, Shafa'at Ahmad Khan warned the Indian historians, ought not to turn the historians into "nationalist writers," and the task of the historian was always "to avoid appeals to racial or national prejudices."[7]

In December 1947, when the Indian History Congress met in Bombay for its tenth meeting, Shafa'at Ahmad Khan's dire prophecy had come true. The subcontinent was now a partitioned world between India and Pakistan, comprising East and West Pakistan. The medievalist Mohammad Habib now gave the presidential address. Habib was undoubtedly the most prominent historian of the second millennium of the subcontinent at that time. He had worked on Mahmud Ghazni, on

Khusrau, critiqued and corrected Elliot's assessments of Muslim historians, and even attempted a translation of Firishta's *Tarikh*.[8]

It is difficult to imagine the task facing Habib, to speak about the role of historians in the face of, as he put, "this hideous criminality, the like of which is not to be found in the whole history of our ancient land."[9] He was shaken by "the horrors with which this Partition has been accompanied—of the six million people or more uprooted from the homes of their ancestors, of corpses that no one has been able to count, and of crimes seen and credibly reported."[10] Even in this dire moment, even facing the tearing apart of the subcontinent on the basis of a separate homeland for Muslims, Habib's conviction was to argue for Muslim belonging in "our ancient land," as he asserted. Habib repeatedly spoke as a historian to declare that "the overwhelming mass of the Muslims of this land have an undoubted Indian paternity," that the Muslim is not foreign to the soil of the subcontinent.[11]

As a medieval historian, Habib rejected the idea that the subcontinent had historically housed two distinct and separate civilizations. He stressed that, "it is absolutely unnecessary to state that, so far as the historian of India is concerned, the country has always been one and indivisible, and will always continue to be so."[12] The Partition, which had been enacted as the condition of decolonization, Habib hoped would be a temporary one, and the land would one day soon be reunited through peaceful means. Like Shafa'at Ahmad Khan, Habib prescribed a restorative role for the historian: that the historian would work to create a common basis for understanding history, to popularize the notion of a peopled past, with common roots. He prompted historians to stand with the Indian people against their rulers, regardless of faith, to create a "National Community" that would create unity where there was now division.

In that immediate moment after Partition, Habib hoped a new national future would come to be governed by "a creation of laws consciously planned for the public good."[13] History would be one of those public goods. Habib wanted the historian of the future to promote diversity of thought, to not be cowed by sectarianism, and to focus on giving voice to those who were silenced—the working class. He declared, "It is not our duty to knock down old temples, every element of value in them must be preserved. But we have to build a new shrine."[14] He wanted the historian to speak out, and he harkened back to the ethics of history writing given by Barani hundreds of years before him. "History, as a Persian writer has rightly remarked," Habib spoke, "is quickly exported from the academy to the bazar and shopkeepers, who cannot distinguish white from black and black from white, [and] confidently venture to pass judgements on historical matters."[15]

Mohammad Habib's address in 1947 gives us a sense of continuity in the ethics and work of the comity of Hindustani historians across the second millennium. Mohammad Habib and the generation of intellectuals and historians who came after him were to rethink their world in the aftermath of Partition. They faced the challenge of how to write in the aftermath of the many violences—from the violence of Partition itself, to the war of 1965, to the creation of Bangladesh in 1971, to the destruction of the Babri mosque in 1992. There were further separatist demands—nationalisms from Kashmir to Naga to Sindh to Khalistan to Baluchistan. Through this turmoil, the trajectories of the discipline of history between the two partitioned nation-states was also starkly divergent. In the Republic of India, prominent historians flourished in departments in Calcutta, Delhi, Aligarh, Pune, and so on, shaping not only the national conversation but also becoming internationally renowned experts. In India, historians like Satish Chandra (1922–2017), Irfan Habib (b. 1931), Romila Thapar (b. 1931), and more continued to demonstrate the ways in which the medieval remained a part of the fabric of Indian history. Pakistan's military dictatorships, on the other hand, shut down thriving spaces at Peshawar University, Karachi University, Dhaka University, and Punjab University. In Pakistan, despite the efforts of Mubarak Ali (b. 1941), or K. K. Aziz (1927–2009), a national origin story took root—that Pakistan was a homeland for Muslims of the subcontinent since the eighth century. This meant that, in the textbooks of Pakistan, much of the second millennium of the history of the subcontinent was simply erased. Since the 1950s, historians of the premodern period in India, in Pakistan, in the UK, and in the United States, have continued to write against the majoritarian politics, and a new generation of specialists is now continuing that work. In no uncertain terms, the subject of history writing itself emerged as the most generative vein of scholarship in the last fifty years.[16]

Yet, across the subcontinent we now confront a crisis of the past, with an explicit understanding of difference as destiny. The majorities of the subcontinent have accumulated power to govern, and they have condemned the minorities to be marginalized or to be expunged. The majoritarians believe that this current state of exception, where one's religion and linguistic heritage determine belonging and exclusion in Pakistan, India, and Bangladesh, is the rule. The majoritarian Sunni or Hindutva projects ask that we, as historians, consider them inevitable and immutable. Yet, this cannot stand. It is instructive for us to reengage with the urgency with which Shafa'at Ahmad Khan laid out the collective intellectual project facing the colonized historian, in 1935. While we face differently articulated versions in majoritarian readings of the medieval, we ought to recognize the same sense of despair, the same urgency to take collective action in the face of majoritarian claims on the past.

If "an acknowledgment of loss is one way forward," then the history I have sketched here is a prompt to imagine ways forward that do not yield to the majoritarian present, that do not inherit the past as a certainty, and do not romanticize that which is lost.[17] It is essential that, as historians, artists, activists, and thinkers, we turn to the medieval period and recognize the ways in which it continues to organize how current prejudices are articulated. Undoubtedly, as post-colonized historians we have inherited the colonial episteme, but we are also inheritors of a deep archive of history writing that stretches from Juzjani to Firishta to Mohammad Habib—from the thirteenth century to the twentieth. In this archive is an ethics of writing history that ought to be our greatest resource in launching new intellectual projects. It is, as Habib declared, our collective responsibility to speak against the conformism of prejudice. It is our collective task to re-imagine the past.

NOTES

1. Introduction: The End of Hindustan

1. In 1499, when Vasco da Gama returned to Lisbon from Calicut, Dom Manuel I became "Senhor de Guine e da Conquista Navegação e Comércio de Etiópia, Arábia, Pérsia, e da Índia."

2. See Ian J. Barrow, "From Hindustan to India: Naming Change in Changing Names," *South Asia: Journal of South Asian Studies* 26, no. 1 (2003): 37–49.

3. For instance, Joan Josua Ketelaar, *Instructie of onderwijsinghe der Hindousta- anse en Persiaanse taalen* (ca. 1698), ms. 1478 (1 E 21), Utrecht University Library; John Zephaniah Holwell, *Interesting Historical Events, Relative to the Provinces of Bengal, and the Empire of Indostan* (London: T. Beckett and P. A. De Hondt, 1765); John Rennell, *A Map of Hindoostan, or the Mogul Empire: From the Latest Authorities* (1788); John Gilchrist, *Hindoostanee Philology* (London: Kingsbury, Parbury, and Allen, 1796); Antoine Fabre D'Olivet, *Le Sage de l'Indostan: Drame philosophique, en un acte et en vers* (Paris: Dufay, 1796).

4. Though V. D. Savarkar, in 1925, re-imagined Shivaji as claiming the "throne of all Hindustan." See V. D. Savarkar, *Hindu-Pad-Padashahi or A Critical Review of the Hindu Empire of Maharashtra* (Madras: B. G. Paul, 1925), 56.

5. See Kalidas Gupta Raza, *Dīvān-e ġhālib kāmil nuskhah-e guptā raẓā, tārīkhī tartīb se* (Bombay: Sakar Publications, 1995), 225. On wider resonances between Hindustan as a garden and Mughal rulers, see Stephen Frederic Dale, *The Garden of the Eight Paradises: Bābur and the Culture of Empire in Central Asia, Afghanistan and India (1483–1530)* (Leiden: Brill, 2004); and Ebba Koch, "My Garden Is Hindustan: The Mughal Emperor's Realization of a Political Metaphor," in *Middle East Garden Traditions: Unity and Diversity,* ed. Michael Conan (Washington, DC: Dumbarton Oaks, 2007), 159–175. Also see Sunil Sharma, *Mughal Arcadia: Persian Literature in an Indian Court* (Cambridge, MA: Harvard University Press, 2017).

6. In North America at the turn of the century there existed newspapers like *The Hindustanee: The Official Organ of the United India League,* organizations like the Hindustanee's Welfare and Reform Society of America, and student journals like the *Hindusthanee Student.* Poetry was published in the *Ghadar* newsletter that celebrated Hindustan as a political and social entity: "Hindus, Sikhs and Muslims and Bengalis, we are all sons of Hindustan / Let us keep religion and doctrinaires aside, we will deal with them later, first is the task of war." Virinder S. Kalra, "Poetic Politics: From Ghadar to the Indian Workers' Association," in *Routledge Handbook of the Indian Diaspora,* ed. Radha Sarma Hegde and Ajaya Kumar Sahoo (London: Routledge, 2018), 209. My thanks to Ken Chen for this citation.

7. One historian who has consistently argued against this truism is Irfan Habib. See, for example, Irfan Habib, "The Formation of India: Notes on the History of an Idea," *Social Scientist* 25, nos. 7–8 (July–August 1997): 3–10; and "The Envisioning of a Nation: A Defense of the Idea of India," *Social Scientist* 27, nos. 9–10 (September–October 1999): 18–29.

8. B. D. Verma, "Inscriptions from the Central Museum, Nagpur," in *Epigraphia Indica: Arabic and Persian Supplement, 1955 and 1956* (Calcutta: Government of India Press, 1960), 109–118.

9. On the idea of "Turk," see Joo-Yup Lee, "The Historical Meaning of the Term *Turk* and the Nature of the Turkic Identity of the Chinggisid and Timurid Elites in Post-Mongol Central Asia," *Central Asiatic Journal* 59, nos. 1–2 (2016): 101–132. Also see Mana Kia, *Persianate Selves: Memories of Place and Origin before Nationalism* (Stanford, CA: Stanford University Press, 2020), 104–122.

10. One can even begin from outside the subcontinent. See Matthew Mosca, "Hindustan as a Geographic and Political Concept in Qing Sources," *China Report* 47, no. 4 (2011): 263–277.

11. A point made forcefully in Michel-Rolph Trouillot, *Silencing the Past: Power and the Production of History* (Boston: Beacon, 1995).

12. Hence the politics of A. L. Basham's *The Wonder That Was India: A Survey of the History and Culture of the Indian Sub-continent before the Coming of the Muslims* (New York: Grove Press, 1954). See, as well, Nandy's critique of South Asia in Ashis Nandy, "The Idea of South Asia: A Personal Note on Post-Bandung Blues," *Inter-Asia Cultural Studies* 6, no. 4 (2005): 541–545.

13. Historians and intellectuals who have grappled with such issues and shown methodological frameworks that this work follows include C. L. R. James, *The Black Jacobins: Toussaint L'Ouverture and the San Domingo Revolution* (New York: The Dial Press, 1938); Greg Dening, *Islands and Beaches: Discourse on a Silent Land: Marquesas 1774–1880* (Chicago: Dorsey Press, 1980); Gloria Anzaldúa, *Borderlands / La Frontera: The New Mestiza* (San Francisco: Aunt Lute Books, 1987); and Paul Gilroy, *The Black Atlantic: Modernity and Double Consciousness* (Cambridge, MA: Harvard University Press, 1993), to highlight a few.

14. See Marisa J. Fuentes, *Dispossessed Lives: Enslaved Women, Violence, and the Archive* (Philadelphia: University of Pennsylvania Press, 2016), 138–143.

15. On a case for political forgetting, see Ashis Nandy, "History's Forgotten Doubles," *History and Theory* 34, no. 2 (May 1995): 44–66.

16. Walter Benjamin, "Theses on the Philosophy of History," in *Illuminations,* ed. Hannah Arendt, trans. Harry Zohn (1968; New York: Schocken Books, 2007), 255. Emphasis in the original.

17. For an overview, see Prathama Banerjee, "Histories of History in South Asia," in *A Companion to Global Historical Thought,* ed. Prasenjit Duara, Andrew Sartori, and Viren Murthy (West Sussex, UK: Wiley-Blackwell, 2014), 293–307.

18. The details of this meeting are taken from Tauqir Ahmad Khan, *Iqbāl aur Hindūstān* (New Delhi: Na'ī Kitāb Pablisharz, 2007), 13–25.

19. "Sare Jahan se Achcha," *Itihad* 1, no. 10, August 1–12, 1904, 3–4. My gratitude to C. Ryan Perkins for providing me with a digital copy of the issue.

20. Muhammad Iqbal, *Bāng-i-darā: Majmū'ah-yi kalām-i Urdū murattabah-yi muṣannif,* 2nd ed. (Lāhor: Maqbūl-i-'āmm Press, 1926), 82.

21. Gandhi sent a letter of condolence at the death of Iqbal, which was published in *Jauhar* on June 9, 1938, reported in Khan, *Iqbāl aur Hindūstān,* 14. Gandhi refers to Iqbal's song in a speech at the Women's Meeting in August 21, 1947, in Calcutta. The meeting was opened with the song: "Gandhiji drew attention to the two flags of Pakistan and the Indian Union that were being prominently flown among the audience and hoped that that pleasing sight would be universal in India. He was glad too that Shaheed Sahib had suggested the revival of the slogan 'Hindu-Muslim ki Jai,' for it was started during the balmy Khilafat days. He recalled the memory of the old days when a Muslim fellow-prisoner used to sing Iqbal's *Sare Jahan se Achcha.* He used to have it sung equally sweetly by the late Saraladevi Chowdharani. The third time was this evening when he heard it sung with equal sweetness and force. The words of the poem were as sweet as the tune. And among them what could be sweeter than that religion never taught mutual hatred?" Quoted in *The Collected Works of Mahatma Gandhi,* electronic book, 98 vols. (New Delhi: Publications Division Government of India, 1999), 96:259–260, https://www.gandhiashramsevagram.org/gandhi-literature/mahatma-gandhi-collected-works-volume-96.pdf.

22. Muhammad Iqbal, *Speeches, Writings, and Statements of Iqbal,* comp. and ed. Latif Ahmed Sherwani (Lahore: Iqbal Academy, 1977), 11.

23. Ibid., 21.

24. Ibid., 13.

25. I address the orthography of "Hindusthan" below. For the translation, see Sisir Kumar Das, *A History of Indian Literature: 1911–1956, Struggle for Freedom, Triumph and Tragedy* (New Delhi: Sahitya Akademi, 1995), 364–365. Also see Anurapa Cinar, "Translation of Savarkar Poems: Priyakar Hindusthan," AnurupaCinar.com, http://anurupacinar.com/otherworks/translations-of-savarkars-poems/.

26. See Gyanendra Pandey, "Hindus and Other: The Militant Hindu Construction," *Economic & Political Weekly* 26, no. 52 (December 28, 1991): 2997–3009; and Vinayak Chaturvedi, "A Revolutionary's Biography: The Case of V. D. Savarkar," *Postcolonial Studies* 16, no. 2 (2013): 124–139. Also see Janaki Bakhle, "Country First? Vinayak Damodar Savarkar (1883–1966) and the Writing of Essentials of Hindutva," *Public Culture* 22, no. 1 (January 2010): 149–186.

27. V. D. Savarkar, *Hindutva: Who Is a Hindu?* (Bombay: Veer Savarkar Prakashan, 1969), 71.

28. Ibid., 10.

29. Ibid., 81–82.

30. Ibid., 42–43.

31. Ibid., 45.

32. Ibid., 113. Emphasis added.

33. Jadunath Sarkar, *India through the Ages: A Survey of the Growth of Indian Life and Thought* (Calcutta: M.C. Sarkar & Sons, 1928), 68.

34. Ibid.

35. Ibid., 70–71. Emphasis added.

36. Ibid., 135. On Sarkar, see Kiran Pawar, *Sir Jadunath Sarkar: A Profile in Historiography* (New Delhi: Books & Books, 1985); and Dipesh Chakrabarty, *The Calling of History: Sir Jadunath Sarkar and His Empire of Truth* (Chicago: University of Chicago Press, 2015).

37. Iqbal, *Speeches, Writings, and Statements,* 9.

38. The supremacist argument had its own response from the Muslim side. Maulana Hussain Ahmad Madani, one of the leaders of the Deobandi religious school and an opponent of the partition of the subcontinent, published in 1946 his own claim in *Hindustan Hamara* (Hindustan is ours). Madani said, contra Savarkar, that only Muslims can claim Hindustan as their fatherland and holy land, for two reasons. First, that Adam, the first human created, landed in Hindustan when he was cast out of Heaven. Second, that Muslims bury their dead in the soil of Hindustan, as opposed to other communities who burn or expose their dead. Thus, Muslim bodies have made a material contribution to the earth of Hindustan. For Savarkar, a Hindustani was the product of the Hindu earth, and for Madani, a Hindustani was the product of a Muslim soil. See Sayyid Ḥusain Aḥmad Madnī and Sayyid Muḥammad Miyān, *Hamārā Hindustān aur uske fazā'il* (Delhi: Delhi Printing Press, 1946). Certainly, there were many voices against the Partition, led by M. K. Gandhi himself. Kanaiyalal Maneklal Munshi's 1940 speech "Akhand Hindustan," published in *Harijan,* is a good overview of the nonseparatist arguments. See K. M. Munshi, *Akhand Hindustan* (Bombay: New Book, 1942), 16–24.

39. T. V. Mahalingam, "Presidential Address," *Proceedings of the Indian History Congress* 14 (1951): 103.

40. See *A Short History of Hind-Pakistan* (Karachi: Pakistan Historical Society, 1955). The title *Hind-Pakistan* came under criticism and was subsequently revised to *Pak o Hind* in the Urdu edition.

41. The Battle of Plassey, in 1757, is usually central to such simplified timelines, but as Ranajit Guha writes, "For India was not conquered in a nine-hour battle on one single day. . . . Indeed, it would take nearly one hundred more years of war, intrigue, and piecemeal annexation—region by region and often locality by locality—for conquest to be consummated in British paramountcy over the subcontinent as a whole." Ranajit Guha, "A Conquest Foretold," *Social Text* 54 (Spring 1998): 85–86.

42. See Bernard S. Cohn, *Colonialism and Its Forms of Knowledge: The British in India* (Princeton, NJ: Princeton University Press, 1996); Ronald B. Inden, *Imagining India* (Cambridge, MA: Blackwell, 1990); and, more recently, Sanjay Subrahmanyam, *Europe's India: Words, People, Empires, 1500–1800* (Cambridge, MA: Harvard University Press, 2017).

43. See Lata Mani, *Contentious Traditions: The Debate on Sati in Colonial India* (Berkeley: University of California Press, 1998).

44. There is a wide scholarship on the "making" of British India. A key text is Sudipta Sen, *A Distant Sovereignty: National Imperialism and the Origins of British India* (London: Routledge, 2002).

45. I prefer and use "rendering" or "versioning" rather than "translation" to indicate the movement of Persian histories into English during the colonial period. Other scholars have used "tellings" and "transcreation" or "transmutation." For a nuanced discussion on this issue, and a case for "rendering," see Ronit Ricci, *Islam Translated: Literature, Conversion, and the Arabic Cosmopolis of South and Southeast Asia* (Chicago: University of Chicago Press, 2011), 31–32. Also see Finbarr Barry Flood, *Objects of Translation: Material Culture and Medieval "Hindu-Muslim" Encounter* (Princeton, NJ: Princeton University Press, 2008).

46. Alexander Dow, *The History of Hindostan; from the Earliest Account of Time, to the death of Akbar; translated from the Persian of Mahummud Casim Ferishta of Delhi: Together with a Dissertation Concerning the Religion and Philosophy of the Brahmin with an Appendix containing the History of the Mogul Empire, from its decline in the Reign of Mahummud Shaw to the Present Times,* 2 vols. (London: T. Becket and P. A. De Hondt, 1768), n.p. (dedication).

47. Ibid., iii.

48. Ibid., vi.

49. Ibid.

50. Alexander Dow, *The History of Hindostan, from the Death of Akbar, to the Complete Settlement of the Empire under Aurungzebe. To which are prefixed, I. A Dissertation on the Origin and Nature of Despotism in Hindostan. II. An Enquiry into the State of Bengal; with a Plan for Restoring that Kingdom to Its Former Prosperity and Splendor* (London: Printed for T. Becket and P. A. De Hondt in the Strand, 1772).

51. James Anderson, "Account of Malabar, and the Rise and Progress of the Mussulman Religion in that Country, from Ferishtah's General History of Hindostan," *Asiatick Miscellany* 2 (1786): 279–305.

52. Jonathan Scott, *Ferishta's History of Dekkan, from the First Mahummedan Conquests* (Shrewsbury: J. and W. Eddowes, 1794), n.p. (dedication).

53. John Briggs, *History of the Rise of the Mahomedan Power in India, till the Year A.D. 1612* (London: Longman, Rees, Orme, Brown, and Green, 1829), xiii.

54. I deploy "soldier-scribe" to both foreground the role of military officers in creating colonial knowledge and to resist the literary convention of having "secretary" or "scribe" be categories reserved for Hindustani intellectuals and scholars, while even a condemnatory "Orientalist" being somehow a sign of scholarly recognition. There should never be a distinction made between the violence of colonialism and its knowledge product. As Abdelmajid Hannoum writes for the French case in Algeria, "French colonialism engaged in the conquest of knowledge from the earliest stages of its long history, and it turned soldiers into scholars and administrators into historians and ethnographers. It became a machine of thought despite its sustained and violent physical practices." See Abdelmajid Hannoum, *Violent Modernity: France in Algeria* (Cambridge, MA: Harvard University Press, 2010), 95.

55. Dow was in Voltaire's library. See Daniel S. Hawley, "L'Inde de Voltaire," *Studies on Voltaire and the Eighteenth Century* 120 (January 1974): 139–178.

56. Urs App, *The Birth of Orientalism* (Philadelphia: University of Pennsylvania Press, 2010), 72–74.

57. Immanuel Kant, *Idee zu einer allgemeinen Geschichte in weltbürgerlicher Absicht* (Leipzig: Meiner, ca. 1917), 18n. See translation in Immanuel Kant, *Anthropology, History, and Education,* ed. and trans. Günter Zöller and Robert B. Louden (Cambridge: Cambridge University Press, 2007), 118.

58. Johann Gottfried von Herder, *Ideen zur Geschichte der Menschheit,* 2 vols. (Leipzig: F.A. Brockhaus, 1869), 2:187–188. See translation at Johann Herder, *Outlines of a Philosophy of the History of Man,* trans. T. Churchill (London: J. Johnson / L. Hansard, 1803), 307.

59. Herder, *Outlines of a Philosophy of the History of Man,* 309–310.

60. Georg Wilhelm Friedrich Hegel, *Lectures on the Philosophy of World History,* ed. and trans. Robert F. Brown and Peter C. Hodgson (Oxford: Clarendon Press, 2011), 1:286–287.

61. Frederick von Schlegel, *The Philosophy of History: In a Course of Lectures, Delivered at Vienna,* vol. 1, trans. James Burton Robertson (London: Saunders and Otley, 1835), 197.

62. The historiography of the postcolonial critique of the European philosophy of history and its relationship to the Orient is immense. My work here is guided by Ranajit Guha, *History at the Limit of World-History* (New York: Columbia University Press, 2003); and Velcheru Narayana Rao, David Dean Shulman, and Sanjay Subrahmanyam, *Textures of Time: Writing History in South India, 1600–1800* (Delhi: Permanent Black, 2001).

63. There is a parallel question of what even is "Islamic history." For a discussion of recent historiography, see Rian Thum, "What Is Islamic History?," *History and Theory* 57 (December 2019): 7–19. Also see Tarif Khalidi, "Premodern Arabic / Islamic Historical Writing," in *A Companion to Global Historical Thought,* ed. Prasenjit Duara,

Viren Murthy, and Andrew Sartori (Chichester, Sussex, UK: Wiley-Blackwell, 2014), 78–91; Shahzad Bashir, "A Perso-Islamic Universal Chronicle in Its Historical Context: Ghiyas al-Din Khwandamir's Habib al-siyar," in *Historiography and Religion,* ed. Jörg Rüpke, Susanne Rau, and Bernd-Christian Otto (Berlin: Walter de Gruyter, 2015), 207–223; and Christopher Markiewicz, "History as Science: The Fifteenth-Century Debate in Arabic and Persian," *Journal of Early Modern History* 21, no. 3 (2017): 216–240.

64. Marshall G. S. Hodgson, "Two Pre-Modern Muslim Historians: Pitfalls and Opportunities in Presenting Them to Moderns," in *Toward World Community,* ed. John Nef (The Hague: Dr. W. Junk N.V., 1968), 53–68.

65. Franz Rosenthal's *A History of Muslim Historiography,* also from 1968, would theorize further distinctions such as "classical" (works in Arabic) and "later" (works in Persian) histories. Other significant works on Muslim historiography, such as R. Stephen Humphreys's *Islamic History: A Framework for Inquiry* (1988) and Julie Meisami, *Persian Historiography* (1998), developed stricter genre distinctions between the Arabic and Persian literary cultures, which coincided with the geographical distinction between the "Middle East" and "South Asia." For a more enlightened take, see Sanjay Subrahmanyam, "On World Historians in the Sixteenth Century," *Representations* 91, no. 1 (Summer 2005): 26–57.

66. Sanjay Subrahmanyam has long been the lone voice in raising the status and prominence of Firishta. See Sanjay Subrahmanyam, *Courtly Encounters: Translating Courtliness and Violence in Early Modern Eurasia* (Cambridge, MA: Harvard University Press, 2012); Peter Hardy, *Historians of Medieval India: Studies in Indo-Muslim Historical Writing* (New Delhi: Munshiram Manoharlal Publishers, 1997); and C. P. Melville, *Persian Historiography,* vol. 10, *A History of Persian Literature* (London: I. B. Tauris, 2012).

67. For a full listing, see François De Blois and C. A. Storey, *Persian Literature: A Bio-Bibliographic Survey* (London: Luzac, 1939), 2:446–447.

68. See the lists in W. H. Morley, *A Descriptive Catalogue of the Historical Manuscripts in the Arabic and Persian Languages* (London: John W. Parker, 1854); Otto Loth, *A Catalogue of the Arabic Manuscripts in the Library of the India Office* (London: n.p., 1877); Charles Rieu, *Catalogue of the Persian Manuscripts in the British Museum* (London: British Museum, 1883); J. F. Blumhardt, *Catalogue of the Hindi, Panjabi and Hindustani Manuscripts in the Library of the British Museum* (London: British Museum, 1899); E. D. Ross and E. G. Brown, *Catalogue of Two Collections of Persian and Arabic Manuscripts Preserved in the India Office Library* (London: Eyre and Spottiswoode, 1902); Mohammed Hukk, *A Descriptive Catalogue of the Arabic and Persian Manuscripts in Edinburgh University Library* (Edinburgh: Printed for the University of Edinburgh, 1925); Nasiruddin Hashmi, *Europe mein Dakhani Makhtūthāt* (Hyderabad, the Deccan: Shamsul Mutaba' 'Usman, 1932); and A. J. Arberry, "Hand-List of Islamic Manuscripts Acquired by the India Office Library (1936–1938)," *Journal of the Royal Asiatic Society* 3 (1939): 353–396.

69. John Briggs, "Essay on the Life and Writings of Ferishta," *Transactions of the Royal Asiatic Society of Great Britain and Ireland* 2, no. 1 (1829): 341–361.

70. For a convincing argument in support of this, see Shaikh Chānd Husain, "When and Where Was Ferishta Born?," *Annals of the Bhandarkar Oriental Research Institute* 22, nos. 1–2 (1941): 74–78. The presence of historians, poets, and other notables from Shiraz or Astrabad remains a significant part of Deccan history. See Sanjay Subrahmanyam, "Iranians Abroad: Intra-Asian Elite Migration and Early Modern State Formation," *Journal of Asian Studies* 51, no. 2 (May 1992): 340–365; Shaikh Musak Rajjak, "Mir Mohammad Momin Astrabadi's Contribution to Qutb Shahi Deccan History," *Journal of the Research Society of Pakistan* 52, no. 2 (2015): 203–209; and Ali Anooshahr, "Shirazi Scholars and the Political Culture of the Sixteenth-Century Indo-Persian World," *Indian Economic and Social History Review* 51, no. 3 (2014): 331–352.

71. See Emma J. Flatt, *The Courts of the Deccan Sultanates: Living Well in the Persian Cosmopolis* (Cambridge: Cambridge University Press), 74–120.

72. See Henry Cousens, *Bijapur: The Old Capital of the Adil Shahi Kings* (Poona: Orphanage Press, 1889); Navina Najat Haidar and Marika Sardar, eds., *Sultans of the South: Arts of India's Deccan Courts, 1323–1687* (New Haven, CT: Yale University Press, 2012); and Deborah S. Hutton, *Art of the Court of Bijapur* (Bloomington: Indiana University Press, 2007).

73. The literature is vast, but for a recent overview, see Richard M. Eaton, *India in the Persianate Age, 1000–1765* (Oakland: University of California Press, 2019), 142–190. Also see Haroon Khan Sherwani, P. M. Joshi, and Ghulam Yazdani, *History of Medieval Deccan, 1295–1724*, 2 vols. (Hyderabad: Govt. of Andhra Pradesh, 1973); Carl W. Ernst, *Eternal Garden: Mysticism, History, and Politics at a South Asian Sufi Center* (Albany: State University of New York Press, 1992); Hiroshi Fukazawa, *The Medieval Deccan: Peasants, Social Systems and States, Sixteenth to Eighteenth Centuries* (New Delhi: Oxford University Press, 1991); Richard M. Eaton, *The Social History of the Deccan, 1300–1761: Eight Indian Lives* (Cambridge: Cambridge University Press, 2005).

74. For an overview of the early seventeenth century, see Muzaffar Alam and Sanjay Subrahmanyam, "The Deccan Frontier and Mughal Expansion, ca. 1600: Contemporary Perspectives," *Journal of the Economic and Social History of the Orient* 47, no. 3 (2004): 357–389. For the later seventeenth century, see John F. Richards, "The Imperial Crisis in the Deccan," *Journal of Asian Studies* 35, no. 2 (1976): 237–256. For the continuation of Deccani sultanate modes of political formulations into the eighteenth century, see Hannah Lord Archambault, "Geographies of Influence: Two Afghan Military Households in 17th and 18th Century South India" (PhD diss., University of California, Berkeley, 2018), 131–156.

75. See, for example, G. T. Kulkarni, "A Note on a Unique Adil Shahi Farman Bestowing Madad-Ma'ash on Hindus (1653 A.D.)," *Proceedings of the Indian History Congress* 68, no. 1 (2007): 313–318.

76. This book takes its inspiration from the Mughal historian M. Athar Ali's seminal article, "The Evolution of the Perception of India: Akbar and Abu'l Fazl," in which he

argues that "the case for the study of a history of the concept of India is strong" (80). While I do take exception to his usage of "India" for Hindustan, and while my emphasis on Firishta differs from his on Abu'l Fazl and the Mughals, I am undertaking precisely the project that he gestured toward. Let me briefly explain my two substantial differences with M. Athar Ali. First, on the usage of "Hindustan" rather than "India," I believe that it is important to re-enliven concepts translated out of existence during the colonial period, with the semantic richness of their usage in the source languages. This is an important difference that is elided if we insist on reading "Hindustan" simply as "India." A concept history of "India," for instance, would be based solely on European source materials and trace the Latin, Greek, and, later, French, German, Dutch, and English employment and emplotment of the term "India." In that regard, it would be a history of the colonial encounter of the subcontinent and / or the modern state of India, such as Sunil Khilnani's *The Idea of India* (1997). In contrast, a history of the concept "Hindustan" would rely on close examination of subcontinental languages (Sanskrit to Persian, Arabic, Urdu, Bengali, Marathi, and so on). My second major difference with Ali is that he relies on Mughal sources alone to investigate the history of this concept. Even if the Mughal were, for a while, the largest territorial polity in the subcontinent, Hindustan was, as a concept, employed outside the Mughal polity. On Firishta's importance for such a history, M. Athar Ali concludes that "the constant underlying assumption of historical unity of India is remarkable (in Firishta)" (83). Yet, he privileges Mughal sources and maintains that Firishta is merely "inspired" by Nizamuddin Ahmad's *Tabaqat-i Akbari*. As I show in this book, the idea that Firishta's text is a derivation from older histories is born out of its first encounter with colonial scholars. See M. Athar Ali, "The Evolution of the Perception of India: Akbar and Abu'l Fazl," *Social Scientist* 24, nos. 1–3 (January–March 1996): 80–88.

77. My own approach is very much shaped by Sheldon Pollock's considerations. See Sheldon I. Pollock, "Towards a Political Philology: D. D. Kosambi and Sanskrit," in *Unsettling the Past: Unknown Aspects and Scholarly Assessments of D.D. Kosambi,* ed. Meera Kosambi (Delhi: Permanent Black, 2012), 34–61; and Sheldon I. Pollock, "Philology in Three Dimensions," *Postmedieval: A Journal of Medieval Cultural Studies* 5, no. 4 (December 2014): 398–413.

78. I take heed from Walter Benjamin, who wrote that "this state of unrest refers to the demand on the researcher to abandon the tranquil contemplative attitude toward the object in order to become conscious of the critical constellation in which precisely this fragment of the past finds itself in precisely this present." See Walter Benjamin and Knut Tarnowski, "Eduard Fuchs: Collector and Historian," *New German Critique* 5 (Spring 1975): 28.

79. Bernard S. Cohn made fun of historians for using the metaphor of "digging," so I will say that we can just as well imagine the historian as a baker, and these chapters as three-layer cakes. See Bernard S. Cohn, "History and Anthropology: The State of Play," *Comparative Studies in Society and History* 22, no. 2 (April 1980): 208–210.

2. The Question of Hindustan

1. The colonial episteme was challenged in the nineteenth century by Hindustani historians—from Sayyid Ahmad Khan to Kaviraj Shyāmal Dās. It was also challenged and reassessed by historians in the twentieth century, such as Mohammad Habib. Contemporary scholarship's reassessment includes many of the prominent historians of the last fifty years: Romila Thapar, Irfan Habib, Muzaffar Alam, Sanjay Subrahmanyam, Shahid Amin, and many more.

2. Elphinstone defined Hindostan as "composed of the basin of the Indus, that of the Ganges, the desert towards the Indus, and the high tract recently called Central India." See Mountstuart Elphinstone, *The History of India: The Hindú and Mahomatan Periods* (London: John Murray, 1843), 1.

3. The creation of a mythic Hindu king is addressed in Cynthia Talbot, *The Last Hindu Emperor: Prithviraj Chauhan and the Indian Past, 1200–2000* (Cambridge: Cambridge University Press, 2015). For the mythic Muslim invader, see Romila Thapar, *Somanatha: The Many Voices of a History* (New Delhi: Penguin, 2004). The origin of Muslims is addressed in Shahid Amin, *Conquest and Community: The Afterlife of Warrior Saint Ghazi Miyan* (Chicago: University of Chicago Press, 2016); and Manan Ahmed Asif, *A Book of Conquest: Chachnama and Muslim Origins in South Asia* (Cambridge, MA: Harvard University Press, 2016). On the invention of tradition in the Deccan, see Richard M. Eaton and Phillip B. Wagoner, *Power, Memory, Architecture: Contested Sites on India's Deccan Plateau, 1300–1600* (Delhi: Oxford University Press, 2014).

4. This chapter specifically, and my thinking on this question generally, is indebted to the scholarship of Bernard S. Cohn, Nicholas B. Dirks, Ronald B. Inden, Muzaffar Alam, Cynthia Talbot, Shahid Amin, Partha Chatterjee, Sanjay Subrahmanyam, and Romila Thapar.

5. In Hindi, the Constitution reads, "Bhārat arthāt Indiyā, rājyon ka sangh hoga," and in Urdu, "hind, yāni bhārat, riyāsatōn ki aik yunion hogā." For more on the constitutional debates, see Catherine Clémentin-Ojha, "'India, That Is Bharat . . .': One Country, Two Names," *South Asia Multidisciplinary Academic Journal* (December 2014).

6. The *Constituent Assembly of India (Legislative) Debates,* vol. 4 (New Delhi: Government of India, 1948), 740. Also see Roy Srirupa, "'A Symbol of Freedom': The Indian Flag and the Transformations of Nationalism, 1906–2002," *Journal of Asian Studies* 65, no. 3 (August 2006): 495–527. I am grateful to Rohit De for these references.

7. Mohan Sinha Mehta (Udaipur State), *Constituent Assembly of India (Legislative) Debates,* 4:747. Emphasis added.

8. Jawaharlal Nehru, *Glimpses of World History: Being Further Letters to His Daughter, Written in Prison, and Containing a Rambling Account of History for Young People* (New York: Asia Publishing House, 1962), 124.

9. "In other words, the coherence of South Asia as a world region in our current perception is largely a legacy of British colonialism. The British were the first and only

political power to ever extend their sway over all of South Asia and the limits of their dominion now define the boundaries of the region." Catherine B. Asher and Cynthia Talbot, *India before Europe* (Cambridge: Cambridge University Press, 2008), 8.

10. See W. Norman Brown, "South Asia Studies: A History," *Annals of the American Academy of Political and Social Science* 356 (1964): 54–62. Also see Nicholas B. Dirks, "South Asian Studies: Futures Past," in *The Politics of Knowledge: Area Studies and the Disciplines,* ed. David Szanton (Berkeley: University of California Press, 2004), 341–385.

11. Quoted in Samuel Purchas, *Purchas His Pilgrimes: In Five Books* (London: William Stansby, 1625), 205. I have slightly updated the spelling conventions.

12. On early ideas on despotism, see Piyel Haldar, "The Jurisprudence of Travel Literature: Despotism, Excess, and the Common Law," *Journal of Law and Society* 31, no. 1 (2004): 87–112; and Roger Boesche, "Fearing Monarchs and Merchants: Montesquieu's Two Theories of Despotism," *Western Political Quarterly* 43, no. 4 (1990): 741–761.

13. On Jones and his work, see Bernard S. Cohn, *India: The Social Anthropology of a Civilization* (Englewood Cliffs, NJ: Prentice-Hall, 1971), reproduced in *The Bernard Cohn Omnibus* (Oxford: Oxford University Press, 2004); and Ronald B. Inden, "Orientalist Constructions of India," *Modern Asian Studies* 20, no. 3 (1986): 401–446.

14. Jones translates the couplet, which he made famous, from Hafiz: "Agar ān turk-i shirāzi be dast ārad del-i mā rā / Ba khāle hindū-ash bakhsham Samarkhand o Bukharā rā," as "If the fair damsel of Shiraz would accept my heart/I would give for the black mole on her cheek the cities of Samarkand and Bukhāra." See William Jones, *A Grammar of the Persian Language* (London: W. and J. Richardson, 1771), 101. He translates "hindu" as "black" as well on page 43. In the third, expanded edition, he added an index where he lists "hindu" as "black, an Indian." For a discussion on Jones's grammar, see Mohamad Tavakoli-Targhi, *Refashioning Iran: Orientalism, Occidentalism and Historiography* (New York: Palgrave, 2001), 23–26. A proper deconstruction of Jones awaits a scholar, though it is useful to remember that Jones's celebrated linking between Latin, Greek, and Sanskrit is a European project of imagining an origin myth set in the East of some durability. See, for instance, John Webb, *An Historical Essay Endeavoring a Probability That the Language of the Empire of China Is the Primitive Language* (London: Printed for Nath. Brook, 1669); and Jean-Jacques Rousseau, *Essai sur l'origine des langues* (ca. 1755).

15. William Jones, *A Grammar of the Persian Language,* 3rd ed. (London: J. Murray, 1783), 151–154.

16. William Jones, *The Works of Sir William Jones* (London: John Stockdale, 1807), 2:3–4. On this point, also see Edward Said, *Orientalism* (New York: Vintage Books, 1979), 78.

17. See William Jones, "The Third Anniversary Discourse," in *Sir William Jones: Selected Poetical and Prose Works,* ed. Michael J. Franklin (Cardiff: University of Wales Press, 1995), 355–371. Further see the discussion of geography in texts like the *Mahabharata, Kamasutra,* and *Arthasastra* in Haran Chandra Chakladar, "The Geography

of Vātsyāyana," *Annals of the Bhandarkar Oriental Research Institute* 7, nos. 1/2 (1926): 129–152; and Haran Chandra Chakladar, "The Geography of Vātsyāyana (Continued)," *Annals of the Bhandarkar Oriental Research Institute* 8, no. 1 (April 1926): 43–62. Incidentally, this is precisely how Bernard S. Cohn describes India in "India as a Geographic Entity," *India: The Social Anthropology of a Civilization* (Englewood Cliffs, NJ: Prentice-Hall, 1971), 8. See also Manu V. Devadevan, "From Lineage to Territory: The Making of Territorial Self-Consciousness in Kaliṅga," *Indian Historical Review* 44, no. 2 (2017): 181. In medieval Latin, there is "India Minor/India Major," which roughly corresponds to differentiations across the river Indus. See J. M. Bigwood, "Ctesias' 'Indica' and Photius," *Phoenix* 43, no. 4 (Winter 1989): 302–316; and Fernando Tola and Carmen Dragonetti, "India and Greece before Alexander," *Annals of the Bhandarkar Oriental Research Institute* 67, nos. 1–4 (1986): 159–194. For Roman India, see Matthew Fitzpatrick, "Provincializing Rome: The Indian Ocean Trade Network and Roman Imperialism," *Journal of World History* 22, no. 1 (2011): 27–54; and Dick Whittaker, "Conjunctures and Conjectures: Kerala and Roman Trade," *Journal of Asian History* 43, no. 1 (2009): 1–18. For Avestan and Pahlavi connections, see B. D. Mirchandani, "Ancient Sindhu and Sauvīra," *Annals of the Bhandarkar Oriental Research Institute* 57, nos. 1–4 (1976): 81–93. For China, see Liu Xinru, *Ancient India and Ancient China: Trade and Religious Exchanges, A.D. 1–600* (Oxford: Oxford University Press, 1988); and Tansen Sen, *Buddhism, Diplomacy, and Trade: The Realignment of Sino-Indian Relations, 600–1400* (Honolulu: University of Hawai'i Press, 2003). For the variety of references to "al-Hind" (and related words based on the *h-n-d* stem: *mūhind, mūhindā, hindi, hindūvan*), see Nada 'Abd al-Raḥmān Yūsuf al- Shāyī', *Mu'jam alfāẓ al-ḥayāt al-ijtimā'īyah fī dawāwīn shu'arā' al-Mu'allaqāt al-'ashar* (Beirut: Maktab Lebanon, 1991), 313–314.

18. Paul Thieme, "Sanskrit *sindhu-/Sindhu-* and Old Iranian *hindu-/Hindu-*," in *W. B. Henning Memorial Volume*, ed. Mary Boyce and Ilya Gershevitch (London: Lund Humphries, 1970), 447–450.

19. Jones, "The Third Anniversary Discourse," 358.

20. Alok Rai, *Hindi Nationalism* (New Delhi: Orient Longman, 2000).

21. Karl Marx, "The British Rule in India," *New York Daily Tribune* 13 (June 25, 1853), in *Dispatches for the New York Tribune* (Stilwell: Neeland Media, 2014), 218.

22. This particular version was told to me by Ronald B. Inden.

23. See Garland Cannon, "Sir William Jones's Indian Studies," *Journal of the American Oriental Society* 91, no. 3 (July–September 1971): 418–425.

24. On the concept of female deviance as episteme in colonial British India, see Durba Mitra, *Indian Sex Life: How Sexuality Shaped the Science of Society* (Princeton, NJ: Princeton University Press, 2020).

25. Jones, "The Enchanted Fruit; or, The Hindu Wife: An Antediluvian Tale. Written in the Province of Bahar," in *Sir William Jones: Selected Poetical and Prose Works*, 80–97.

26. Ibid., 81. Orthography in the original.

27. Ibid., 82. Orthography in the original.

28. Ibid., 83. Emphasis in the original.

29. Ibid.

30. Jones, *The Works of Sir William Jones* (London: G. G. and J. Robinson, 1799), 6:240.

31. Francis Wilford, "On the Chronology of the Hindus," *Asiatick Researches,* vol. 5 (London: Vernor and Hood, 1798), 263.

32. Manmatha Nath Dutt, *Prose English Translation of Vishnupuranam* (Varanasi: Chowkhamba Sanskrit Series Office, 1972), 308. H. H. Wilson first translated the *Vishnupurana* in 1840.

33. Jonathan Duncan, "An Account of the Discovery of Two Urns in the Vicinity of Benares," and "Inscriptions on the Staff of Fi'ruz Shah. Translated from the Sanscrit, as explained by Ra'dha'ca'nta Sarman," in *Asiatick Researches or Transactions of the Society Instituted in Bengal for Enquiring into the History and Antiquities, the Arts, Sciences, and Literature, of Asia* (London: Vernor and Hood, 1798), 5:131–132 and 5:379–382.

34. The mounds outside Benares provided the raw material for many a construction project: Markham Kittoe used stones and bricks for his construction of Queen's College in Benares in 1847, and much of Cunningham's excavations were put in the nearby river to change its course by W. H. Davidson. See *Archaeological Survey of India, Annual Report, 1904–1905* (Calcutta: Superintendent Government Printing, 1908), 63–64.

35. F. E. Oertel, "Excavations at Sārnāth," in ibid., 69. Emphasis added.

36. See Patrick Olivelle, *King, Governance, and Law in Ancient India: Kauṭilya's Arthásāstra* (New York: Oxford University Press, 2013), 6.

37. As Olivelle explains: "Identifying the historical figure linked to the first Maurya emperor with Kauṭilya, the author of *AŚ,* did not happen until the rise of the next major empire in north India, the Gupta, which also arose in the same geographical region as the Maurya and probably occupied the same capital, Pāṭaliputra. . . . Such associations, especially as powerful a historical association of a text on political science with one of the most powerful operatives of ancient India linked closely to the most powerful Indian empire, do not happen by accident. . . . I want to propose the hypothesis that the identity of Cāṇakya with Kauṭilya was forged during the Gupta rule as one way of connecting the new dynasty to the fabled Maurya empire as its legitimate successor." Ibid., 33–34.

38. With the modern "discovery" of the ideal king Ashoka, a field was inaugurated that investigates the idea of Hindu kingship—from the Ashokan edicts, to the various *Purana* texts—such as the *Matsayapurana, Brahmandapurana* and *Vishnupurana*—to the *Arthasastra*. On Hindu kingship, see John F. Richards, ed., *Kingship and Authority in South Asia* (Madison: Center for South Asian Studies, University of Wisconsin–Madison, 1978).

39. The nationalist historians, like the British, imagined that the "Hindu" Indic past would come alive from texts such as the *Mahabharata* and *Ramayana,* and arguments

were made to view the *Puranas* as the true sources of history. R. C. Majumdar and R. C. Hazra are two exemplars of this strategy. The major intervention in the theories of kingship for medieval India were led by B. D. Chattopadhyaya, Thomas Trautmann, Burton Stein, Ronald B. Inden, Hermann Kulke, and others. These scholars are largely very careful in thinking about Hindu kingship as deriving from texts that predate the Muslim period in the subcontinent. See, for example, Ronald Inden's work on the *Viṣṇudharmottarapurāṇa*, composed in Kashmir, Peshawer, or northern Punjab between 600 and 1000, and the *Aparājitaprcchā* of Bhuvanadeva composed in Gujarat between 1100 and 1200. However, the fact remains that extant copies of these texts were composed / reinscribed or even commented on during a historical period when there was a Muslim political and social presence.

40. James Mill, *The History of British India* (London: Baldwin, Cradock, and Joy, 1817), 1:90–91. Also see Javed Majeed, *Ungoverned Imaginings: James Mill's* The History of British India and Orientalism (Oxford: Clarendon Press, 1992).

41. Mill, *The History of British India,* 1:93n1.

42. Ibid., vol. 2.

43. Elphinstone, *History of India,* 19.

44. On Vincent Smith, see Ronald B. Inden, *Imagining India* (Cambridge, MA: Blackwell, 1990), 7–11. Also see Vincent Arthur Smith, *The Oxford History of India* (Oxford: Clarendon Press, 1920).

45. Fred Donner has recently raised the call to reconsider the "conquest paradigm." See Fred M. Donner, "Visions of the Early Islamic Expansion: Between the Heroic and the Horrific," in *Byzantium in Early Islamic Syria,* ed. Nadia Maria El Cheikh and Shaun O'Sullivan (Beirut: American University of Beirut and University of Balamand, 2011), 9–29.

46. As quoted in Walter Emil Kaegi, "Initial Byzantine Reactions to the Arab Conquest," *Church History* 38, no. 2 (June 1969): 139–149.

47. The history of Islam as imagined and written in Europe begins with Muhammad as a heretic, as an epileptic, as a savant, as a degenerate. Interspersed with that figuration are translations of the Qur'an, the Crusades, the emergence of the Ottoman Empire, the expulsion of Muslims and Jews from the Iberian peninsula. And then there is Muhammad the conqueror or, more broadly, Islam as the faith of an ever-expanding military.

48. The late Shahab Ahmed's book is the first real attempt at a corrective. See Shahab Ahmed, *What Is Islam?: The Importance of Being Islamic* (Princeton, NJ: Princeton University Press, 2017). As a thought experiment, compare the scholarship on Muslim Spain to that of Muslim Sindh. This despite the fact that the Arabian peninsula and the subcontinent had centuries of contact prior to Islam.

49. Henry Miers Elliot, *Appendix to The Arabs in Sind,* vol. 3, part 1, of *The Historians of India* (Cape Town: Saul Solomon, 1853), 1–2.

50. See Henry Miers Elliot, *Bibliographical Index to the Historians of Muhammedan India,* vol. 1 (Calcutta: Baptist Mission Press, 1849), xiii–xiv.

51. As cited in Nayanjot Lahiri, *Ashoka in Ancient India* (Cambridge, MA: Harvard University Press, 2015), 168–169.

52. Edward Gibbon, *The History of the Decline and Fall of the Roman Empire* (London: W. Strahan and T. Cadell, 1788), 5:647.

53. Elphinstone, *History of India,* 542.

54. H. M. Elliot and John Dowson, *The History of India, as Told by Its Own Historians,* vol. 2, *The Muhammedan Period* (London: Trübner, 1869), 2:435.

55. The most significant treatments are in Finbar Barry Flood, *Objects of Translation: Material Culture and Medieval "Hindu-Muslim" Encounter* (Princeton, NJ: Princeton University Press, 2009); and Asif, *A Book of Conquest.*

56. Aḥmad ibn Yahya al-Balādhurī, *Futūḥ al-Buldān* (Beirut: Dar wa-Maktabāh al-Hilāl, 1988), 425.

57. Buzurg ibn Shaharyār and Muḥammad Sa'īd Ṭurayḥī, *'Ajā'ib al-Hind: Barruhā wa-baḥruhā wa-jazā'iruhā* (Abu Dhabi: al-Mujamma' al-Thaqāfī, 2000), 19.

58. Ibid., 20.

59. These letters are reproduced in various other compilations and histories, though often truncated. See S. Q. Fatimi, "Two Letters from the Mahārājā to the Khalifāh: A Study in the Early History of Islam in the East," *Islamic Studies* 2, no. 1 (March 1963): 121–140. The best treatment of these sources is in Flood, *Objects of Translation,* 19–21.

60. Aḥmad ibn 'Alī Ibn al-Zubayr, *Kitāb Al-Dahā'ir wa-l-tuhaf* (Al-Kuwayt: Dā'irat al-Maṭbū'āt wa-l-Našr, 1959), 21.

61. Ibid., 22. Also compare the translation in Ghada Hijjawi Qaddumi, *Book of Gifts and Rarities* (Cambridge, MA: Harvard University Press, 1996), 73–74.

62. Zubayr, *Kitāb Al-Dahā'ir wa-l-tuhaf,* 26. Also compare the translation in Qaddumi, *Book of Gifts and Rarities,* 76.

63. Abū Zayd al-Sīrāfī and Aḥmad Ibn Faḍlān, *Two Arabic Travel Books: Accounts of China and India and Mission to the Volga,* ed. and trans. Tim Mackintosh-Smith and James Edward Montgomery (New York: New York University Press, 2014), 38–39.

64. Ziyaud-Din A. Desai, "Some Fourteenth Century Epitaphs from Cambay in Gujarāt," *Epigraphia Indica: Arabic and Persian Supplement* (Delhi: Government of India Press, 1971), 1–59.

65. See S. Jabir Raza, "Coinage and Metallurgy under the Ghaznavid Sultan Mahmud," *Proceedings of the Indian History Congress* 75 (2014): 224–231; and Waleed Ziad, "'Islamic Coins' from a Hindu Temple: Reconsidering Ghaznavid Interactions with Hindu Sacred Sites through New Numismatic Evidence from Gandhara," *Journal of the Economic and Social History of the Orient* 59, no. 4 (2016): 618–659.

66. See Muḥammad bin Abdūl Jabbar 'Utbi, [Kitāb al-Yamini] *akhbār dawlāt al-mulk Yamin-al-Dawla abi-al-Qasim Maḥmud bin Nāsir al-Dawla abi Mansūr Subuktkin,* ed. Yusuf al-Hādi (Tehran: Markaz al-Buḥūth wa-al-Dirāsāt lil-Turāth al-Makhṭūṭ, 2008), 578; and Muḥammad bin Abdūl Jabbar 'Utbi and Nāsih bin Zafār bin Sa'ād Jorfādeqāni, *Tārīkh-i Yamīnī,* ed. Y. Qayyum (Tehran: Chāpkhānah-i Muḥammad 'Alī Fardīn, 1956), 250.

67. See Abu al-Kalam Azad, *Albiruni aur jugrāfiyā-i ʿālam* (Karachi: Idarā-i Tasnīf o Tahqīq Pakistan, 1980).

68. Nazir Ahmad, "The Earliest Persian Work Completed in Gujarat," in *The Growth of Indo-Persian Literature in Gujarat*, ed. M. H. Siddiqi (Baroda: M. S. University of Baroda Press, 1985), 1–10.

69. ʿAlī ibn Ḥāmid Kūfī, *Fathnamah-i Sind*, ed. Nabi Baksh Khan Baloch (Islamabad: Institute of Islamic History, Culture and Civilization, Islamic University, 1983), 7.

70. For an examination of the *Chachnama* and its geography, see Asif, *A Book of Conquest*, 23–47.

71. On Delhi during this period, see the classic Khaliq Ahmad Nizami, *Religion and Politics in India during the Thirteenth Century* (Delhi: Idarah-i Adabiyat-i Delli, 1974). On Khusrau, see Syed Hasan Askari "Historical Matters in Ijaz-i Khusravi," *Proceedings of the Indian History Congress* 26, no. 2 (1964): 11–20.

72. Qutban Suhravardi, *The Magic Doe: Quṭban Suhravardī's Mirigāvatī: A New Translation*, trans. Aditya Behl, ed. Wendy Doniger (New York: Oxford University Press, 2012), 195.

73. See Dominik Wujastyk, "Indian Manuscripts," in *Manuscript Cultures: Mapping the Field*, ed. Jörg Quenzer, Dmitry Bondarev, and Jan-Ulrich Sobisch (Berlin: Walter de Gruyter, 2014), 159–181. My thanks to Whitney Cox for the reference. Also see Jatindrabimal Chaudhri, *Muslim Patronage to Sanskritic Learning* (Delhi: Idarah-i Adabiyat-i Delli, 1981).

74. See Deborah Hutton, *Art of the Court of Bijapur* (Bloomington: Indiana University Press, 2006), 107–119. On *rasa*, see Sheldon I. Pollock, *A Rasa Reader: Classical Indian Aesthetics* (New York: Columbia University Press, 2016).

75. See Navina Najat Haidar, "The Kitab-i Nauras: Key to Bijapur's Golden Age," in *Sultans of the South: Arts of India's Deccan Courts, 1323–1687*, ed. Navina Najat Haidar and Marika Sardar (New York: Metropolitan Museum of Art, 2011), 26–44.

76. Ibrahim ʿAdil Shah II, *Kitab-i Nauras*, ed. Nazir Ahmad (New Delhi: Bharatiya Kala Kendra, 1956), 111.

77. "No people whose word for 'yesterday' is the same as their word for 'tomorrow' can be said to have a firm grip on the time," quips Salman Rushdie in *Midnight's Children* (New York: Knopf, 1980), 106.

78. Flood's formulation of "Hindu-Muslim Encounter" as a composite and in quotations speaks to this same impulse. See Flood, *Objects of Translation*.

3. AN ARCHIVE FOR HINDUSTAN

1. Muḥammad Qāsim Hindū Shāh Astarābādī Firishta, *Tārīkh-i Firishta*, ed. Muḥammad Riẓā Naṣīrī (Tehran: Anjuman-i Āsār va Mafākhir-i Farhangī, 2009), 3:269.

2. Thomas Babington Macaulay, *Macaulay: Prose and Poetry,* ed. G. M. Young (Cambridge, MA: Harvard University Press, 1952), 722.

3. Ibid., 728.

4. For a full biographical note, see Muhammad Akram Chughtai, *Qadīm Delhī Kallīj* (Lahore: Oriental Publications, 2012), 30–34. See also Gail Minault, "Aloys Sprenger: German Orientalism's 'Gift' to Delhi College," *South Asia Research* 31, no. 1 (2011): 7–23.

5. See George FitzClarence, *Journal of a Route across India, through Egypt, to England, in the Latter End of the Year 1817, and the Beginning of 1818* (London: John Murray, 1819), 11, 254.

6. Aloys Sprenger, *El-Mas'údí's Historical Encyclopædia, Entitled "Meadows of Gold and Mines of Gems,"* vol. 1 (London: Oriental Translation Fund, 1841), ix.

7. Ibid., xi–xii

8. Aloys Sprenger, *A Catalogue of the Bibliotheca Orientalis Sprengeriana* (Giessen: Wilhelm Keller, 1857), iv.

9. Ibid., v.

10. Ibid., vi. Emphasis added.

11. The Tabari is specifically important because it completed the "missing" text of Tabari in Europe. Morley writes, "The chronicle of At-Tabarí, as originally written in Arabic, comprised about twenty parts, of which, until very lately, only the third, fifth, tenth, eleventh, and twelfth were known. Dr. Sprenger has however recently discovered some of the lost portions containing that part of the annals which relates to the origin of Islám. This lost part was found by Dr. Sprenger at Cawnpore, in January, 1850." William Hook Morley, *A Descriptive Catalogue of the Historical Manuscripts in the Arabic and Persian Languages: Preserved in the Library of the Royal Asiatic Society of Great Britain and Ireland* (London: John W. Parker & Sons, 1854), 17.

12. Aloys Sprenger, *A Catalogue of the Arabic, Persian and Hindu'stan'y Manuscripts, of the Libraries of the King of Oudh, compiled under the Orders of the Government of India,* vol. 1 (Calcutta: Baptist Mission Press, 1854), iii.

13. Henry Miers Elliot, *Bibliographical Index to the Historians of Muhammedan India,* vol. 1 (Calcutta: Baptist Mission Press, 1849), x–xii.

14. Ibid., xxvi.

15. Ibid., xxx.

16. These details have been compiled from Elliot's papers. Charles Rieu's third volume of the *Catalogue* (1883) describes in detail the notable "contributors" to the Persian collections—namely Warren Hastings, Charles Hamilton, Nathaniel Brassey Halhed, William Erskine, Henry Elliot, and others. For Elliot's papers, see Charles Rieu, *Catalogue of the Persian Manuscripts in the British Library* (London: British Museum, 1883), 3:1030–1062. Also see the notice of compilation from a family library in the city of Thatta, at the behest of Elliot, in "List of MSS Persian," British Library, London, APAC Or 2073, fl. 14. My thanks to Nur Sobers Khan and Roy Bar Zadeh for providing access to this ledger.

17. Not without *some* resistance. Here is one such protector of Hindustani heritage: "Copies of the *Tárikh Yamini* are not uncommon in India. One of the best is in the Library of Nawẃab Siráju-l Mulk, of Haidarábad; and Sir H. Rawlinson has a very good copy. . . . I only know one copy from which I have made the Extracts given hereafter. This belongs to a pertinacious old lady at Belgrám, who, without knowing what it is, scrupulously guards it from leaving her house, ever since my enquiries respecting the work have led her to look upon it as of exceeding value." Somehow I believe the "pertinacious old lady" knew exactly what was at stake in Elliot's enquiries. See Henry Miers Elliot and John Dowson, eds., *The History of India* (London: Trübner, 1869), 2:16.

18. Sprenger put together the catalog for Elliot's own personal collection after Elliot's death in which he listed 222 manuscripts in Elliot's possession. These are also now in the British Library. See Aloys Sprenger, "Manuscripts of the late Sir H. Elliot, K. C. B.," *Journal of the Asiatic Society* 23, no. 3 (1854): 225–263. See Rieu, *Catalogue of the Persian Manuscripts in the British Library*, xxii.

19. Elliot, *Bibliographical Index*, 310.

20. Ibid., xxxi.

21. Ibid., 317.

22. Ibid., 314.

23. Firishta, *Tarikh-i Firishta*, 1:9.

24. Firishta, *Tarikh-i Firishta*, 1:8.

25. Ahmad Nizamuddin, *The Ṭabaqāt-i-Akbarī of Khwājah Niẓāmuddīn Aḥmad*, ed. Baini Prashad, Brajendranath De, vol. 1 (Calcutta: Asiatic Society of Bengal, 1931), 2–3.

26. Ibid., 3.

27. An argument for Nizamuddin is in M. Athar Ali, "The Evolution of the Perception of India: Akbar and Abu'l Fazl," *Social Scientist* 24, nos. 1–3 (January–March 1996): 80–88.

28. Muhammad ibn 'Abd al-Jabbār al-'Utbī and Nāṣiḥ ibn Ẓafr Jurfādhaqānī, *Tārīkh-i Yamīnī* (Tehran: Chāpkhānah-i Muḥammad 'Alī Fardīn, 1956), 23.

29. Nazir Ahmed, "The Earliest Persian Work Completed in Gujarat," in *The Growth of Indo-Persian Literature in Gujarat*, ed. M. H. Siddiqi (Baroda: M.S. University of Baroda Press, 1985), 2; and Muhammad Nizamu'd-din, *Introduction to the Jawāmi'u'l-Ḥikāyāt wa Lawāmi'u'r-Riwāyāt of Sadīdu'd-dīn Muḥammad al-'Awfī* (London: Luzac, 1929), 15–16.

30. 'Alī ibn Ḥāmid Kūfī, *Fathnama-i Sind*, ed. Nabi Baksh Khan Baloch (Islamabad, Pakistan: Institute of Islamic History, Culture and Civilization, Islamic University, 1983), 17.

31. See Blain Auer, "Civilising the Savage: Myth, History and Persianisation in the Early Delhi Courts of South Asia," in *Islamisation: Comparative Perspectives from History*, ed. A. C. S. Peacock (Edinburgh: Edinburgh University Press, 2017), 393–419.

32. Tajuddin Hasan Nizami, *Tāj Al-Ma'āṣir* (Delhi: Markaz-i Taḥqiqāt-i Fārsi, 2008), 40.

33. The historiography on Baihaqi as a historian is formidable. The most important works are Marilyn Robinson Waldman, *Toward a Theory of Historical Narrative: A Case Study in Perso-Islamicate Historiography* (Columbus: Ohio State University Press, 1980); Stephen Humphreys, *Islamic History: A Framework for Inquiry*, rev. ed. (Princeton, NJ: Princeton University Press, 1991), and Julie S. Meisami, *Persian Historiography to the End of the Twelfth Century* (Edinburgh: Edinburgh University Press, 1999). A wide range of historians have consulted the text and worked on it, from Muhammad Nazim, *The Life and Times of Sultan Mahmud of Ghazna* (Cambridge: Cambridge University Press, 1931); to Clifford Edmund Bosworth, *The Ghaznavids: Their Empire in Afghanistan and Eastern Iran, 994–1040* (Edinburgh: Edinburgh University Press, 1963); to Ali Anooshahr, *The Ghazi Sultans and the Frontiers of Islam: A Comparative Study of the Late Medieval and Early Modern Periods* (New York: Routledge, 2008), to name just a few.

34. Abu-'l-Faḍl Muḥammad Ibn-Ḥusain Baihaqī, *Tārīkh-i Baihaqī* (Tehran: Chāpkhānah-i Bānk-i Millī-i Īrān, 1945), 108.

35. Ibid., 109.

36. Ibid., 96.

37. Ibid., 106.

38. Ibid., 36.

39. Minhāj Sirāj Jūzjānī, *Ṭabaqāt-i Nāṣirī*, ed. 'Abd al-Ḥayy Ḥabībī (Tehran: Intishārāt-i Asāṭīr, 1989), 1:6–7.

40. Ibid., 1:8.

41. Ibid., 1:8.

42. Ibid., 1:8–9.

43. He is often considered the first Hindustani historian, based on his birth. Baran is between Meerut and Aligarh in Uttar Pradesh. However, if birth in the north Indian subcontinent is the determining factor, Juzjani's father, having been born in Lahore, should have given honorary Hindustani status to him, or for that matter, the historians from Ghazni. For the Hindustani historian claim, see Syed Hasan Barani, *Ziaduddin Barani* (Delhi: Maktabā Jami'a Milli Islamiya, 1930), 1.

44. Ziyā al-Dīn Baranī, *Tārīkh-i Fīrūz Shāhī: Tārīkh-i Fārsī* (Rāmpūr: Kitābkhānah-i Razā Rāmpūr, 2013), 15.

45. Ibid., 2; Qur'an 36:12 and 12:3.

46. Barani, 5–7.

47. Ibid., 9.

48. Ibid., 17.

49. Ibid.

50. Mīr Khwānd, *Tārīkh-i rawẓat al-ṣafā fī sīrat al-anbiyā' va al-mulūk va al-khulafā'*, ed. Jamshīd Kiyānfar (Tehran: Intesharat Aṣāṭīr, 2001), 1:7.

51. Ibid., 1:10.

52. Ibid.

53. Ibid., 1:12.

54. Ibid.

55. Ibid., 1:4–15.

56. Ibid., 1:17.

57. See Peter Hardy, "Abul Fazl's Portrait of the Perfect Padshah: A Political Philosophy for Mughal India—or a Personal Puff for a Pal?," in *Islam in India: Studies and Commentaries*, ed. Christian W. Troll (New Delhi: Vikas, 1985), 2:114–137.

58. Abu'l Fazl, *The History of Akbar*, ed. and trans. Wheeler M. Thackston (Cambridge, MA: Harvard University Press, 2018), 4:525.

59. Ibid., 4:526–527.

60. Ibid.

61. Ibid., 4:529.

62. Ibid., 4:541.

63. Firishta, *Tarikh-i Firishta*, 1:6–7.

64. See Shaikh Chānd Husain, "When and Where Was Firishta Born?," *Annals of the Bhandarkar Oriental Research Institute* 22, nos. 1–2 (1941): 74–78.

65. Firishta, *Tarikh-i Firishta*, 1:7.

66. Qur'an 12:4.

67. Qur'an 12:5.

68. Qur'an 12:100.

69. An important reading of Yusuf's story is in Gayane Karen Merguerian and Afsaneh Najmabadi, "Zulaykha and Yusuf: Whose 'Best Story'?," *International Journal of Middle East Studies* 29, no. 4 (November 1997): 485–508.

70. Ishaq ibn Bishr (d. 821), *Mubtada' al-Dunyā wa-Qiṣaṣ al-Anbiyā'* (The beginning of the world and the tales of the prophets); Tabari, *Ta'rīkh al-Rusul wa'al Mulūk* (History of prophets and kings); and al-Tha'labī (d. 1036), *'Arā'is al-Majālis: Qiṣaṣ al-Anbiyā'* (Brides of gatherings: Tales of the prophets) are some of the earliest collections. The genre went on to become the most significant repository of Muslim historical and theological knowledge around the world. For an overview, see J. Knappert, "The Qiṣaṣu'l-Anbyā'i as Moralistic Stories," *Proceedings of the Seminar for Arabian Studies* 6 (1976): 103–116; and Roberto Tottoli, *Biblical Prophets in the Qur'ān and Muslim Literature* (London: Routledge, 2002), 86–101.

71. See Thibaut d'Hubert and Alexandre Papas, eds., *Jāmī in Regional Contexts: The Reception of 'Abd al-Raḥmān Jāmī's Works in the Islamicate World, ca. 9th/15th–14th/20th Century* (Leiden: Brill, 2018).

72. For such stories in Dakhani, see M. A. M. Khan and C. H. Shaikh, "A Dakhani Manuscript," *Bulletin of the Deccan College Research Institute* 2, nos. 3–4 (June 1941): 302. For Śrīvara's Sanskrit version of the *Yusuf Zulaykha* story, see Richard Schmidt, *Śrīvara's Kathākāutumkam: Die Geschichte von Joseph in persisch-indischem Gewande* (Kiel: C. F. Haeseler, 1898). Also see Luther Obrock, "Śrīvara's Kathākautuka Cos-

mology, Translation, and the Life of a Text in Sultanate Kashmir," in d'Hubert and Papas, *Jāmī in Regional Contexts*, 752–777.

73. Firishta, *Tarikh-i Firishta*, 1:11.

74. While Naqib Khab did one rendering in Persian, Faizi also completed a separate rendition of the *Mahabharata*. Abu'l Faiz Faizi, the brother of Abu'l Fazl, was also a close adviser of Akbar and the poet laureate of Akbar's court. The Rampur manuscript of Firishta's *Tarikh* quotes Faizi's version. On Faizi's version, see Shaikh Chand Husain, *A Descriptive Handlist of the Arabic, Persian and Hindusthānī Mss., Belonging to the Satara-Historical Museum, at Present Lodged at the Deccan College Research Institute, Poona* (Poona: Katre, 1943), 247–248. See Shaikh Chand Husain, "Translations of the Mahābhārata into Arabic and Persian," *Bulletin of the Deccan College Research Institute* 5, no. 3 (1943–1944): 274.

75. For details on Akbar's project, see M. Athar Ali, "Translation of Sanskrit Works at Akbar's Court," *Social Scientist* 20, nos. 9–10 (September–October 1992): 38–45; and Jivanji Jamshedji Modi, "King Akbar and the Persian Translations of Sanskrit Books," *Annals of the Bhandarkar Institute* 6, no. 1 (1925): 83–107. Also see Muhammad Riza Jalali Na'ini and N. S. Shukla, eds., *Mahabharat: Buzurgtarin Manzumah-i Kuhnah-i Mawjud-i Jahan bih Zaban-i Sanskrit* (Tehran: Kitabkhanah-i Tahuri, 1980), 1:1–42. For literary responses to the Mughal projects, also see Allison Busch, "Literary Responses to the Mughal Imperium: The Historical Poems of Kesavdas," *South Asian Research* 25, no. 1 (2005): 31–54.

76. Jalali Na'ini and Shukla, *Mahabharat*, 1:18.

77. Ibid.

78. Ibid., 1:19.

79. Firishta, *Tarikh-i Firishta*, 1:25.

80. Ibid., 1:12.

81. Ibid., 1:25–26.

82. Ibid., 1:31.

83. "Contrapuntal" comes from the musical composition practice of "counterpoint," which emerged in the seventeenth century (most famously used by J. S. Bach), wherein melodies are harmonically (or dis-harmonically) interdependent while being independent in rhythm and contour. The application of a musical term to a historical / material setting is motivated by the centrality of music theory and performance for Firishta's courtly milieu in the early seventeenth century.

84. On Viyasa performing an author function in the *Mahabharata*, see Alf Hiltebeitel, *Rethinking the Mahābhārata: A Reader's Guide to the Education of the Dharma King* (Chicago: University of Chicago Press, 2001), 46–92.

85. The seminal work on the Ghaznavids remains Bosworth, *The Ghaznavids*.

86. Firishta, *Tarikh-i Firishta*, 1:61.

87. Ibid.

88. Ibid., 1:63.

89. Ibid.

90. Muḥammad ibn ʿAbd al-Jabbār al-ʿUtbī, *Kitāb al-Yamini akhbār dawlāt al-mulk Yamin-al-Dawla abi-al-Qasim Maḥmud bin Nāsir al-Dawla abi Mansūr Subuktkin*, ed. Yusuf al-Hādi (Tehran: Markaz al-Buḥūth wa-al-Dirāsāt lil-Turāth al-Makhṭūṭ, 2008), 221–222. In the Persian translation of ʿUtbi, compiled by Jurbādhaqāni in the 1180s, the generic "pollutant" (*al-najasat*) from Arabic is rendered as the more specific "wine flasks," which are thrown into the spring. See Muhammad ibn ʿAbd al-Jabbār al-ʿUtbī and Nāṣiḥ ibn Ẓafr Jurfādhaqānī, *Kitāb-i mustatāb-i tarjumah-ʾi Tārīkh-i Yamīnī* (Tehran: n.p., 1856), 30ff.

91. Nizamuʾd-din, *Introduction to the Jawāmiʿuʾl-Ḥikāyāt*, 252.

92. Juzjānī, *Ṭabaqāt-i Nāṣirī*, 1:229.

93. Ibid.

94. Ibid., 1:231.

95. Firishta, *Tarikh-i Firishta*, 1:109.

96. Ibid., 1:113.

97. Ibid., 1:114.

98. Ibid.

99. Juzjānī, *Ṭabaqāt-i Nāṣirī*, 1:230–31.

100. Firishta, *Tarikh-i Firishta*, 1:125.

4. The Places in Hindustan

1. Muḥammad Qāsim Hindū Shāh Astarābādī Firishta, *Tārīkh-i Firishta*, ed. Muḥammad Riẓā Naṣīrī (Tehran: Anjuman-i Āsār va Mafākhir-i Farhangī, 2009), 1:8.

2. I am relying here on Michel de Certeau's distinction between "space" and "place," in which place indicates a fixity, as through the origins that Firishta invents for cities. See Michel de Certeau, "Practices of Space," in *On Signs*, ed. Marshall Blonsky (Baltimore, MD: Johns Hopkins University Press, 1985), 122–146. See further in Michel de Certeau, *The Writing of History*, trans. Tom Conley (New York: Columbia University Press, 1988), 17–115.

3. Firishta, *Tārīkh-i Firishta*, 4:153.

4. See John Donne, *A Sermon upon the Eight Verse of the First Chapter of the Acts of the Apostles. Preached to the Honourable Company of the Virginia Plantation, 13th of November 1622, by John Donne Deane of Saint Pauls* (1624), in *The Sermons of John Donne*, ed. G. R. Potter and Evelyn M. Simpson (Berkeley: University of California Press, 1953–1962), vol. 4 (no. 10): 264–282; and John Locke, *Two Treatises of Government*, ed. Peter Laslett (Cambridge: Cambridge University Press, 1988).

5. Richard Hakluyt, *The Second Volvme of the Principal Navigations, Voyages, Traffiques and Discoueries of the English Nation, made by Sea or ouer-land, to the South and South-east parts of the World, at any time within the compasse of these 1600 yeres:*

Diuided into two seuerall parts (London: George Bishop, Ralph Newbery, and Robert Barker, 1599), 250.

6. See Radhika Seshan, "Routes and Towns in the Deccan 15th to 17th Centuries," *Proceedings of the Indian History Congress* 75 (2014): 331–335.

7. Hakluyt, *The Second Volvme of the Principal Navigations, Voyages, Traffiques and Discoueries of the English Nation*, 253. For the ease of reading, I have slightly modernized the diction from the original material.

8. Ibid., 254.

9. See Samuel Purchas, *Hakluytus Posthmus or Purchas His Pilgrimes. Contayning a History of the World, in Sea voyages. & lande-Trauells, by Englishmen & others* (London: Henry Fetherston, at ye signe of the rose in Pauls Churchyard, 1625), 216. Also see William Foster, ed., *Early Travels in India, 1583–1619* (Oxford: Oxford University Press, 1921), 100.

10. Ibid.

11. William Foster, *The Embassy of Sir Thomas Roe to the Court of the Great Mogul, 1615–1619, as Narrated in His Journal and Correspondence* (London: Hakluyt Society, 1899), 2:531.

12. Ibid., 2:537.

13. The standard history of the cartographic imagination of empire in British India remains Matthew H. Edney, *Mapping an Empire: The Geographical Construction of British India, 1765–1843* (Chicago: University of Chicago Press, 1997).

14. "You, who are Roman, recall how to govern mankind with your power. These will be your special 'Arts': the enforcement of peace as a habit, Mercy for those cast down and relentless war upon proud men." See Virgil, *Aeneid*, trans. Frederick Ahl (Oxford: Oxford University Press, 2007), 155.

15. Louis Stanislas d'Arcy Delarochette, "Hind, Hindoostan, or India" (London: William Faden, 1788), map.

16. Ibid.

17. Joseph Tieffenthaler, *Description Historique et Géographique De L'Inde qui présente en Trois Volumes*, vol. 1, trans. M. Jean Bernoulli (Berlin: Pierre Bourdeaux, 1786).

18. Delarochette, "Hind, Hindoostan, or India." These labels had lasting impact. See, for example, S. Chartres Macpherson, "An Account of the Religion of the Khonds in Orissa," *Journal of the Royal Asiatic Society of Great Britain and Ireland* 13 (1852): 216–274. Macpherson's account would be later used by British ethnologists to construct ideas of primitivity.

19. Edney, *Mapping an Empire*, 9–16.

20. James Rennell, *Memoir of a Map of Hindoostan, or, The Mogul Empire: With an Introduction, Illustrative of the Geography and Present Division of that Country, and a Map of the Countries Situated between the Head of the Indus and the Caspian Sea* (London: M. Brown for the author, 1788).

21. Ibid., lxxi.

22. Ibid., ix.

23. Ibid., xx.

24. Ibid., xl.

25. Ibid., xli.

26. Ibid.

27. James Rennell, J. I. Phillips, and W. Harrisson, "Hindoostan" (London: Published according to act of Parliament by J. Rennell, December 1, 1782), map.

28. Rennell, *Memoir of a Map of Hindoostan*, iv.

29. A key effort was led in Madras by Colonel Colin Mackenzie. See Phillip B. Wagoner, "Precolonial Intellectuals and the Production of Colonial Knowledge," *Comparative Studies in Society and History* 45, no. 4 (October 2003): 783–814.

30. Mas'ūdī, Abu'l Ḥasan 'Ali, and Charles Pellat, *Murūj al-Dhahab wa Ma'āden al-Jawhar* (Beirut: Manshurat al-Jami'ah al-Lubnaniyah, 1966), 71–72.

31. Ibid.

32. Ibid. A *mun* (maund) is roughly twenty-one kilograms.

33. Ibid., 72. I am translating the Arabic word *kafir* not as "infidel" or "unbeliever" (as is generally done), but closer to its intended meaning in *kufr* as "pagan" or "polytheist."

34. Abu'l Qasem Ferdowsi, *The Shahnameh*, ed. Djalal Khaleghi-Motlagh (New York: Bibliotheca Persica, 1988), 1:18.

35. Sunil Sharma, in his study on Mas'ud Sa'ad Salman, notes the poet Khaqani's caustic comment on 'Unsari, who received riches from Mahmud: "With ten couplets for one victory in Hindustan / 'Unsari earned a hundred bags of gold and slaves." Cited in Sunil Sharma, *Persian Poetry at the Indian Frontier: Mas'ûd Sa'd Salmân of Lahore* (New Delhi: Permanent Black, 2000), 41.

36. 'Abd al-Ḥayy ibn Ẓaḥḥāk Gardīzī, *Zayn al-Akhbār*, ed. Raḥīm Riẓāzādah-'i Malik (Tehran: Anjuman-i Āsār va Mafākhir-i Farhangī, 2005), 412.

37. Ibid.

38. Muḥammad Manṣūr bin Sa'īd Mubārakshāh, *Ādāb al-ḥarb wa-l-shujā'a* (Tehran: Intishārāt-i Iqbāl, 1967), 240–270. Also see *Encyclopaedia Iranica*, s.v. "Ādāb al-ḥarb wa'l-šajā'a"; *Encyclopaedia of Islam, THREE*, s.v. "Fakhr-i Mudabbir"; Iqbal M. Shafi, "Fresh Light on the Ghaznavīds," *Islamic Culture* 12, no. 2 (1938): 189–234.

39. Minhāj Sirāj Jūzjānī, *Ṭabaqāt-i Nāṣirī*, ed. 'Abd al-Ḥayy Ḥabībī (Tehran: Intishārāt-i Asāṭīr, 1989), 1:6.

40. Ibid., 1:449.

41. Ibid., 1:8.

42. Ibid., 1:11.

43. Ibid., 1:39.

44. Ibid., 1:415.

45. Ibid., 1:417.

46. Ibid., 1:428.

47. Ibid., 1:452.

48. Ibid., 1:449.

49. The scholarship on Khusrau is vast. See Sunil Sharma, *Amir Khusraw: The Poet of Sultans and Sufis* (London: One World Publications, 2005), for an overview. Also see Zoe Ansari, ed., *Life, Times and Works of Amīr Khusrau Dehlavi* (New Delhi: National Amir Khusrau Society, 1975).

50. Amir Khusrau, *Khaza'in al-futuh of Hazrat Amir Khusrau Dihlawi*, trans. Mohammad Wahid Mirza (Calcutta: Asiatic Society of Bengal, 1953), 5–6. See also Amir Khusrau, *The Campaigns of 'Alā'u;d-dīn Khiljī, Being the Khaẓā'inul Fuṭūḥ (Treasures of Victory) of Hazrat Amīr Khusrau of Delhi*, trans. Mohammad Habib (Madras: Diocesan Press, 1931), 3.

51. Khusrau, *Khaza'in al-futuh of Hazrat Amir Khusrau Dihlawi*, 6.

52. Ibid., 8.

53. Ibid.

54. Ibid., 24.

55. Ibid.

56. Ibid., 40.

57. Ibid., 49.

58. Ibid., 47.

59. Ibid., 77.

60. Ibid., 49.

61. Ibid.

62. Ibid., 171.

63. Amir Khusrau, *The Nuh Sipihr of Amir Khusraw: Persian Text*, ed. Muhammad Wahid Mirza (Oxford: Oxford University Press, 1950), 151. See also Hazrat Ameer Khusro Dehlavi, *Masnavi Nuh Siphar*, trans. Mohammad Rafiq Abid (New Delhi: Maktaba Jami'a, 2012).

64. Khusrau, *The Nuh Sipihr of Amir Khusraw*, 150.

65. Ibid., 147.

66. Ibid., 149.

67. Ibid., 151–152.

68. Ibid., 153.

69. Ibid., 154.

70. Ibid.

71. Ibid., 155–156.

72. Ibid., 157.

73. Ibid., 172.

74. Ibid., 175.

75. Ibid., 178.

76. Ibid., 175.

77. Ibid., 179.

78. Ibid., 179–180.

79. Ibid., 181.

80. Ibid., 184.

81. Ẓiyā' ad-Dīn Baranī, *Tarīkh-i-Firoz Shāhī*, ed. Syed Ahmed (Aligarh: Sir Syed Academy, 2005), 50–51.

82. Ibid., 51–52.

83. Ibid.

84. Ibid.

85. Ibid., 529.

86. Ibid., 531.

87. Ibid.

88. Ibid., 567–568.

89. See Shams Sirāj 'Afīf, Ishrat Husain Ansari, and H. A. Qureshi, *Tarikh-i-Firoz Shahi of Shams Siraj Afif* (Rampur: Rampur Raza Library, 2015).

90. Throughout his text, Babur uses *badshah* to mean Muslim rulers. See Ali Anooshahr, *The Ghazi Sultans and the Frontiers of Islam: A Comparative Study of the Late Medieval and Early Modern Periods* (New York: Routledge, 2008), 49–51.

91. Ẓahīr-ud-Dīn Muḥammad Bābur, *Bāburnāma: Chaghatay Turkish Text with Abdul-Rahim Khankhanan's Persian Translation, Turkish Transcription, Persian Edition, and English Translation* by W. M. Thackston, Jr., 3 vols. (Cambridge, MA: Department of Near Eastern Languages and Civilizations, Harvard University, 1993), 3:178.

92. Ibid.

93. Ibid., 3:179.

94. Abu'l Fazl, *The A'in i Akbari of Abul Fazl 'Allami*, ed. Hienrich Blochmann (Piscataway, NJ: Gorgias Press, 2010), 5:1.

95. Abu'l Fazl, *The History of Akbar*, ed. and trans. Wheeler M. Thackston (Cambridge, MA: Harvard University Press, 2006), 2:479.

96. Abu'l Fazl, *The A'in i Akbari of Abul Fazl 'Allami*, 5:1.

97. Ibid., 5:4.

98. Ibid.

99. Ibid.

100. Ibid., 5:58.

101. Ibid., 5:16.

102. Ibid., 5:29–48.

103. Firishta, *Tarikh-i Firishta*, 1:28.

104. Ibid., 1:29.

105. Ibid.

106. Ibid., 1:31.

107. Ibid., 1:34.

108. Ibid., 1:43.

109. See Roy S. Fischel, *Local States in an Imperial World: Identity, Society and Politics in the Early Modern Deccan* (Edinburgh: Edinburgh University Press, 2020).

110. Firishta, *Tarikh-i Firishta*, 1:189.

111. Ibid., 1:190–193.

112. Ibid., 1:237–238.

113. Ibid., 1:503.

114. Ibid., 1:569.

115. Ibid., 2:43.

116. Ibid., 2:105–106.

117. Ibid., 2:240–241.

118. Ibid., 2:230.

119. Ibid., 2:252.

120. Ibid., 2:357.

121. Ibid., 2:383.

122. Ibid.

123. Ibid., 3:4. Also see M. A. Nayeem, *External Relations of the Bijapur Kingdom, 1489–1686 A.D.* (Hyderabad: Bright Publishers, 1974), iiin2.

124. Firishta, *Tarikh-i Firishta*, 3:35.

125. Ibid.

126. Ibid., 3:140.

127. Ibid., 3:269.

128. Ibid., 3:321.

129. Ibid., 3, 381–382.

130. Ibid., 3:529.

131. Ibid.

132. Ibid., 3:529–530.

133. Ibid., 3:530.

5. THE PEOPLES IN HINDUSTAN

1. Muḥammad Qāsim Hindū Shāh Astarābādī Firishta, *Tārīkh-i Firishta*, ed. Muḥammad Riẓā Naṣīrī (Tehran: Anjuman-i Āsār va Mafākhir-i Farhangī, 2009), 4:56–88. On the making of Gujarat in the fifteenth century, see Jyoti Gulati Balachandran, *Narrative Pasts: The Making of a Muslim Community in Gujarat, c. 1400–1650* (New Delhi: Oxford University Press, 2020), 63–95; and Aparna Kapadia, *In Praise of Kings: Rajputs, Sultans and Poets in Fifteenth-Century Gujarat* (Cambridge: Cambridge University Press, 2018).

2. Ferñao Lopes de Castanheda, *História del descobrimento e conquista de India pelos Portugueses* (Coimbra: João de Barreira e Álvares, 1552).

3. See Heidi Brayman Hackel and Peter C. Mancall, "Richard Hakluyt the Younger's Notes for the East India Company in 1601: A Transcription of Huntington Library Manuscript EL 2360," *Huntington Library Quarterly* 67, no. 3 (2004): 423–436; and Samuel Purchas, *Purchas His Pilgrimage. Or Relations of the world and the religions obserued in all ages and places discouered, from the Creation vnto this present In foure partes* (London: William Stansby for Henrie Fetherston, 1613), 418.

4. See Sanjay Subrahmanyam, "Intertwined Histories: 'Crónica' and 'Tārīkh' in the Sixteenth Century Indian Ocean World," *History and Theory* 49, no. 4 (2010): 129. On the history of the early Portuguese encounters in Hindustan, also see Sanjay Subrahmanyam, *Courtly Encounters: Translating Courtliness and Violence in Early Modern Eurasia* (Cambridge, MA: Harvard University Press, 2012).

5. Nicholas Lichefeld, *The first booke of the historie of the discouerie and conquest of the East Indias* (London: Thomas East, 1582), iv.

6. In recounting the history of Portuguese arrivals, Castanheda peoples the subcontinent with the understood enemies of the Muslims, his fellow Christians: "There were in that Island such Christians which also had wars with the Moores. Moreover they carried our men to the Merchant's house of the Indias, which were Christians, who having information that ours also were people Christened, showed themselves to be joyfull thereof, both embracing and banqueting them, showing them painted in a Paper, the figure of the holy Ghost, which they did worship, and before them made their Prayers upon their knees." Ibid., 23.

7. Ibid., 20. For ease of reading, I have slightly modernized the diction from the original material.

8. Ibid., 31.

9. Ibid., 32.

10. Ibid.

11. Ibid., 33. For ease of reading, I have slightly modernized the diction from the original material.

12. Ibid., 38.

13. Ibid., 47.

14. Ibid.

15. Sergio J. Pacifici, trans., *Copy of a Letter to the King of Portugal Sent to the King of Castile Concerning the Voyage and Success of India* (Minneapolis: University of Minnesota Press, 1955), 9.

16. Cristina Osswald, "On Otherness and India: O Livro de Duarte Barbosa (c. 1516) Seen in Context," *CEM: Cultura, Espaço & Memória* 6, no. 6 (2015): 23–38.

17. Duarte Barbosa, *The Book of Duarte Barbosa*, ed. and trans. Mansel Longworth Dames, vol. 2 (London: Hakluyt Society, 1921), 2–3.

18. Luís Vaz de Camões, *The Lusiads*, trans. Landeg White (Oxford: Oxford University Press, 1997), 142.

19. Camões, *The Lusiads*, 144.

20. The "Moor" sailor from Malindi who actually guided the Portuguese ships to Calicut is already written out of history.

21. Camões, *The Lusiads,* 145.

22. Ibid., 146.

23. Ibid., 147.

24. Ibid., 150.

25. Ibid., 167.

26. Sushil Srivastava, "Situating the Gentoo in History: European Perception of Indians in the Early Phase of Colonialism," *Economic and Political Weekly* 36, no. 7 (2001): 579.

27. Women being burned on the funeral pyre has been variously termed "Suttee," "Sati," and "Widow Burning." All of these terms originate from, and participate in, the colonizing spectacle of the peoples of Hindustan in Europe. I have chosen to not use any of these terms, unless the source material uses them. I use the term "immolation" (but pointedly not "self-immolation"), with its implicit understanding of death by fire. See Gayatri Chakravorty Spivak, "Can the Subaltern Speak?," in *Marxism and the Interpretation of Culture,* ed. Cary Nelson and L. Grossberg (Urbana: University of Illinois Press, 1988), 304–305. In terms of European gendering of India, see Rosa Maria Perez, "The Rhetoric of Empire: Gender Representations in Portuguese India," *Portuguese Studies* 21 (2005): 126–141.

28. Strabo, *Geography,* trans. Horace Leonard Jones (Cambridge, MA: Harvard University Press, 1930), 107–109.

29. Dames, *The Book of Duarte Barbosa,* 216.

30. Ibid., 214.

31. Samuel Purchas, *Hakluytus Posthmus or Purchas His Pilgrimes* (London: Henry Fetherston at ye signe of the rose in Pauls Churchyard, 1625), 482–486; and Nicholas Withington, *A Briefe Discoverye of Some Things best worth Noteinge in the Travels of Nicholas Withington & c.* (London: C. Rivington, at the Bible and Crown in St. Paul's Church yard, 1735). Also see William Foster, ed., *Early Travels in India, 1583–1619* (Oxford: Oxford University Press, 1921), 188–284.

32. Purchas, *Purchas His Pilgrimes,* 483.

33. Ibid., 484. For the ease of reading, I have slightly modernized the diction from the original material.

34. Ibid., 485.

35. Ibid.

36. Also see Lata Mani, *Contentious Traditions: The Debate on Sati in Colonial India* (Berkeley: University of California Press, 1998); and Norbert Schürer, "The Impartial Spectator of Sati, 1757–84," *Eighteenth-Century Studies* 42, no. 1 (2008): 19–44.

37. Samuel Johnson, Oliver Goldsmith, and Christopher Smart, eds., *The World Displayed or, A Curious Collection of Voyages and Travels, Selected from the Writers of All Nations,* vol. 16 (London: J. Newbery, 1760), 61–62.

38. Adam Olearius, *Offt begehrte Beschreibung Der Newen Orientalischen Reise, So durch Gelegenheit einer Holsteinischen Legation an den König in Persien geschehen* (Schleswig: Bey Jacob zur Glocken, 1647).

39. Vincent Arthur Smith, "The Credit Due to the Book Entitled 'The Voyages and Travels of J. Albert de Mandelslo into the East Indies,'" *Journal of the Royal Asiatic Society of Great Britain and Ireland* (April 1915): 245–254.

40. John Locke, *John Locke: Essays on the Law of Nature: The Latin Text with a Translation, Introduction, and Notes; Together with Transcripts of Locke's Shorthand in His Journal for 1676,* ed. W. von Leyden (Oxford: Oxford University Press, 2002), 172–173. Emphasis mine.

41. John Dryden, *Aureng-Zebe: A Tragedy Acted at the Royal Theatre* (London: T. N. for Henry Herringman, 1676), 84–85. Emphasis in original.

42. Dryden and Davies both made a living from rendering texts into English from other languages. Joseph E. Tucker, "John Davies of Kidwelly (1627?–1693), Translator from the French: With an Annotated Bibliography of His Translations," *Papers of the Bibliographical Society of America* 44, no. 2 (1950): 119–152.

43. Dryden, however, was not the sole storyteller. It was almost certainly the case that Davies created, compiled, or invented a composite account of descriptions of the peoples and customs of Hindustan, which he published under Mandelslo's name. Where Olearius's had some 30 folio pages for Mandelslo, Davies had three books of 240-odd pages. In light of this invention, it is important to read Mandelslo's account as a robust extension of the English will to narrate that sought to see the landscape of the subcontinent embodied as women undergoing extreme violence. Locke's dismissal of excess violence as tedious deserves a further reading in light of Davies's Mandelslo.

44. Adam Olearius, John Davies, and Johann Albrecht von Mandelslo, *Mandelslo's Travels into the Indies,* the first book of *The Voyages and Travells of the Ambassadors Sent by Frederick Duke of Holstein, to the Great Duke of Muscovy, and the King of Persia: Begun in the Year M.DC.XXXIII, and Finish'd in M.DC.XXXIX* (London: John Starkey, 1669), 25.

45. Ibid.

46. Ibid.

47. Ibid., 26.

48. Ibid.

49. Ibid.

50. Ibid.

51. Ibid.

52. Ibid., 31–32.

53. Ibid.

54. Ibid.

55. Ibid., 58.

56. Robert Orme, *Historical Fragments of the Mogul Empire, of the Morattoes, and of the British Concerns in Indostan; From the Year MDCLIX* (London: F. Wingrave in the Strand, 1805), 391.

57. Ibid., 407.

58. Ibid., 422.

59. Ibid., 452–453.

60. Ibid., 459n.

61. Ibid.

62. Ibid., 463.

63. Ibid., 465.

64. Ibid., 470.

65. Ibid., 472.

66. Immanuel Kant, *Anthropology, History, and Education,* ed. and trans. Günter Zöller and Robert B. Louden (Cambridge: Cambridge University Press, 2007), 94.

67. Buzurg ibn Shaharyār and Muḥammad Saʿīd Ṭurayḥī, *ʿAjāʾib al-Hind: Barruhā wa-baḥruhā wa-Jazāʾiruhā* (Beirut: Dār al-Qāriʾ, 1987), 148.

68. Abū Zayd al-Sīrāfī and Aḥmad Ibn Faḍlān, *Two Arabic Travel Books: Accounts of China and India and Mission to the Volga,* ed. and trans. Tim Mackintosh-Smith and James Edward Montgomery (New York: New York University Press, 2014), 38–39.

69. Ibid., 39–43.

70. Abu'l Ḥasan ʿAli Masʿūdī and Charles Pellat, *Murūj al-Dhahab wa Maʿāden al-Jawhar* (Beirut: Manshurat al-Jami'ah al-Lubnaniyah, 1966), 70–80.

71. Shaharyār and Ṭurayḥī, *ʿAjāʾib al-Hind,* 136–137.

72. Sīrāfī and Faḍlān, *Two Arabic Travel Books,* 30–31.

73. Ibid., 56–57.

74. Ibid., 58.

75. Abdularahamāna, *The Saṃdeśarāsaka of Abdul Rahman,* trans. Colin M. Mayrhofer (Delhi: Motilal Banarsidass Publishers, 1998), 6–7.

76. Ibid., 2–3.

77. "Praise belongs to God, Lord of the Worlds, the Lord of Mercy, the Giver of Mercy." Qur'an 1:2.

78. Abdularahamāna, *The Saṃdeśarāsaka,* 4–5.

79. Ibid., 10–11.

80. Pushpa Prasad, *Sanskrit Inscriptions of the Delhi Sultanate, 1191–1526* (Delhi: Oxford University Press, 1990), 5. Also see Ghulam Yazdani, "The Inscriptions of the Turk Sultans of Delhi (Plates IV-XVI)," in *Epigraphia Indo-Moslemica 1913–14* (Calcutta: Government Printing, 1917), 13–46.

81. Prasad, *Sanskrit Inscriptions of the Delhi Sultanate,* 14.

82. Ibid., 12.

83. Ibid.

84. Ibid., 14.

85. Ibid., 15.

86. Ibid., 25.

87. Ibid.

88. Ibid., 26.

89. Ibid.

90. Minhāj Sirāj Jūzjānī, *Ṭabaqāt-i Nāṣirī*, ed. ʿAbd al-Ḥayy Ḥabībī (Tehran: Intishārāt-i Asāṭīr, 1989), 1:435.

91. Ibid., 1:442.

92. Ibid., 1:460.

93. Ibid., 1:461.

94. Ibid.

95. Also see Abhishek Kaicker, *The King and the People: Sovereignty and Popular Politics in Mughal Delhi* (New York: Oxford University Press, 2020).

96. Jūzjānī, *Ṭabaqāt-i Nāṣirī*, 1:459–460.

97. Ziyā ad-Dīn Baranī, *Tārīkh-i Firūz Shāhi: Tārīkh-i Fārsī* (Rampūr: Rampur Raza Library, 2013), 247.

98. Ibid., 250.

99. Ibid., 257.

100. Ibid., 258.

101. Ibid., 268.

102. Firishta, *Tārīkh-i Firishta*, 4:464.

103. Ibid., 4:466.

104. Ibid., 4:473.

105. Ibid., 4:468.

106. Ibid., 3:221.

107. Ibid., 3:269.

108. Ibid., 2:251.

109. Ibid., 4:292.

110. Ibid., 3:265–266.

111. See Richard Maxwell Eaton and Phillip B. Wagoner, *Power, Memory, Architecture: Contested Sites on India's Deccan Plateau, 1300–1600* (Delhi: Oxford University Press, 2014).

112. Firishta, *Tārīkh-i Firishta*, 3:515.

113. Ibid., 3:521.

114. Ibid.

115. Ibid., 3:520–521.

116. Ibid., 4:541.

117. Ibid., 4:542.

118. Ibid., 4:548.

6. A History for Hindustan

1. Sujan Rai Bhandari, *The Khulāṣat-ut-Tawārīkh*, edited by M. Zafar Hasan (Delhi: J. & Sons Press, 1918), 6.

2. Ibid., 6–7.

3. Ibid., 10.

4. Muzaffar Alam and Sanjay Subrahmanyam also argue for this history's importance, but they credit Abu'l Fazl as the model. See Muzaffar Alam and Sanjay Subrahmanyam, "Witnesses and Agents of Empire: Eighteenth-Century Historiography and the World of the Mughal Munshī," *Journal of the Economic and Social History of the Orient* 53, nos. 1–2, (2010): 398.

5. See Sudipta Sen, "Historian as Witness: Ghulam Husain Tabatabai and the Dawning of British Rule in India," in *India and Iran in the Longue Durée*, ed. Alka Patel and Touraj Daryaee (Irvine, CA: Jordan Center for Persian Studies, 2017), 103–125; and Kumkum Chatterjee, "History as Self-Representation: The Recasting of a Political Tradition in Late Eighteenth-Century Eastern India," *Modern Asian Studies* 32, no. 4 (October 1998): 913–948.

6. Alexander Dow, *The History of Hindostan; From the Earliest Account of Time, to the Death of Akbar* (London: Printed for T. Becket and P. A. De Hondt, in the Strand, 1768), 1:A2.

7. Ibid.

8. Ibid., 1:xiii.

9. Ibid., 1:viii.

10. Alexander Carlyle, *The Autobiography of Dr. Alexander Carlyle of Inveresk, 1722–1805*, edited by John Hill Burton (London: T. N. Foulis, 1910), 529.

11. Ibid., 530.

12. Ibid. There are further accounts of Dow's competence in the "Moorish" tongue in his servant's memoirs. See John Macdonald, *Travels, in Various Parts of Europe, Asia, and Africa, during a Series of Thirty Years and Upwards* (London: J. Forbes, 1790), 160–168.

13. Carlyle, *The Autobiography*, 530.

14. Dow, *The History of Hindostan*, vol. 1.

15. Dow, *The History of Hindostan*, vol. 2.

16. Dow, *The History of Hindostan*, 1:ii. Emphasis added.

17. Dow, *The History of Hindostan*, 2:1. Emphasis added.

18. Alexander Dow, *Tales, Translated from the Persian of Inatulla of Delhi* (London: T. Becket and P. A. de Hondt, 1768), 1:vii–viii.

19. *The Gentleman's Magazine, and Historical Chronicle* 41, March 1771, 141. Also see Vinita Damodaran, "The East India Company, Famine and Ecological Conditions in Eighteenth-Century Bengal," in *The East India Company and the Natural World*, ed. V. Damodaran, A. Winterbottom, and A. Lester (London: Palgrave Macmillan, 2015), 80–101.

20. *The Gentleman's Magazine, and Historical Chronicle* 41, March 1771, 141.

21. See Nandini Bhattacharyya-Panda, *Appropriation and Invention of Tradition: The East India Company and Hindu Law in Early Colonial Bengal* (New Delhi: Oxford University Press, 2008), 36–82.

22. See Susan Gole, *Maps of Mughal India: Drawn by Colonel Jean-Baptiste-Joseph Gentil, Agent for the French Government to the Court of Shuja-ud-daula at Faizabad, in 1770* (New Delhi: Manohar Publications, 1988). Also see Jean Baptiste Joseph Gentil, *Mémoires sur L'Indoustan ou Empire Mogol* (Paris: Petit, 1822).

23. See Sanjay Subrahmanyam, "The Career of Colonel Polier and Late Eighteenth-Century Orientalism," *Journal of the Royal Asiatic Society* 10, no. 1 (April 2000): 43–60; and Taymiya R. Zaman, "Visions of Juilana: A Portuguese Woman at the Court of the Mughals," *Journal of World History* 23, no. 4 (December 2012): 761–791. Also see Chanchal Dadlani, "The 'Palais Indiens' Collection of 1774: Representing Mughal Architecture in Late Eighteenth Century India," *Ars Orientalis* 39 (2010): 175–197.

24. Ranajit Guha, *A Rule of Property for Bengal: An Essay on the Idea of Permanent Settlement* (Paris: Mouton, 1963), 25.

25. Dow, *The History of Hindostan*, 1:xiii.

26. Ibid., 1:cxvi.

27. Ibid., 1:xiv.

28. Ibid.

29. Ibid.

30. Ibid., 3:cxx.

31. Ibid., 1:xxix.

32. Ibid., 1:xxiii.

33. Ibid., 1:xlix.

34. Ibid.

35. See Claude François Bergier, *Dissertation sur les mœurs, les usages, le langage, la religion et la philosophie des Hindous: Suivie d'une exposition générale et succincte du gouvernement & de l'état actuel de l'Hindostan* (Paris: Pissot, 1769).

36. Dow, *The History of Hindostan*, 3:394.

37. Ibid., 3:xxxv.

38. Ibid., 2:79.

39. Ibid.

40. See Mrinalini Sinha, *Colonial Masculinity: The "Manly Englishman" and the "Effeminate Bengali" in the Late Nineteenth Century* (Manchester: Manchester University Press, 1995).

41. Dow, *The History of Hindostan*, 3:xx–xxi.

42. Ibid., 3:xxxvi.

43. Jonathan Scott, *Ferishta's History of Dekkan: From the First Mahummedan Conquests: With a Continuation from Other Native Writers, of the Events in That Part of India, to the Reduction of Its Last Monarchs by the Emperor Aulumgeer Aurungzebe: Also, the Reigns of His Successors . . . to the Present Day: And the History of Bengal,*

from the Accession of Aliverdee Khan to the Year 1780. Comprised in Six Parts (Shrewsbury: J. & W. Eddowes, 1794), 1:vi.

44. Ibid.

45. Ibid., 2:461.

46. Ibid., 1:31.

47. Ibid.

48. John Briggs, *History of the Rise of the Mahomedan Power in India, Till the Year A.D. 1612. Translated from the Original Persian of Mahomed Kasim Ferishta . . . to Which Is Added, an Account of the Conquest, by the Kings of Hyderabad, of the Ceded Districts and Northern Circars. With Copious Notes* (London: A. & R. Spottiswoode, 1829), 1:vii.

49. Ibid., 1:xiii.

50. Ibid., 1:xi–xii.

51. Thomas Maurice, *The History of Hindostan: Its Arts, and Its Sciences, as Connected with the History of the Other Great Empires of Asia, during the Most Ancient Periods of the World* (London: W. Bulmer, 1795), 1:12.

52. See Major David Price, *Chronological Retrospect or Memoirs of the Principal Events of Mahommedan History*, 3 vols. in 4 books (London: J. Booth, 1811–1820).

53. See "Proceedings of the Royal Asiatic Society," *Journal of the Royal Asiatic Society of Great Britain and Ireland* 3, no. 2 (1836): xii–xiv.

54. See Cyril Henry Philips, "James Mill, Mountstuart Elphinstone and the History of India," in *Historians of India, Pakistan and Ceylon* (London: Oxford University Press, 1961), 217–229; and Ronald Inden, "Orientalist Constructions of India," *Modern Asian Studies* 20, no. 3 (1986): 401–446.

55. Mountstuart Elphinstone, *The History of India: The Hindú and Mahometan Periods* (London: John Murray, 1841), 1:527.

56. Henry Miers Elliot, *Bibliographical Index to the Historians of Muhammedan India*, vol. 1 (Calcutta: Baptist Mission Press, 1849), 336.

57. Henry Miers Elliot, *Kitāb-i Miṣbāḥ aṭ-ṭālibīn dar bāb-i tawārikh-i Hindustān-i maṭluba wa gair-i maṭlūba* (Simla: Maṭbaʻa-i Kūh-i Šimla, 1849).

58. See Arshad Islam, "The Backlash in Delhi: British Treatment of the Mughal Royal Family following the Indian 'Sepoy Mutiny' of 1857," *Journal of Muslim Minority Affairs* 31, no. 2 (June 2011): 197–215.

59. See Bernard S. Cohn, *Colonialism and Its Forms of Knowledge: The British in India* (Princeton, NJ: Princeton University Press, 1996); and Ranajit Guha, *Dominance without Hegemony: History and Power in Colonial India* (Cambridge, MA: Harvard University Press, 1997).

60. See Narayani Gupta, "From Architecture to Archaeology: The 'Monumentalising' of Delhi's History in the Nineteenth Century," in *Perspectives of Mutual Encounters in South Asian History*, ed. Jamal Malik (Leiden: Brill, 2000), 49–65.

61. See Seema Alavi, *Muslim Cosmopolitanism in the Age of Empire* (Cambridge, MA: Harvard University Press, 2015).

62. See Manan Ahmed Asif, "Quarantined Histories: Sindh and the Question of Historiography in Colonial India—Part II," *HIC3 History Compass* 15, no. 8 (August 2017): 1–7.

63. These issues are raised and assessed in Muzaffar Alam and Sanjay Subrahmanyam, *Writing the Mughal World: Studies on Culture and Politics* (New York: Columbia University Press, 2011), 1–33.

64. See Khaliq Ahmad Nizami, *Sayyid Ahmad Khan* (New Delhi: Publications Division, Ministry of Information and Broadcasting, Government of India, 1966), 37–39.

65. Sayyid Ahmad Khan, *Maqālat-i Sar Sayyid*, ed. Muḥammād Ismāʿil Panīpatī (Lahore: Majlis Taraqqī Adab, 1965), 16:1–73.

66. Elliot was skeptical that Sayyid Ahmad Khan had consulted all of the histories. See Henry M. Elliot and John Dowson, *The History of India as Told by Its Own Historians* (London: Trubner, 1877), 8:430–431.

67. Sayyid Ahmad Khan, *Maqālat-i Sar Sayyid*, ed. Muḥammād Ismāʿil Panīpatī (Lahore: Majlis Taraqqī Adab, 1962), 6:166–232.

68. Sayyid Ahmad Khan, *Asār-ul-Sanādid: ʿImārāt-i Delhī Kī Mustanad Tārīkh*, ed. Syed Moinul Haq (Karachi: Pakistan Historical Society, 1966), 1.

69. See James Tod, "Translation of a Sanscrit Inscription, Relative to the Last Hindu King of Delhi, with Comments Thereon," *Transactions of the Royal Asiatic Society of Great Britain and Ireland* 1, no. 1 (1824): 133–154.

70. For a rich discussion of the differences and convergences between these two editions, see C. M. Naim, "Syed Ahmad and His Two Books Called 'Asar-al-Sanadid,'" *Modern Asian Studies* 45, no. 3 (May 2011): 669–708. Also see Christian W. Troll, "A Note on an Early Topographical Work of Sayyid Aḥmad Khān: Āsār al-Ṣanādīd," *Journal of the Royal Asiatic Society of Great Britain & Ireland* 104, no. 2 (1972): 135–146.

71. The society dedicated this translation to the Duke of Argyll. See Mountstuart Elphinston, *Tarikh-i Hindustan* (Aligarh: Secretary Syed Ahmad's Private Press, 1866).

72. See David Lelyveld, *Aligarh's First Generation: Muslim Solidarity in British India* (Princeton, NJ: Princeton University Press, 1977).

73. Shiblī Nuʿmānī, *Al-Fārūq: Mukammal* (Aʿzamgaḍh: Shiblī Akaiḍmī, 2008), 10. On Ranke, see Arnaldo Momigliano, "A Hundred Years after Ranke," *Diogenes* 2, no. 7 (June 1954): 52–58.

74. ʿAbdul Halim Sharar, *Mulk al-ʿAzīz Varjiniā* (Lahore: Mājlis Tarāqi-i Adāb, 1964), 64.

75. See C. M. Naim, "Interrogating 'The East,' 'Culture,' and 'Loss,' in Abdul Halim Sharar's Guzashta Lakhna'u," in *Indo-Muslim Cultures in Transition*, ed. Alka Patel and Karen Leonard (Leiden: Brill, 2012), 189–204. Also see C. Ryan Perkins, "A New Pablik: Abdul Halim Sharar, Volunteerism and the Anjuman-e Dar us Salam in Late Nineteenth-Century India," *Modern Asian Studies* 49, no. 4 (July 2015): 1049–1090.

76. 'Abdul Halim Sharar, *Tarikh-i Sindh* (Karachi: City Book Point, 2011), 9.

77. Ibid., 141.

78. Indeed, in 1888, when Sayyid Ahmad Khan embarked on a tour of Punjab to raise funds for Aligarh, it was almost as if he was traveling to London. Nu'mani wrote the preface to the *Safarnama-i Punjab* and even commented that the travelogue, as a genre for Muslim intellectuals, had focused exclusively on travels abroad, and that the publication of Sayyid Ahmad's journey to Punjab should open up the travelogue to areas within the subcontinent. See Sayyid Iqbāl 'Alī, *Sayyid Aḥmad Khān kā safarnāmah-yi Panjāb* (Aligarh: 'Alīgaḍh Insṭīṭyūṭ Press, 1884), 1. My thanks to David Lelyveld for calling attention to this travelogue.

79. Charles Freer Andrews, *Zaka Ullah of Delhi* (Cambridge: W. Heffer & Sons, 1929), xxv.

80. For a full list of his works, see Rifat Jamal, *Zakā'ullāh: Hayāt aur un ke 'ilmī va adabī kārnāme* (Delhi: Taqsīmkār Sāqī Buk Ḍipo, 1990), 179–244.

81. Andrews, *Zaka Ullah of Delhi*, 99.

82. In 2010, *Tarikh-i Hindustan* was reprinted in Pakistan, but it was not typeset and is largely illegible to readers of Urdu not trained in reading lithographs.

83. Mushirul Hasan, *A Moral Reckoning: Muslim Intellectuals in Nineteenth-Century Delhi* (Oxford: Oxford University Press, 2007), 228–229.

84. Maulvi Muḥammad Zakā'ullāh, *Tārīkh-i Hindustān*, vol. 1 (Aligarh: Matba' Institute, 1915), 3.

85. Ibid., 77.

86. Ibid.

87. Ibid., 58.

88. Ibid., 29.

89. Ibid., 58.

90. See Tara Chand, *The Problem of Hindustani* (Allahabad: Indian Periodicals, 1944); Christopher R. King, *One Language, Two Scripts: The Hindi Movement in Nineteenth Century North India* (Bombay: Oxford University Press, 1994).

91. See Cemil Aydin, *The Idea of the Muslim World: A Global Intellectual History* (Cambridge, MA: Harvard University Press, 2017).

92. See Gail Minault, *The Khilafat Movement: Religious Symbolism and Political Mobilization in India* (New York: Columbia University Press, 1982).

7. Afterword

1. See S. P. Sen, "History of the Indian History Congress (1935–1963)," *Proceedings of the Indian History Congress* 25 (1963): 19–56.

2. Shafā'at Ahmad Khan, "Presidential Address of Sir Shafā'at Ahmad Khān," *Proceedings of the Indian History Congress* 1, no. 1 (June 1935): 6.

3. Ibid., 9.

4. Ibid.

5. Ibid., 10.

6. Ibid.

7. Ibid., 45.

8. See the biographical essay penned by Muhammad Habib's son—who is currently the most prominent Indian medievalist—Irfan Habib, "Introduction: Professor Mohammad Habib by Irfan Habib," in Mohammad Habib, *Studies in Medieval Indian Polity and Culture: The Delhi Sultanate and Its Times*, ed. Irfan Habib (New Delhi: Oxford University Press, 2016), 1–17.

9. Mohammad Habib, *Studies in Medieval Indian Polity and Culture: The Delhi Sultanate and Its Times*, ed. Irfan Habib (New Delhi: Oxford University Press, 2016), 18.

10. Ibid.

11. Ibid., 22.

12. Ibid., 19.

13. Ibid., 26.

14. Ibid., 30.

15. Ibid., 27.

16. The study of the histories produced in the 1900s to the 1940s shaped the very field of "South Asian studies" in the United States (and to a lesser degree in the UK and Europe) from the 1980s onward. Some of the works that have shaped my own thinking on the question of history writing and medieval history are the following: J. S. Grewal, *Medieval India: History and Historians* (Amritsar: Guru Nanak University, 1975); Ranajit Guha, *An Indian Historiography of India: A Nineteenth-Century Agenda and Its Implications* (Calcutta: Centre for Studies in Social Sciences, 1988); Kumkum Sangari and Sudesh Vaid, eds., *Recasting Women: Essays in Indian Colonial History* (New Brunswick, NJ: Rutgers University Press, 1990); Velcheru Narayana Rao, David Shulman, and Sanjay Subrahmanyam, *Textures of Time: Writing History in South India, 1600–1800* (Delhi: Permanent Black, 2001); Ranajit Guha, *History at the Limit of World-History* (New York: Columbia University Press, 2003); Shahid Amin, *Alternative Histories: A View from India* (Calcutta: Center for Studies in Social Sciences, 2002); Partha Chatterjee, "A Tribute to the Master," in *Empire and Nation: Selected Essays* (New York: Columbia University Press, 2010), 153–161; Ramnarayan S. Rawat, "Colonial Archive versus Colonial Sociology: Writing Dalit History," in *Dalit Studies*, ed. Ramnarayan S. Rawat and K. Satyanarayana (Durham, NC: Duke University Press, 2016), 53–74.

17. Taymiya R. Zaman, "Nostalgia, Lahore, and the Ghost of Augrangzeb," *Fragments: Interdisciplinary Approaches to the Study of Ancient and Medieval Pasts* 4 (2015): 19.

BIBLIOGRAPHY

Abdularahamāna. *Saṃdeśarāsaka of Abdala Rahamāna.* Edited by H. C. Bhayani. Ahmedabad: Prakrit Text Society, 1999.

———. *The Saṃdeśarāsaka of Abdul Rahman.* Translated by Colin M. Mayrhofer. Delhi: Motilal Banarsidass Publishers, 1998.

ʿAbdulghanī, Muḥammad. *Pre-Mughal Persian in Hindūstān: A Critical Survey of the Growth of Persian Language and Literature in India from the Earliest Times to the Advent of the Mughal Rule.* 2 vols. Gurgaon, Haryana: Vintage Books, 1994.

ʿAbdul Qayyūm. *Tārīkh-i Hindūstān, 1526 Tak.* Ḥaidarābād: Niṣāb Pablīshars, 2008.

Abdul Razak, P. P. "Vernacular Histories and the History of Remembering: A Study of Historical Consciousness of the Muslims of Malabar." *Proceedings of the Indian History Congress* 72, no. 1 (2011): 875–883.

ʿAbdurraḥmān, Ṣabāḥuddīn. *Mughal Bādshāhon Ke ʿAhd Men Hindūstān Se Maḥabbat Va Sheftgī Ke Jazbāt.* Aʿẓamgaṛh: Dar al-Muṣannifīn, 1988.

ʿĀbidī, Sayyid Amīr Ḥasan. *Hindustānī Fārsī Adab: Taḥqīqī ʿIlmī Aur Adabī Maqālāt Kā Intikhab.* Delhi: Indo Persian Society, 1984.

Abū al-Fazl, Mubārak ibn. *Āʾīn-i Akbarī.* Edited by Sayyid Ahmad Khan. Aligarh: Sir Sayyid Akīdimī, 2005.

———. *The Aʾin i Akbari of Abul Fazl ʾAllami.* Edited by Hienrich Blochmann. 5 vols. Piscataway, NJ: Gorgias Press, 2010.

———. *Akbārnāmah.* Edited by Agha Ahmad ʿAli and ʿAbd-ur-Rahim. 3 vols. Calcutta: Urdu Guide Press, 1877–1886.

———. *Ayeen Akbery: The Institutes of the Emperor Akber.* Translated by Francis Gladwin. London: Printed by G. Auld, 1800.

———. *The History of Akbar.* Edited and translated by Wheeler M. Thackston. 6 vols. Cambridge, MA: Harvard University Press, 2015–2020.

ʿAdil Shah II, Ibrahim. *Kitab-i Nauras.* Edited by Nazīr Aḥmad. New Delhi: Bharatiya Kala Kendra, 1956.

ʿAfīf, Shams Sirāj, Ishrat Husain Ansari, and H. A. Qureshi. *Tarikh-i-Firoz Shahi of Shams Siraj Afif.* Rampur: Rampur Raza Library, 2015.

Ahmad, Nazir. "The Earliest Persian Work Completed in Gujarat." in *The Growth of Indo-Persian Literature in Gujarat,* edited by M. H. Siddiqi, 1–10. Baroda: M. S. University of Baroda Press, 1985.

Ahmad, Nizamuddin, *The Tabaqāt-i-Akbarī: A History of India from the Early Musalman Invasions of the Thirty-Eighth Year of the Reign of Akbar.* Edited by Brajendranath De and Baini Prashad. 3 vols. Calcutta: Asiatic Society of Bengal, 1913–1935.

Ahmad Khan, Sayyid. *Āsār-us Sanādīd: ʿImārāt-i Delhī Kī Mustanad Tārīkh.* Edited by Syed Moinul Haq. Karachi: Pakistan Historical Society, 1966.

——. *Maqālat-i Sar Sayyid.* Edited by Muḥammād Ismāʿil Panīpatī. 16 vols. Lahore: Majlis-i Taraqqī Adab, 1961–.

Ahmed, Shahab. *What Is Islam? The Importance of Being Islamic.* Princeton, NJ: Princeton University Press, 2017.

Alam, Muzaffar. "Zamindars and Mughal Power in the Deccan, 1685–1712." *Indian Economic & Social History Review* 11, no. 1 (1974): 74–91.

Alam, Muzaffar, and Sanjay Subrahmanyam. "The Deccan Frontier and Mughal Expansion, ca. 1600: Contemporary Perspectives." *Journal of the Economic and Social History of the Orient* 47, no. 3 (2004): 357–389.

——. *Indo-Persian Travels in the Age of Discoveries: 1400–1800.* Cambridge: Cambridge University Press, 2007.

——. "Witnesses and Agents of Empire: Eighteenth-Century Historiography and the World of the Mughal Munshī." *Journal of the Economic and Social History of the Orient* 53, nos. 1–2 (2010): 393–423.

——. *Writing the Mughal World: Studies on Culture and Politics.* New York: Columbia University Press, 2011.

Alavi, Seema. *Muslim Cosmopolitanism in the Age of Empire.* Cambridge, MA: Harvard University Press, 2015.

Ali, Daud. "The Idea of the Medieval in the Writing of South Asian History: Contexts, Methods and Politics." *Social History* 39, no. 3 (July 3, 2014): 382–407.

Ali, M. Athar. "The Evolution of the Perception of India: Akbar and Abu'l Fazl." *Social Scientist* 24, nos. 1–3 (January–March 1996): 80–88.

——. "Translation of Sanskrit Works at Akbar's Court." *Social Scientist* 20, nos. 9–10 (September–October 1992): 38–45.

——. "The Use of Sources in Mughal Historiography," *Journal of the Royal Asiatic Society,* 3rd ser., 5, no. 3 (November 1995): 361–373.

ʿAlī, Sayyid Iqbāl. *Sayyid Aḥmad Khān kā safarnāmah-yi Panjāb.* Aligarh: Aligarh Institute Press, 1884.

Ali Qalqashandi, Ahmed ibn. *Arab Account of India in the 14th Century: A Translation of the Chapters on India from Al-Qalqashadī's Ṣubḥ Ul-Aʿshā.* Translated by Otto Spies. Stuttgart: W. Kohlhammer, 1936.

Allen, Charles. *Ashoka: The Search for India's Lost Emperor.* London: Abacus, 2013.

Amin, Shahid. *Alternative Histories: A View from India.* Calcutta: Center for Studies in Social Sciences, 2002.

———. *Conquest and Community: The Afterlife of Warrior Saint Ghazi Miyan.* Chicago: University of Chicago Press, 2016.

Anderson, James. "Account of Malabar, and the Rise and Progress of the Mussulman Religion in that Country, from Ferishtah's General History of Hindostan." *Asiatick Miscellany* 2 (1786): 279–305.

Andrews, Charles Freer. *Zaka Ullah of Delhi.* Cambridge: W. Heffer & Sons, 1929.

Anooshahr, Ali. *The Ghazi Sultans and the Frontiers of Islam: A Comparative Study of the Late Medieval and Early Modern Periods.* New York: Routledge, 2008.

———. "Shirazi Scholars and the Political Culture of the Sixteenth-Century Indo-Persian World." *Indian Economic and Social History Review* 51, no. 3 (2014): 331–352.

Ansari, Zoe, ed. *Life, Times and Works of Amir Khusrau Dehlavi.* New Delhi: National Amir Khusrau Society, 1975.

Antrim, Zayde. *Routes and Realms: The Power of Place in the Early Islamic World.* Oxford: Oxford University Press, 2012.

Anzaldúa, Gloria. *Borderlands / La Frontera: The New Mestiza.* San Francisco: Aunt Lute Books, 1987.

App, Urs. *Birth of Orientalism.* Philadelphia: University of Pennsylvania Press, 2015.

Aquil, Raziuddin, ed. *Sufism and Society in Medieval India.* New Delhi: Oxford University Press, 2010.

Arberry, A. J. "Hand-List of Islamic Manuscripts Acquired by the India Office Library, 1936–1938." *Journal of the Royal Asiatic Society* 3 (1939): 353–396.

Archaeological Survey of India, Annual Report 1904–1905. Calcutta: Superintendent Government Printing, 1908.

Archambault, Hannah Lord. "Geographies of Influence: Two Afghan Military Households in 17th and 18th Century South India." PhD diss., University of California, Berkeley, 2018.

Asher, Catherine B., and Cynthia Talbot. *India before Europe.* Cambridge: Cambridge University Press, 2008.

Ashraf, Kunwar Muhammad. *Life and Conditions of the People of Hindustan.* New Delhi: Munshiram Manoharlal, 1969.

Ashraf, Kunwar Muhammad, and Jaweed Ashraf. *Indian Historiography and Other Related Papers.* New Delhi: Sunrise Publications, 2006.

The Asiatic Annual Register: Or, a View of the History of Hindustan, and . . . Asia, for the Year 1799. London: Printed for J. Debrett, by Andrew Wilson, 1800.

The Asiatick Miscellany. Calcutta: Printed by Daniel Stuart, 1785–1786.

Asif, Manan Ahmed. *A Book of Conquest: Chachnama and Muslim Origins in South Asia.* Cambridge, MA: Harvard University Press, 2016.

——. "Quarantined Histories: Sindh and the Question of Historiography in Colonial India—Part II." *HIC3 History Compass* 15, no. 8 (2017): 1–7.

Askari, Syed Hasan. *Amir Khusrau as a Historian*. Patna: Khuda Baksh Public Library, 1988.

——. "Historical Matters in Ijaz-i Khusravi." *Proceedings of the Indian History Congress* 26, no. 2 (1964): 11–20.

——. *On Awfi's Jawami-Ul Hikayat*. Patna: Khuda Bakhsh Oriental Public Library, 1995.

Auer, Blain H. "Civilising the Savage: Myth, History and Persianisation in the Early Delhi Courts of South Asia." In *Islamisation: Comparative Perspectives from History*, edited by A. C. S. Peacock, 393–419. Edinburgh: Edinburgh University Press, 2017.

——. *Symbols of Authority in Medieval Islam: History, Religion and Muslim Legitimacy in the Delhi Sultanate*. London: I. B. Tauris, 2012.

'Awfī, Muḥammad. *Jāmiʿ Al-Hikāyāt-i Hindī*. Edited by Muhammad Baqir. Lahore: Majilis Taraqi-yi Adab, 1963.

——. *Javāmiʿ Al-Hikāyāt: Bakhsh-i Marbūt Bih Tārīkh Irān*. Tehran: Dānishsarā-yi ʿĀlī, 1971.

——. *Javāmiʿ Al-Hikāyāt va Lavāmiʿi Al-Rivāyāt: Taʾlīf-i Sadīd Al-Dīn Muḥammad ʿAwfī. Aknūn Az Rū-Yi Nusakh-i Qadīmah-ʾi Muʿtabarah Bi-Muqaddamah Va Taṣḥīḥ-i Muḥammad Niẓām Al-Dīn*. Delhi: Manager of Publications, 1966.

——. *Javāmiʿ Al-Hikāyāt*. ed. Muḥammad Muʿīn Tehran: Ibn Sina, 1961.

——. *The Lubabul-Albab*. Edited by Edward G. Browne and Mirza Muhammad ibn Abdu'l-Wahhāb-i Qazwīnī. Leiden: Brill, 1903.

Aydin, Cemil. *The Idea of the Muslim World: A Global Intellectual History*. Cambridge, MA: Harvard University Press, 2017.

Azad, Abu al-Kalam. *Albiruni aur jugrāfiyā-i ʿĀlam*. Karachi: Idarā-i Tasnīf o Tahqīq Pakistan, 1980.

Bābur, Ẓahīr-ud-Dīn Muḥammad. *Bāburnāma: Chaghatay Turkish Text with Abdul-Rahim Khankhanan's Persian Translation*. Turkish transcription, Persian edition, and English translation by W. M. Thackston, Jr. 3 vols. Cambridge, MA: Department of Near Eastern Languages and Civilizations, Harvard University, 1993.

Bābur, Ẓahīr-ud-Dīn Muḥammad, and W. M. Thackston. *The Baburnama: Memoirs of Babur, Prince and Emperor*. New York: Modern Library, 2002.

Badāʾūnī, 'Abdulqādir ibn Mulūk Shāh. *Muntakhāb al-Tavārikh: Tārīkh-i Mubārak Shāhī Aur Niẓām Al-Tavārikh Kā Saḥīḥ Intikhāb*. Lahore: Sheikh Ghulam Ali and Sons, 1962.

Baihaqī, Abu-ʿl-Faḍl Muḥammad Ibn-Ḥusain. *Tārikh-i Baihaqī*. Tehran: Chāpkhānah-i Bānk-i Millī-i Īrān, 1945.

Bakhle, Janaki. "Country First? Vinayak Damodar Savarkar (1883–1966) and the Writing of Essentials of Hindutva." *Public Culture* 22, no. 1 (January 2010): 149–186.

Balachandran, Jyoti Gulati. *Narrative Pasts: The Making of a Muslim Community in Gujarat, c. 1400–1650.* New Delhi: Oxford University Press, 2020.

Balādurī, Aḥmad Ibn-Yaḥyā al-. *Futūḥ al-Buldān.* Beirut: Dar wa-Maktabat al-Hilal, 1988.

———. *The Origins of the Islamic State.* Translated by Philip Khuri Hitti. 2 vols. New York: Columbia University, 1916.

Banerjee, Prathama. "Histories of History in South Asia." In *A Companion to Global Historical Thought,* edited by Prasenjit Duara, Andrew Sartori, and Viren Murthy, 293–307. West Sussex, UK: Wiley-Blackwell, 2014.

Banerjee, Sushmita. "Conceptualising the Past of the Muslim Community in the Sixteenth Century: A Prospographical Study of the Akhbār al-Akhyār." *Indian Economic and Social History Review* 54, no. 4 (2017): 423–456.

Barani, Syed Hasan. *Ziaduddin Barani.* Delhi: Maktabā Jamiʿa Milli Islamiya, 1930.

Baranī, Ziyāʾ ad-Dīn. *Fatāvā-yi Jahāndārī.* Edited by Afsar Umar Salim Khan. Lahore: Idārah-ʾi Taḥqīqāt-i Pākistān, 1972.

———. *Tārīkh-i Fīrūz Shāhī: Tārīkh-i Fārsī.* Rāmpūr: Rampur Raza Library, 2013.

———. *Tarīkh-i-Firoz Shāhī.* Edited by Syed Ahmed. Aligarh: Sir Syed Academy, 2005.

———. *Tarikh-i Firoz Shahi.* Translated by Ishtiyaq Ahmad Zilli. New Delhi: Primus Books, 2015.

Barbosa, Duarte. *The Book of Duarte Barbosa; An Account of the Countries Bordering on the Indian Ocean and Their Inhabitants.* Edited and translated by Mansel Longworth Dames. 2 vols. London: Printed for the Hakluyt Society, 1921.

Barrow, Ian J. "From Hindustan to India: Naming Change in Changing Names." *South Asia: Journal of South Asian Studies* 26, no. 1 (2003): 37–49.

Basham, A. L. *The Wonder That Was India: A Survey of the History and Culture of the Indian Sub-continent before the Coming of the Muslims.* New York: Grove Press, 1954.

Bashir, Shahzad. "On Islamic Time: Rethinking Chronology in the Historiography of Muslim Societies." *History and Theory* 53, no. 4 (2014): 519–544.

———. "A Perso-Islamic Universal Chronicle in Its Historical Context: Ghiyas al-Din Khwandamir's Habib al-siyar." In *Historiography and Religion,* edited by Jörg Rüpke, Susanne Rau, and Bernd-Christian Otto, 207–223. Berlin: Walter de Gruyter, 2015.

Bednar, Michael Boris. "The Content and the Form in Amīr Khuraw's Duval Rānī va Khiẕr Khān." *Journal of the Royal Asiatic Society* 24, no. 1 (2014): 17–35.

Benjamin, Walter. *Illuminations.* Edited by Hannah Arendt. Translated by Harry Zohn. New York: Schocken, 2007. Originally published 1968.

Benjamin, Walter, and Knut Tarnowski. "Eduard Fuchs: Collector and Historian." *New German Critique* 5 (Spring 1975): 27–58.

Bergier, Claude François. *Dissertation sur les mœurs, les usages, le langage, la religion et la philosophie des Hindous: Suivie d'une exposition générale et succincte du gouvernement & de l'état actuel de l'Hindostan.* Paris: Pissot, 1769.

Bhandari, Sujan Rai. *The Khulāṣat-ut-Tawārīkh*. Edited by M. Zafar Hasan. Delhi: J & Sons, 1918.

———. *The Khulāṣat-ut-Tawārīkh*, Critical Edition, Translation, and Annotation of Khulasat-ut-Tawarikh of Sujan Rai Bhandari. New Delhi: Indian Council for Cultural Relations, 2006.

Bhandarkar, D. R. "Slow Progress of Islam Power in Ancient India." *Annals of the Bhandarkar Oriental Research Institute* 11, no. 2 (1930): 128–148.

Bhattacharyya-Panda, Nandini. *Appropriation and Invention of Tradition: The East India Company and Hindu Law in Early Colonial Bengal*. New Delhi: Oxford University Press, 2008.

Bigwood, J. M. "Ctesias' 'Indica' and Photius." *Phoenix* 43, no. 4 (1989): 302–316.

Bīrūnī, Abu'r Raihān Muḥammad Ibn-Aḥmad al-. *Kitāb Al-Bīrūnī Fī Taḥqīq Mā Li'l-Hind Min Maqūla Maqbūla Fī'l-'aql Au Mardūla*. Ḥaidārabād: Da'irat al-Maʿārif al-ʿUtmānīya, 1978.

Björkman, W. "Kāfir." In *Encyclopaedia of Islam*. 1st ed. (1913–1936).

Blochet, Edgar. *Catalogue des manuscrits persans de la Bibliothèque nationale*. 4 vols. Paris: Imprimerie nationale, E. Leroux, 1905–1934.

Blumhardt, J. F. *Catalogue of the Hindi, Panjabi and Hindustani Manuscripts in the Library of the British Museum*. London: British Museum, 1899.

Boesche, Roger. "Fearing Monarchs and Merchants: Montesquieu's Two Theories of Despotism." *Western Political Quarterly* 43, no. 4 (1990): 741–761.

Bosworth, Clifford Edmund. *The Ghaznavids: Their Empire in Afghanistan and Eastern Iran, 994–1040*. Edinburgh: Edinburgh University Press, 1963.

Braudel, Fernand. *On History*. Chicago: University of Chicago Press, 1980.

Braw, J. D. "Vision as Revision: Ranke and the Beginning of Modern History." *History and Theory* 46, no. 4 (December 2007): 45–60.

Bray, Julia. *Writing and Representation in Medieval Islam: Muslim Horizons*. London: Routledge, 2010.

Briggs, John. "Essay on the Life and Writings of Ferishta." *Transactions of the Royal Asiatic Society of Great Britain and Ireland* 2, no. 1 (1829): 341–361.

———. *History of the Rise of the Mahomedan Power in India, till the Year A.D. 1612. Translated from the Original Persian of Mahomed Kasim Ferishta . . . to Which Is Added, an Account of the Conquest, by the Kings of Hyderabad, of the Ceded Districts and Northern Circars. With Copious Notes*. 4 vols. London: Longman, Rees, Orme, Brown, and Green, 1829.

Brown, Charles Philip. *Carnatic Chronology: The Hindu and Mahomedan Methods of Reckoning Time Explained*. London: Bernard Quaritch, 1863.

Brown, W. Norman. "South Asia Studies: A History." *Annals of the American Academy of Political and Social Science* 356 (1964): 54–62.

Browne, Edward G. *A Hand-List of the Muhammadan Manuscripts, including all those written in the Arabic character, preserved in the Library of the University of Cambridge*. Cambridge: Cambridge University Press, 1900.

Bry, Theodor de, Johann Israel de Bry, and Johann Theodor de Bry. *Historiarum Orientalis Indiae tomus XII in tres libros siue tractatus distributus.* Francofurti: Apud Wilhelmum Fizzerum Anglum, bibliopolam, 1628.

Busch, Allison. "Literary Responses to the Mughal Imperium: The Historical Poems of Kesavdas." *South Asian Research* 25, no. 1 (2005): 31–54.

Buzurg ibn Shahriyār and Muḥammad Saʿīd Ṭurayḥī. *ʿAjāʾib al-Hind: Barruhā wa-baḥruhā wa-Jazāʾiruhā.* Beirut: Dār al-Qāri, 1987.

Camões, Luís Vazde. *The Lusíads.* Translated by Landag White. New York: Oxford University Press, 1997.

Cannon, Garland. "Sir William Jones's Indian Studies." *Journal of the American Oriental Society* 91, no. 3 (July–September 1971): 418–425.

Carey, Daniel. "The Problem of Sati: John Locke's Moral Anthropology and the Foundations of Natural Law." *Journal of Early Modern History* 18 (2014): 69–100.

Carlyle, Alexander. *The Autobiography of Dr. Alexander Carlyle of Inveresk, 1722–1805.* Edited by John Hill Burton. London: T. N. Foulis, 1910.

Carlyle, Thomas. *On Heroes, Hero-Worship and the Heroic in History.* London: Chapman and Hall, 1883.

Castanheda, Fernão. *História del descobrimento e conquista de India pelos Portugueses.* Coimbra: João de Barreira e Álvares, 1552.

Certeau, Michel de. "Practices of Space." In *On Signs,* edited by Marshall Blonsky, 122–146. Baltimore, MD: Johns Hopkins University Press, 1985.

———. *The Writing of History.* Translated by Tom Conley. New York: Columbia University Press, 1988.

Chakladar, Haran Chandra. "The Geography of Vātsyāna." *Annals of the Bhandarkar Oriental Research Institute* 7, nos. 1/2 (1926): 129–152.

———. "The Geography of Vātsyāna (Continued)." *Annals of the Bhandarkar Oriental Research Institute* 8, no. 1 (April 1926): 43–62.

Chakrabarty, Dipesh. *The Calling of History: Sir Jadunath Sarkar and His Empire of Truth.* Chicago: University of Chicago Press, 2015.

Chand, Tara. *The Problem of Hindustani.* Allahabad: Indian Periodicals, 1944.

Chartier, Roger. *On the Edge of the Cliff: History, Language, and Practices.* Baltimore, MD: Johns Hopkins University Press, 1997.

Chatterjee, Kumkum. "History as Self-Representation: The Recasting of a Political Tradition in Late Eighteenth-Century Eastern India." *Modern Asian Studies* 32, no. 4 (October 1998): 913–948.

Chatterjee, Partha. "Claims on the Past: The Emergence of Nationalist Historiography in Nineteenth-Century Bengal." In *Subaltern Studies VIII,* edited by David Arnold and David Hardiman. Delhi: Oxford University Press, 1994.

———. "History and the Nationalization of Hinduism." In *Representing Hinduism: The Construction of Religious Traditions and National Identity,* edited by

Vasudha Dalmia and Heinrich von Stietencron. New Delhi: Sage Publications, 1995.

———. "A Tribute to the Master." In *Empire and Nation: Selected Essays,* 153–161. New York: Columbia University Press, 2010.

Chattopadhyaya, Brajadulal. *The Concept of Bharatavarsha and Other Essays.* Ranikhet: Permanent Black, 2017.

Chaturvedi, Vinayak. "A Revolutionary's Biography: The Case of V. D. Savarkar." *Postcolonial Studies* 16, no. 2 (2013): 124–139.

Chaudhuri, Jatindrabimal. *Muslim Patronage to Sanskritic Learning.* Delhi: Idarah-i Adabiyat-i Delli, 1981.

Chekuri, Christopher. "'A Share in the World Empire': Nayamkara as Sovereignty in Practice at Vijayanagara, 1480–1580." *Social Scientist* 40, nos. 1–2 (2012): 41–67.

Chughtai, Muhammad Akram. *Qadīm Delhī Kallīj.* Lahore: Oriental Publications, 2012.

Clémentin-Ojha, Catherine. "India, That Is Bharat . . .': One Country, Two Names." *South Asia Multidisciplinary Academic Journal* (December 2014): 1–21.

Cobb, Matthew Adam. *Rome and the Indian Ocean Trade from Augustus to the Early Third Century.* Leiden: Brill, 2018.

Cohn, Bernard S. *The Bernard Cohn Omnibus.* Oxford: Oxford University Press, 2004.

———. *Colonialism and Its Forms of Knowledge: The British in India.* Princeton, NJ: Princeton University Press, 2006.

———. "History and Anthropology: The State of Play." *Comparative Studies in Society and History* 22, no. 2 (April 1980): 198–221.

———. *India: The Social Anthropology of a Civilization.* Englewood Cliffs, NJ: Prentice-Hall, 1971.

Collingwood, Robin George. *Essays in the Philosophy of History.* Austin: University of Texas Press, 1965.

———. *The Principles of History: And Other Writings in Philosophy of History.* New York: Oxford University Press, 1999.

The Constituent Assembly of India (Legislative) Debates. 12 vols. *Second Session of the Constituent Assembly of India.* Vol. 4. Simla: H. S. House, 1948.

Cousens, Henry. *Bijapur: The Old Capital of the Adil Shahi Kings.* Poona: Orphanage Press, 1889.

Dadlani, Chanchal. "The 'Palais Indiens' Collection of 1774: Representing Mughal Architecture in Late Eighteenth Century India." *Ars Orientalis* 39 (2010): 175–197.

Dale, Stephen Frederic. *The Garden of the Eight Paradises: Bābur and the Culture of Empire in Central Asia, Afghanistan and India (1483–1530).* Leiden: Brill, 2004.

Dalmia, Vasudha. "Vernacular Histories in Late Nineteenth-Century Banaras: Folklore, Purānas and the New Antiquarianism." *Indian Economic & Social History Review* 38, no. 1 (March 2001): 59–79.

Damodaran, Vinita. "The East India Company, Famine and Ecological Conditions in Eighteenth-Century Bengal." In *The East India Company and the Natural World,* edited by V. Damodaran, A. Winterbottom, and A. Lester, 80–101. London: Palgrave Macmillan, 2015.

Dapper, Olfert. *Asia, of Naukeurige Beschryving van Het Rijk Des Grooten Mogols En een groot gedeelte van Indien.* Amsterdam: J. Van Meurs, 1672.

Das, Sisir Kumar. *A History of Indian Literature: 1911–1956, Struggle for Freedom, Triumph and Tragedy.* New Delhi: Sahitya Akademi, 1995.

Deambi, B. K. Kaul. *Corpus of Sarada Inscriptions of Kashmir by B.K. Kaul Deambi.* Delhi: Agam Kala Prakashan, 1982.

De Blois, François, and Charles A. Storey. *Persian Literature: A Bio-Bibliographical Survey.* 2 vols. London: Luzac, 1939.

Delarochette, Louis Stanislas d'Arcy. "Hind, Hindoostan, or India." London: William Faden, 1788.

Dening, Greg. *Islands and Beaches: Discourse on a Silent Land: Marquesas 1774–1880.* Chicago: Dorsey Press, 1989.

Desai, Ziyaud-Din A. *Epigraphia Indica: Arabic and Persian Supplement.* Delhi: Government of India Press, 1971.

———. *Published Muslim Inscriptions of Rajasthan.* Jaipur: Directorate of Archaeology and Museums, Government of Rajasthan, 1971.

———. "Some Fourteenth Century Epitaphs from Cambay in Gujarāt." In *Epigraphia Indica: Arabic and Persian Supplement* (Delhi: Government of India Press, 1971), 1–59.

Devadevan, Manu V. "From Lineage to Territory: The Making of Territorial Self-Consciousness in Kaliṅga." *Indian Historical Review* 44, no. 2 (2017): 173–197.

D'Hubert, Thibaut, and Alexandre Papas, eds. *Jāmī in Regional Contexts: The Reception of ʿAbd al-Raḥmān Jāmī's Works in the Islamicate World, ca. 9th/15th-14th/20th Century.* Leiden: Brill, 2018.

Dirks, Nicholas, B. *Castes of Mind: Colonialism and the Making of Modern India.* Princeton, NJ: Princeton University Press, 2001

———. "South Asian Studies: Futures Past." In *The Politics of Knowledge: Area Studies and the Disciplines,* edited by David Szanton, 341–385. Berkeley: University of California Press, 2004.

Donne, John. *The Sermons of John Donne.* Edited by G. R. Potter and Evelyn M. Simpson. Vol. 4 of 10 vols: 264–282. Berkeley: University of California Press, 1953–1962.

Donner, Fred McGraw. *The Early Islamic Conquests.* Princeton, NJ: Princeton University Press, 1981.

———. *Narratives of Islamic Origins: The Beginnings of Islamic Historical Writing.* Studies in Late Antiquity and Early Islam 14. Princeton, NJ: Darwin Press, 1998.

———. "Talking About Islam's Origins." *School of Oriental and African Studies, University of London* 81, no. 1 (2018): 1–23.

———. "Visions of the Early Islamic Expansion: Between the Heroic and the Horrific." In *Byzantium in Early Islamic Syria*, edited by Nadia Maria El Cheikh and Shaun O'Sullivan, 9–29. Beirut: American University of Beirut and University of Balamand, 2011.

Dow, Alexander. *The History of Hindostan; From the Earliest Account of Time, to the Death of Akbar; Translated from the Persian of Mahummud Casim Ferishta of Delhi; Together with a Dissertation Concerning the Religion and Philosophy of the Brahmins; with an Appendix Containing the History of the Mogul Empire, from its Decline in the Reign of Mahummud Shaw, to the present Times*. 2 vols. London: Printed for T. Becket and P. A. De Hondt, in the Strand, 1768.

———. *The History of Hindostan, from the Death of Akbar, to the Complete Settlement of the Empire under Aurungzebe. To which are prefixed, I. A Dissertation on the Origin and Nature of Despotism in Hindostan. II. An Enquiry into the State of Bengal; with a Plan for Restoring that Kingdom to Its Former Prosperity and Splendor*. London: Printed for T. Becket and P. A. De Hondt in the Strand, 1772.

———. *Tales, Translated from the Persian of Inatulla of Delhi*. 2 vols. London: T. Becket and P. A. de Hondt, 1768.

Dryden, John. *Aurenge-Zebe: A Tragedy Acted at the Royal Theatre*. London: T. N. for Henry Herringman, 1676.

Duncan, Jonathan. "An Account of the Discovery of Two Urns in the Vicinity of Benares." In *Asiatick Researches or Transactions of the Society Instituted in Bengal for Enquiring into the History and Antiquities, the Arts, Sciences, and Literature, of Asia*, 5:131–132. London: Vernor and Hood, 1798.

———. "Inscriptions on the Staff of Fi'ruz Shah. Translated from the Sanscrit, as explained by Ra'dha'ca'nta Sarman." In *Asiatick Researches or Transactions of the Society Instituted in Bengal for Enquiring into the History and Antiquities, the Arts, Sciences, and Literature, of Asia*, 5: 379–382. London: Vernor and Hood, 1798.

Dutt, Manmatha Nath. *Prose English Translation of Vishnupuranam*. Varanasi: Chowkhamba Sanskrit Series Office, 1972.

Eaton, Richard Maxwell. *India in the Persianate Age, 1000–1765*. Oakland: University of California Press, 2019.

———. *The Social History of the Deccan, 1300–1761: Eight Indian Lives*. Cambridge: Cambridge University Press, 2005.

———. *Sufis of Bijapur, 1300–1700: Social Roles of Sufis in Medieval India*. Princeton, NJ: Princeton University Press, 1977.

———. "Temple Desecration and Indo-Muslim States." *Journal of Islamic Studies* 11, no. 3 (2000): 283–319.

Eaton, Richard Maxwell, and Phillip B. Wagoner. *Power, Memory, Architecture: Contested Sites on India's Deccan Plateau, 1300–1600*. Delhi: Oxford University Press, 2014.

Edney, Matthew H. *Mapping an Empire: The Geographical Construction of British India, 1765–1843*. Chicago: University of Chicago Press, 1997.

El Cheikh, Nadia Maria, and Shaun O'Sullivan. *Byzantium in Early Islamic Syria*. Beirut: American University of Beirut Press, 2011.

Elliot, Henry Miers. *Appendix to the Arabs in Sind*. Vol. 3, part 1, of *The Historians of India*. Cape Town: S. Solomon, 1853.

———. *Bibliographical Index to the Historians of Muhammedan India*. Vol. 1. Calcutta: Baptist Mission Press, 1849.

———, ed. *Historians of Sind*. Translated by John Dowson. Lahore: Sang-e-Meel Publications, 2006.

———. *Kitāb-i Miṣbāḥ aṭ-ṭālibīn dar bāb-i tawārikh-i Hindustān-i maṭluba wa gair-i maṭlūba*. Simla: Maṭbaʿa-i Kūh-i Šimla, 1849.

Elliot, Henry Miers, and John Dowson, eds. *The History of India: As Told by Its Own Historians*. 8 vols. London: Trübner, 1867–1877.

Elphinstone, Mountstuart. *The History of India: The Hindú and Mahometan Periods*. 2 vols. London: John Murray, 1841.

———. *Tarikh-i Hindustan*. Aligarh: Secretary Syed Ahmad's Private Press, 1866.

Ernst, Carl W. *Eternal Garden: Mysticism, History, and Politics at a South Asian Sufi Center*. Albany: State University of New York Press, 1992.

———. "Muslim Studies of Hinduism? A Reconsideration of Arabic and Persian Translations from Indian Languages." *Iranian Studies* 36, no. 2 (2003): 173–195.

Fabre D'Olivet, Antoine. *Le Sage de l'Indostan: Drame philosophique, en un acte et en vers*. Paris: Dufay, 1796.

Farīdābādī, Sayyid Hāshmī. *Tārīkh-i Hind*. Hyderabad: Jāmiʿah ʿUsmāniyah, 1922.

Fatimi, S. Q. "Two Letters from the Mahārājā to the Khalifāh: A Study in the Early History of Islam in the West." *Islamic Studies* 2, no. 1 (March 1963): 121–140.

Ferdowsi, Abu'l Qasem. *The Shahnameh*. Edited by Djalal Khaleghi-Motlagh. 8 vols. New York: Bibliotheca Persica, 1988–2008.

Firishta, Muḥammad Qāsim Hindū Shāh Astarābādī. *Tārīkh-i Firishta / Taʾlīf-i Muḥammad Qāsim Hindū Shāh Astarābādī; taṣḥīḥ va taʿlīq va tawẕīḥ va izāfāt-i Muḥammad Riẕā Naṣīrī*. Edited by Muḥammad Riẕā Naṣīrī. 4 vols. Tehran: Anjuman-i Āsār va Mafākhir-i Farhangī, 2009.

Fischel, Roy S. *Local States in an Imperial World: Identity, Society and Politics in the Early Modern Deccan*. Edinburgh: Edinburgh University Press, 2020.

FitzClarence, George. *Journal of a Route across India, through Egypt, to England, in the Latter End of the Year 1817, and the Beginning of 1818*. London: John Murray, 1819.

Fitzpatrick, Matthew P. "Provincializing Rome: The Indian Ocean Trade Network and Roman Imperialism." *Journal of World History* 22, no. 1 (2011): 27–54.

Flatt, Emma J. *The Courts of the Deccan Sultanates: Living Well in the Persian Cosmopolis*. Cambridge: Cambridge University Press, 2019.

Flood, Finbarr Barry. *Objects of Translation: Material Culture and Medieval "Hindu-Muslim" Encounter.* Princeton, NJ: Princeton University Press, 2009.

Flores, Jorge. "The *Mogor* as a Venomous Hydra: Forging the Mughal–Portuguese Frontier." *Journal of Early Modern History* 19, no. 6 (2015): 539–562.

Foster, William, ed. *Early Travels in India, 1583–1619.* Oxford: Oxford University Press, 1921.

———, ed. *The Embassy of Sir Thomas Roe to the Court of the Great Mogul, 1615–1619, as Narrated in His Journal and Correspondence.* 2 vols. London: Hakluyt Society, 1899.

Fuentes, Marisa J. *Dispossessed Lives: Enslaved Women, Violence, and the Archive.* Philadelphia: University of Pennsylvania Press, 2016.

Fukazawa, Hiroshi. *Medieval Deccan: Peasants, Social Systems and States: Sixteenth to Eighteenth Centuries.* Delhi: Oxford University Press, 1991.

———. "A Study of the Local Administration of ĀdilShāhī Sultanate (A.D. 1489–1686)." *Hitotsubashi Journal of Economics* 3, no. 2 (June 1963): 37–67.

Gandhi, Mohandas K. *The Collected Works of Mahatma Gandhi.* Electronic book, 98 vols. New Delhi: Publications Division Government of India, 1999. https://www.gandhiashramsevagram.org/gandhi-literature/collected-works-of-mahatma-gandhi-volume-1-to-98.php.

Gardīzī, ʿAbd al-Ḥayy ibn Ẓaḥḥāk. *The Ornament of Histories: A History of the Eastern Islamic Lands AD 650–1041: The Original Text of Abû Saʿîd ʿAbd al-Ḥayy Gardīzī.* London: I. B. Tauris, 2011.

———. *Zayn al-akhbār.* Edited by Raḥīm Riẓāzādah-ʾi Malik. Tehran: Anjuman-i Āsār va Mafâkhir-i Farhangī, 2005.

Genette, Gérard. *Palimpsests: Literature in the Second Degree.* Lincoln: University of Nebraska Press, 1997.

Gentil, Jean Baptiste Joseph. *Mémoires sur L'Indoustan ou Empire Mogol.* Paris: Petit, 1822.

Ghulāmussaiyidain, Khvājah. "Epigraphia Indica: Arabic and Persian Supplement." New Delhi: Archaeological Survey of India Publication, 1952.

———. *Mughal Shahanshāh Akbar Ke ʿAhd Men Fārsī Tārīkh Navesī.* Nāgpūr, Delhi: Urdu Publications, 2009.

Gibb, H. A. R. *The Arab Conquests in Central Asia.* London: Royal Asiatic Society, 1923.

Gibbon, Edward. *The History of the Decline and Fall of the Roman Empire.* 6 vols. London: W. Strahan and T. Cadell, 1777–1788.

Gilani, Mukhtar Ahmad. *Ghaznī Se Somnāt: Sulṭān Maḥmūd Ghaznavī Ke Hind Par Satrah Hamlon Kā Jaʾizah.* Rawalpindi: Jamilah Talʾat Gilani, 1982.

Gilchrist, John Borthwick. *Hindoostanee Philology Comprising a Dictionary, English and Hindoostanee; with a Grammatical Introduction.* London: Kingsbury, Parbury, and Allen, 1796.

Gilroy, Paul. *The Black Atlantic: Modernity and Double Consciousness.* Cambridge, MA: Harvard University Press, 1993.

Ginzburg, Carlo. *Threads and Traces: True, False, Fictive.* Berkeley: University of California Press, 2012.

Gole, Susan. *Maps of Mughal India: Drawn by Colonel Jean-Baptiste-Joseph Gentil, Agent for the French Government to the Court of Shuja-ud-daula at Faizabad, in 1770.* New Delhi: Manohar Publications, 1988.

Grewal, J. S. *Medieval India: History and Historians.* Amritsar: Guru Nanak University, 1975.

Groesen, Michiel van. "Interchanging Representations: Dutch Publishers and the De Bry Collection of Voyages (1596–1610)." *Dutch Crossing* 30, no. 2 (2006): 229–242.

Guha, Ranajit. "A Conquest Foretold." *Social Text* 54 (Spring 1998): 85–99.

———. *Dominance without Hegemony: History and Power in Colonial India.* Cambridge, MA: Harvard University Press, 1997.

———. *History at the Limit of World-History.* New York: Columbia University Press, 2003.

———. *An Indian Historiography of India: A Nineteenth Century Agenda and Its Implications.* Calcutta: Centre for Studies in Social Sciences, 1988.

———. *A Rule of Property for Bengal: An Essay on the Idea of Permanent Settlement.* Paris: Mouton, 1963.

Guha, Sumit. *History and Collective Memory in South Asia, 1200–2000.* Seattle: University of Washington Press, 2019.

Gunderson, Lloyd. *Alexander's Letter to Aristotle about India.* Meisenheim am Glan: Hain, 1980.

Gupta, Narayani. "From Architecture to Archaeology: The 'Monumentalising' of Delhi's History in the Nineteenth Century." In *Perspectives of Mutual Encounters in South Asian History,* edited by Jamal Malik, 49–65. Leiden: Brill, 2000.

Habib, Irfan. "The Envisioning of a Nation: A Defense of the Idea of India." *Social Scientist* 27, nos. 9–10 (September–October 1999): 18–29.

———. "The Formation of India: Notes on the History of an Idea." *Social Scientist* 25, nos. 7–8 (July–August 1997): 3–10.

———. "India: Country and Nation—An Introductory Essay." In *India—Studies in the History of an Idea,* edited by Irfan Habib, 1–19. New Delhi: Munshiram Manoharlal Publishers, 2005.

———. *Interpreting Indian History.* Shillong: North-Eastern Hill University Publications, 1988.

———. "Introduction: Professor Mohammad Habib by Irfan Habib." In *Studies in Medieval Indian Polity and Culture: The Delhi Sultanate and Its Times,* by Mohammad Habib, edited by Irfan Habib, 1–17. New Delhi: Oxford University Press, 2016.

——, ed. *Medieval India: Researches in the History of India, 1200–1750*. Delhi: Oxford University Press, 1992.

Habib, Irfan, and Aligarh Historians Society. *India: Studies in the History of an Idea*. New Delhi: Munshiram Manoharlal Publishers, 2005.

Habib, Mohammad. *The Political Theory of the Delhi Sultanate: Including a Translation of Ziauddin Barani's Fatawa-i Jahandari, Circa 1358–9 A.D.* Allahabad, India: Kitab Mahal, 1940.

——. *Studies in Medieval Indian Polity and Culture: The Delhi Sultanate and Its Times*. Edited by Irfan Habib. New Delhi: Oxford University Press, 2016.

——. *Sultan Mahmud of Ghaznin*. Aligarh: Muslim University, 1927.

——. *Tari'kh-i Hindustan ki Tamhid*. Delhi: Maktaba-i Jamia Milli, 1937.

Habib, Mohammad, and Hayatullah Ansari. *Savanih-i Hayat-i Amir Khusraw*. Ilāhābād: Hindustānī Academy, 1948.

Hackel, Heidi Brayman, and Peter C. Mancall. "Richard Hakluyt the Younger's Notes for the East India Company in 1601: A Transcription of Huntington Library Manuscript EL 2360." *Huntington Library Quarterly* 67, no. 3 (2004): 423–436.

Haidar, Navina Najat. "The Kitab-i Nauras: Key to Bijapur's Golden Age." In *Sultans of the South: Arts of India's Deccan Courts, 1323–1687*, edited by Navina Najat Haidar and Marika Sardar, 26–44. New York: Metropolitan Museum of Art, 2011.

Haidar, Navina Najat, and Marika Sardar, eds. *Sultans of the South: Arts of India's Deccan Courts, 1323–1687*. New York: Metropolitan Museum of Art, 2011.

Haig, Sir Wolseley, and ʿAli ibn ʿAziz Allah. *History of the Nizam Shahi Kings of Ahmadnagar*. Bombay: Education Society's Press, 1923.

Hakluyt, Richard. *The Principal Navigations, Voyages and Discoveries of the English Nation*. London: George Bishop and Ralph Newberie, deputies to Christopher Barker, printer to the Queenes most excellent Maiestie, 1589.

——. *The Second Volvme of the Principal Navigations, Voyages, Traffiques and Discoveries of the English Nation, made by Sea or ouer-land, to the South and South-east parts of the World, at any time within the compasse of these 1600 yeres: Diuided into two seuerall parts*. George Bishop, Ralph Newbery, and Robert Barker, 1599.

Haldar, Piyel. "The Jurisprudence of Travel Literature: Despotism, Excess, and the Common Law." *Journal of Law and Society* 31, no. 1 (2004): 87–112.

Halhed, Nathaniel Brassey. *A Letter to the Rt. Hon. Edmund Burke, on the Subject of His Late Charges Against the Governor-General of Bengal*. London: Printed by J. Johnson, 1783.

Hannoum, Abdelmajid. *Violent Modernity: France in Algeria*. Cambridge, MA: Harvard University Press, 2010.

Hardy, Peter. "Abul Fazl's Portrait of the Perfect Padshah: A Political Philosophy for Mughal India—or a Personal Puff for a Pal?" In *Islam in India: Studies and*

Commentaries. 2 vols. Edited by Christian W. Troll, 2:114–137. New Delhi: Vikas, 1985.

———. *Historians of Medieval India: Studies in Indo-Muslim Historical Writing.* New Delhi: Munshiram Manoharlal Publishers, 1997.

Harriot, Thomas, John White, and Theodor de Bry. *A Briefe and True Report of the New Found Land of Virginia.* Francoforti ad Moenum: Typis Ioannis Wecheli, sumptibus vero Theodori de Bry anno CIC IC XC. Venales reperiuntur in officina Sigismundi Feirabendii, 1590.

Hasan, Mohibbul. *Historians of Medieval India.* Meerut: Meenakshi Prakashan, 1982.

Hasan, Mushirul. *A Moral Reckoning: Muslim Intellectuals in Nineteenth-Century Delhi.* Delhi: Oxford University Press, 2007.

Hashmi, Nasiruddin. *'Ahd-i Āsafi ki Qadīm Ta'līm.* Hyderabad, Deccan: Intizāmi Press, 1946.

———. *Europe mein Dakhani Makhtūthāt.* Hyderabad, Deccan: Shamsul Mutaba' 'Usman, 1932.

Hawley, Daniel S. "L'Inde de Voltaire." *Studies on Voltaire and the Eighteenth Century* 120 (January 1974): 139–178.

Hegde, Radha Sarma, and Ajaya Kumar Sahoo. *Routledge Handbook of the Indian Diaspora.* New York: Routledge, 2018.

Hegel, Georg Wilhelm Friedrich,. *Lectures on the Philosophy of World History.* Edited and Translated by Robert F. Brown and Peter C. Hodgson. Vol. 1, *Manuscripts of the Introduction and the Lectures of 1822–1823.* Oxford: Clarendon Press, 2011.

Herder, Johann Gottfried von. *Ideen zur Geschichte der Menschheit.* 2 vols. Leipzig: F. A. Brockhaus, 1869.

———. *Outlines of a Philosophy of the History of Man.* Translated by T. Churchill. London: J. Johnson / L. Hansard, 1803.

Hiltebeitel, Alf. *Rethinking the Mahābhārata: A Reader's Guide to the Education of the Dharma King.* Chicago: University of Chicago Press, 2001.

Hindusthan Association of America. "The Hindusthanee Student." *Hindusthanee Student* 1 (1914): 17.

Hirschler, Konrad. *Medieval Arabic Historiography: Authors as Actors.* London: Routledge, 2006.

Hodgson, Marshall G. S. "Two Pre-Modern Muslim Historians: Pitfalls and Opportunities in Presenting Them to Moderns." In *Toward World Community,* edited by John Nef, 53–68. The Hague: Dr. W. Junk N.V., 1968.

Holwell, J. Z. *Interesting Historical Events, Relative to the Provinces of Bengal, and the Empire of Indostan. With a Seasonable Hint and Perswasive to the Honourable the Court of Directors of the East India Company. As Also the Mythology and Cosmogony, Fasts and Festivals of the Gentoo's, Followers of the Shastah; Part I.* London: Printed for T. Becket and P. A. De Hondt, 1765.

Hukk, M. *A Descriptive Catalogue of the Arabic and Persian Manuscripts in Edinburgh University Library.* Edinburgh: Printed for the University of Edinburgh, 1925.

Humphreys, R. Stephen. *Islamic History: A Framework for Inquiry.* Rev. ed. Princeton, NJ: Princeton University Press, 1991.

Hunter, William Wilson. *A Brief History of the Indian Peoples.* London: Trübner, 1882.

Husain, Shaikh Chānd. *A Descriptive Handlist of the Arabic, Persian and Hindusthānī Mss., Belonging to the Satara-Historical Museum, at Present Lodged at the Deccan College Research Institute, Poona.* Poona: Katre, 1943.

———. "Some Literary Personages of Ahmadnagar." *Bulletin of the Deccan Research Institute* 3, no. 3 (March 1942): 212–218.

———. "Translations of the Mahābharatā into Arabic and Persian." *Bulletin of the Deccan College Research Institute* 5, no. 3 (1943–1944): 267–280.

———. "When and Where Was Firishta Born?" *Annals of the Bhandarkar Oriental Research Institute* 22, nos. 1–2 (1941): 74–78.

Husaini, Khalidah. *Īshyāṭik Sūsāʾiṭī: Kalkattah Kī Khidmāt-i Fārsī.* Calcutta: Qāzī Davākhānah, 1997.

Hussain, Muhammad Khader, and Moreshwar Gangadhar Dikshit. *Catalogue of Coins of the Mughal Emperors.* Bombay: Directorate of Archives and Archaeology, Maharashtra State, 1968.

Hutton, Deborah S. *Art of the Court of Bijapur.* Bloomington: Indiana University Press, 2006.

Hyppolite, Jean. *Introduction to Hegel's Philosophy of History.* Translated by Bond Harris and Arkady Plotnitsky. Gainesville: University Press of Florida, 1996.

Ibn Khaldūn, Franz Rosenthal, and N. J. Dawood. *The Muqaddimah, an Introduction to History.* Princeton, NJ: Princeton University Press, 1981.

Ikrām, Muḥammad. *Armaghān-i Pāk: Islāmī Hind va Pakistān kī Fārsī shāʿirī kā intikhāb.* Karāchī: Idāra-e Maṭbūʿāt-i Pākistān, 1953.

Inden, Ronald B. *Imagining India.* Cambridge, MA: Blackwell, 1990.

———. "Orientalist Constructions of India." *Modern Asian Studies* 20, no. 3 (1986): 401–446.

Iqbal, Muhammad. *Bāng-i-darā: Majmūʿah-yi kalām-i Urdū murattabah-yi muṣannif.* 2nd ed. Lāhor: Maqbūl-i-ʿāmm Press, 1926.

———. *Speeches, Writings, and Statements of Iqbal.* Compiled and edited by Latif Ahmed Sherwani. Lahore: Iqbal Academy, 1977.

ʿIṣāmī, ʿAbd al-Malik, Āghā Mahdī Ḥusain. *The Futuh-us-Salatin: Or the Shahnama of Medieval India of ʿIsami.* Agra: Educational Press, 1938.

———. *Futūh-us-Salātīn: Or, Shāh Nāmah-i Hind of ʿIsāmī; Translation and Commentary.* Bombay: Asia Publishing House, 1967.

Islam, Arshad. "The Backlash in Delhi: British Treatment of the Mughal Royal Family following the Indian 'Sepoy Mutiny' of 1857." *Journal of Muslim Minority Affairs* 31, no. 2 (June 2011): 197–215.

Jalali Na'ini, Muhammad Riza, and N. S. Shukla, eds. *Mahābhārat: Buzurgtarin manzumah-'i kuhnah-'i mawjud-i jahan bih zaban-i Sanskrit.* Tehran: Kitabkhanah-'i Tahuri, 1980.

Jalali, S. Farrukh Ali. "Place Names and Territorial Divisions in the Sultanate Period Inscriptions." *Proceedings of the Indian History Congress* 38 (1977): 793–805.

Jamal, Rif'at. *Zakā'ullāh: Hayāt Aur Un Ke 'Ilmī Va Adabī Kārnāme.* Delhi: Taqsīmkār Sāqī Buk Dipo, 1990.

James, C. L. R. *The Black Jacobins: Toussaint L'Ouverture and the San Domingo Revolution.* New York: The Dial Press, 1938.

Janaki, Vengalil A. *Gujarat as the Arabs Knew It: A Study in Historical Geography.* Baroda: M.S. University of Baroda, 1969.

Johnson, Samuel, Oliver Goldsmith, and Christopher Smart. *The World Displayed or, a Curious Collection of Voyages and Travels, Selected from the Writers of All Nations.* 20 vols. London: J. Newbery, 1759–1761.

Jokic, Olivera. "Commanding Correspondence: Letters and the 'Evidence of Experience' in the Letterbook of John Bruce, the East India Company Historiographer." *The Eighteenth Century* 52, no. 2 (2011): 109–136.

Jones, William. *A Grammar of the Persian Language.* London: W. and J. Richardson, 1771.

———. *A Grammar of the Persian Language.* 3rd ed. London: J. Murray, 1783.

———. "The Third Anniversary Discourse." In *Sir William Jones: Selected Poetical and Prose Works,* edited by Michael J. Franklin, 355–371. Cardiff: University of Wales Press, 1995.

———. *The Works of Sir William Jones.* 13 vols. London: John Stockdale, 1807.

Jones, William, and John Shore Teignmouth. "On the Chronology of the Hindus." In *The Works of Sir William Jones.* Vol. 6. London: Stockdale, 1807.

Jordanus, Catalani, bishop of Columbum, Henry Yule, and Hakluyt Society. *Mirabilia Descripta. The Wonders of the East.* London: Printed for the Hakluyt Society, 1863.

Jūzjānī, Minhāj Sirāj. *Ṭabaqāt-i Nāṣirī.* Edited by 'Abd al-Ḥayy Ḥabībī. 2 vols. Tehran: Intishārāt-i Asāṭīr, 1989.

Kaegi, Walter Emil. "Initial Byzantine Reactions to the Arab Conquest." *Church History* 38, no. 2 (1969): 139–149.

Kaicker, Abhishek. *The King and the People: Sovereignty and Popular Politics in Mughal Delhi.* New York: Oxford University Press, 2020.

Kalhana, M A. *Kalhaṇa's Rājataraṅgiṇi: A Chronicle of the Kings of Kashmīr.* Mirpur, Azad Kashmir: Verinag Publishers, 1991.

Kant, Immanuel. *Anthropology, History, and Education.* Edited and translated by Günter Zöller and Robert B. Louden. Cambridge: Cambridge University Press, 2007.

———. *Idee zu einer allgemeinen Geschichte in weltbürgerlicher Absicht.* Leipzig: Meiner, ca. 1917.

Kapadia, Aparna. *In Praise of Kings: Rajputs, Sultans and Poets in Fifteenth-Century Gujarat.* Cambridge: Cambridge University Press, 2018.

Kejariwal, Om Prakash. *The Asiatic Society of Bengal and the Discovery of India's Past, 1784–1838.* New York: Oxford University Press, 1988.

Ketelaar, Joan Josua. *Instructie of onderwijsinghe der Hindoustaanse en Persiaanse taalen,* ca. 1689. Ms. 1478 (1 E 21), Utrecht University Library.

Khaldun, Ibn. *Muqaddimah: An Introduction to History.* Edited by Franz Rosenthal. New York: Pantheon Books, 1958.

Khalidi, Tarif. "Premodern Arabic / Islamic Historical Writing." In *A Companion to Global Historical Thought,* edited by Prasenjit Duara, Viren Murthy, and Andrew Sartori, 78–91. Chichester, Sussex, UK: Wiley-Blackwell, 2014.

Khālidiyān, and Muḥammad ibn Hāshim Khālidī, eds. *Kitāb al-tuḥaf wa-hadāyā.* Miṣr: Dār al-Maʿārif, 1956.

Khan, M. A. M., and C. H. Shaikh. "A Dakhanī Manuscript." *Bulletin of the Deccan College Research Institute* 2, nos. 3–4 (June 1941): 300–313.

Khan, Shafāʾat Ahmad. "Presidential Address of Sir Shafāʾat Ahmad Khān." *Proceedings of the Indian History Congress* 1, no. 1 (June 1935): 1–63.

Khan, Tauqir Ahmad. *Iqbāl aur Hindūstān.* New Delhi: Naʾī Kitāb Publishers, 2007.

Khan, Yusuf Husayn. *Farāmīn Va Asnād-i Salāṭīn-i Dakin: Min Ibtidāʾī Sanah 1408 Li-Ghāyat 1687 ʿIsavī.* Hyderabad: State Archives Government Andhra Pardesh, 1980.

Khusrau, Amir. *The Campaigns of ʿAlāʾud-dīn Khiljī, Being the Khaẓāʾinul Futūḥ (Treasures of Victory) of Hazrat Amīr Khusrau of Delhi.* Translated by Mohammad Habib. Madras: Diocesan Press, 1931.

———. *Duvālrāni-i Khiẓr Khān.* Delhi: Idarah-yi Adabiyat-i Dilli, 1988.

———. *Khazaʾin al-Futuh of Hazrat Amir Khusrau Dihlawi. A Short History of the Reign of Sultan Alaʾuddin Khalji from the Date of His Accession up to the Year 711 H. Persian Text.* Edited by Mohammad Wahid Mirza. Calcutta: Asiatic Society, 1953.

———. *Khazāyīn Al-Futūḥ: Mushtamal Bar Aḥvāl Va Kavāʾif-i ʿAhd-i Sulṭān ʿAlāʾ Al-Dīn Khiljī.* Islamabad: National Book Foundation of Pakistan, 1976.

———. *Masnavi Nuh Siphar.* Translated by Mohammad Rafiq Abid. New Delhi: Maktaba Jamiʾa, 2012.

———. *Masnavī Tughlug Nāma-yi Khusraw Dihlavī.* Aurangābād: Deccan Publishers, 1933.

———. *The Nuh Sipihr of Amir Khusraw. Persian Text.* Edited by Muhammad Wahid Mirza. London: Oxford University Press, 1950.

Kia, Mana. *Persianate Selves: Memories of Place and Origin before Nationalism.* Stanford, CA: Stanford University Press, 2020.

King, Christopher R. *One Language, Two Scripts: The Hindi Movement in Nineteenth Century North India.* Bombay: Oxford University Press, 1994.

Kinra, Rajeev. *Writing Self, Writing Empire: Chandar Bhan Brahman and the Cultural World of the Indo-Persian State Secretary.* Oakland: University of California Press, 2015.

Knappert, J. "The Qisasu'l-Anbiyā'i as Moralistic Stories." *Proceedings of the Seminar for Arabian Studies* 6 (1976): 103–116.

Koch, Ebba. "My Garden Is Hindustan: The Mughal Emperor's Realization of a Political Metaphor." In *Middle East Garden Traditions: Unity and Diversity,* edited by Michael Conan, 159–175. Washington, DC: Dumbarton Oaks, 2007.

Kūfī, ʿAlī ibn Ḥāmid. *Fathnamah-i Sind.* Edited by Nabi Baksh Khan Baloch. Islamabad, Pakistan: Institute of Islamic History, Culture and Civilization, Islamic University, 1983.

———. *Fatḥnāma-i Sind: Maʿrūf bi Čačnāma.* Edited and translated by Dāwūd Pūta. Tehran: Intišārāt-i Asāṭīr, 2005.

Kulkarni, G. T. "A Note on a Unique Adil Shahi Farman Bestowing Madad-Ma'ash on Hindus (1653 A.D.)." *Proceedings of the Indian History Congress* 68, no. 1 (2007): 313–318.

Kulke, Hermann, and Dietmar Rothermund. *A History of India.* London: Routledge, 2016.

Lahiri, Nayanjot. *Ashoka in Ancient India.* Cambridge, MA: Harvard University Press, 2015.

Lal, Vinay. *The History of History: Politics and Scholarship in Modern India.* New Delhi: Oxford University Press, 2003.

Lee, Joo-Yup, "The Historical Meaning of the Term *Turk* and the Nature of the Turkic Identity of the Chinggisid and Timurid Elites in Post-Mongol Central Asia." *Central Asiatic Journal* 59, nos. 1–2 (2016): 101–132.

Lees, W. Nassau, and H. W. Hammond. "Materials for the History of India for the Six Hundred Years of Mohammadan Rule Previous to the Foundation of the British Indian Empire." *Journal of the Royal Asiatic Society of Great Britain and Ireland* 3, no. 2 (1868): 414–477.

Lelyveld, David. *Aligarh's First Generation: Muslim Solidarity in British India.* Princeton, NJ: Princeton University Press, 1977.

———. "Colonial Knowledge and the Fate of Hindustani." *Comparative Studies in Society and History* 35, no. 4 (1993): 665–682.

Lichefeld, Nicholas. *The first booke of the historie of the discouerie and conquest of the East Indias, enterprised by the Portingales, in their daungerous nauigations, in the time of King Don Iohn, the second of that name VVhich historie conteineth much varietie of matter, very profitable for all nauigators, and not vnpleasaunt to the readers. Set foorth in the Portingale language, by Hernan Lopes de Castaneda. And now translated into English, by N.L. Gentleman.* London: Thomas East, 1582.

Linschoten, Jan Huygen van, Johann Adam Lonicerus, and Theodor de Bry. *Ander Theil der Orientalischen Indien, Von allen Völckern, Insulen, Meerporten, fliessenden Wassern vnd anderen Orten, so von Portugal auss, lengst dem Gestaden Aphrica, biss in Ost Indien vnd zu dem Landt China, sampt andern Insulen zu sehen seynd.* Franckfurt am Meyn: Durch Erasmum Kempffer, 1613.

Liu, Xinru. *Ancient India and Ancient China: Trade and Religious Exchanges AD 1–600.* Oxford: Oxford University Press, 1988.

Locke, John. *John Locke: Essays on the Law of Nature: The Latin Text with a Translation, Introduction, and Notes; Together with Transcripts of Locke's Shorthand in His Journal for 1676.* Edited by W. von Leyden. Oxford: Oxford University Press, 2002.

———. *Two Treatises of Government.* Edited by Peter Laslett. Cambridge: Cambridge University Press, 1988.

Loth, Otto. *A Catalogue of the Arabic Manuscripts in the Library of the India Office.* London: n.p., 1877.

Macaulay, Thomas Babington. *Macaulay: Prose and Poetry.* Edited by G. M. Young. Cambridge, MA: Harvard University Press, 1952.

MacDonald, John. *Travels, in Various Parts of Europe, Asia, and Africa, during a Series of Thirty Years and Upwards.* London: J. Forbes, 1790.

Mackenzie, C. F. *The Romantic Land of Hind.* London: W. H. Allen. 1882.

Macpherson, S. Chartres. "An Account of the Religion of the Khonds in Orissa." *Journal of the Royal Asiatic Society of Great Britain and Ireland* 13 (1852): 216–274.

Madnī, Sayyid Ḥusain Aḥmad, and Sayyid Muḥammad Miyān. *Hamārā Hindustān aur uske faẓā'il.* Delhi: Delhi Printing Press, 1946.

Mahalingam, T. V. "Presidential Address." *Proceedings of the Indian History Congress* 14 (1951): 103–110.

Mahdi, Muhsin. *Ibn Khaldūn's Philosophy of History: A Study in the Philosophic Foundation of the Science of Culture.* Chicago: University of Chicago Press, 1964.

Māhrū, 'Ainuddīn 'Ainulmulk 'Abdullāh, and Abdur Rashid. *Inshā-yi Māhrū.* Lahore: Intishārāt-i Taḥqiqāt-i Pakistān, 1965.

Maine, Henry Sumner. *Village-Communities in the East and West: Six Lectures Delivered at Oxford.* London: Murray, 1871.

Majeed, Javed. *Ungoverned Imaginings: James Mill's* The History of British India *and Orientalism.* Oxford: Clarendon Press, 1992.

Majumdar, Ramesh Chandra. *Historiography in Modern India.* New York: Asia Publication House, 1970.

Mancini-Lander, Derek J. "Tales Bent Backward: Early Modern Local History in Persianate Transregional Contexts." *Journal of Royal Asiatic Society* 28, no. 1 (January 2018): 23–54.

Mani, Lata. *Contentious Traditions: The Debate on Sati in Colonial India.* Berkeley: University of California Press, 1998.

Markiewicz, Christopher. "History as Science: The Fifteenth-Century Debate in
    Arabic and Persian." *Journal of Early Modern History* 21, no. 3 (2017): 216–240.

Marx, Karl. *Dispatches for the New York Tribune.* Stilwell: Neeland Media, 2014.

Mas'ūdī, Abu'l Ḥasan 'Ali. *Murūj al-dhahab wa maʿāden al-jawhar.* Edited by
    Charles Pellat. Beirut: Manshurat al-Jami'ah al-Lubnaniyah, 1966.

Maurice, Thomas. *The History of Hindostan; Its Arts, and Its Sciences, as Connected
    with the History of the Other Great Empires of Asia, during the Most Ancient
    Periods of the World.* 3 vols. London: W. Bulmer, 1795.

Mayerson, Philip. "A Confusion of Indias: Asian India and African India in the
    Byzantine Sources." *Journal of the American Oriental Society* 113, no. 2 (1993):
    169–174.

McGetchin, Douglas T. *Indology, Indomania, and Orientalism: Ancient India's
    Rebirth in Modern Germany.* Madison, NJ: Fairleigh Dickinson University
    Press, 2009.

Meisami, Julie S. *Persian Historiography to the End of the Twelfth Century.* Edin-
    burgh: Edinburgh University Press, 1999.

Melville, C. P., ed. *Persian Historiography.* Vol. 10 of *A History of Persian Literature.*
    London: I. B. Tauris, 2012.

Merguerian, Gayane Karen, and Afsaneh Najmabadi. "Zulaykha and Yusuf:
    Whose 'Best Story'?" *International Journal of Middle East Studies* 29, no. 4
    (November 1997): 485–508.

Mernissi, Fatima. *The Forgotten Queens of Islam.* Translated by Mary Jo Lakeland.
    Karachi: Oxford University Press, 2003.

Mill, James. *The History of British India.* 2 vols. London: Baldwin, Cradock, & Joy, 1817.

Minault, Gail. "Aloys Sprenger: German Orientalism's 'Gift' to Delhi College." *South
    Asia Research* 31, no. 1 (2011): 7–23.

——. *The Khilafat Movement: Religious Symbolism and Political Mobilization in
    India.* New York: Columbia University Press, 1982.

Minkowski, Christopher. "Sanskrit Scientific Libraries and Their Uses: Examples and
    Problems of the Early Modern Period." In *Looking at It from Asia: The Processes
    That Shaped the Sources of History of Science,* edited by Florence Bretelle-Establet,
    81–114. Dordrecht: Springer Netherlands, 2010.

Mirchandani, B. D. "Ancient Sindhu and Sauvīra." *Annals of the Bhandarkar
    Oriental Research Institute* 57, nos. 1–4 (1976): 81–93.

Mīr Khwānd. *Tārīkh-i rawẓat al-ṣafā fī sīrat al-anbiyā' va al-mulūk va al-khulafā'.*
    Edited by Jamshīd Kiyānfar. 10 vols. in 15 books. Tehran: Intesharat Aṣāṭīr,
    2001.

Misra, Satish Chandra. *Muslim Communities in Gujarat: Preliminary Studies in Their
    History and Social Organization.* New York: Asia Publication House, 1964.

Miśra, Vidyānivāsa, and N. S. S. Raman, eds. *Purāṇas: History and Itihāsas.* New
    Delhi: Centre for Studies in Civilizations for the Project of History of Indian
    Science, Philosophy and Culture, 2014.

Mitra, Durba. *Indian Sex Life: How Sexuality Shaped the Science of Society.* Princeton, NJ: Princeton University Press, 2020.

Modi, Jivanji Jameshdji. "King Akbar and the Persian Translation of Sanskrit Books." *Annals of the Bhandarkar Oriental Research Institute* 6, no. 2 (March 1925): 83–107.

Mohan, Jyoti. "La Civilisation la plus Antique: Voltaire's Images of India." *Journal of World History* 16, no. 2 (2005): 173–185.

Momigliano, Arnaldo. "A Hundred Years after Ranke." *Diogenes* 2, no. 7 (June 1954): 52–58.

———. *Studies in Historiography.* London: Weidenfeld and Nicolson, 1966.

Moraes, George. "Early Relations of the Portuguese with the Syrian Christians of Malabar 1500–1552." *Proceedings of the Indian History Congress* 21 (1958): 640–647.

Morley, William Hook. *A Descriptive Catalogue of the Historical Manuscripts in the Arabic and Persian Languages: Preserved in the Library of the Royal Asiatic Society of Great Britain and Ireland.* London: John W. Parker & Sons, 1854.

Morris, Rosalind C. *In the Place of Origins: Modernity and Its Mediums in Northern Thailand.* Durham, NC: Duke University Press, 2000.

Mosca, Matthew W. "Hindustan as a Geographic and Political Concept in Qing Sources, 1700–1800," *China Report* 47, no. 4 (2011): 263–277.

Mubārakpūrī, Qāẓī Aṯhar. *Khilāfat-i Umviyyah Aur Hindūstān.* Dehli: Nadvat al-Muṣannifīn, 1975.

Mubārakshāh, Fakhr al-Dīn. *Ta'rikh-i Fakhru'd-Din Mubarakshah: Being the Historical Introduction to the Book of Genealogies of Fakru'd-Dín Mubarak-shah Marvar-Rúdi Completed in A.D. 1206.* Edited by E. Denison Ross. Ed. from a unique manuscript. James G. Forlong Fund (Series) 4. London: Royal Asiatic Society, 1927

Mubārakshāh, Muḥammad Manṣūr bin Saʻid. *Ādāb al-ḥarb wa-l-shujāʻa.* Tehran: Intishārāt-i Iqbāl, 1967.

Mukhia, Harbans. *Historians and Historiography during the Reign of Akbar.* New Delhi: Vikas Publishing House, 1976.

Mukhopadhyay, Subodh Kumar. *Evolution of Historiography in Modern India, 1900–1960: A Study of the Writing of Indian History by Her Own Historians.* Calcutta: K. P. Bagchi, 1981.

Munshi, Kanaiyalal Maneklal. *Akhand Hindustan.* Bombay: New Book, 1942.

Mushtaqui, Shaikh Rizq Ullah. *Wāqiʻāt-e Mushtāquī.* Rāmpūr: Rāmpūr Raẓā Library, 2002.

———.*Waqiʻat-e Mushtaqui of Shaikh Rizq Ullah Mushtaqui: A Source of Information on the Life and Conditions in the Pre-Mughal India.* New Delhi: Indian Council of Historical Research and Northern Book Centre, 1993.

Nadvī, Masʻūd ʻAlī. *Hindustān ʻArabon Kī Nazar Mein.* ʻAzamgaṛh: Dar Al-Muṣanifen, 1960.

Naik, J. V. "Instant Indian Nationalist Reaction to James Mill's 'The History of India.'" *Proceeedings of the Indian History Congress* 63 (2002): 587–595.

Naim, C. M. "Interrogating 'The East,' 'Culture,' and 'Loss,' in Abdul Halim Sharar's *Guzashta Lakhna'u*." In *Indo-Muslim Cultures in Transition*, edited by Alka Patel and Karen Leonard. Leiden: Brill, 2012.

———. "Syed Ahmad and His Two Books Called 'Asar-Al-Sanadid.'" *Modern Asian Studies* 45, no. 3 (May 2011): 669–708.

Na'imuddīn. *Hindūstān Mein Fārsī Adab: Dihlī Saltanat Se Qabl*. Delhi: M. S. Publications, 1985.

Nainar, S. Muhammad Husayn. *Arab Geographers' Knowledge of Southern India*. Madras: University of Madras, 1942.

Naqvi, Sadiq. *Iranian Afaquies Contribution to the Qutb Shahi and Adil Shahi Kingdoms*. Hyderabad: A.A. Hussain Book Shop, 2003.

Naqvī, Sakhī Hasan. *Hamārā Qadīm Samāj*. New Delhi: National Book Trust, 1972.

Nandy, Ashis. "History's Forgotten Doubles." *History and Theory* 34, no. 2 (May 1995): 44–66.

———. "The Idea of South Asia: A Personal Note on Post-Bandung Blues." *Inter-Asia Cultural Studies* 6, no. 4 (2005): 541–545.

Nayeem, M. A. *External Relations of the Bijapur Kingdom, 1489–1686 A.D.* Hyderabad: Bright Publishers, 1974.

Nayeem, M. A., Aniruddha Ray, Kuzhippalli Skaria Mathew, and A. Rā Kulakarṇi, eds. *Studies in History of the Deccan: Medieval and Modern: Professor A.R. Kulkarni Felicitation Volume*. Delhi: Pragati Publications, 2002.

Nazim, Muhammad. *The Life and Times of Sultan Mahmud of Ghazna*. Cambridge: Cambridge University Press, 1931.

Nedungatt, George. "The Apocryphal 'Acts of Thomas' and Christian Origins in India." *Gregorianum* 92, no. 3 (2011): 533–57.

Nehru, Jawaharlal. *Glimpses of World History: Being Further Letters to His Daughter, Written in Prison, and Containing a Rambling Account of History for Young People*. New York: Asia Publishing House, 1962.

Nizami, Khaliq Ahmad. *Religion and Politics in India during the Thirteenth Century*. Delhi: Idarah-i Adabiyat-i Delli, 1974.

———. *Sayyid Ahmad Khan*. New Delhi: Publications Division, Ministry of Information and Broadcasting, Government of India, 1966.

Nizami, Tajuddin Hasan. *Tāj Al-Ma'āsir*. Delhi: Markaz-i Taḥqīqāt-i Fārsī, Rāyzanī Farhangī, Jamhūrī Islāmī Īrān, 2008.

Nizami, Tajuddin Hasan, M. Aslam Khan, and Chander Shekhar. *Taj ul Ma'athir*. Delhi: Saud Ahmad Dehlavi, 1998.

Niẓāmu'd-Dīn, Muḥammad. *Introduction to the Jawāmi'u'l-Ḥikāyāt wa Lawāmi'u'r-Riwāyāt of Sadīdu'd-dīn Muḥammad al-'Awfī*. London: Luzac, 1929.

Noth, Albrecht, and Lawrence I. Conrad. *The Early Arabic Historical Tradition: A Source-Critical Study*. Princeton, NJ: The Darwin Press, 1997.

Nuʿmānī, Shiblī. *Al-Fārūq: Mukammal.* Aʿẓamgaḍh: Shiblī Akaiḍmī, 2008.

Obrock, Luther. "Śrīvara's Kathākautuka Cosmology, Translation, and the Life of a Text in Sultanate Kashmir." In *Jāmī in Regional Contexts,* edited by Thibaut d'Hubert and Alexandre Papas, 752–777. Leiden: Brill, 2018.

Olearius, Adam, John Davies, and Johann Albrecht von Mandelslo. *Mandelslo's Travels into the Indies.* The first book of *The Voyages and Travells of the Ambassadors Sent by Frederick Duke of Holstein, to the Great Duke of Muscovy, and the King of Persia: Begun in the Year M.DC.XXXIII, and Finish'd in M.DC.XXXIX.* London: John Starkey, 1669.

Olearius, Adamus. *Offt begehrte Beschreibung der newen orientalischen Reise so durch Gelegenheit einer holsteinischen Legation an den König in persien Geschehen.* Schleswig: Bey Jacob zur Glocken, 1647.

Olivelle, Patrick. *King, Governance, and Law in Ancient India: Kauṭilya's Arthaśāstra.* New York: Oxford University Press, 2013.

Orme, Robert. *Historical Fragments of the Mogul Empire, of the Morattoes, and of the British Concerns in Indostan; From the Year MDCLIX.* London: F. Wingrave in the Strand, 1805.

Osswald, Cristina. "On Otherness and India: O Livro de Duarte Barbosa (c. 1516) Seen in Context." *Cem: Cultura, Espaço & Memória* 6, no. 6 (2015): 23–38.

Pacifici, Sergio J., trans. *Copy of a Letter to the King of Portugal Sent to the King of Castile Concerning the Voyage and Success of India.* Minneapolis: University of Minnesota Press, 1955.

Pandey, Gyanendra. "Hindus and Other: The Militant Hindu Construction." *Economic & Political Weekly* 26, no. 52 (December 28, 1991): 2997–3009.

Patel, Alka, and Tūrağ Daryāyī. *India and Iran in the Longue Durée.* Irvine: University of Califonia, Irvine, Jordan Center for Persian Studies, 2017.

Patton, Laurie, ed. *Jewels of Authority: Women and Textual Tradition in Hindu India.* Oxford: Oxford University Press, 2002.

Pawar, Kiran. *Sir Jadunath Sarkar: A Profile in Historiography.* New Delhi: Books & Books, 1985.

Peacock, Andrew C. S. *Islamisation Comparative Perspectives from History.* Edinburgh: Edinburgh University Press, 2017.

———. *Mediaeval Islamic Historiography and Political Legitimacy: Bal'ami's Tarikhnama.* New York: Routledge, 2007.

———. "'Utbī's al-Yamīnī: Patronage, Composition and Reception." *Arabica* 54, no. 4 (October 2007): 500–525.

Perez, Rosa Maria. "The Rhetoric of Empire: Gender Representations in Portuguese India." *Portuguese Studies* 21 (2005): 126–141.

Perkins, C. Ryan. "A New Pablik: Abdul Halim Sharar, Volunteerism and the Anjuman-e Dar us Salam in Late Nineteenth-Century India." *Modern Asian Studies* 49, no. 4 (July 2015): 1049–1090.

Pertsch, Wilhelm. *Verzeichniss der Persischen Handscriften der Königlichen zu Berlin.* Berlin: A. Asher, 1888.

Philips, Cyril Henry. "James Mill, Mountstuart Elphinstone and the History of India." In *Historians of India, Pakistan and Ceylon,* 217–229. London: Oxford University Press, 1961.

Pickthall, Muhammad M., trans. *The Meaning of the Glorious Qur'an.* New York: Muslim World League, n.d.

Pierce, Leslie P. *The Imperial Harem: Women and Sovereignty in the Ottoman Empire.* New York: Oxford University Press, 1993.

Pollock, Sheldon I. *The Language of the Gods in the World of Men: Sanskrit, Culture, and Power in Premodern India.* Berkeley: University of California Press, 2009.

———. "Philology in Three Dimensions." *Postmedieval: A Journal of Medieval Cultural Studies* 5, no. 4 (December 2014): 398–413.

———. *A Rasa Reader: Classical Indian Aesthetics.* New York: Columbia University Press, 2016.

———. "Towards a Political Philology: D. D. Kosambi and Sanskrit." In *Unsettling the Past: Unknown Aspects and Scholarly Assessments of D.D. Kosambi,* edited by Meera Kosambi. Delhi: Permanent Black, 2012.

Postans, Thomas. *Personal Observations on Sindh; the manners and customs of its inhabitants, and its productive capabilities: with a sketch of its history, a narrative of recent events, and an account of the connection of the British Government with that country, etc.* London: Longman, Brown, Green & Longmans, 1843.

Prakashū, Motī. *Sindhī Shiʿra Men Istarīʾa Jo Ciṭu.* Bambaʾī: Shrīkānt, 1988.

Prasad, Pushpa. *Sanskrit Inscriptions of the Delhi Sultanate, 1191–1526.* Delhi: Oxford University Press, 1990.

Price, Major David. *Chronological Retrospect or Memoirs of the Principal Events of Mahommedan History, from the Death of the Arabian Legislator, to the Accession of the Emperor Akbar, and the Establishment of the Moghul Empire in Hindustan. From Original Persian Authors.* 3 vols. in 4 books. London: J. Booth, 1811–1820.

Priestley, Johnson. *Disquisitions relating to matter and spirit: to which is added, The history of the philosophical doctrine concerning the origin of the soul, and the nature of matter; with its influence on Christianity, especially with respect to the doctrine of the pre-existence of Christ.* London: Printed for J. Johnson, 1777.

Pritchett, Frances W. *Marvelous Encounters: Folk Romance in Urdu and Hindi.* Riverdale, MD: Riverdale Company, 1985.

"Proceedings of the Royal Asiatic Society." *Journal of the Royal Asiatic Society of Great Britain and Ireland* 3, no. 2 (1836): xii–xiv.

Purchas, Samuel. *Hakluytus Posthmus or Purchas His Pilgrimes. Contayning a History of the World, in Sea voyages. & lande-Trauells, by Englishmen & others.* London: Henry Fetherston, at ye signe of the rose in Pauls Churchyard, 1625.

————. *Purchas His Pilgrimage. Or Relations of the world and the religions obserued in all ages and places discouered, from the Creation vnto this present In foure partes.* London: William Stansby for Henrie Fetherston, 1613.

Qaddumi, Ghada Hijjawi. *Book of Gifts and Rarities: Selections Compiled in the Fifteenth Century from an Eleventh-Century Manuscript on Gifts and Treasures.* Cambridge, MA: Harvard University Press, 1996.

Quenzer, Jörg B., Dmitry Bondarev, and Jan-Ulrich Sobisch. *Manuscript Cultures: Mapping the Field.* Berlin: Walter de Gruyter, 2014.

Qutban. *The Magic Doe: Qutban Suhravardi's Mirigavati: A New Translation.* Translated by Aditya Behl. Edited by Wendy Doniger. New York: Oxford University Press, 2012.

Rai, Alok. *Hindi Nationalism.* New Delhi: Orient Longman, 2000.

Rajjak, Shaikh Musak. "Mir Mohammad Momin Astrabadi's Contribution to Qutb Shahi Deccan History." *Journal of the Research Society of Pakistan* 52, no. 2 (2015): 203–209.

Raleigh, Walter. *The Life and Death of Mahomet; the Conquest of Spaine, Together with the Rysing and Ruine of the Sarazen Empire.* London: Printed by R.H. for D. Frere, 1637.

Ramani, Hashoo Kewal, ed. *Sindhi Short Stories.* New Delhi: Hashmat Publications, 1963.

Rangachari, Devika. *Invisible Women, Visible Histories: Gender, Society, and Polity in North India, Seventh to Twelfth Century AD.* New Delhi: Manohar Publishers, 2009.

Ranke, Leopold von. *Theory and Practice of History.* London: Routledge, 2011.

Rao, Velcheru Narayana, David Shulman, and Sanjay Subrahmanyam. *Textures of Time: Writing History in South India, 1600–1800.* Delhi: Permanent Black, 2001.

Raverty, Henry George. *The Mihran of Sind and Its Tributaries.* Calcutta: Baptist Mission Press, 1897.

Rawat, Ramnarayan S. "Colonial Archive versus Colonial Sociology: Writing Dalit History." In *Dalit Studies,* edited by Ramnarayan S. Rawat and K. Satyanarayana, 53–74. Durham, NC: Duke University Press, 2016.

Raza, Kalidas Gupta. *Dīvān-e ghālib kāmil nuskhah-e guptā raẓā, tārīkhī tartīb se.* Bombay: Sakar Publications, 1995.

Raza, S. Jabir, "Coinage and Metallurgy under the Ghaznavid Sultan Mahmud." *Proceedings of the Indian History Congress* 75 (2014): 224–231.

Rennell, James. *Memoir of a Map of Hindoostan, or, the Mogul Empire: With an Introduction, Illustrative of the Geography and Present Division of That Country, and a Map of the Countries Situated between the Head of the Indus, and the Caspian Sea.* London: M. Brown for the author, 1788.

Rennell, James, J. I. Phillips, and W. Harrisson. "Hindoostan." London: Published according to act of Parliament by J. Rennell, December 1, 1782. Map.

Rezavi, Syed Ali Nadeem. "The Idea of India in Amir Khusrau." In *India—Studies in the History of an Idea,* edited by Irfan Habib, 121–128. Delhi: Munshiram Manoharlal Publishers, 2005.

Ricci, Ronit. *Islam Translated: Literature, Conversion, and the Arabic Cosmopolis of South and Southeast Asia.* Chicago: University of Chicago Press, 2011.

Richards, John F. "The Imperial Crisis in the Deccan." *Journal of Asian Studies* 35, no. 2 (1976): 237–256.

———, ed. *Kingship and Authority in South Asia.* Madison: Center for South Asian Studies, University of Wisconsin, Madison, 1978.

Rieu, Charles. *Catalogue of the Persian Manuscripts in the British Museum.* 3 vols. London: British Museum, 1879–1883.

Risley, Herbert Hope. *The People of India.* London: Thacker, Spink, 1908.

Ross, E. D., and E. G. Browne, *Catalogue of Two Collections of Persian and Arabic Manuscripts preserved in the India Office Library.* London: Eyre and Spottis-woode, 1902.

Rousseau, Jean-Jacques. *Oeuvres posthumes de Jean-Jacques Rousseau; ou, Recueil de pièces manuscrites.* Vol. 3, 211–327. Geneve [s.n.], 1781–1782.

Roy, Srirupa. "'A Symbol of Freedom': The Indian Flag and the Transformation of Nationalism, 1906–2002." *Journal of Asian Studies,* 65, no. 3 (2006): 495–528.

Rushdie, Salman. *Midnight's Children.* New York: Knopf, 1980.

Sachau, Eduard, and Carl Hermann Ethé. *Catalogue of the Persian, Turkish, Hindûstânî, and Pushtû Manuscripts in the Bodleian Library.* 2 vols. Oxford: Clarendon Press, 1889.

Sadiq, Qaiyum. *Dakan Zindah Kardam: Dakanī Nāyāb Makhṭūṭāt Aur Dīgar Tabṣire.* Gulbargah: Urdu Research Center, 2004.

Said, Edward. *Orientalism.* New York: Vintage Books, 1979.

Saldanha, Arun. "The Itineraries of Geography: Jan Huygen van Linschoten's "Itinerario" and Dutch Expeditions to the Indian Ocean, 1594–1602." *Annals of the Association of American Geographers* 101, no. 1 (2011): 149–177.

Sangari, Kumkum, and Sudesh Vaid, eds. *Recasting Women: Essays in Indian Colonial History.* New Brunswick, NJ: Rutgers University Press, 1990.

Sarkar, Jadunath. *India through the Ages: A Survey of the Growth of Indian Life and Thought.* Calcutta: M. C. Sarkar & Sons, 1928.

Śāstrī, Hariprasāda Gaṅgāśaṅkara. *Historical and Cultural Study of the Inscriptions of Gujarat: From Earliest Times to the End of the Caulukya Period (Circa 1300 A.D.).* Ahmedabad: B. J. Institute of Learning & Research, 1989.

Savarkar, Vinayak Damodar. *Hindu-Pad-Padashahi, or A Critical Review of the Hindu Empire of Maharashtra.* Madras: B. G. Paul., 1925.

———. *Hindutva: Who Is a Hindu?* Bombay: Veer Savarkar Prakashan, 1969.

Schlegel, Friedrich von. *The Philosophy of History: In a Course of Lectures Delivered at Vienna.* Translated by James Burton Robertson. London: Saunders and Otley, 1835.

Schmidt, Richard. *Śrīvara's Kathākautukam: Die Geschichte von Joseph in persisch-indischem Gewande.* Kièl: C. F. Haeseler, 1898.

Schürer, Norbert. "The Impartial Spectator of Sati, 1757–84." *Eighteenth-Century Studies* 42, no. 1 (2008): 19–44.

Scott, Jonathan. *Ferishta's History of Dekkan: From the First Mahummedan Conquests: With a Continuation from Other Native Writers, of the Events in That Part of India, to the Reduction of Its Last Monarchs by the Emperor Aulumgeer Aurungzebe: Also, the Reigns of His Successors . . . to the Present Day: And the History of Bengal, from the Accession of Aliverdee Khan to the Year 1780. Comprised in Six Parts.* Shrewsbury: J. and W. Eddowes, 1794.

Sen, S. P., "History of the Indian History Congress (1935–1963)." *Proceedings of the Indian History Congress* 25 (1963): 19–56.

Sen, Sudipta. *A Distant Sovereignty: National Imperialism and the Origins of British India.* London: Routledge, 2002.

———. "Historian as Witness: Ghulam Husain Tabatabai and the Dawning of British Rule in India." In *India and Iran in the Longue Durée,* edited by Alka Patel and Touraj Daryaee, 103–125. Irvine, CA: Jordan Center for Persian Studies, 2017.

Sen, Tansen. *Buddhism, Diplomacy, and Trade: The Realignment of Sino-Indian Relations, 600–1400.* Honolulu: University of Hawai'i Press, 2003.

Seshan, Radhika. "Routes and Towns in the Deccan 15th to 17th Centuries." *Proceedings of the Indian History Congress* 75 (2014): 331–335.

Sezgin, Fuat. *Pseudo-Aristotelica Preserved in Arabic Translation: Texts and Studies.* Vols. 1 and 2. Frankfurt: Institute for the History of Arabic-Islamic Science at Johann Wolfgang Goethe University, 2000.

Shafi, Iqbal M. "Fresh Light on the Ghaznavīds." *Islamic Culture* 12, no. 2 (1938): 189–234.

Shāhu, 'Ināyatu. *Mīyunu Shāhu 'Ināta Jo Kalāmu: Ilahī! 'ināyāta Jā Aghīyan Kalāmu.* Edited by Nabī Bakhshu K̲h̲ānu Balocu. Jāmshoro: Sindhī Adabī Borḍ, 2010.

Sharar, 'Abdul Halim. *Mulk al-'Azīz Varjiniā.* Lahore: Mājlis Tarāqi-i Adāb, 1964.

———. *Tārīkh-i Sindh.* Karachi: City Book Point, 2011.

Sharma, Sunil. *Amir Khusraw: The Poet of Sultans and Sufis.* London: Oneworld Publications, 2005.

———. *Mughal Arcadia: Persian Literature in an Indian Court.* Cambridge, MA: Harvard University Press, 2017.

———. *Persian Poetry at the Indian Frontier: Mas'ûd Sa'd Salmân of Lahore.* Delhi: Permanent Black, 2000.

Shauqi, Ḥasan. *Divān-i Ḥasan Shauqī: Dasvīn ṣadī Hijrī Men Urdū Shā'irī Kī Rivāyat Kā Surāgh.* Edited by Jamil Jalibi. Karachi: Anjuman Taraqqi-yi Urdu Pakistan, 1971.

Shāyi', Nada 'Abd al-Raḥmān Yūsuf al-. *Mu'jam alfāẓ al-ḥayāt al-ijtimā'īyah fī dawāwīn shu'arā' al-Mu'allaqāt al-'ashar.* Beirut: Maktab Lebanon, 1991.

Sherwani, Haroon Khan, P. M. Joshi, and Ghulam Yazdani, eds. *History of Medieval Deccan: 1295–1724*. 2 vols. Hyderabad: Director of Print and Publication Bureau, Govt. of Andhra Pradesh, 1973.

A Short History of Hind-Pakistan. Karachi: Pakistan Historical Society, 1955.

Sibṭ-i Ḥasan, Sayyid. *Pākistān Men Tahẓīb Kā Irtiqā'*. Karachi: Maktabā Daniyāl, 1977.

Siddiqi, Iqtidar Husain. *Indo-Persian Historiography up to the Thirteenth Century*. Delhi: Primus Books, 2010.

Siddiqi, M. H. *The Growth of Indo-Persian Literature in Gujarat*. Baroda: M. S. Sayajirao University, 1985.

Sinha, Mrinalini. *Colonial Masculinity: The "Manly Englishman" and the "Effeminate Bengali" in the Late Nineteenth Century*. Manchester: Manchester University Press, 1995.

Sīrāfī, Abū Zayd al-, and Aḥmad Ibn Faḍlān. *Two Arabic Travel Books: Accounts of China and India and Mission to the Volga*. Edited and translated by Tim Mackintosh-Smith and James Edward Montgomery. New York: New York University Press, 2014.

Sīrāfī, Abū Zayd Ḥasan ibn Yazīd, Yūsuf Shārūnī, and Sulaymān al-Tājir. *Akhbār al-Ṣīn wa-al-Hind*. al-Qāhirah: al-Dār al-Miṣrīyah al-Lubnānīyah, 2000.

Smith, Vincent Arthur. "The Credit Due to the Book Entitled 'the Voyages and Travels of J. Albert de Mandelslo into the East Indies.'" *Journal of the Royal Asiatic Society of Great Britain and Ireland* (April 1915): 245–254.

———. *The Oxford History of India*. Oxford: Clarendon Press, 1920.

Sorley, Herbert Tower. *Shāh Abdul Latīf of Bhit: His Poetry, Life and Times; a Study of Literary, Social and Economic Conditions in Eighteenth Century Sind*. London: H. Milford, Oxford University Press, 1940.

Spivak, Gayatri Chakravorty. "Can the Subaltern Speak?" In *Marxism and the Interpretation of Culture*, edited by Cary Nelson and L. Grossberg, 271–313. Urbana: University of Illinois Press, 1988.

Sprenger, Aloys. *A Catalogue of the Arabic, Persian and Hindu'stan'y Manuscripts, of the Libraries of the King of Oudh, Compiled under the Orders of the Government of India*. Vol. 1. Calcutta: Baptist Mission Press, 1854.

———. *A Catalogue of the Bibliotheca Orientalis Sprengeriana*. Giessen: Wilhelm Keller, 1857.

———. *El-Mas'udí's Historical Encyclopaedia, Entitled "Meadows of Gold and Mines of Gems."* Vol. 1. London: Oriental Translation Fund, 1841.

———. "Manuscripts of the Late Sir H. Elliot, K. C. B." *Journal of the Asiatic Society of Bengal* 23, no. 3 (1854): 225–263.

Srivastava, Sushil. "Situating the Gentoo in History: European Perception of Indians in the Early Phase of Colonialism." *Economic and Political Weekly* 36, no. 7 (2001): 576–594.

Strabo. *Geography*. Translated by Horace Leonard Jones. Cambridge, MA: Harvard University Press, 1930.

Stuurman, Siep. "Cosmopolitan Egalitarianism in the Enlightenment: Anquetil Duperron on India and America." *Journal of the History of Ideas* 68, no. 2 (2007): 255–278.

Subrahmanyam, Sanjay. "The Career of Colonel Polier and Late Eighteenth-Century Orientalism." *Journal of the Royal Asiatic Society* 10, no. 1 (April 2000): 43–60.

———. *Courtly Encounters: Translating Courtliness and Violence in Early Modern Eurasia*. Cambridge, MA: Harvard University Press, 2012.

———. *Europe's India: Words, People, Empires, 1500–1800*. Cambridge, MA: Harvard University Press, 2017.

———. "Golden Age Hallucinations," *Outlook India*, August 20, 2001.

———. "Intertwined Histories: Cróonica and Tārīkh in the Sixteenth Century Indian Ocean World." *History and Theory* 49, no. 4 (2010): 118–145.

———. "Iranians Abroad: Intra-Asian Elite Migration and Early Modern State Formation." *Journal of Asian Studies* 51, no. 2 (May 1992): 340–365.

———. "On World Historians in the Sixteenth Century." *Representations* 91, no. 1 (Summer 2005): 26–57.

Tabarī, Abū Ja'far Muhammad b. Jarīr. *The History of Al-Tabari*. Vol. 1, *General Introduction and from the Creation to the Flood*. Translated by Frank Rosenthal. Albany: State University of New York Press, 1989.

Talbot, Cynthia. *The Last Hindu Emperor: Prithviraj Chauhan and the Indian Past, 1200–2000*. Cambridge: Cambridge University Press, 2015.

Tavakoli-Targhi, Mohamad. *Refashioning Iran: Orientalism, Occidentalism and Historiography*. New York: Palgrave, 2001.

Thackston, Wheeler M., ed. *Three Memoirs of Humayun*. Translated by W. M. Thackston. Costa Mesa, CA: Mazda Publishers, 2009.

Thapar, Romila. *Somanatha: The Many Voices of a History*. New Delhi: Penguin, 2004.

Thieme, Paul. "Sanskrit *sindhu-/Sindhu-* and Old Iranian *hindu-/Hindu-*." In *W. B. Henning Memorial Volume*, edited by Mary Boyce and Ilya Gershevitch, 447–450. London: Lund Humphries, 1970.

Thomas, Paul. *Indian Women through the Ages: Historical Survey of the Position of Women and the Institutions of Marriage and Family in India from Antiquity to the Present Day*. New York: Asia Publishing House, 1964.

Thum, Rian, "What Is Islamic History?" *History and Theory* 57 (December 2019): 7–19.

Tibebu, Teshale. *Hegel and the Third World: The Making of Eurocentrism in World History*. Syracuse, NY: Syracuse University Press, 2011.

Tieffenthaler, Joseph. *Description Historique et Géographique De L'Inde qui présente en Trois Volumes*. Vol. 1, translated by M. Jean Bernoulli. Berlin: Pierre Bourdeaux, 1786.

Tod, James. "Translation of a Sanscrit Inscription, Relative to the Last Hindu King of Delhi, with Comments Thereon." *Transactions of the Royal Asiatic Society of Great Britain and Ireland* 1, no. 1 (1824): 133–154.

Tola, Fernando, and Carmen Dragonetti. "India and Greece before Alexander." *Annals of the Bhandarkar Oriental Research Institute* 67, nos. 1–4 (1986): 159–194.

Tottoli, Roberto. *Biblical Prophets in the Qur'an and Muslim Literature*. London: Routledge, 2002.

Trautmann, Thomas R. *Does India Have History?* New Delhi: Nehru Memorial Museum and Library, 2012.

Troll, Christian W. "A Note on an Early Topographical Work of Sayyid Aḥmad Khān: Āsār al-Ṣanādīd." *Journal of the Royal Asiatic Society of Great Britain & Ireland* 104, no. 2 (1972): 135–146.

Trouillot, Michel-Rolph. *Silencing the Past: Power and the Production of History*. Boston: Beacon, 1995.

Truschke, Audrey. "The Power of the Islamic Sword in Narrating the Death of Indian Buddhism." *History of Religions* 57, no. 4 (2018): 406–435.

Tucker, Joseph Eagon. "John Davies of Kidwelly, 1627?–1693, Translator from the French: With an Annotated Bibliography of His Translations." *Papers of the Bibliographical Society of America* 44, no. 2 (1950): 119–152.

'Utbi, Muḥammad ibn 'Abd al-Jabbār al-. *Kitāb al-Yamini fi akhbār dawlāt al-mulk Yamin-al-Dawla abi-al-Qasim Maḥmud bin Nāsir al-Dawla abi Mansūr Subuktkin*. Edited by Yusuf al-Hādi. Tehran: Markaz al-Buḥūth wa-al-Dirāsāt lil-Turāth al-Makhṭūṭ, 2008.

'Utbi, Muḥammad ibn 'Abd al-Jabbār al-, and Nāṣiḥ ibn Ẓafr Jurfādhaqānī. *Kitāb-i mustaṭāb-i tarjumah-i Tārīkh-i Yamīnī*. Tehran: Dār 'al-Ṭibā'ah, 1856.

———. *Tarikh-i Yamini*. Tehran: Chāpkhānah-i Muḥammad 'Alī Fardīn, 1956.

Vacca, Alison. *Non-Muslim Provinces under Early Islam: Islamic Rule and Iranian Legitimacy in Armenia and Caucasian Albania*. Cambridge: Cambridge University Press, 2017.

Vajdī al-Ḥusainī, Sayyid 'Ābid 'Alī. *Hindūstān Islām ke sā'e men*. Bhopāl: Bhopāl Buk Hā'ūs, 1989.

Varayāṇī, Prītama. *Sindhi Folk Tales*. Translated by Mohan Gehāṇī. Kutch: Indian Institute of Sindhology, 2009.

Verma, B. D. "Inscriptions from the Central Museum, Nagpur." In *Epigraphia Indica: Arabic and Persian Supplement, 1955 and 1956*, 109–118. Calcutta: Government of India Press, 1960.

Virgil. *Aeneid*. Translated by Frederick Ahl. Oxford: Oxford University Press, 2007.

Visvanathan, Susan. "The Legends of St. Thomas in Kerala." *India International Centre Quarterly* 22, nos. 2–3 (1995): 27–44.

Voltaire. *Essai sur l'Histoire générale et sur les moeurs et l'esprit des nations, depuis Charlemagne jusqu'à nos jours*. Amsterdam: Aux dépens de la Compagnie, 1764.

Wagoner, Phillip B. "Precolonial Intellectuals and the Production of Colonial Knowledge." *Comparative Studies in Society and History* 45, no. 4 (October 2003): 783–814.

Wajhī, Asadullah, and Humera Jalīlī. *Quṭb Mushtarī*. New Delhi: Taraqqī-yi Urdū Biyūro, 1992.

Waldman, Marilyn Robinson. *Toward a Theory of Historical Narrative: A Case Study in Perso-Islamicate Historiography*. Columbus: Ohio State University Press, 1980.

Wallis, H. W. *Cosmology of the Rigveda, an Essay*. London: Williams and Norgate, 1887.

Waseem, Shah Mohammad. *Development of Persian Historiography in India: From the Second Half of the 17th Century to the First Half of the 18th Century*. New Delhi: Kanishka Publishers, 2003.

Webb, John. *An Historical Essay Endeavoring a Probability That the Language of the Empire of China Is the Primitive Language*. London: Printed for Nath. Brook, 1669.

Wellen, Kathryn. "The Danish East India Company's War against the Mughal Empire, 1642–1698," *Journal of Early Modern History* 19, no. 5 (September 2015): 439–461.

Wheeler, Mortimer. *Early India and Pakistan: To Ashoka*. New York: Praeger, 1959.

White, Hayden V. "The Politics of Historical Interpretation: Discipline and De-Sublimation." *Critical Inquiry* 9, no. 1 (September 1982): 113–137.

———. *Tropics of Discourse: Essays in Cultural Criticism*. Baltimore: Johns Hopkins University Press, 1978.

Whittaker, Dick. "Conjunctures and Conjectures: Kerala and Roman Trade." *Journal of Asian History* 43, no. 1 (2009): 1–18.

Withington, Nicholas. *A Briefe Discoverye of Some Things best worth Noteinge in the Travels of Nicholas Withington & c.* London: C. Rivington, at the Bible and Crown in St. Paul's Church yard, 1735.

Wujastyk, Dominik. "Indian Manuscripts." In *Manuscript Cultures: Mapping the Field*, edited by Jörg Quenzer, Dmitry Bondarev, and Jan-Ulrich Sobisch, 159–181. Berlin: Walter de Gruyter, 2014.

Yazdani, Ghulam. *The Early History of the Deccan*. London: Oxford University Press, 1960.

———. "The Inscriptions of the Turk Sultans of Delhi (Plates IV-XVI)." In *Epigraphia Indo-Moslemica 1913–14*, 13–46. Calcutta: Government Printing, 1917.

Zadeh, Travis E. *Mapping Frontiers across Medieval Islam: Geography, Translation, and the 'Abbāsid Empire*. London: I. B. Tauris Publishers, 2011.

Zakā'ullāh, Muhammad. *Tārīkh-i Hindustān*. 10 vols. Aligarh: Matba' Institute, 1915–1919.

———. *Tārīkh-i Hindustān: Saltanat-i islāmiyyah Kā Bayān*. 5 vols. Lahore: Sang-i Mīl Publications, 1998.

Zaman, Taymiya R. "Nostalgia, Lahore, and the Ghost of Aurangzeb." *Fragments: Interdisciplinary Approaches to the Study of Ancient and Medieval Pasts* 4 (2015): 1–27.

———. "Visions of Juliana: A Portuguese Woman at the Court of the Mughals." *Journal of World History* 23, no. 4 (December 2012): 761–791.

Ziad, Waleed. "'Islamic Coins' from a Hindu Temple: Reconsidering Ghaznavid Interactions with Hindu Sacred Sites through New Numismatic Evidence from Gandhara." *Journal of the Economic and Social History of the Orient* 59, no. 4 (2016): 618–659.

Zubayr, Aḥmad ibn ʿAlī Ibn. *Kitāb Al-Ḏaḵā'ir wa-l-tuḥaf.* Al-Kuwayt: Dā'irat al-Maṭbūʿāt wa-l-Našr, 1959.

ACKNOWLEDGMENTS

The debts of support and kindness I have accumulated over the last two decades—from graduate school and beyond—remain on my shoulders, and I acknowledge them with the hope that I can pay them forward. I dedicate this work to the guidance and mentorship of Professors C. M. Naim, Muzaffar Alam, and Shahid Amin and to their ethical and engaged scholarship, which remains a road map for all of us students.

I am grateful to all who gave their time, intellectual labor, and goodwill to this project: Purnima Dhavan, Projit Mukerji, David Lelyveld, Ronald B. Inden, Anubhuti Maurya, Rebecca Goetz, Sanjay Subrahmanyam, Samia Khatun, Abhishek Kaicker, Rajeev Kinra, Gaiutra Bahadur, Whitney Cox, Prithvi Chandra Datta Shobhi, Kitty Ahmed, Aamir Naveed, Chris Carmichael, Eric Beverley, Sarah Neilson, Prachi Deshpande, Bodhisattva Kar, Bilal Tanweer, Shahnaz Rouse, Ali Raza, Taymiya Zaman, and Cynthia Talbot.

I received invaluable material support from Jennifer Ivers, Sunil Amrith, Nur Sobers Khan, Anisha Padma, Pushkar Sohoni, Rahul Sarwate, Joslyn DeVinney, Roy Bar Zadeh, Gianni Sievers, M. Salim Mohammad, C. Ryan Perkins, Jamal Jafri, and Esmat Elhalaby. I want to thank Rochona Majumdar, Kishwar Rizvi, Jisha Menon, Hajnalka Kovacs, and Sunil Sharma for inviting me to their respective fora and giving me the opportunity to share portions of this work.

My colleagues at Columbia's Butler Library Reservations Desk were gracious, extremely kind, and instrumental to the success of this project.

My thanks to Catherine T. Parker-Thomas, Isacio Cedeno, and Mayra E. Alvarez. Colleagues at the libraries of the University of Pennsylvania, Harvard, Princeton, and Yale and the British Library helped at short notice. I immensely appreciate the staff and resources made available by Interlibrary Loan and by Borrow Direct. Much of the work would have been impossible without the digital repositories of the Internet Archive, Rekhta, HathiTrust, Early English Books Online, Center for Research Libraries, as well as the digitization of holdings at the British Library (especially the Early Indian Printed Books and Endangered Archives Program), Qatar Digital Library, Staatsbibliothek zu Berlin, and Bibliothèque Nationale de France. The streaming Bombay Talkies and Binaca Geetmala, watched with dear comrades, were a key source of inspiration and sustenance for this project.

At Columbia University, I benefit from colleagues who have consistently supported my work and helped make it possible: Partha Chatterjee, Anupama Rao, Kavita Sivaramakrishnan, Mahmood Mamdani, Sheldon Pollock, Carol Gluck, Adam Kosto, Mark Mazower, Seth Schwartz, Rashid Khalidi, Lien-Hang Nguyen, Frank Guridy, Marwa Elshakry, Line Lillevik, Mae Ngai, Karl Jacoby, Patricia Morel, Lawino Lurum, Sia Mensah, Patrick McMorrow, Hanh Angela To, Bethany Schwartz, Abril Gallego, Edyaline Tejeda, Cody Frank, Saeeda Islam, Michael Adan, Emma Scheinbaum, Kimberly Soloman, Richie Rodriguez, Felvin Recio, Vishakha Desai, Mana Kia, Avinoam Shalem, Kathryn Spellman Poots, S. Akbar Zaidi, Eileen Gillooly, and Brinkley Messick. A special shout-out to my fellow migrants Dennis Yi Tenen, Alex Gil, Moacir P. de Sá Pereira, and a big thank you to all the wonderful friends at Brownie's Café and Taqueria y Fonda.

This book was made possible by Sharmila Sen at Harvard University Press. I am utterly grateful to her and to Heather Hughes. David "Raver" Emmanuel does the first round of copy edits on much of what I write, and I am grateful for his friendship and his clear-eyed approach. I want to thank Hannah Lord Archambault, Shahnur Said, Virginia Perrin, Judy Loeven, and Derek Gottlieb for making this manuscript better.

I am honored by the care, intellectual generosity, and commitment that Durba Mitra offers to my work. There is no idea in this book that was not shaped by our conversation, nor any sentence that did not benefit from her reading and insight. I thank her. As always, my love to Maha Shaista Ahmed and Kavi Kashmiri Ahmed; to Junaid, Mukarram, and Talal Ahmed; to my dearest amma, Shaista Ahmed, and my late father, Sultan Ahmed Asif.

Kavita Saraswathi Datla (1975–2017), Annie Ali Khan (1980–2018), Meena Alexander (1951–2018), and Allison Busch (1969–2019) are my lost interlocuters—intellectuals whose own work echoes within this book, within me. I inscribe their names here, so that they will always be carried, wherever these ideas carry.

INDEX